THE CURIOUS LIFE AND WORK OF scott walker

THE CURIOUS LIFE AND WORK OF scott walker

Paul Woods

OMNIBUS PRESS

London / New York / Paris / Sydney / Copenhagen / Berlin / Madrid / Tokyo

Exclusive Distributors
Music Sales Limited,
14/15 Berners Street,
London, W1T 3LJ.

Music Sales Corporation
180 Madison Avenue, 24th Floor,
New York,
NY 10016,
USA.

Macmillan Distribution Services,
56 Parkwest Drive
Derrimut, Vic 3030,
Australia.

Every effort has been made to trace the copyright holders of the photographs in this book but one or
two were unreachable. We would be grateful if the photographers concerned would contact us.

Typeset by Phoenix Photosetting, Chatham, Kent
Printed in the EU

A catalogue record for this book is available from the British Library.

Visit Omnibus Press on the web at www.omnibuspress.com

Contents

Contents

Introduction

"I am a formalist. I believe that an artist must work within walls, within boundaries. Greater originality emerges from this rather than from sporadic leaps."

– Scott Walker, 1968

"I'm not really interested in creating tranquillity. There's far too much of that going on in popular culture today… you don't need me for more of the same. I see the work as many layered, not just unsettling."

– Scott Walker, 2012

They can't be the same guy.

Can they?

The name 'Scott Walker' always denoted a rumour – an absence – even a spectral presence, as far back as I can remember. But then some of us were just about old enough to start taking notice in the seventies, a full decade after the reputation that cemented the 'legend' (that much debased term).

He was man who sang 'Amsterdam', that beer-stinking ballad of whores, piss and fish heads, even before Bowie did it. In fact a letter in *Record Mirror* said he did it *years* before, and spoke about another Jacques Brel song, 'Jackie', that was so familiar with subjects us kids liked to think we knew about ("authentic queers and phoney virgins"), although we didn't, that they wouldn't play it on Radio 1. And he did it all in the velvet tones of a real grown-up singer, a 'crooner', that put him almost a decade ahead of Bryan Ferry.

Some of us were seriously impressed, even though we only had a faint recollection of catching one or two of his tunes. So where was he now when we needed him, in this post-hippie pop world?

That was where our musical education began. *He was in The Walker Brothers,* some of our barely elders told us, *they sang 'The Sun Ain't Gonna Shine Anymore' and it was the best thing he ever did.* We remembered it from when we were toddlers, and it was kinda cool: a sad ballad with a cowboy-ish guitar intro, more sulky than mournful, like it was enjoying a good mope but on the verge of leaping up and down.

It also gave you a vague sense, in that one phrase, of what it must be like to be Scott Walker: 'the best thing he ever did'. Like they knew everything he'd ever done and ever would do, and their memories could keep him imprisoned in that one 45rpm groove.

He had a late-night programme on the telly – I think my mother might have told me that, as anything approaching pub closing time was deemed 'late night' in those black-and-white late sixties days. He sang some sophisticated barroom ballads, like the Tony Bennett records our dads and uncles had; in fact some of them were the same songs – songs for world-weary men who expressed their sentimentality by equating years and seasons with the names of girls they'd once known.

Except he didn't look like them and he probably didn't smell like an aftershave-drenched hangover in the morning either. He was still pop-star age, with a slender frame and pop-star looks.

("I really do think... that I was too young recording them," Scott would later tell the Irish rock journalist Joe Jackson, "maybe there is something there to listen to... more so for other people than myself.")

And then, in the mid-to-late seventies, there was another Scott Walker: the MOR and country covers artist looking denim-clad, laid-back and distinctly Californian. When I found one of these albums in the salvage warehouse where I worked as a kid, I didn't even bother to purloin it – that guy surely wasn't the purveyor of overwrought Euro-ballads on solo records you couldn't even buy any more?

English music fans have long held Noel Scott Engel, the artist known as Scott Walker, in high esteem for dignifying our pop music with a certain gravitas. Even some of the lesser moon-in-June ballads he sang with The Walker Brothers sounded like a matter of life and death when the young American applied that precocious baritone.

But then, it seems he didn't want to be an American anyway. *Portrait*, the second Walkers album, included a cheesy sleeve note that claimed Scott was "the existentialist who knows what [existentialism] means and reads Jean-Paul Sartre". Even then it must have made him seem like a leftover from the fifties bebop era, evoking not Albert Camus' philosophical treatise *The Rebel* but Tony Hancock's Brit comedy *The Rebel*. ("Why live for tomorrow when you can die today?" asks the confused beatnik chick in the Breton striped T-shirt.)

As an attitude for living rather than an intellectual fad, however, Engel has maintained the ethos through all his fluctuating fortunes. "A person who needs no other people – a world in himself," is how he defined it for Keith Altham, an *NME* journalist and (later) music PR man who saw the depths in this lanky young drink of water from the get-go. "A belief in existence rather than essence."

The religiosity that can be detected from the time of Engel's earliest compositions, like the neo-gothic love song 'Archangel', with its swelling church organ tones, is no contradiction. Whether or not the lead Walker Brother (as Scott quickly, and inadvertently, became) had read *The Outsider* by Colin Wilson, the closest thing to existentialism we ever had in a nation that regards intellectual ideas as an embarrassment, he fitted that writer's definition of a man who applies the same serious devotion to existence that the faithful devote to a pie-in-the-sky afterlife. Research by this author has detected a

Zionist Lutheran (Old Testament-quoting Protestant) lineage in his family that Engel ('angel' in German) appeared to shrug off. But the seriousness remains.

"How can you relate to something unless you have felt it emotionally?" he asked near the release of his first solo album, 1967's eponymous *Scott*, insisting that all song lyrics had to be extracted (and indeed earned) from personal experience.

It's a strict literalism that he might shun today, when Engel considers internal images and ideas as valid a starting point as the autobiographical approach he seems to totally reject. But for a while – in the cinematically influenced 'big pop' of *Scott 1-3* – it worked beautifully. Fragments of genuine emotion and experience among the orchestrated angst made it all seem so personal, as much for the listener as for the performer.

There was also a studied realism that gave an intentional one in the eye to "that phoney love and flower power scene". When we look back at the commercial success of the first three solo albums, we can see how the popular music of the sixties was the broadest of churches, only partly in thrall to acid-addled smiley faces.

"Life is full of heartbreaks, rain and unsmiling people," said Scott at the time. "I want people to face life not run away from it because some aspects are unpleasant. The first battle is to see things as they are. You can't hide from reality through drugs."

It might seem an unremarkable statement today, but that's because it holds true as much for popular culture as it does for every other strand of existence. At the time, however, its iron-in-the-soul resolve must have been hugely unfashionable – though it's not till we get to the post-hippie era of the late sixties/early seventies, when hair and flares and dope and coke were increasingly common aspects of many people's lives (even, sometimes, of Scott's), that we can see any real commercial damage being done.

This was also a performer who, in his words, "became addicted to classical music", to 'old squares' like Mozart, Schubert, Beethoven, Brahms, Shostakovich, Delius and Sibelius, in a period before 'progressive rock' rehabilitated the classical pretensions of some rock or pop musicians in the public eye. Many of the songs, even Brel's morbid Gallic bravado, were conventional verse-chorus-verse (apart from some of Scott's early 'miniatures', which approached the minimalism of haikus-in-sound) but they still consciously descended from a tradition.

By the time that tradition bled into pop culture, however, it passed through the heightened emotion of written-to-order film and TV soundtracks, through Max Steiner and Elmer Bernstein; as former *Wire* editor Rob Young has noted, the soundtracks of Morricone ("It sounds like bloody spaghetti-western music!" my younger brother has whined) or the mellow eclecticism of Scott's favourite pop album, Dion's 1968 album *Dion* (which in 2007 was retitled *Abraham, Martin And John*), seemed to exert as much of an influence as the traditional classicists.

As producer Peter Walsh and filmmaker Stephen Kijak both note in this volume, Engel has never stopped searching out and assimilating influences, however laterally: fluid arrangements inspired by Gil Evans' work for Miles Davis; obliquely haunting lyrics with the allusional restraint of Kafka; abandoning the folk-influenced songs of Brel for something closer to the 'Schubertian ideal', the symbiotic meshing of words and melody.

And then, after the more rock-influenced but equally searching *Scott 4* and the less ambitious but cleverly catchy *'Til The Band Comes In*, it all seemed to end. Scott has written off the covers albums of his seventies solo period as "useless" – but search them out and you may find that, given the near-impossibility of him putting in a lacklustre performance, there are moments from the artist's unhappiest years that can still soothe the soul.

By the mid-seventies, Noel Scott Engel seemed almost intimidated by the former ambition of the young performer called Scott Walker: "There was one point way back there when I turned back from what I believed in and I was never able to get back around again," he fatalistically admitted in one 1976 interview. He complained that he felt "completely dwarfed" by his own musical interests: by the avant-garde atonality of Boulez, Schoenberg and Stockhausen; the Eastern folk-influenced symphonies of Bartok and the *Twilight Zone* musings of Scriabin; even quintessential seventies singer-songwriters Randy Newman and Joni Mitchell invited feelings of inadequacy.

And then, in an ironic quirk, desperation made it all turn around. The mid-seventies Walker Brothers reunion had yielded only one success (the hit single 'No Regrets') and was about to hit the rocks. Telling his pseudo-siblings they should all write whatever they wanted for their final shot, Engel propelled himself as an artist into the glacial temperature of the modern age. At the time it was a commercial non-event, but at least one resulting track, 'The Electrician', can be counted as an experiment with classical form, its lyrics attuned to the darkness of the human condition.

"'Boy Child' led to the later work," Scott would reflect of the ambitious tone poem from *Scott 4*. "In fact I feel that the whole album… later evolved into albums like *Climate Of Hunter*." It was what his former 'brothers', John and Gary, would refer to as "Scott's dark page" – though the work centred less on morbidity than on obliquely drawn, finely honed images that resonated in the mind; the *Lieder* approach of Schubert, Mahler and their contemporaries, filtered through the decades of modern and popular culture that succeeded them.

For this writer's money, it's the densely atmospheric 'Sleepwalkers Woman', on 1984's *Climate Of Hunter*, that best fulfils the promise of 'Boy Child'. The rest of the album had a coldly modern urgency to the music and the fractured narratives that are suggestive, rather than didactic. In cinematic terms, the effective low-budget video for 'Track Three' has been compared to the Tarkovsky of *Stalker* – but its synchronicitous release at the same time as *The Element Of Crime*, the surreal Euro-noir debut of Lars Von Trier, seems to coincidentally mark a similar vision in a different artform.

By the end of the decade, however, the incongruous commercial failure of *Climate* (the most 'eighties' of albums in its sounds) had made Scott Walker just a rumour again. His marked absence (apart from a nostalgic cinema ad) meant that, even by the time of the re-

release of his classic sixties albums on CD, few expected him to ever re-emerge.

When he actually did reappear, with 1995's *Tilt*, his half-decade spent on fine arts courses seems to have reinforced his aversion to artistic compromise. "You are working with different elements of time and concepts of space," he alluded to his minimally surreal lyrics and the elements of music and sound that sat in isolation, or sometimes in opposition. Citing the spare, physically naturalistic poetry of former 'beat poet' and Zen Buddhist Gary Snyder as an influence, Engel insisted, "All the honing down I've done in the lyric will lead me to just one sound that will tell me – and tell everyone – what that lyric is trying to say. Maybe two or three sounds."

That he wasn't concentrating on, say, the beauty of nature but on the absurdity and contrariness of human existence made *Tilt* a hard listen for some – including some former avid devotees. Tracks like 'The Cockfighter' – transposing elements of Adolf Eichmann's 1962 Nazi war crimes trial and the 1820 trial for adultery of Queen Caroline – and 'Farmer In The City' – which explored the last night of filmic visionary Pier Paolo Pasolini before his murder – had an audio-cinematic quality in themselves that could make them unnerving, even after several listens.

Almost two decades on and Scott Walker is still honing his work down, "moving towards a silence". It can be a particularly noisy silence though: 2006's *The Drift* had an occasional brutalism even in its masterful standout tracks like 'Clara' and 'Jesse'. At the tail end of an artistically productive decade for him, 'Zercon: A Flagpole Sitter' and 'Epizootics', to name but two tracks on *Bish Bosch* at the end of 2012, crank up the absurdist humour and post-humanist disgust to an infernal level.

★★★

So, all of the above just can't be the same guy, right?

This writer would probably go along with that. Whoever 'Scott Walker' happens to be at a particular time depends on which aspect of his artistic muse Noel Scott Engel happens to be concentrating on, or honing to a shard-like point. But there's no doubt that it's the same personage wearing all those different hats: if you've exposed yourself to the energising inner visions of the *Tilt/Drift/Bish Bosch* axis, take a backwards listen to 'The Gentle Rain', the film theme from the 1966 *Solo John, Solo Scott* EP: the *acapella* opening may have you full of foreboding, wondering what aural intrusion comes next. What does actually come next is Johnny Franz's tinkling piano and a gentle lounge bar ballad.

Same worker. Same basic set of tools. But a different artist.

In a sad but inevitable sense, it's probably right that the artist himself has declined to contribute to this book. Forcing him to dig around in the minutiae of his past (some of his earliest family history has been dredged up here from the historical archives of his birthplace) might have been like a jailer trying to coax him back into prison with a wave of the key, expecting him to re-embrace what he'd already been at pains to escape.

But the author is grateful for the participation of those who have worked with the artist, and their insights into the perfection of his method. A method which now seems to have been pushed to the furthest point that it can – but I wouldn't bet on that. There is an artistic war being fought in Engel's head and it seems to have been raging since his own birth during World War Two.

Chapter 1

War Baby Boomer

Today we have not only the responsibility of administering the government of Ohio, but also of aiding to keep Ohio's war production on its farms and in its factories ever increasing and at its peak.

We also have the deep obligation to those hundreds of thousands of boys including those from Ohio who are fighting for us around the world. We have the further duty of doing everything we can to aid the national government in the prosecution of the war and in the winning of the war at the earliest possible time. For the next two years these shall be our solemn and determined duty.

Howard Metzenbaum (Democrat), quoted on his election to the Ohio House of Representatives, *Hamilton Journal News*, Wednesday, January 10, 1943

On the same day that the above announcement was made in the Midwestern city of Hamilton, the local newspaper announced the following birth on the same page:

"Engel, Lieutenant Noel W. and Betty (Fortier), 122 Sherman Avenue, a boy, January 9, Fort Hamilton Hospital."

To 32-year-old Noel Walter Engel and his wife, Elizabeth Marie (née Fortier, familiarly known as Betty and of the same age as

1

her husband) was born a son, Noel Scott Engel. By his mother's account, the boy weighed in at a healthy eight pounds and measured a strapping 24½ inches long. Born as the tide of World War Two had yet to definitively turn, the child would be a privileged offspring of the USA's post-war economic boom and the explosion in popular culture that accompanied it.

His birthday fell one day after that of little Elvis Aaron Presley, then eight years old and living in poverty in Memphis, who would become a hero to the Engel boy in his teens. That same date, four years later, would also see the birth of one David Robert Haywood Stenton Jones in London, England – who would bear the distinction of being one of the few performing artists the adult Engel might regard as a peer.

In 1943, however, much darker spectacles were playing out on the world stage. While his naval lieutenant father faced up to the horrors of war in the Pacific, little Noel and Betty were housed in the grand-paternal family home at Sherman Avenue. For a while, mother and child would live with Noel Sr.'s parents and his big sister – little Noel's Aunt LaNelle.

Grandpa Scott, from whom Noel Jr. took his middle name, ran a dry cleaning business from his home and had been an enthusiastic semi-pro musician, playing the fiddle on Cincinnati Radio. All paternal family members were descended from George Engel Sr., who first migrated to Cincinnati in the mid-19th century. Born in the German principality of Bavaria, George had been schooled in the strict Old Testament teaching of the Zion Lutheran Church – a faith still adhered to by some of his descendants 100 years on.

This was the family environment the little boy was briefly grounded in, before his mother took him off to live an often peripatetic existence. On February 23, 1945, the local *Journal* would read:

"Mrs. Grace Jarrett Engel… 122 Sherman Avenue, died at five o'clock Thursday afternoon in Fort Hamilton hospital. She had been ill one year…

"She leaves the widower, Scott Engel... one son, Lt. Noel W. Engel, serving with the navy in the South Pacific... a daughter-in-law, Betty Engel and grandson, Noel Scott Engel, both of California."

By the time of her son's second birthday, and before the US's conflict with the Imperial Japanese Army was concluded, Betty would take the boy intermittently back to stay with her sister Celia ('Aunt Seal') on her native West Coast.

On Noel Sr.'s honourable discharge from the US Navy at the end of the war, adjustment to civilian life was compounded by difficulties in a marriage he'd hardly known. While Noel Jr. (or Scotty, as he increasingly came to be known) would be doted on by his mother, she could do little to stop him witnessing the trauma of a marital relationship in breakdown.

"I lived in a nice home – but things were always tense," Scott would later tell one of the sixties Brit pop magazines that hung on his every word. "It was a very bad time for me... I held it against Dad – which I shouldn't have... But it had been a violent situation between Mum and Dad."

Added to this was the experience of watching his mother undergo an emotional and nervous breakdown. For the first time, young Scotty Engel would become aware of the fragile nature of human consciousness and the strange ways in which it responded to external pressure.

Noel Sr. and Betty capitulated to the emotional forces destroying their marriage in 1949, divorcing when Scotty was six years old. With Noel now working as a geologist for the Superior Oil Company, his career would take him to Midland, Texas. Betty and Scotty would stay for the time being at the previous family home, 2871 Krameria Avenue, Denver, Colorado, with the boy occasionally staying at Noel's place on the wide open range. Beneath the benign shadow of the Rocky Mountains, Betty would pour all her hope and affection into Scotty, nurturing whatever talents she felt he might possess.

In her son's twenties, as he gradually passed from burning star to cult artist, 'Mrs Betty' briefly became a cult figure herself to

Scott's Japanese fans. In an interview for Nipponese magazine *Music Life*, 'Mimi', as she was now known (an affectionate *nom de plume* bestowed by her son), was described as in her late fifties, elegant, "dressed in a beautiful blue velvet long skirt... the pearl dinner ring from Scott on her finger".

In pedantically translated reminiscences of her son, she describes a "sensible" child who "often bit the nail of his thumb... Compared to others, he was quiet, but he was a vigorous and cheerful boy who moved around very much... He used to play with his friends in sand and being a cowboy and so on."

Inspired by Roy Rogers and his faithful horse Trigger, at the Saturday movie matinees, seven-year-old Scotty was thrown from his steed the first time he tried horse riding when visiting his father's Texas home. According to Scott, he was knocked spark out for a few moments. Such was Betty's faith in her son's physical robustness that she picked him up, dusted him off and put him straight back on the mount.

The Engels were by tradition a sporting family. Noel Sr. had been known as 'Tubby' or 'Tub' at Hamilton High School, but the school's 1928 *Weekly Review* photo shows not a fat boy but a solid-looking kid with a pomaded hair parting and thick lips. He was a stalwart of the school's football team and pitched in with baseball too, while Grandpa Scott served as commissioner of the Butler County Merchants Softball League up to the time of his death, in his mid-eighties.

As a schoolboy, young Scotty would engage in running, athletics, even boxing training – whatever the assumptions about his artistic, introspective nature, by all accounts the Engel boy learned how to land a punch. For all his good health and self-reliance, however, according to Betty, childhood was not without its hazards:

"When he was five years old, he played with matches with his friends in the neighbourhood. And then the fire began to burn the curtains of his bedroom. I took him out through the window at once! He almost got burnt!

"I remember he always came home having small hurts but he had no big hurts," she was quaintly misquoted, evoking a cover version from Scott's first solo album. Mrs Betty describes an active child who (at least then) "wasn't nervous at all":

"He was healthy as he didn't catch a cold... He had only caught a scarlatina that children catch when he was seven years old. And he almost died because of having been very feverish."

As scarlatina is the less serious manifestation of the illness, it's possible that the Japanese translator meant a more dangerous scarlet fever. In any case, his mother describes a healthy childhood suddenly invaded by delirium and fever dream. This may have been the start of the "very bad dreams" that Scott acknowledges suffering from all of his life. Or perhaps the oneiric nightmare side of his existence had already begun, initiated by the unpredictable adult world with all of its conflicts and mood swings.

Modern classical/Broadway composer Leonard Bernstein characterised the post-WW2 era as 'The Age Of Anxiety'. This was the cultural landscape in which Scott Engel spent his formative years; it would permeate his life and work throughout his adult career.

But not all dreams were the stuff of cold sweat. Scotty, far from friendless but too self-absorbed to need much human company, lived out some of his dreams on the screen, moving along from the corny 'horse operas' that were his introduction to cinema.

"I used to watch the movie *The Rocking Horse Winner*, an English film, and I was just fascinated," he later recalled as an adult. "I must have been very young when I had seen this, and it had such a dream-like quality that the American things didn't have for me." An expressionistic 1950 adaptation of a D.H. Lawrence story about a clairvoyant little boy, its unsettling elements are subtly cloaked in shadow and a Mussorgsky-esque orchestral score.

In the *Music Life* interview, any momentary glimpse of fractured consciousness was passed over in favour of the aspects the interviewer had come to talk to Betty about:

When did he begin to be interested in music?
"Well, when he was seven months old, he stopped crying to hear music. He was 11 years old when he studied music really."

Had he a favourite singer?
"Yes, he favoured Bing Crosby so much, as he sang his songs instantly..."

Do you think that he inherits Crosby's spirit now?
"I think that he was impressed by his songs, being a ballad singer... He says that he likes Crosby best still."

In the early fifties, when Scott was a young boy, the baritone-voiced Bing, idol of the thirties/forties, was still the USA's crooner laureate, its nabob of *ba-ba-ba-ba-boom*. Though some of the bobbysoxer idols he influenced were on the way up (particularly the more worldly Frank Sinatra, who would revive his stalled career with the Nelson Riddle-orchestrated *In The Wee Small Hours* in 1955), the almost catatonically laid-back Crosby remained America's biggest seller with his perennial 'White Christmas'.

When did Scott sing in public for the first time?
"When he was about four years old, he appeared at a lot of charity shows. At that time he seemed to get a lot of pleasure from songs which he had first been able to sing."

According to 'Mrs Betty', a small-time neighbourhood impresario picked up on the boy's nascent talent via his schoolmates, getting him to perform regularly in local charity shows. The young trouper took to it so naturally that he would frequently volunteer himself for performances, whether his mother accompanied him or not.

In 1951, *The Denver Post* paid tribute to this precocious talent with a three-column article on page one:

"He has the volume of Mario Lanza, the stage personality and showmanship of the late Al Jolson, and a deep, vibrating, baritone-bass voice that's all his own.

"That's a description of Scotty who is leaving Denver to appear on several television shows in Los Angeles."

An eight year old with the volume of a light opera-singing tenor; with the charisma of a much-loved ragtime jazz singer – though memories of Al Jolson singing 'Sonny Boy' in blackface may today seem a strange anachronism. (Jolson, who died at the beginning of the fifties, would return to surrealistic effect in the lyric 'Jolson And Jones' – then a lifetime of nightmares away.)

"The mite of a boy with the mighty voice brings the low notes from his small chest like a professional. It's almost weird to watch him; you keep looking for a hidden photograph.

"Scotty, who says he is not sure he wants to be a singer when he grows up, is also scheduled for an audition with Bing Crosby.

"The lad, who has been appearing on special programs and U.S.O. [United Service Organizations] shows at service camps since the age of two, never has had a voice lesson.

"According to his parents, Scott has had dancing lessons but no vocal instruction outside the family. His heavy voice just happened."

No record exists of how the audition with Crosby went – or indeed, if it ever took place. By the middle of the fifties, Betty and Scotty would decamp to New York City, seemingly to pursue his talents further.

"I asked him about his year or two on Broadway, in a Rodgers and Hammerstein play when he was 13, and he basically just said, 'I really don't remember anything about that,'" laughs Stephen Kijak, the documentary filmmaker who created the nearest thing to a Walker autobiography in existence. "Okay, moving on..."

The story goes that Scott picked up his Broadway role at random, when attending an audition with a Puerto Rican friend. According to a 1957 article in *American Fan Club Magazine*, these two 'lost years' of the boy's life did not occur quite so casually. Having already appeared in an amateur Texas production entitled *Ten Men In A Barroom*, the nascent trouper's New York stage debut was in a production of *Plain And Fancy* – an almost forgotten 1955 show described as "the best Rodgers and Hammerstein musical not written by Rodgers and Hammerstein".

This in turn led to a singing supporting role in the real deal, a musical entitled *Pipe Dream*, which ran from November 1955 to June 1956 at the Shubert Theatre on Broadway. A sanitised version of the sequel to John Steinbeck's novella *Cannery Row*, it skirted around its female lead's profession as a whore, much in the way that the 1962 film of *Breakfast At Tiffany's* would with its Audrey Hepburn character. It was also Richard Rodgers and Oscar Hammerstein's only commercial flop.

Although Betty seems to have received regular alimony from Noel Sr., their living expenses could still be stretched to the hilt. Scott's stint on Broadway allowed him to become the family breadwinner for the first time in his young life. It also acted as a prelude to his participation in a TV talent contest held at Madison Square Garden, entitled *Star Time*, and his precocious debut as a recording artist.

Scotty Engel would cut his first single disc – 'When Is A Boy A Man?' / 'Steady As A Rock' – for the RKO Unique label in late 1956, issued the following year. The A-side is a show tune-like number which might have originated from any musical or TV variety show of its era. What *is* remarkable about it is the perfectly pitched bellow erupting from the chest of its 13-year-old vocalist (laying down a challenge to the world: "Take me if you can. I'm a man! I'm a man!"). It seemed you could take the boy off Broadway, but traces of the greasepaint and the roaring crowd would remain.

"That wasn't anything serious," a much older Scott protested from a 21st century viewpoint, decades down the line. "A lot of my friends sang at school and stuff. Someone would hear us singing and pick certain guys and say, 'Oh, would you like to make a record?' or whatever."

His dismissive attitude extends to how much 'Scotty Engel' material would later see unauthorised release, including songs intended only as demonstration copies. But it also fails to acknowledge that, just for a brief period, young Scotty's search for stardom would be pushed as far as it would go.

As 'Mrs Betty' would later tell Japanese fans, Scott had cut his first disc with surprising ease and a seemingly total lack of nerves. "As it was pointed out that his voice was good, I had confidence in his voice, a little. But I thought that being a professional singer depended on his luck and that he might face a lot of difficulties. I didn't want him to be a professional singer..."

By the time of Scott's 15th birthday, he and his mother would return permanently (at least in her case) to the West Coast to be close to her family again. For all their drifting around, their surroundings were not nothing short of salubrious.

"Scott lived with his mother, Betty, in a house that looked like a mock castle on Scenic Drive in Hollywood," testifies Gary Leeds, the fellow Californian who would go on to play a major role in Engel's life. "It was very big and contained about 12 apartments. The 'chateau' was painted a light grey and had a dark-grey roof, trimmed in white. Most of the flats had turrets, which is something you don't normally see in LA, except in the movies, so the building had a bit of Hollywood magic. You could see the big white Hollywood sign up in the hills from Scott's bedroom window..."

As a student at Hollywood High School, the boy's musical interests and studies would expand far beyond Tin Pan Alley. For a while, however, he would perform demonstration discs – demos, which would earn him a few dollars for performing the untested new works of commercial songwriters, with an eye toward getting a chart act to perform them.

Scott Engel's own second disc was released in 1958 – 'The Livin' End', by the new (and short-lived) songwriting team of composer Henry Mancini, who would earn fame by creating movie/TV soundtrack music including the *Pink Panther* theme, and lyricist Rod McKuen – who would find fame in the sixties as the self-styled 'most popular poet in the world'.[1] The song was premiered on the TV show hosted by mainstream pop crooner Eddie Fisher and notable solely for being its young singer's first foray into rock'n'roll ("Do you wanna go boppin'? Do you wanna go rockin'?") – albeit closer to Bill Haley than Little Richard. The B-side, 'Good For Nothin', exhibited similar vocal confidence as the young kid got his vocals around a tongue-tying bopper.

This was the era that passes for Scott's rock'n'roll years – roll over Bing Crosby, and tell Sinatra the news. For a brief period, he would be intoxicated by the prowess and excitement of Elvis Presley, Johnny Ace and the doo-wop genre.[2]

"Particularly Elvis. Like a lot of kids in the fifties I was just blown away by those Sun recordings and the whole Elvis thing at the time." That combination of operatic bellow, shit-kicker inflexions and southern bubba charisma would leave its mark.

In later years, Scott would remember his teenage debutant era as mainly a period of recording demo discs of songs later recorded by tame Middle American soft-rock crooners like Paul Anka. The surviving artefacts tell a wider story of a boy who, for a period at least, sought bona fide stardom, playing family-friendly engagements at Coney Island in New York and the Honolulu Civic Auditorium in Hawaii.

In late September 1958, a Honolulu newspaper ran the following story:

"There he is," the teen-age misses screeched, as 15-year-old Scott Engel stepped off the United States Overseas Airlines plane.

"He's so handsome."

The five-foot seven-inch 121-pound singer said he was "very impressed with the wonderful reception".

Kisses were planted on Scott's cheek as female fans presented him with leis.

Just who is Scott Engel? He's a recording star for Hi-Fi Records (the Orbit label), a regular on Eddie Fisher's television show, and a swingin' performer on stage...

Scott plays the guitar, "but I don't use it in my act… I don't think I play it well enough.

"I've always wanted to become a singer," he said. "And I guess I made it.

"I'm not an expert student at school but I get by all right. Being in the business doesn't interfere too much. I often receive stuff through the mail, and I send them back."

Does the blue-eyed, dark-blond, curly-haired youngster go steady?

"No.

"As far as my favourite performers go, I've got to classify them into three groups: For 'rock' Presley is king, he's my favourite; Steve Lawrence [*male half of the schmaltzy Steve & Eydie duo*] is great… other than 'rock'… For girl singers, Peggy Lee's my favourite."

He was dressed in Ivy League trousers, a flashing green sports shirt, a tan sweater, and tan loafers. "I don't like to dress up… unless there's a show."

The article was accompanied by a photo of young Scotty with a brushed-back, James Dean-style DA hairdo, and an intense, unsmiling gaze. It seemed to have been reproduced from his Ohio family's photo album, as it carried the handwritten dedication "To Grandpa, love Scott."

Another surviving historical artefact is a fan club letter on headed paper, featuring a screen print of young Scotty posing with his eyes averted right, a lightly greased quiff and dogtooth box jacket.

"This is dated November '58, the very first Scott Engel fan club," explains Arnie Potts, English arch-fan of The Walker Brothers and collector of Walker ephemera. "He would have been about 14 [*sic – 15*] at the time. This [membership card] was sent out signed by Scott, and by the look of the type I think it was actually typed by Scott. Sent out to one of his fan club members, Elaine [Igarashi] in Honolulu":

Nov. 28, 1958

Dear Elaine

Please forgive me for not answering your nice letter written at the fan club meeting Sept. 27. All I can say is that I am terribly sorry, but have been so busy. I am staying out of school this week to catch up with the mail, as I like to answer them myself.

Thanks for liking my performance, you kids were a great audience, and I loved doing the show. I'll never forget it either, and hope I can get back again real soon, only stay a little longer.

You kids have been really wonderful, putting my records upon the top I can never thank you enough. I had hoped to have a new record out by now, but we are having trouble finding the right songs.

I also want to thank you for joining my fan club, Geri and Gwyne are doing a great job. I owe both of them so much, plus the rest of you kids. Maybe someday I can show my appreciation. I think of you kids lots, and how wonderful you were to me.

Thanks too for writing, and all the good wishes and compliments that were in your letter. Please forgive me for not answering sooner.

Sincerely,

Scott

SCOTT ENGEL
c/o ORBIT Records
7803 Sunset Blvd.
Hollywood 48, Calif.

In fact, Scott had recently issued two more songs on 78/45rpm discs: 'Charley Bop' demonstrated how quickly rock'n'roll rhythms could be adapted into Tin Pan Alley saccharine, while 'All I Do Is Dream Of You' is an old-fashioned show tune by lyricist Arthur Freed. Around the time of the week-long Honolulu residence, Scott also released 'Paper Doll' and 'Blue Bell'. The latter was the type of would-be show tune that showed up on US variety shows or BBC Home Service radio's *Two-Way Family Favourites*. ("On my way to Albuquerque / I'll be feelin' mighty perky!")

The A-side is more interesting, if only because of its origins. An upbeat but self-pitying ballad about desiring a paper doll, instead of a real woman, so that those "flirty, flirty guys with their flirty, flirty eyes will have to flirt with dollies that are real",[3] it sold up to six million copies in versions by the Mills Brothers and a young Sinatra from 1942-44. "What has turned it into a bonanza," claimed *Billboard*, "is the affection and loyalty displayed for the song by boys in uniform during World War Two." But in June 1936, composer Johnny Black left an estate valued at $100. A lifelong resident of Hamilton, Ohio, he died in its Mercy Hospital (not too far from Grandpa Scott's place on Sherman Avenue) after a fight with customers in his club over 25 cents in change.

In the celebrated documentary film, *Scott Walker: 30 Century Man*, Arnie Potts gives further details of his collection onscreen: "That's a 10-inch acetate. Basically, [Scott] started doing demos when he was about 13 or 14 years old, I think he was pushed along by his mother."

Titles on the 'reference record' by 'Scott Engle' (*sic*) include 'Are These Really Mine?', 'Crazy In Love With You', 'Oh What It Seemed To Be', 'Your Eyes' and 'Misery'. Further unreleased acetates shown to this writer include 'Paradise Cove', 'Everybody But Me', 'When I Kiss You Goodnite', 'Too Young To Know', 'Take This Love', 'Till You Return' and 'When You See Her'. By far the most impressive of a largely corny bunch is 'Sing Boy Sing' – Scott's demo rendition of another rhythmic tune co-written by the up-and-coming Rod McKuen. The released hit version would be by its co-composer, young singer Tommy Sands, but it lacks the demonstrative howl of Scotty Engel at this age. Having employed his baritone like a falsetto in reverse, Scott's vocal style seems to have acquired more depth after he hit puberty – his now broken voice has an almost femininely husky quality, not too far from his favourite jazz singer of the time, Peggy Lee (of 'Fever' fame).[4]

Despite the boy's brooding blond good looks (inheriting his father's Nordic tones and his mother's statuesque but slender frame), he was reticent as to how he might actually respond to the love objects he sang about on his 78s and 45s. "He was very negative and was shy," admitted Betty to the Japanese magazine. "The time that I felt Scott had found someone was very late and when he was 17 years old. She lived in Bakersville [CA] and was very charming with blonde hair. Since she married, we have not seen her at all, but I heard that she married someone about two years ago."[5]

And didn't he have a steady girlfriend till then?
"[*with a little prodding*] Yes, he had. In America it is a custom to have a steady girlfriend when one goes to junior high school. When he was 18 years old he was introduced to Miss Janet when she lived in New York. But they were finished before I knew."

It seems that by the ages of 16/17, and the passing of the fifties into the early sixties, the teenage boy had wearied of the path to stardom – if not forsaken it altogether. In a subsequent mid-decade interview for England's *New Musical Express*, he was keener to present himself as an alienated kid on the verge of juvenile delinquency. One might have thought Scott never harboured any showbiz brat aspirations at all.

"School bored me," he complained, "they didn't make it interesting and it wasn't. Nothing they were talking about seemed important to me then and anyway I was into more important things like getting into trouble!"

This hardly sounds like the sensitive soul whose vocal cords would melt hearts in his newly adopted country. But the interviewee was warming to his theme – rebellion without a cause.

"I was expelled from about three or four schools because I was such a nuisance. I was the guy who'd get a group around him and looked for trouble. We'd get up to all sorts of things. I was a horrible son... I disliked school and the stupidity of having to sit in classes, and I suppose having a gang was a way of forgetting what a drag everything was. It was a form of rebellion, though I wasn't rebelling against my home, just school."

In case 'having a gang' carries any modern-day connotations of random violence and meaningless murder, we should let Scott mitigate in his own favour: "I did join in on most school activities. I always liked music and art and sometimes my drawings would be exhibited to others."

While admitting to colour blindness, the intellectually curious but non-academic high school kid was a student of both classical and contemporary fine art, from the devotional painters of Renaissance Europe to Picasso's cubist period and beyond.

Outside the classroom and the family home, however, life seemed to be a situationist prankster's game of chicken.

"Somehow I found a bunch of guys who felt like me so we had something in common. We... got a car and used to go around at nights finding trouble.

"We didn't want to hurt people – just the authorities. Anything that was owned by the authorities – lampposts, seats, anything – we'd damage. But you had to be quick. Part of being in a gang was having the knack of talking your way out of a tight spot if the police caught you...

"We got caught a couple of times and were prosecuted, but I always managed to avoid detention homes or being put on probation. In the States the police are different from [in the UK], and if they catch you, you can usually talk your way out. Also you've got to do something really bad before they send you to a detention home.[6]

"I must have been the worst son ever and my mother had real worries with me. I was horrible, I'd be out late and she wouldn't know where I was, and it was terrible for her when I got into trouble.[7]

"One of our favourite tricks we got up to in the dead of night. In Beverly Hills the fashion then was to have your beautiful home built at the top of a hill cliff and at the bottom of the garden there would be an outhouse. (That's what you call an outside toilet.)

15

"When everyone was asleep and the streets weren't busy, we'd go up to Beverly Hills and push the outhouses over the edge of the cliffs. Some of them were heavy but... we pushed like mad and the thrill of seeing it going over was really great."

As the sixties drew on and the violence endemic in American culture erupted, often irrationally and without warning, Scott and his LA buddies' antics would fade into the memory of a more innocent era. By the end of that psychotic decade, 'pranks' could equate with slaughtering an entire houseful of people in the Hollywood Hills. In contrast, Scott's own 'creative destruction' didn't extend further than purportedly blowing up a telephone booth with cherry bombs smuggled over the Mexican border. Similar pyrotechnics in a toilet cubicle got him suspended for several weeks, but it was the use of 'profane language' in the street that got him expelled from his last public (non-fee paying) school – resulting in Betty paying for his stint at Hollywood High.

Although his attendance could be erratic (as alluded to in the letter to young fan Elaine), Hollywood High's more creative environment eased some of the tedium he'd previously felt in one interchangeable school after another. It was here that he joined the California Youth Orchestra, learning to play the double bass. Already basically competent on the guitar, he would soon combine his two chosen instruments to become a bass guitarist. Scott also found a focus for his musical interests far removed from the Americana of the era, in the florid themes of Mozart and busy sonatas of Haydn.

Modern jazz too offered new avenues of exploration. He started attending the Lighthouse Café underage on Hermosa Beach, a showcase for West Coast jazz since the early forties. It was here he'd listen to the fluid guitar stylings of Barney Kessel, played live. Having switched his own instrumental allegiance from guitar to bass, Scott took occasional lessons with jazz bassist Marty Budwood. It epitomised the 'cool jazz' ethos of LA, a world away from the frenetic storms brewing in New York as John Coltrane and Ornette Coleman took improvisation further and further out. It was also light years away from mainstream pop – which was surely no longer where it was at (daddy-o).

At age 16, however, the sometime demo singer was still issuing single releases. In 1959, grown-up smoocher 'The Golden Rule Of Love' might have made a passable last dance for younger members at a rotary club. More rock'n'roll-inflected were 'Comin' Home'/'I Don't Wanna Know' – both sides of the disc written by original rockabilly Johnny Burnette. Cheesy backing vocals on the A-side dulled its edge, though the flip boasted authentic-sounding hillbilly guitar. 'Take This Love'/'Till You Return' were more schmaltz, underlined by horribly obtrusive backing vocals.

"There's a great story about Scott," be-quiffed English singer/ guitarist Richard Hawley testified much later. "I worked with him... I think it was [at] Metropolis [studios in west London], and there was a little fifties specialist rock'n'roll shop a couple of doors down. I cheekily nipped in there when we should have been doing a session and I bought loads of rock'n'roll stuff, like an Eddie Cochran album. Scott was really interested in these records, 'cos it was stuff that he grew up with, and he pulled the Eddie Cochran one out and he said, 'Shake my hand.' I shook his hand and he said, 'When I was 16 I met Eddie Cochran, so you're shaking Eddie Cochran's hand through me.' That was a bit of a moment."

The late, lamented Eddie, like the young Scott, was recording for Liberty Records at the time. But Scott was still then a protégé of mainstream pop singer Eddie Fisher, cropping up on Fisher's TV series several times from 1957-59. "I sang at a luncheon in Palm Springs and Eddie Fisher was there," he later admitted, "and he kind of adopted me. He took me on a tour of 15, 16 TV shows with him, but then he got burned..."

In 1959, the scandal of Fisher's affair with a friend of his actress wife Debbie Reynolds ('America's sweetheart'), a sultry brunette named Elizabeth Taylor, put the skids on his career. The TV show was dropped; Eddie could do little for young Scott, being too preoccupied with saving himself. The young man's pop–music career seemed stuck in a deep, crackling groove.

The boy initially took some time out to think, indicating to his mother that he might give up singing altogether and enter business school. As the new decade beckoned, however, Scott Engel took the more creative step of enrolling at California's Chouinard Art Institute as a trainee commercial artist, much to Betty's relief. The college's co–director and chief patron was Walt Disney, whose suburban utopia in Burbank mirrored the anodyne fantasy of Disneyland as a living environment for the future.

It could have been a major step toward corporate conformity for the young man. "I liked it at the time," he'd admit. "There seemed to be nothing for me in music, and I'd felt sure there was, but nothing was clear to me." As a newly diligent student, Scott was even given some design assignments by Uncle Walt himself.

But something had to give. As a self-professed cynic who'd lived a largely independent life in several major American cities by his mid-teens, the boy was feeling more worldly (and at the same time more out of place) than his tender age gave him a right to be. His yearning for an indefinable freedom found expression in the books and movies of the age – or at least in its art cinema and hip lit.

"I used to go to these art cinemas on Wishire Boulevard and watch Bergman or Fellini or Bresson," he later recalled. "It was like it was in my blood, y'know?... I had an enormous desire for something that was not American, for something that nobody in my environment really understood."

But one latter-day offshoot of US culture did connect. Even before the coming of the hippie era, 'drop out and hit the road' was becoming something of a cliché. If the idea of cruising America's endless highways and byways retains a romantic feel even to this day, it's due at least in part to Jack Kerouac's *On The Road* – which reads largely as a mythologisation of the author and his beat generation buddies like Burroughs and Ginsberg.

(While Scott picked up on the 1957 novel, like many young students of the time, he reserved his greatest admiration for a writer who was not of the beat generation but served to inspire it. As a kind of godfather figure to the movement, Henry Miller's prose does not suffer from Kerouac's attempts to replicate jazz riffs in print. His matter-of-factness about sex exudes poeticism as well as squalor – something the older Scott would later detect in a certain Belgian songwriter.)

So it was that, before he reached his 17th birthday, Scott Engel decided to 'see America' by hitchhiking all the way back to the East Coast alone. While he later spoke of how he'd blown a $2,000 loan from his dad (who he rarely saw at this stage) on a car, his road trip seems to have been facilitated by sticking out his thumb and doing moonlight flits before his motel bill was due. Noel Sr. may have joked to the *Hamilton High School Review* in 1928, when asked about his 'Predetermined Predicament (20 years hence)', that he'd become a 'hoboe' (sounding more like a woodwind instrument than a freight train rider). But in 1959 he was following the American corporate dream. It was his son who'd become a bum – however temporarily.

On coming to stardom in the UK, Scott would later paint his experience as a sordid view of the USA's underbelly – without describing it in detail, he'd darkly allude to how he was exposed to people and situations that only worsened the cynicism which made many people take against him. At best, the drifting characters he'd met along the way might turn up, disguised, in some later song lyric.

But by the time he briefly became a television personality, in the late sixties, he was taking an altogether more sentimental view:

"I came from the beatnik era in America," he liltingly told the audience of his TV show, *Scott*. "They labelled it the beatnik era anyway. I read Jack Kerouac and dug progressive jazz and got kicked out of schools and hitchhiked across America, the whole bit you see. Met a lot of wonderful people, the relationships were ephemeral but some of the best I've ever known, and this is a song about it."

(The song is 'It's Raining Today', from Scott's third solo album.)

Scott Engel never specifically indicated how long this period lasted. His art studies would soon resume – and, perhaps most incongruous of all, the early sixties would see further detours down Tin Pan Alley. 'Anything Will Do' was issued in 1961 on the Liberty label; Scott's voice may have matured, but the material is just as cheesy (a dance number referencing contemporary crazes like the Twist – "Wah-ooh! Wah-ooh!").

In 1962, the final recordings by a teenage Scott Engel comprised four tracks on an EP – though its release would be deferred for four years, until the vocalist had achieved some renown all the way across the Atlantic. Standing out from the other slices of American cheese, lead track 'I Broke My Own Heart' is a swinging aw-shucks number, complete with tinkling barroom piano and brush drums. 'What Do You Say?' is a country-tinged ballad of regret which perhaps comes closest to the early part of Scott's professional singing career. For all his exploration of other forms of music, this track testifies to his growing admiration of Jack Jones – a crooner with perfect pitch and vocal control who took the genre to a new technical level.[8]

And then it was over. Or, if we shift our perspective, it was just beginning.

"It happened for so many people around the same time," reflects Scott of his early years, "when Elvis appeared, of course, and then everybody thought yes, I'd like to do this, because he inspired everybody. So it didn't really start happening for me till I started joining bands, and I was in a lot of bands – blues bands and all kinds of bands, just as a player."

Scott Engel the student had resumed his art studies. Scott Engel the musician was now strictly a jobbing bassist. For all his dismissal of his earliest recordings, it seems that by then he'd experienced a taste of stardom on a micro-scale – and found it wanting.

Notes

1   No one ever talked their way through a lyric like McKuen. In the sixties, he would collide again with Scott's personal orbit by becoming the first lyricist to translate a *chansonnier* named Jacques Brel into English. At this stage, however, both men's European digressions seemed like a lifetime away – and half a world away, for Scott at least.

2   "The first record I ever bought was Frankie Lymon's 'Why Do Fools Fall In Love?'" It can be safely assumed that records by the older crooners that young Scott learned his technique from were supplied by Betty.

3   Roxy Music's 'In Every Dream Home A Heartache' this is *not*.

4   In 1968, Scott would take out an injunction against Ember Records who planned to release a compilation of early demo and single cuts under the title *Scott Walker* – including 'Too Young', a gruesome teen ballad previously a hit for DJ Jimmy Young in the UK and later for Donny Osmond, and Rodgers and Hammerstein's 'Sunday', from their musical *Flower Drum Song*. The offence was avoided by adding *Looking Back With...* to the album title.

5   This interview took place in the late sixties.

6   What Scott said at the time (1966) was contrary to the prevailing wisdom. While an old-fashioned 'clip round the ear' by British bobbies might more realistically translate as a kick in the balls, it was less harsh than being sent to one of the USA's scarier reformatories – which were often hunting grounds for predatory gang members.

7   "Because... we moved from place to place, he was not used to school," Betty later told the Japanese fans. "We don't say he was a good student. But I am to blame. It made him negative."

   Is it the reason he converted to music?

   "I think so. From the first he liked music. But he had much time to play the guitar alone, I think he dreamed of being a singer."

8   If Sinatra sang songs for swinging lovers, it can be argued that Jones produced hi-fi music for hip insurance salesmen.

Chapter 2

Walker See Walker

Meet the Hippies… the Teenyboppers with their too-tight capris… and the Pot-Partygoers – out for a new thrill… a new kick!

Poster blurb for *Riot On Sunset Strip*, a sixties exploitation movie featuring LA band the Standells

Since settling in Los Angeles, Scott Engel had found a near-constant companion in his best friend John Stewart. To some extent John was a kind of doppelganger: young, good-looking; literate and artistic, with an interest in the performing arts; aloof but not quite too cool for school.

He also shared Scott's precociously cynical view of the local entertainment scene – though he wasn't above looking for the main chance, if there was one to be found.

It was later claimed that young Engel was accompanying his pal Stewart when they attended an audition for bit-part players on a TV show, *Playhouse 90*. It was here, in 1960, that Scott would first encounter another significant figure in his life – a rangy blond beach-boy type named John Maus, who'd won a gig as an extra in the TV play.

Maus was also a local musician with Teutonic roots, like Scott. Before appearing on camera, he was killing time and calming his nerves by strumming his guitar. It may have been the similarities between them that caused a near-clash, the anti-magnetic repulsion of two people close enough in time and place to feel the need to outdo each other.

"He asked me if he could play something too and did some up-tempo rock song," John Maus later recalled of his first meeting with Scott Engel. "I thought he was posing a bit too much and taking himself a bit too seriously, generally overdoing the cool-kid act."

They took their leave with the detachment of two young men who'd just entered into a who-can-piss-furthest contest, without quite knowing why.

This 'other John' was irked by the Engel kid, who'd boasted of knowing more guitar chords than his new acquaintance. As a guitarist, however, Scott's activities remained strictly on the hobby level. As a bassist, he'd find a small niche on the local music scene with the instrumental groups flowering in the wake of non-singing (or rarely singing) guitarists like Duane Eddy and Link Wray. Surf rock had not yet found its wave, but the riffing dance bands Scott occasionally performed with paved the way for the likes of The Surfaris.

Maus was no slouch in that department either. He was proficient enough to give guitar lessons to his friend Carl Wilson, who'd soon form a band called The Beach Boys with his brothers Brian and Dennis. (The latter also buddied up with John over a shared love of the hot-rod and beach-bum lifestyle.)

It was to be another couple of years before the two young Californians met again. By 1962, all of Scott's tentative steps toward becoming a crooning star had been put behind him, in favour of laying down a solid bass rhythm on the Hollywood band scene. Although he'd cut his last vocal tracks that same year, it seems to have been viewed by him as something from his past – something he'd never seriously intended.

John Maus had no such misgivings. He continued to play guitar and sing wherever there was an opportunity – though the early sixties vogue for girl groups led to his photogenic sister Judy taking over vocals. Originally a duo, in the summer of '62 John & Judy expanded into a full band line-up.

"We changed our name to Judy & The Gents," recalled John, "and had this residency at this coffee-house called Pandora's Box every Sunday night. The Beach Boys played on Fridays and Saturdays, and on Sundays, we'd be supported by a guest recording act...

"One night, later in 1962, the guest group at Pandora's Box were The Routers, a surf band who had a hit called 'Let's Go'. The bass player was Scott Engel."

The Routers were, like their contemporaries The Ventures, more of a musical franchise than a fulltime band. With pickup members who could work the studio or the clubs, there was no permanent line-up. For this reason, it's still a moot point to some pop-music historians as to whether the bassist on their rudimentary cheerleader chant (bah–bah, bah–bah–bah, bah–bah–bah–bah, "*Let's go!*"[1]) was actually Scott rather than some other session man.

There is no doubt that the ex-crooner was then cutting out a new life for himself on the Hollywood music scene. He also claimed credit for the bass on Sandy Nelson's instrumental 45 'Let There Be Drums' – a far superior piece to The Routers', anchored by a heavy bass riff as drummer Nelson scattered himself over the tom-toms and hi-hats. Scott and John Stewart (on guitar and occasional vocals) were playing backing gigs for Phil Spector-produced artists like Ike and Tina Turner and (more significantly) The Righteous Brothers, as well as cutting occasional instrumental tracks under a variety of names including The Moongooners, The Newporters and, a little later, The Dalton Brothers. Scott even did gofer work for wunderkind Spector at his Gold Star Studios and drove a van for Liberty Records, his former record label.

But all this disparate activity wasn't enough to keep a boy occupied. "The next day Scott asked if he could join my band as a bass player,"

John Maus recalled the aftermath of the Routers gig. "I wasn't happy with either my bass player or drummer at the time, so the deal was for Scott to find a good drummer then they would both be hired. He found a guy named Spider Webb, a flamboyant drummer reminiscent of Gene Krupa, one of the best in LA at the time."

Judy & The Gents soon procured bookings at the Kismet, one of downtown LA's most 'in' nightclubs. John remained the lead singer, but sister Judy stepped forward to sing and dance as their 'Twist girl'. Maus also encouraged his new bandmate to sing backing vocals to his sister and harmonies with himself, although "he seemed to have a hang-up about singing". In 1963, being a vocalist seemed to be all in the past for Scott Engel. He was now a working musician for a gigging rock'n'roll band.

Around this time, Hollywood photographer John Reed took publicity photos of Judy & The Gents which showed the young Engel with a goatee beard. This may have had an ulterior purpose. "Scott and I were both 20 – a year shy of the legal age to be in a club," acknowledged Maus. Due to the USA's puritanical licensing laws, both risked arrest by developing a taste for drinking hard spirits below the age of 21. As John also noted, Scott "had a decent phoney draft card" to ensure he got served. The eventual arrival of his genuine draft card would prove rather more problematic.

In the summer of 1963, Maus also joined Engel on the surf instrumental scene when they formed a pickup band to capitalise on the massive singles hit 'Wipeout' by The Surfaris. As The Surfaris were every bit as amorphous a grouping as The Routers, the foursome could pretend to be the real McCoy and fill a string of dates (apparently fraudulently) in the Midwest. It would be the last tour Engel would undertake for some time.

Maus found his new sidekick less interested in rehearsing with the group than with continuing his art studies. Gary Leeds, who was yet to show up on Scott's radar, later noted how he "had a natural ability to draw what he saw; he did portraits of Ray Charles and other famous people that looked just like photographs, but he was never satisfied and would always change them or throw them in the trash."

Any gigs outside of Hollywood – even in LA County – were treated as an unwelcome distraction and avoided where possible. It would not be the last time his distaste for the touring routine was made manifest.

The young Engel remained something of a rock'n'roll dilettante, however. Rather than commit to one band, he continued to record intermittently with Stewart. The following year, 1963, saw them cut an original single with the small independent Martay label. For their song, they went to a mercurial young Texan who had come to LA to make a splash in the record industry.

Of the dozen or more songs they listened to by Jim Smith, it was 'I Only Came To Dance With You' which won their favour. Smith, a charismatic showman who, under the name P.J. Proby, would later come on like a rougher hewn Elvis, was not yet a star – like Scott Engel himself, he was an American performer whose period of stardom would be a strictly British phenomenon.

Scott first tested out the song on his new bandmate, 'the other John'. Its twin Stewart/Engel harmonies still stand up today as one of the more atmospheric teen ballads of the early sixties, blown along on a burst of mariachi trumpet that Proby's musical memory exported from the Tex-Mex border. Maus would later claim Engel never revealed who was behind the track he played, crediting it to The Dalton Brothers – named after the Wild West lawmen-turned-outlaws. "I told him it was OK, and no big deal, which it wasn't," said John.

His bandmate took it on the chin and kept his counsel to himself. The record would not see wide release till three years later – by which point the Engel-Maus musical alliance would be well established. It became the title track of a Dalton Brothers album which, when issued by Capitol Records' Tower subsidiary in 1966,[2] featured mostly instrumentals of unknown origin – and the single's B-side, 'Without Your Love', a heartbroken Everly Brothers-type ballad with a heavy Western-style bass. One other notable exception is a surf-rock instrumental called 'Devil Surfer'[3] which, when first issued by Martay in 1963, appears to have been the final single credited to one-time family entertainer Scott Engel.

To their peers of the time, it must have looked as though the Engel-Stewart musical partnership would endure – whether they made the leap to pro songwriters/record producers or else just faded into obscurity. Production credits for this period include 1962's 'Jump Down' c/w 'Wish You Were Here' by a band called Chosen Few – the B-side of which sounds as if its la-la backing was pastiched by Elton John on 'Crocodile Rock' a decade later. 1963's 'Have I Lost My Touch?' c/w 'Tell Me In The Sunlight' by Margie Day resembled a WASP-ish take on Spector's work with The Ronettes, the semi-cinematic production credited to 'Alec Noel' (Stewart's middle name/Engel's forename).

Despite this welter of activity, 20-year-old Scott Engel maintained a distinctly un-rock'n'roll demeanour. "Scott never displayed any wild behaviour," a mature John Maus would acknowledge. "He was a quiet, laid back, normal guy with a good sense of humour. He didn't seek attention, or garner any extra attention either… He liked foreign films, and listened to classical and jazz music. Aside from John Stewart, I never met or heard of any other friends he had. He was quite a private person."

The show at which the 'Walker' stage name first appeared was on November 30, 1963 at the Trolley-Ho! club. This was the debut of The Walker Family – the 'family name' taken from the pseudonym John derived from his mother's maiden name, irritated by how his surname Maus (which the family pronounced 'Moss') was spoken in a way that make him sound like Uncle Walt's creation Mickey. From the get-go, it was accepted by an audience who took it as read that fair-skinned/fair-haired John, Judy and Scott were all related.

One of their regular gigs was the Come To The Party club – later to become the celebrated Whisky A Go Go – on Hollywood's Sunset Strip. P.J. Proby (then trading under the brash moniker Jet Powers) would join them there for drinking sessions, where ingénue boozers Scott and John got their palates used to rum and Coke, or vodka and 7-Up.

Then The Walker Family went on apparently permanent hiatus for a few months. The strong-willed Judy, finding her ambitions stifled, decamped to be a singer/dancer with a band working in Las Vegas. It looked like everyone would just go their separate ways, but the LA band scene was a small solar system. John eventually found his personal trajectory colliding with Scott's orbit.

"In early 1964, I got a call from Donnie Brooks," recalled John, "who asked me to play guitar for him at an audition at a hotel on the Strip. I asked him about the line-up and he told me that Scott Engel was on bass."

Brooks was a young be-suited Mr Showbiz type on the scene, performing white-boy retreads of the Twist and R&B standards like Ray Charles' 'What'd I Say'. Donnie and Scott would not remain best of friends, but John was happy enough to be back working with his bandmate – who, he noted, was taking a more musicianly approach to his bass amp equipment than in his surf rock days.

"Donnie was hired permanently for the gig – he was the headliner and we were his backing group," confirmed John. "We also played our own sets, six nights a week for two weeks, with Al 'Tiny' Schneider as our new drummer."

The former Walker Family members now formed the nucleus of The Walker Brothers Trio. With their classic smart-casual look of black polo-neck sweaters, black blazers and black boots, 'John Walker' and 'Scott Walker' were yet to transform into the handsome androgynes with tumbledown moptops inspired by The Beatles.[4]

With a vigour born of his hard-working family's healthy hunger for the dollar, John naturally fell into the role of band leader and business negotiator. "Donnie Brooks called to ask if he could bring in some club owners so he could audition for them, using us as his backup band," he'd later recall. "It was lucky for us that one of the club owners was Bill Gazzarri."

As the owner of Gazzarri's nightclub on La Cienega Boulevard, the Italianate entrepreneur would be one of the accidental overseers of the sixties rock explosion. As the decade evolved, The Byrds, The Doors and Buffalo Springfield would all play early gigs in the club – as would the original Walker Brothers.[5]

"It only really started getting serious when I sang with The Walker Brothers," Scott now acknowledges. "Nights when John couldn't sing, I would sing at the clubs, because I was the bass player. So we started to work sessions and I think I've said this before, but if I hadn't have been a singer I would have probably been a session musician by now."

It seems a wistful notion, perhaps reflecting on a life that might have been lived away from the madness of the spotlight. But it echoes with the emptiness of unrealised ideas and unfulfilled projects. Whatever the intensity of what was to follow, this would not be the case.

The Walker Brothers was now a band with two singers – neither taking a fulltime role as lead, each adapting to the same R&B tunes or pop hits of the day as the occasion required. As John defined it, "We would alternate harmonies, depending on who was more comfortable doing the lead part. I usually sang the rock stuff because I've got a scratchier voice. Scott sang the ballads."

John and genial bruiser Tiny were often unnerved by how Scott would go on a walkabout in the 15-minute break between their two sets, but could always drag him back to the stage – even if it meant starting the next set without him. His idiosyncratic approach to timekeeping would follow John throughout the Walkers' career.

The Walker Brothers Trio was a danceable hit at Gazzarri's. For the first time since his fifties tours of civic centres and TV studios, Scott Engel was at the centre of something that was becoming a palpable success.

"This was the beginning of the disco[theque] era, so the places in Hollywood were very, very packed all the time," he reminisces. "They were packed seven nights a week. People were queuing round the block, especially at the weekends, to get in. And I mean big movie stars, Lana Turner and all these people, would come in.

So you had that kind of thing every night, it was fantastic. It was an incredible scene, there were four big clubs at that time and they were all just really jamming. We're talking about the Whisky A Go Go, that had just opened on the Strip, we used to alternate and play there on weekends. It was a great time."

And yet Scott's closest bandmate – who'd now called him a friend for over a year – found it hard to get close to him on a personal level. "Scott never got into discussing his personal relationships or girlfriends," reflected John. "I know there was a waitress at Gazzarri's named Ann who fancied him, and that they became a quiet item. Aside from commenting about some attractive woman we'd all seen, he kept his thoughts about the ladies to himself."

Gary Leeds agrees. "Scott never discussed his private life with me. I think he had one or two girlfriends, but I can't remember their names. One was also going with... Donnie Brooks; I think she was cheating on him with Scott."

It may be apt that he kept the secrets of the heart so tightly locked up inside. In the years that followed, Scott Walker as a singer would become synonymous with the insanity and drama of the experience commonly known as love. His flair for the dramatic might never have been so pronounced if personal attraction and sex had been merely casual matters.

The Walkers would soon become regular performers on US TV, initially in January 1964 on local TV pop show *9th Street A Go-Go* – which would soon be retitled as the less parochial *Hollywood A Go-Go*. On their first TV appearance, the two white Californians sang the negro–spiritual derived 'Cotton Fields', with John strumming acoustic guitar and taking lead vocal. It was the start of a regular residency, performing three songs a show (sometimes in truncated versions) while playing Gazzarri's five nights a week, where the dancers also featured onscreen.

"Later in 1964, Nik Venet came to see us at Gazzarri's," said John. "Nik was an A&R man at Mercury Records; he had a lot of clout and expressed an interest in signing Scott and me... At the time, there were so many phoneys coming in the club each night, and they were always offering us deals, so we disregarded his advances and didn't take him seriously."

After negotiations between Venet and the patriarchal Gazzarri, whose wife was doing her best to beef up slender Engel with pasta, the gently Mafioso-like club owner convinced them to sign. The Walker Brothers were now a Mercury recording duo – John and Scott only, contracted as vocalists but not as musicians, "which was fine with us at the time as we both considered ourselves singers who played instruments, and not the other way around," John later explained. "Tiny seemed pleased for both of us..."[6]

With staged photographic portraits of the two singers, Mercury seemed set on promoting them as a more photogenic counterpart to The Righteous Brothers. While there was never any disputing the fact that the 'Brothers' were in fact two unrelated boys named Maus and Engel, there was still an aesthetic uniformity to Scott and John that just wasn't there with the totally dissimilar Bill Medley and Bobby Hatfield.

As with virtually all of the Walkers' repertoire at the time, the first single selected by the record label for release was a cover version. 'Pretty Girls Everywhere' had been a 1958 hit for Eugene Church, a simple pop celebration of boys cruising for chicks. ("If I make it to the show... / Even at the rodeo they come on horses.") With a vaguely flamenco-ish backing and parping sixties brass replacing the original call-and-response vocals, it's sung as a duet where it's difficult to distinguish John's voice from Scott's or vice versa.

Surviving footage from the TV show *Shindig* shows them in suits and ties with button-down collars, their hair still quiffed, miming unconvincingly without mikes or leads as Scott follows John around a bevy of conventional sixties chicks, looking vaguely embarrassed. They were not yet The Walker Brothers that would go down in pop history, either visually or musically.

The B-side, 'Doin' The Jerk', is remarkable only in that it's the first Walker Brothers songwriting credit of Scott Engel. Beyond that, it's akin to finding that, say, as compelling a performer as

Lou Reed started out as a record company songwriter by writing about a silly (and in his case imaginary) dance craze.[7] The Jerk was another parochial five-minute fad, and The Walker Brothers secured a slot in a teen movie called *Beach Ball* (one of many cash-ins on successful teen-exploitation movie *Beach Party*) to tell the world all about it – alongside, rather impressively, The Righteous Brothers, The Supremes and The Four Seasons. Otherwise it was as per the A-side – thin but blaring brass and vocal harmonies that could have been either singer. "There's a new dance, the hippies call it the Jerk," sang Scott and John – referring to beach party hipsters, rather than the psychedelic pseudo-beats who would soon arrive in California.

(Scott would never be quite so tolerant of *them*.)

Shindig was the US brainchild of British pop TV producer Jack Good, who had a hit show at home with *Oh Boy!* The toothsome, blonder-than-blond Walkers became intermittent regulars. On the third show they gave a creditable account of Larry Williams' R&B number 'Slow Down' – as recently covered by The Beatles.[8] On the same edition they covered Brit band Manfred Mann's catchy but irritating 'Do Wah Diddy Diddy'. The musical agenda was, by 1964, being set by English beat groups and the so-called 'British invasion'. In an audacious act of cultural appropriation, bands from the northwest and southeast of England were re-exporting rhythm and blues to the USA – which, given the white-bread nature of so much early sixties pop, must have sounded like an authentically foreign phenomenon to many young American ears.

Shindig also marked the first exposure of The Walker Brothers in the US national media, when they were photographed on set. "I remember when Scott walked into Gazzarri's around nine o'clock one night," recalled John, "with the magazine rolled up in his hand, asking me if I had seen the latest *Newsweek*, to which I said no, and he proudly showed me the photo." Fame was not yet anathema to one half of the Walker Brothers duo – but at that stage it was only of the most ephemeral kind.

The Walkers also started copping their sartorial licks from the Brits. Among the second wave of British invaders (after The Beatles) were The Rolling Stones, the epitome of white boys singing the blues. As new habitués of Gazzarri's, the surly suburban Brits, with long fringes that met their eyebrows and ass-freezer jackets, made John and Scott's rock'n'roll hairstyles look very old-fashioned. The former responded by growing his hair out; his bassist partner went the whole nine yards, restyling his hair in an approximation of the look Astrid Kirchherr developed for The Beatles in Hamburg.

As with any decade, the early sixties were really the tail end of the era that preceded them. It was still seen as subversive – if not all-out 'faggy' – for Scott and John to walk down a Hollywood street with silky hair gravitating towards their shoulders. "Guys would whistle at us, and folks very likely questioned our sexual orientation," acknowledged John. "We just blew it off, but I guess we were each a little too chicken to face the stares and flak alone, so we always went in together for moral support."

In late 1964, the Walkers also made the closer acquaintance of a fellow Sunset Strip anglophile. Gary Leeds was the drummer of The Standells, an LA beat band whose name was reputedly derived from standing around waiting for club bookings. The Standells would write their own footnote to pop-music history with 'Dirty Water', a 1966 white-boy R&B single inspired by the Stones.[9]

But that was still in the future, when Gary had long since vacated the drum seat. For now, the goofy guy with the dark Beatle haircut and Chelsea boots was more interested in networking at Gazzarri's and getting to know The Walker Brothers – both of whom were distant acquaintances of his from the LA scene. It wouldn't take long for him to become best of friends with both – including the usually reticent Scott.

"I was always friendly with Gary because he has a great sense of humour," Scott later confirmed, comparing his zaniness to the idiot-savant humour of Jerry Lewis. John claimed that Gary was known to have donned one of the popular Don Post monster masks of the time, springing out on unsuspecting 'victims' in the Hollywood Hills dressed as the Wolfman.

"Gary was playing with a group called The Standells at the Peppermint Lounge," Scott recalls, "and [he] decided I guess to come to England with P.J. Proby. It was a big mistake evidently, because he came back."

Gary Leeds left The Standells to drum for Proby (who had now adopted his latest stage alias fulltime), following him to England for a support slot on a Beatles special directed by *Oh Boy!/Shindig* producer Jack Good. It was an eye-opening experience.

It was the start of a period of British stardom for Proby, the Elvis-alike who infused standard tunes like 'Hold Me' with a manic zest and Beatlesque undertones to suit his newly adopted market.[10] New drummer Leeds was a firsthand witness to P.J.'s insatiable appetite for girls and booze: "P.J. and I moved into a mews house owned by Shirley Bassey, a stone's throw from the Royal Albert Hall. P.J. threw a few parties at this house, and they would sometimes last all night long. When I came downstairs in the morning, I would not be surprised to find a couple of girls passed out on the floor with hardly any clothes on, empty beer bottles everywhere, cigarettes, panties and bras strewn all over the floor."

Ultimately, Gary would be unable to play onstage for Proby, citing problems with work permits and Musicians Union rules. Proby, for his part, claims the genial Leeds had hoodwinked him as to how well he could actually play the drums. In any case, before the end of 1964 Gary was back home in California.

"But he'd been over here[11] and he'd seen the scene," testifies Scott, "he knew what was going on, so he came over to see us one night and he said, 'Would you be interested in going?', because he had a financier. So I said, 'Of course.'"

The 'financier' was actually Gary's generous stepfather, who was prepared to fund the Walkers to the tune of $5,000, with supplements up to a total of $10,000. (No small amount of money in the mid-sixties.) The corresponding condition was that Gary would replace the hapless Tiny on drums.

"I approached Scott and John, laid out the deal, and left it with them," confirms Gary. "Scott really did want to take up the offer, because he loved Europe, its films, its culture and everything about it…

"There were also a lot of meetings with all the parents. When we finally made up our minds to go to England, Scott's mother, Betty, wasn't too happy."

"Scott and I lapped up every detail as we had been considering going to Britain to check out English groups," elaborated John. "Scott and I thought British music was very cool, and started using the top UK songs in our sets. The audiences loved them too, regularly requesting Rolling Stones and Beatles hits."

In fact one of their final *Shindig* appearances, dated January 20, 1965, featured Scott and John singing an uptempo truncation of The Beatles' 'I'm A Loser', John Lennon's sulkily defiant lost-love song.

At the same time, The Walker Brothers had no counterpart UK contract to match their US deal with Mercury, nor did they have any contacts in the UK music industry. As Maus attested, to him and Engel the visit was to be strictly exploratory.

"On February 16, 1965, the day before we left for England," said John, "we finished up recording our second single, 'Love Her', at RCA studios; it was backed with 'Theme From *The Seventh Dawn*'. Again it was Nik Venet who chose the songs. 'The Seventh Dawn' was originally meant to be the A-side, but 'Love Her' was chosen because Nik decided it was the more commercial of the two."

The arranger chosen by Venet was Jack Nitzsche, due to his fundamental role in creating the Spector 'Wall of Sound'. As Engel commented in the mid-sixties, his brief seemed to be to create an aural environment that might both resemble and outstrip The Righteous Brothers.

"In fact I wasn't the lead vocal with [The Walker Brothers]," Scott acknowledges of this pivotal moment, "John was the lead vocalist, but there was this ballad they wanted to do called 'Love Her'. And so they switched it around because they had to go with the guy with the lowest voice. So it was kind of accidental."

Gary Leeds claims to have suggested the choice of Brill Building songwriters Barry Mann and Cynthia Weil's 'Love Her',[12] formerly the B-side of The Everly Brothers' 'The Girl Sang The Blues'. Mann and Weil had composed 'You've Lost That Lovin' Feelin' for Spector/The Righteous Brothers and the idea was clearly to emulate that track for its emotional drama. But what came out was an exercise in understatement.

"When Nik said, 'I'll have Scott sing solo with the bass,' Scott was terrified," John later recollected. "He was looking at me as if to say, 'Don't make me do this, it's not working. Don't leave me out here.'… But I knew it was working."

Whereas Don and Phil Everly's trademark harmonies had suggested brotherly support and a hand around the shoulder in this lyric of lost love and regret, Scott's voice reverberates alone in the finely balanced mix of orchestra and rhythm guitar, like a stray planetoid of solitude. As he moodily instructs his girl's new lover to "love her like I couldn't do", John's high-pitched backing shadows him as if several light years away while still managing to underline the emotion.

This is the point in time and aural space when the Walker Brothers' sound was truly born.

Gary Leeds, by then still only a theoretical member of the Walkers, was present at RCA Studios for the recording – which directly followed The Rolling Stones cutting 'The Last Time', also with Nitzsche. "Scott asked me if I knew that this was also where Elvis recorded; I was very impressed… Scott had a voice more in the vein of Frank Sinatra or Tony Bennett, smooth and mellow and deep. John's was a little higher, gravelly, and ideally suited to rock'n'roll."

Nitzsche utilised the same 38-piece orchestra that he'd used for Spector's records, overdubbing the players until they all came together in two and a half minutes of tuneful mournfulness. For all that, he was underwhelmed by the performance, describing Scott's vocal style as "too white" and praising instead the version by demo singer Freddie Scott.

On the flip side, 'The Seventh Dawn' crystallised that fading point of the late fifties/early sixties when Hollywood themes always dripped with sentimentality – even if set during a violent crisis like the Malayan war, as with this martial love story.[13] Singing a lyric by Broadway songwriter Paul Francis Webster, Scott and John's vocals are stereophonically separate but so sweetly close in tone as to be indistinguishable.

The sugary string arrangement would have made *Family Favourites* fare on either side of the Atlantic, harking back to Scott's discarded crooning days as a teenager. (It truly *was* 'white music'.) But Nik Venet's decision to flip 'The Seventh Dawn' had made the Walkers take a more interesting turn.

When Scott Engel and John Maus flew to London with Gary Leeds, on February 17, 1965, the former was one step ahead of being drafted into the intensifying Vietnamese war. He later also alluded to relief at leaving what he saw as an increasingly brutal and philistine American culture behind.

Not everyone was as thrilled, however.

Several years later, Scott's mother, 'Mrs Betty', was interviewed on the subject by the Japanese fanzine *Scott Times*:

How did she think about it when he told her?
"I doubted my senses for a moment... and also I wondered about him leaving [art] school."

How did he tell you about it?
"He said that he had a chance to go to England and that he would like me to let him go there. And he said that I must not worry about him as he would come back after six weeks. But he won't come back yet after six years."

If it now seems remarkable for a 22-year-old man to be seeking permission to travel abroad from his mother, bear in mind that Betty Engel also extended a maternal hand towards John and Gary. She addressed a letter to all three young men, which the Japanese quaintly translated as follows:

"If you're having troubles come to us. Your parents and I will wait for you but Scott gets along alone. So please help each other… but if you cannot do anything at all, please come back to us."

Notes

1   The chant-style rhythm predated the English soccer chants that soon became commonplace across the Atlantic. Once Scott crossed the ocean, he may have found something oddly familiar in the football crowd noise that sometimes jangled his nerves: duh-duh, duh-duh-duh, duh-duh-duh-duh, "*Chel-sea!*"

2   Credited on the cover to 'John Stewart and Scott Engel, Original Members of The Walker Brothers'. This seemingly catchpenny 'error' was compounded by a cover portrait of a grinning Scott and pensive John, their similar brown hair (Scott does not appear blond in the least) underlining the suggestion of them as siblings. It also lends credence to sixties buff journalists who see Stewart as a kind of silent 'fourth Brother'.

3   'Devil Surfer' contains the controlled trebly hysteria of the best surf instrumentals – verging on the cinematic quality that, much later, led Quentin Tarantino to compare Dick Dale (composer of 'Misirlou', the *Pulp Fiction* theme) with Ennio Morricone.

4   The 'Brothers'' hair was growing long – though they still had the brushed-back semi-quiffs, as styled by trendy Hollywood hairdresser Jay Sebring. A photo from this time has them looking like grown-up versions of the spooky blond kids in 1960 movie *Village Of The Damned*.

5   After a move to Sunset Boulevard, Gazzarri's would also be instrumental in the late seventies launch of heavy metal band Van Halen – followed by a decade as epicentre of the cheesy LA glam/'hair metal' scene.

6   Tiny Schneider may have demurred. "I just wasn't asked," he was later quoted as saying. "I guess they knew which way it was going… They just didn't say anything."

7   'The Ostrich', for Pickwick Records.

8   In 1977, sixties beat band revivalists The Jam also featured 'Slow Down' on their debut album.

9   Written by producer Ed Cobb, 'Dirty Water' featured a dirty Farfisa organ riff by keyboard player Larry Tamblyn, brother of actor Russ (*West Side Story*) Tamblyn. It attained minor classic status with its inclusion on *Nuggets* – Lenny Kaye's compilation of sixties US 'punk rock' and would become a staple in the live sets of seventies R&B revival bands ('pub rock', as it became known in the UK).

10 Proby's mid-sixties period of stardom also encompassed two show tunes from *West Side Story*, before a steady decline in popularity. The beginning of the end was first flagged by the incident that brought him notoriety – splitting his trousers onstage in Croydon, in the same month that The Walker Brothers came to England. (Some cynics suggested the apparent accident was staged.) He later headed off into obscurity and alcoholism, before being rescued by stage roles as Roy Orbison and Elvis, taking the latter role at age 58 – 16 years older than Presley at the time of his death. Between the latter two periods, his reputation was kept afloat in the eighties by maverick Manchester publishers Savoy Books, who recruited him to sing lead on an admirably intense series of cover versions ranging from Phil Collins' 'In The Air Tonight' to Joy Division's 'Love Will Tear Us Apart'. Few former sixties pop stars have had such a singularly strange career – except perhaps for Scott Walker.

11 Scott uses the term 'over here' to describe the UK, after more than four decades of voluntary exile.

12 Scott asserted it was the selection of Jack Nitzsche – although the arranger had a strangely dismissive attitude toward the recording. As a close associate of the Stones in the sixties (to the extent that he contributed to the mixed score for Mick Jagger in classic cult movie *Performance*), he seemed to adopt a similar inverted snobbery to Keith Richards in not listening to 'white music'.

13 The original version of the theme was performed by The Lettermen. Its cover version by The Walker Brothers marked the first of a number of cinematic themes sung by Scott Walker, whether in original or covered form.

Chapter 3

All-American Alien Boys

My Brother, my poor Brothers, it is thus,
This life holds nothing good for us
But it ends soon and never more can be.
I ponder these thoughts and they comfort me.

James Thomson – *The City Of Dreadful Night* (1873)

On Wednesday February 17, 1965, the American pop world staged a small-scale counter invasion of Britain. This was when The Walker Brothers – aka John Maus and Scott Engel, with their unofficial/unsigned new recruit Gary Leeds – crossed the Atlantic to a pre-swinging London.

"I had no second thoughts about the trip," John later claimed, "regardless of the fact that I was newly engaged and my family didn't want me to leave America. Scott was also leaving behind his girlfriend, Ann, the waitress at Gazzarri's, but was excited about seeing the art galleries, museums, and historical sites we had read about in books."

"We took a gamble when we came over," Scott would tell the Brit pop press. "We walked out of a 20-week coast-to-coast TV

40

series – we nearly got sued – and other things were goin'[1] for us too."

The arrival of his draft induction papers was no small spur either. But for Engel, another attraction was the reputed British respect for traditional 'quality' performers – the suggestion that London might be a working environment where he could practise the painstaking vocal techniques of a Jack Jones or Sinatra, without record company compulsion to, say, cut a Twist or surf single.

The garrulous Gary shared his new bandmate's enthusiasm for the 'ultimate adventure', chatting with him all through the transatlantic flight. As they began to descend into London Heathrow airport, the first signs of what they were about to experience became visible.

"As we came out of the clouds and were coming in to land," recalled Leeds, "we noticed white stuff on the ground. Scott said, 'Is that snow?' I said, 'I think it is!'"

"Jesus, it was cold," Scott shuddered in recollection. Neither was the climate the only aspect the three Californians had to adapt to.

"Scott and I stared quietly out of the windows of the cab, taking in the dreary, bleak surroundings," John reflected. "I think he was as shocked as I was by what we saw. All the buildings and homes looked old, worn and smoke-stained."

Two decades on from the end of World War Two, London had not yet escaped from the near-bankruptcy that followed it. While Britain had suffered less than some continental European nations, the legacy of the Blitz left pockets of bomb damage dotted around that no one had quite got around to repairing or redeveloping. On the taxi journey from the airport in the outer suburbs, the three young men watched as the dilapidated state of the city's inner boroughs became gradually more apparent. Even in 1965, some council-built homes were actually the improvised prefab housing erected in the immediate post-war years.

No such criticism applied to 13 Courtfield Gardens in the bedsit land of Earl's Court. This was a traditional old house converted into separately austere little flats. "The only saving grace was that our building was across the street from a beautiful church with well-kept grounds," recalled John. "Unfortunately, the church bells rang loudly at all hours of the day and night."

At first, the clean-shaven but longhaired trio had to share one tiny room with the chaperone sent by Gary's stepfather, a strait-laced businessman by the name of Claude Powell,[2] enjoying the luxuries of a shared communal toilet and bathroom out in the hallway.

On their second day of acclimatisation, the Walkers began to make journeys by tube train and bus into the nearby West End. Scott would naturally gravitate towards the National Gallery and the British Museum, but on early excursions with his two 'brothers' it was more a case of finding what was happening in London *now* rather than delving into its past.

The neon-lit traffic of Piccadilly Circus must have reminded Engel of the Times Square of his early youth; the trio checked out the musical equipment stores of Shaftesbury Avenue and Denmark Street; they passed the seedy clip joints of Soho to sample its many pubs, able to get merrily half-drunk in a city that regarded young men in their twenties as way above the legal drinking age.

Then there was music.

It was Gary who first discovered the Marquee Club in Wardour Street, taking Scott and John to their first live gig there – The Who, promising 'Maximum R&B' on a poster depicting the young Pete Townshend windmill-flailing his arm over his guitar neck. It epitomised the mix of electric feedback and youthful articulacy that the London scene seemed to offer.

After checking out the West End's clubs, Gary's pseudo-siblings would gravitate toward their own venue of choice: John to The Flamingo, where white R&B flourished in the wake of a slightly passé mod scene and Georgie Fame & The Blue Flames often headlined; Scott would find himself more at home in a quiet corner of Ronnie Scott's jazz club, a more satisfactory counterpart to the Lighthouse Café in LA, where he could legally drink to the background of Euro-jazz or the occasional touring US artist.

After the first weeks, the Walkers (with Claude in tow) moved into a high-ceilinged second-floor flat at 1 Onslow Gardens in South Kensington. With the chill British winter only just passed, they assembled their beds like a wagon train around a two-bar electric fire.

"London was the weirdest thing I'd seen in my life," John would later complain, "a real culture shock. I was a California surfer, man! It was cold, you put shillings in the gas meter, the food was weird. It took me a long time to get used to England."

Scott had far less trouble adapting, in part because he was able to continue the culture-vulture habits he'd developed in LA. The National Film Theatre on London's Southbank became another home away from home. When Gary Leeds first buddied up with him, he'd impressed Engel by telling of his stepdad's acquaintance with maverick Hollywood genius Orson Welles: "When studios invited guests on board Welles' boat for a party, he'd sneak away and hide on my father's because he didn't like those Hollywood party people."

The parallels with Engel's own sensitivities would later become obvious to his bandmate. For his part, the long, skinny 'Stretch' (as Scott was sometimes called as a kid) admired the larger-than-life Orson for how he'd incorporated European cinematic and artistic sensibilities into his films (much as the makers of film noir had done). Welles' filmmaking career took place under a state of financial siege, but in his first masterpiece, *Citizen Kane*, he was able to incorporate elements of German expressionism and Freudian symbolism.[3] This sense of symbolic allusion, of what an image signifies being greater than the literal 'thing in itself', would have a growing influence on Engel.

"Scott has a presence that's hard to define. I also experienced this with Orson Welles," Leeds said much later, inherently flattering his bandmate by comparison.

By 1965, however, Scott was more enraptured by European art cinema. He'd been mesmerised by *The Seventh Seal*, the 1957 masterpiece of Swedish director Ingmar Bergman. Centring on the return to his plague-ridden homeland of a knight who plays chess with the spirit of Death, its medieval imagery burned slowly in the mind. Bergman's brooding 1960 film *The Virgin Spring* reinforced Scott's devotion to the director's vision.[4] By the mid-sixties, Scott would have been able to view the Swedish *auteur*'s trilogy on religious faith and doubt, *Through A Glass Darkly*, *Winter Light* and *The Silence*. If Gary was still attending the NFT with him the following year, he might have endured actress Liv Ullman withdrawing into catatonia and an internal reality in *Persona*.

But for the Walkers, the most significant cultural event of early 1965 was a more accessible affair. On their arrival in February, 'You've Lost That Lovin' Feeling' by The Righteous Brothers was number one in the UK charts.

"Neither Scott nor myself believed we were leaving [the USA] to become stars and have hit records," remembered John Maus. But for Gary Leeds, thus far the only non-musical member of the band, the Spector-produced record was both the touchstone and the competition.

By the time the Walkers had their first windy London photoshoot in March 1965 – at Marble Arch, the gateway between Oxford Street and Hyde Park – Gary was hustling the band's name for all he was worth. Their first UK TV appearance followed soon after, as surprise guests on *Juke Box Jury* where 'Pretty Girls Everywhere' got a hearing. The unexceptional record was voted a hit, but John and Scott's faces stayed out of frame when the cameraman (presumably used to less nourished Brits) misjudged their six-foot-plus frames. This was followed by a slot singing the song on the ultimate 'weekend starts here' pop show, *Ready Steady Go!* with Cathy McGowan. The record still made no showing on the singles chart.

The tide suddenly started to turn at the end of the month, when the Walkers got a call from Philips Records. Philips' head of A&R, one John Franz, was suitably impressed by a tape of 'Love Her' sent over by Mercury, the label's US counterpart. With no live dates scheduled, their funds starting to run down and not even any UK work permits, the 45's April release came in the nick of time. At a gradual pace it entered the Top 50 for a three-month stay, peaking at number 18. On a modest level at least, The Walker Brothers had arrived.

"Scott never wanted to go home," Gary Leeds remembers of that ebullient time. "He liked it in Europe, as did I. John found it a little hard here because of the lack of sun and the cold climate. Nevertheless, after 'Love Her' made the charts we decided to stay."

While warm-blooded Maus clearly missed his native living environment, to a melancholic the unrelenting sunshine of California (and the expectation that one should respond positively to it) may have been almost oppressive. He may have made regular phone calls home to his mother, but Scott Engel seemed to have adapted to Britain's slate-grey skies and the general bleakness of her winter.

"He was over here, but he was reading Nietzsche and going out to Bergman movies," observes California-based filmmaker Stephen Kijak. As director of the lauded documentary *Scott Walker: 30 Century Man*, Kijak has come closest to creating an authorised biography with the subject's participation.

"It was well documented that in those years he was digging nonstop and had a real fondness for European culture – which is a really strange thing for a young guy in the sixties out here in California. I have a similar feeling – maybe because I've listened a lot to [British] music and I've worked a lot out there, but to me London has always felt like a second home. I like it here too, but you get pangs for it to rain once in a little while, you want to feel the cold. You can miss the variance of the seasons, which I think a melancholy temperament needs. So it was a total homecoming in so many ways. [After the mid-sixties] I don't think he ever really spent any time here at all."

If, as Kijak suggests, the young Engel had been reading the tragic German philosopher Nietzsche, then he likely heeded the clarion call of "God is dead – we have killed Him" that challenged the Lutheran faith of his ancestors. He may also have noted Nietzsche clinging to one supernatural belief – that of his Buddhist-influenced 'law' of endless recurrence.

If all that was acted out on humankind's stage was yet to be repeated, then Scott may have found his brief juvenile taste of stardom a forerunner for what was about to occur. Whether it would be any more desirable this time around remains a moot point.

Ever homesick for California, John returned that spring for 10 days, only to rush back to meet the Walkers' first UK recording date for Philips. "I got a cab at Heathrow back to Onslow Gardens and knocked on our flat door," he later recounted, "only to be told that Scott and Gary had moved. They had assumed I wasn't coming back. Fortunately... the landlady knew they had moved to Chelsea. They had definitely decided to stay in England; I found out later that they had cashed in their return tickets."

The unlikely double act of Engel and Leeds, introspective chalk and happily buffoonish cheese, had put down new roots in a flat just off the Fulham end of the Kings Road. Pop journalists would later describe the vaguely surrealistic décor – unidentified marble bust, huge aspidistra plant, 15 mirrors filling one of the bedrooms – as if Antonioni's *Blow Up* had arrived a year early.

The world may not have been at their feet, but it seemed increasingly as if England might be there for the taking. Return visits to *Ready Steady Go!* became a regular showcase. Pop-managerial luminary Simon Napier-Bell (co-writer of Dusty Springfield's hit 'You Don't Have To Say You Love Me') noted how stage and screen director Michael Lindsay-Hogg (the biological son of Orson Welles – unknown to Scott), then working in-house on the show, first created a Walkers visual aesthetic by making "them look like trees waving in the wind, filming them from the floor up". It emphasised the stoic stillness of John, while Scott's nervous emotiveness would become increasingly pronounced on stage.

"Success – and what Scott much later called his personal nightmare... – really began the first time we appeared on the TV show *Thank Your Lucky Stars*," acknowledged Gary, "when we were mobbed. Within a very short time, and with interest being increasingly driven by the popular Radio London pirate station, The Walker Brothers had become an essential part of the London scene."

The transference from small screen to provincial stage first came at Leeds Odeon on May 25, 1965, when the Walkers deputised for The Kinks[5] on a package tour, along with The Yardbirds and The Hollies. Nervous of disappointing beat-loving Kinks fans, The Walkers discarded 'Love Her' and reverted to their old role of R&B covers band, with Gary replacing Tiny on drums. They played the standard 15-minute slot of the time, without even an encore, before hysteria erupted.

"This was the beginning of 'Walkermania'," John later recounted, still sounding incredulous after all these years, "and we played all three nights to hysterical fans. The girls mobbed us, security couldn't handle it, and we were in shock. Scott and I had never experienced anything remotely like this before."

"I've got 10 youngsters on my back trying to rip the shirt off my back," Scott put it in tersely dramatic terms. "I'm lucky to be alive."

After three dates as a three-piece band, the trio took time out to reconsider the situation. It was Engel who urged the other two to be more selective in their approach, playing special gigs rather than just more fodder for the beat music circuit. "We came near to starvation," Scott would admit. "The other guys thought I'd gone mad."

In fact this avoidance of beat group status would very quickly fall in line with what Philips, their new UK record label, had in mind. Press coverage correspondingly followed. In those smudged inky days, titles like *Disc* and *Fab 208*,[6] the Radio Luxembourg magazine, supplemented the more hardy perennials. These pushed the Walkers as heartthrobs as hard as they could, but it was in the more established titles that they found a musically sympathetic hearing. As the pressures of youthful fame began to grow, Scott would often talk candidly with Chris Welch of the *Melody Maker*, while Keith Altham of the

New Musical Express became a long-term ally up to and beyond the end of the Walkers era.

As for live performances, they were about to undergo a transformation.

"The Walker Brothers' shows that came later were heavy workouts," recalled Gary Leeds, "and we did lose a lot more weight than in the earlier part of our career. Scott and John were no longer playing their instruments and were required to dance and perform."

It was a discipline that the nervy Engel took to surprisingly naturally. Writhing before an audience of mostly teenage girls, he unleashed a tension that could whip them all the way up to madness. Sometimes resembling a stylish scarecrow in loosely fitting suit jacket and cord trousers, pointing and gesticulating with his hands in a manner part Dusty Springfield and part Marcel Marceau, he released an emotional genie from its bottle which would ultimately terrify him.

"Even in those days, he was straight out the back door after a show," Gary acknowledged, "and nobody could ever find him. Maybe he wanted to escape the crowds, or maybe it was because he was so dependent on his mother, or afraid of being let down."

For all their differences of temperament, Engel and Leeds found natural allies in each other.

"The only reason why most people can't get to know Scott is because he doesn't want them to. But he and I were friends. We probably wouldn't have become such close friends if we hadn't been forced to spend so much time in Britain when the fan hysteria stopped us from going anywhere. We had to depend on each other because there was nobody else."

As Gary and John socialised at sixties nightclubs like the Scotch of St James in Mayfair, Scott, initially a part of the same night-time world, sometimes withdrew into seclusion to continue reading the great works of 20th-century literature. Hemingway marked a point when modern novelists put away their florid 19th-century affectations and reported the world face-on as they saw it; the verse prose of Dylan Thomas, whose *Under Milk Wood* embraced a phonetic love of language for its own sake, led back to James Joyce and his more substantial literary experiments with *Ulysses* and *Finnegans Wake*.

And then there were the existentialists.

The sleeve notes of The Walker Brothers' second LP would refer to Scott as "the existentialist who knows what it [i.e. the term 'existentialism'] means". At the time, Scott's reading of Jean-Paul Sartre must have seemed about as relevant to pop fans as, say, if Bobby Darin had espoused an unlikely fascination with Kierkegaard.

In the mid-sixties, however, Sartre was still a formidable force in European culture. As a philosopher, author, playwright, journalist and critic, he and his near-contemporary, the French-Algerian Albert Camus (killed in a 1960 car crash), articulated what they saw as the crises of the times: the smothering influence of bourgeois capitalist ethics; the importance of acting on individual conscience in an age of mass conformity; the essential question of what 'existence' really is, and what we are to do with it.[7]

("Scott was increasingly portrayed as the intellectual one, and he was in fact interested in Jean-Paul Sartre and existentialism, Albert Camus, Ingmar Bergman and jazz," confirms the fun-loving Gary. "John and I found all that a bit – dare I say it? – boring.")

The influence of both men – particularly Camus, who broke with Sartre by refusing to commit to Marxism as an article of faith – would wield an influence over the songwriting of Scott Engel in his early solo years. In the mid-sixties, however, just reading their works must have fostered a perception of himself as a Man of the Left, who had left the cultural influence of his native United States behind.

***

The bourgeois capitalist ethics of the music industry were fully embraced when the Walkers went looking for professional management. After a recommendation from Beatles manager Brian Epstein, who'd been briefly sniffing round the Walkers himself, they hit upon Capable Management, which represented Philips recording star Shirley Bassey and Them – the Irish beat group fronted by a young Van Morrison, who'd hit the British charts with 'Baby Please Don't Go' and 'Here Comes The Night'.

Capable was based at 185 Bickenhall Mansions in Baker Street, opposite Madame Tussaud's waxworks. It was run by two polar-opposite London Jews – Barry Clayman, a mild-mannered showbiz administrator, and Maurice King, Essex-born/East End-raised, who carried the look and cultivated the impression of a heavy.[8]

When they eventually parted company, Scott would damn their setup in a throwaway quip as 'Incapable Management'. In the early days, however, he would be as intoxicated as his 'brothers' by what he saw as a flirtation with the seamy side of the city.

"[Maurice] had a club off Oxford Street in the West End of London, where we would occasionally practise in the daytime," reminisced Gary. "We suspected that people traded in illegal goods there, which we found quite romantic, but we never knew for certain. The Kray twins came down there a few times, as well as George Raft, who played gangsters in the old black-and-white movies, but we never got to see any of them, and, when we asked to meet the Krays, we weren't allowed to. Unsurprisingly, we suspected that Maurice had some connections in the underworld: Scott would push him on it, and Maurice would tell Scott to shut up..."

Scott, while well-read and well-travelled, was still relatively naïve as to the characters populating his newly adopted city. At the time, he seemed to fall hook, line and sinker for the villainous air that a man like Maurice King would exude.[9] King, for his part, would come to see the young Engel as a main contender for the much coveted role of the 'new Sinatra' – something a man of his background and generation could appreciate.

As The Walker Brothers' Anglo career picked up, their one-on-one relationships with women were less intense than the reactions they were starting to elicit from their young audiences. "Our faces were becoming known and some girls in the neighbourhood found out we lived there, and would come around and talk to us," Gary would later admit, "[though] we were too shy to chat any of them up. But that would soon change."

As John had noted, Gary found that his flatmate kept his thoughts about women to himself. He did note, however, how much Scott admired Francoise Hardy, the flaxen-haired French brunette whose international hit, 'All Over The World', was a favourite in their apartment. Like a breathy Gallic counterpart of the similarly fragile Marianne Faithfull, the translation of her Francophone hit was promoted by Ms Hardy singing from the back of a truck in Piccadilly, scant months before Scott Engel arrived. (Alas, said Gary, "He never got to meet her.")

More immediately pressing was the Walkers' initial British recording session at the end of the spring. It was to be held under the auspices of John Franz, who was not only Philips' A&R head but its chief house producer.

At the Philips studio in Stanhope Place, near Marble Arch, the commercial protocol was to record a minimum three/maximum four tracks per session. Franz presided over recordings with a firm but gentle nicotine-stained hand. Then 43 years old, he was a native of the genteel inner north London village of Hampstead. Said to be blessed with perfect pitch, he'd started his career as a pianist working alongside jazzman Georgie Shearing at Tottenham Court Road tube station during the Blitz, before becoming an accompanist at the BBC for popular singer Anne Shelton.[10]

Since becoming the head of A&R at Philips, Franz had presided over an artists' roster that ran from light operatic ex-Goon Harry Secombe to phenomenal new discovery Dusty Springfield – formerly Mary O'Brien from Hampstead, who graduated from her brother's folk group The Springfields to become the pop world's first credible white soul singer.

"When we came over, we were going to do our first session and I met John Franz," remembers Scott. "He'd been producing Dusty Springfield over here and people like that." Franz was also expecting to meet a much more mature combo than the Walkers, going by the tones of 'Love Her'. When he first clapped eyes on the three young longhairs, the potential of combining the technical finesse of the crooner/torch song/cabaret generation with the immediacy of sixties pop must have become apparent.

"John and I were very concerned that the rhythm section was going to be, like, we didn't know," recalls Scott of his own immediate immersion in the recording process. "A British rhythm section in those days, we didn't know. We knew the strings would be great, we knew the brass would be great, [but] we didn't know about that. And John Franz says, 'Don't worry, I'm going to line up some great people,' and we got to the studio and they were just fantastic – fantastic guitar players, you know. After that we were just sailing."

Though they were a generation apart, the producer and his protégé formed a natural alliance. Brilliantined, moustached, a compulsive tea drinker and chain smoker (which must have irritated lifelong non-smoker Engel), the veteran producer would become a friend and confidant for the nervy young American, and also a dining partner at the Lotus House Chinese restaurant in Edgware Road or his home on Hampstead Heath.

Gary Leeds has described how he'd often find Engel and Franz together at the baby grand piano in the producer's office, gentlemanly Johnny providing an accompaniment to Scott's rendition of the songs of his parents' generation: "I'd be there, giving 'em the most obscure numbers I could think of – you know, old standards and such, and I couldn't catch 'em out. They knew 'em all!"[11]

Accompanying Franz in the studio was an intense young engineer of eastern European extraction, Peter Olliff. It was as if the progress of British pop music had been placed in the hands of the backroom boffins who built the bouncing bomb in *The Dambusters*.

"They also had natural echo chambers," recollects Scott, "which they don't have any more. It was down the hall and you opened it up and it was a tiled room with a microphone in it, with a speaker in

front of it. But it was one of the best echo chambers in the country
– if not the best."

Indeed, it was these facilities that would soon establish the famous
Walker vibrato: "*Oh, breakin' up is so-o-o very hard to do-oo-ooh!*"

Engel credits Olliff and Franz equally with the innovative measures
that outdid diminutive American control freak and production genius
Phil Spector in the studio: guitar, bass, drums, separate keyboards,
orchestra – all would be claustrophobically squeezed into the same
studio for simultaneous recording. Unlike Spector's hit factory in the
US, there was little time for multiple taping.

As for the song selection at this historic session, John Maus took
credit. He played a Burt Bacharach and Hal David tune from *The
Best Of Jerry Butler*, a greatest hits anthology from a powerful soul
ballad singer.

According to Gary, "We had wanted to do Burt Bacharach's
'Don't Make Me Over', and the only reason we didn't was that we
thought Dionne Warwick had got there first. Scott was really pissed
off when we found out that her version was released only in the US."

As indeed was her version of 'Make It Easy On Yourself' – her
primly enunciated take on the heartbreak lyric that Butler made into
a quietly masculine howl of despair. With Bacharach and David's
'I Just Don't Know What To Do Myself' a classic hit for Dusty
the previous year, the sixties 'big pop' sound owed much to their
formula of simple-but-affecting lyric and epic melody.

"For 'Make It Easy On Yourself' we actually used the same
arrangement that was on Jerry Butler's album," John later asserted,
"but with a bigger orchestra and a more dynamic rhythm section.
The most noticeable difference was obviously Scott singing lead, and
the addition of harmony, which I created and sang."

This moody mope, in which the narrator urges his girlfriend, "Don't
try to spare my feelings," was enhanced by Scott's liquid vibrato and
John's soprano shadow. Behind them both, a ghostly feminine backing
takes lyrical regret into the space age, pitched somewhere between
an eerie Theremin sound and the female vocal that announced the

Scott Walker

Star Trek TV series two years later. It was the same song as Butler's heartfelt plea, but somehow it was so much bigger.

"My father was in the sixties renowned as one of the top string arrangers for pop hits," explains Simon Raymonde – formerly the bassist of ethereal eighties band The Cocteau Twins,[12] now director/ producer of Bella Union records. "[Ivor Raymonde] worked on 'The Sun Ain't Gonna Shine Anymore' and 'Make It Easy On Yourself' – that was 1965, I suppose. I was three, so it wasn't on my radar. But I know that Scott Engel, as my parents used to refer to him, came to our house [in Tottenham, north London]… I don't know how I would have remembered at that age but I know he was there – Dusty Springfield came, and Scott Engel came, and I remember those two events. But it didn't mean anything to me, his name didn't really register till I was in my twenties.

"I learned more about my father after he died than when he was alive. I didn't really pay attention, I was so wrapped up in what I was doing."

The younger Raymonde has come to recognise how his father was one of a team of innovators who turned the pop song into a two-and-a-half-minute symphony of heartbreak; into a deep audio well of sweet melancholy.

"And I think I only realised how good the stuff was when he wasn't there, when he wasn't around any more. Those recording sessions, how they were constructed, is more like how I would want to do it now. I think the influence is coming through to me more now than it did at the time."

In the years that followed, the late Raymonde senior described how, "Between Scott and myself, we devised an orchestra that would be The Walker Brothers' band… So we had three pianos, four guitars, umpteen Latin American instruments, percussion… a sound that we hoped would be 'The Walker Brothers' – and, of course, it worked."

"The end result… was this big swirling noise which became quite famous," reflected Reg Guest, who played keyboards on the track and would later take over from Raymonde as the Walkers' arranger. "It

54

was very… boring to actually play. Scott was fond of literally flattening you with noise and yet on top of it would be a tender vocal with a heavy emotional feel… The actual sound was in Scott's head."

That sound would enter the public consciousness at the end of the summer.

Between the single's recording and its release, the Walkers – and in particular the cynical young blond who had (almost by default) become their lead singer – also became a fixture on the London pop scene. Scott would complain (half-jokingly) to the *Melody Maker* that some drunk had come to his flat door in the early hours of the morning and punched him out. He may have left the random gun violence he despised behind in the USA,[13] but, as he was learning, London was the place for drunken fisticuffs.

He also bitched about the 'Swinging London' club set ("They're all such nothing people and the people that have really got something are probably walking about in the street") and reserved most of his praise for just one contemporary performer, a French-Armenian *chansonnier* he'd recently discovered named Charles Aznavour ("He looks like a dustman with a five o'clock shadow but his songs are beautiful").

That summer, the brothers were booked to play a series of seaside concerts by promoter Arthur Howes. No longer an R&B club band but purveyors of emotional teenage psychodrama, they were at first augmented by a keyboard player named Jimmy O'Neil – then soon after by The Quotations, who would become their regular backing band onstage, with a leader/keyboardist going under the humble moniker of Johnny B. Great.

Gary Leeds remembers how Scott Engel, always a sporting type, would drag hungover band members up in the morning to play tennis with him. That was in their quieter moments, which were becoming increasingly rare: "In July, riots erupted at Walker Brothers concerts, and the fan mania began to get out of hand. Shows could not be completed; our clothes were ripped, our cars vandalised. Privacy, for us, was now a thing of the past."

It was at the Philips reception for the launch of 'Make It Easy On Yourself', in August, that Scott met the young woman who'd be in and out of his life for the next couple of years. Irene Dunford was a 19-year-old model, a striking blonde with backcombed hair and mascara'd eyes whose looks epitomised the glamour of when London was starting to swing.[14]

At first theirs was a friendship and nothing more, as Irene was seeing someone else. However, "He was genuinely lonely and would invite me round to his flat for conversations. He had quite a funny side to him too, but he had to trust you first before this side of his character came out. He could become a bit of a prankster after downing a bottle of bourbon. It did loosen him up."

As their relationship grew closer, Irene would share drunken evenings with her new companion, including one occasion when she risked her neck by breaking into his fourth-floor flat when he'd lost his key. For a while, she became his steadying influence as fame began to grow and its absurdities became part of the everyday.

But even she couldn't steel his nerve at those moments when it seemed expedient to withdraw into his flat, or disappear off the map for a few days.[15]

"I think it's just the straitjacket of fame itself," remarks Stephen Kijak of his subject's growing reticence during this period. "Some people just aren't suited to it. Some people take to it and some people just can't deal [with it]; they don't want to, it can only repel them or they repel fame."

One of the prices of fame became clear after 'Make It Easy On Yourself' knocked the Stones' 'Satisfaction' off the top of the charts. When Scott and Irene were sitting at a table in the Scotch of St James one night, they suddenly found themselves pelted with unlit fags from the table behind. The Dartford bluesmen felt sufficiently threatened by the Walkers to humiliate their frontman.

"[Mick Jagger] uses my cigarettes to throw at Scott," acknowledged Gary, then a friend of the rock aristocracy. "I can't smoke 'em afterwards because they're full of Scott's hair."

It's hard to see why the R&B revisionists should feel challenged by the brothers' smoothly symphonic hit. But maybe their differences explain it – Scott wasn't putting on a white negro act like Jagger; to Mick and Keith he may have seemed like the resurgence of the Sinatra generation. Word also had it that the liver-lipped Stones vocalist's girlfriend, model Chrissie Shrimpton, had let slip how attractive she found Engel.

(Scott's cynicism about the London club scene was later aired in the Walkers' 'Saturday's Child' – though, in keeping with the times, the target of his lyric was a girl.)

Whatever his discomfort, Scott Engel and his pseudo-siblings were now propelled into the world of celebrity. 'After the Beatles and Stones – we're next!' say Walkers' ran one 1965 pop press headline.

"The Walker Brothers' success lies in one main factor – sex," oozed the copy that followed. "They are loaded with sex appeal. It positively pervades the air that surrounds them. They are all tall, slim, handsome..."

After 'Make It Easy On Yourself' rocketed north up the charts, Scott would protest to *Disc* that, in his own eyes, he did not regard himself as 'good-looking'. (That praise was reserved for Gallic film star Alain Delon.)

But the newly initiated Walker Brothers Fan Club was growing in size, and the fans (mostly girls, so it seems) who were buying the record begged to differ. "Scott has got such dreamy eyes," sighed a young miss named Pat Mackenzie of Wandsworth SW18. "On stage and TV, [Scott] always looks so calm and relaxed, manly and strong, the best looking. His hair is always so shiny, he must wash it every day," observed Christina Robertson of Fife.

At least Lynne Milligan of Stockport, Cheshire praised the musical atmospherics: "When they slow down to do a ballad like 'Make It Easy On Yourself', they give the impression that they're going through it themselves." Besides, she added, "Who else would risk their lives at those personal appearances?"

Who else indeed?

The Walkers were becoming increasingly recognisable in public. Even dark-haired Gary, whose musical contribution was restricted to drumming onstage, had picked up a fan contingent that forced the Tower of London to close when they descended on their man out on a day's sightseeing.

Onstage, fever pitch was maintained by show comperes who'd invariably draw out the introduction of each of the boys to a nerve-snapping point. The Quotations could spend up to a quarter of an hour playing the riff to an R&B number like 'Land Of A Thousand Dances', a duration not much less than the show itself. Gary would be the first to take his place, at a drum kit that seemed somehow superfluous when he had The Quotations' drummer playing behind him.

By the time that John, and finally Scott, had been introduced and took their place in the formerly vacant spotlights, the band upped the tension by breaking into the James Bond theme music – then the most contemporary of signature themes. Scott would propel the audience further with his gyrations and expressionistic hand gestures, as symptomatic of his nervous energy as his stagecraft.

"Really, people didn't come to see you, they came to scream," reflects Scott several decades after the experience. "And it was loud so you could sing anything, virtually, 'cos they couldn't hear you. We didn't take advantage of that, as a lot of people did.[16]

"But it was crazy because we'd be on the stage for one minute, or maybe two minutes, and then the whole gig would be over, because the stage would be rushed and you would be swamped and torn to ribbons. So that was the life."

In *30 Century Man*, rock manager Ed Bicknell, who would look after Scott's affairs in the eighties, laughingly describes one specific instance: "He told me a story once about when they were in Dublin, and they'd done a show as the Walkers and they came out and got in the car and the audience, the kids, turned the car upside down with them in it. And he added the line, 'And there were no seatbelts either.' So presumably they were all lying in a crushed state in the roof space, being rescued by big Irish bobbies."

"They got to us and they turned the van over," confirms Scott with rather less levity. "They literally turned it over, and we had thousands and thousands of people on this van, beating on it. It was particularly frightening, we didn't know we were going to get out."

The Walkers adopted a strategy of wearing motorcycle crash helmets on their way to live shows. "Of course, everybody thought it was a big publicity thing," said Gary Leeds, "but it wasn't. That was for real. They were ripping your hair out and everything. John's head was cut wide open about three times."

"Scott had his shirt in ribbons, and they scalped Gary," described John Maus of another such occasion. "They wanted noses, pieces of cheeks, stuff like that."

John's words evoke the chilling climax of Nathanael West's interwar novel, *The Day Of The Locust*[17] – in which a crowd of celebrity watchers outside an LA movie theatre turn on the two main characters, tearing one of them to pieces. But West's crowd hysteria was born of their disappointment and animosity.

The girls of sixties Britain were living out their own frustrations, trying to emerge from their parents' black-and-white wartime world. In the USA, the media had witnessed teen hysteria, knicker-wetting and an almost orchestrated cacophony of screams as The Beatles took their country in 1964. In the British Isles, where the populace were supposedly more tight-lipped and repressed, the girls tried to stake a personal claim to the objects of their dreams. To possess. To physically own. Seemingly, if needs be, to devour them.

"The reason you don't have it today is that everyone has videos and can watch people," Scott deduces from hindsight. "It was so rare. We had a few television shows and it was so rare to see them; The Beatles and everybody got mobbed like that because they had to see you, they had to get to you.

59

"I don't like pop people that bitch about what's happened to them, but it does change [you] dramatically. There's no way to describe it to anyone else because it's phenomenal."

★★★

At the end of the Walkers' summer tour, John Maus took another of his lightning trips back to California. What his bandmates, his management and his public didn't know, before he returned in October 1965, was that his purpose had been to get married to girlfriend Kathy Young, a former pop singer herself.

There were mildly bitter undertones to his postnuptial reception, with a suggestion that the marriage might have been kept from the fans (as that of John and Cynthia Lennon initially was). Scott was even somewhat reproachful – "I'd get very, very annoyed if Kathy started to travel around with us on dates."

But then, from the group's point of view, there were more compelling matters to attend to.

'Make It Easy On Yourself' had proved to be that elusive career-changing hit, staying at number one throughout September. The need for a follow-up was an industry prerequisite – both in terms of a 45 and an album showcase that might grant the Walkers some longevity.

In *30 Century Man*, telling use is made of some vintage mid-sixties black-and-white Walkers footage. "Pop is good for money," asserts a slightly slurring John, "that's what pop is good for."

"'Pop' spelled backwards is 'money'," bullshits clown prince Gary.

"'Pop' backwards spells 'pop'," retorts John rather too literally.

Scott is seen reclining in the silver-framed shades that were becoming a permanent appendage, swigging from a beer bottle. "I'm in it for different things, I'm not in it for money," he insists, displaying his earnestness of the time. "I don't care about money, which sounds ridiculous but I really actually don't. I'm in it strictly from a creative point of view. I can do records. Produce records. Write music."

"I started writing B-sides for The Walker Brothers because our manager was always saying, 'We've got to get the publishing for this so somebody's got to do it,'" Scott reflected decades later. "Gradually I got more confident and of course I had these great forces at my disposal, so my imagination could really soar."

Scott's first songwriting collaborator at this time was far from an obvious choice. Lesley Duncan was a folksy northern English songstress who'd been singing backing vocals for Dusty and, latterly, was working with the Walkers and for John Franz at Philips. After meeting at a nightclub owned by notorious band manager Don Arden, they decided to take the creative plunge.

"We wrote 'You're All Around Me' at his flat, I think," the elfin Ms Duncan later recalled. "I think we had a guitar and just tossed some ideas back and forth, you know? I sang backing on some of their records, but we didn't write together again.[18] He wasn't a particularly likeable person... he didn't have many social niceties about him."

'You're All Around Me' is the kind of dramatically descriptive love song that the Walkers were now specialising in: "In the morning when everything has ended / And night's cover has lifted without you," Scott begins his emotional vignette to sweetly sympathetic strings.

It made a more than creditable B-side to the latest Walkers 45 – which was already starting to follow something of a pattern. 'My Ship Is Coming In' had been a commercial misfire for Jimmy Radcliffe, written by his musical partner Joey Brooks. Like Jerry Butler, he was of the generation of soul singers who could enunciate lyrics clearly, strongly, with a very masculine emotional insistence.[19]

A lyric of defiant optimism, from its thudding opening piano chords it praises the woman who's suffered alongside the narrator, now rising out of material poverty. It may not be classic Scott Walker subject matter but its title provides a strong hook, operatically emoted (like all the Walkers' sixties hits) with a higher-pitched backing by John.

It gave the Walkers their second big hit (albeit only reaching number three this time), in November 1965. At the same time, their corresponding debut album was also reaching fruition.

When *Take It Easy With The Walker Brothers* was released the next month, just in time for the Christmas market ("The title Scott and I immediately changed to *Take It Greasy*, because we were not too happy with it," said Gary, "and later to *Take It Cheesy*"), it provided a showcase for a teen-scream group whose melodic gift and professionalism also endeared them to a good few mums and dads.

Alongside standard sixties Motown/R&B cover fare like 'Dancing In The Street', Scott applied his crushed velvet tones to 'First Love Never Dies',[20] a country-inflected ballad co-written by Jimmy Seals (later of Seals and Crofts) that failed to hit with its original version in 1961. 'The Girl I Lost In The Rain' is a notable gem, reclaiming an obscure 45 sung by C.J. Russell (aka the then-unknown Leon Russell) and written by David Gates (later of Bread) and imbuing it, via the cinematic production/arrangement by Franz/Raymonde, with a film-noir ambience ("Last night I walked through town / The rain was tumbling down and I could hardly see").

At a time when Bob Dylan's *Bringing It All Back Home* was the acoustic folk/electric rock crossover which led to him being called 'Judas' at Newport Folk Festival, the Walkers took that album's poetic paean, 'Love Minus Zero', and enhanced the jangly melody in a Scott-John duet. ("Subconscious alliteration" was Scott's sneering summary of the man dubbed the voice of his generation.[21] This particular track had obviously *not* been his selection.)

"I picked 75 per cent of the material, because I was a kind of 'producer in disguise' in those days," Scott explained years later. At the time he'd given the pop press a statement of intent: "We were tryin' to find songs which are good from people who aren't very well known yet, and give 'em a kind of showcase and start-off."

While this didn't apply to Dylan, it gave Scott the first opportunity to tip his hat to a New Orleans-born contemporary then working as a professional songwriter. Randy Newman's 'I've Been Wrong Before' had recently been a hit for young Liverpudlian ballad singer Cilla Black, but it was 'I Don't Want To Hear It Anymore' that displayed the ear for melody of a traditionalist (his uncle was soundtrack composer Alfred Newman) and the eye for detail of a novelist.

Originally recorded by Jerry Butler (again, it was John's selection), 'I Don't Want To Hear It Anymore' is the anguished cry of a guy who hears his neighbours discussing his disintegrating love life in a place where "the walls are much too thin". It provided perfect dramatic substance for the young Scott, and would be the first song in a series of occasional crossovers between the careers of Scott Walker and Dusty Springfield (though Dusty got there several years later, with her classic *Dusty In Memphis* in 1969).

"It was a very demanding piece and, during the recording, he shot me that look that I had come to know meant he was uncomfortable or nervous," John later claimed. "It was a certain expression in his eyes that inevitably ended with a questioning look at the end of a performance, waiting for feedback from Gary and me."

John's own contributions to the album were R&B covers, duets with Scott and backing vocals. While his performances on later Walkers recordings would be more memorable, there was already a definite sense that the former leader of the band had become a secondary figure.

As to his own performance, Scott later reflected: "After we made 'Make It Easy On Yourself', after we had that first album, I started thinking maybe I'd better go and learn how to sing – really, like, get some lessons.

"Then I went to this – I don't say 'poor man' because he was a poor man, but he was a poor man because of the way I treated him. A man called Freddie Winrose, good vocal coach. So I went to him a few times initially, but because I was younger and everything else I never went constantly. I would turn up like six months later for another lesson, so the whole thing was ridiculous. I eventually drifted away from it. I'm not a trained singer."

It was John Franz who first recommended his young protégé to Winrose, who ran his business from the old Tin Pan Alley neighbourhood of Denmark Street, telling him, "Freddie, we are going to have the finest ballad singer in the world."

"I had to agree with him," Winrose reflected later. "Scott's potential was enormous." The young Engel would return the sentiment, gifting his tutor with a gold chain inscribed, "To Freddie – the maestro."

Ultimately, however, Winrose was forced to agree with the futility of giving sporadic lessons. "I probably worked with Scott for about 18 months during the sixties but we never could quite get rid of that vibrato. Just when I thought we had it licked he'd disappear for a couple of months."

Meanwhile, a generation of record buyers who were still children would lock onto that vibrato, some of them trying to replicate it as they cut their own records in the decades that followed.

Back at the time, Scott was finding himself increasingly the focus of the spotlight both on and offstage. He seemed to respond to it in the manner of many sensitive souls – albeit the more demonstrative rather than timid kind.

Although it would be heavily disputed by his bandmates,[22] Scott claimed in an interview with *Disc & Music Echo* the following year that he'd got into trouble on a pub crawl along the King's Road. Drinking with "a bunch of freeloaders and a couple of beatnik artistic types", he'd hit the beer and whisky chasers with enthusiasm. It led to him getting verbally aggressive (an apparently drunken Engel attribute of the time) and thrown out of the pub on his arse. According to the interview, he then "started throwing rocks at cars.[23] The police picked me up and locked me up, saying I should be ashamed of myself."

The incident never made the mainstream press, but reputedly set a precedent for Scott's behaviour for a while – he was cautioned another time for shouting and singing along Oxford Street, as if he was some poor down-and-out. How much of this is accurate is lost in time – it is, after all, the recollection of a drunken man. But it chimes with Scott's mid-seventies quote that "we were probably the drunkest group ever" (stated at a time when his drinking was at its worst, ironically enough), and it resonates in 'Such A Small Love' on his first solo LP, with its "drunken madman nights ending up in jail" – or at least a police cell.

His friendship with Irene Dunford had by now stabilised into a regular relationship – though the model apparently didn't regard her boyfriend as the most stable of characters.

"Scott and I would meet lots of girls in clubs, and because we were famous they would talk and flirt with us all the time," John later recalled. "[He] became quite distrustful of women. As a result of his celebrity, he could never be quite sure that women liked him for himself, or because he was famous… Once he found a lady he trusted, he stayed with her for a long time."

Such was the case with Ms Dunford, who Engel would pick up from her Islington flat in an ex-US Army open-top jeep he'd recently purchased for £180. "Scott's driving mirrored his personality," she'd later complain. "He was very erratic: always swerving in front of cars and pulling up in the nick of time cursing the other drivers."

(In one of the first interviews he gave to the British music press, he admitted: "I'm so nervous about driving. I've been in five accidents this year and been in hospital five times.")

John and Gary later claimed to be sceptical of Scott's unenviable reputation for stage fright, saying that he never exhibited it in front of them. While it's likely that he exorcised his nervous state via his very physical stage performances, the press headlines of the time tell a radically different story:

'SADNESS OF THE WALKER BROTHERS' – "It's not just a publicity gimmick"; 'SCOTT: TERRIFIED OF LIVE AUDIENCES' – "[To be] faced with the prospect of meeting Scott Walker for the first time is apt to send many erstwhile interviewers into a cold sweat. Their ears ring with tales of moodiness, abruptness and instant dismissal of those he does not like."

Scott later told loyal Walkers supporter Keith Altham, then at the *NME*: "When you see me out there shakin' in front of the camera you know why. It's because I'm frightened – you can't fight that kind of thing if it is inside you… When they throw me out on to a TV set or stage it's like puttin' a hermit who has lived all his life in isolation suddenly in the middle of Times Square."

Creating music, for Scott Engel, was less and less about making himself accessible, putting himself up for grabs. Likely influenced by the rigorous approach of his new friend Johnny Franz, he saw himself increasingly as a creative backroom boy.

This was consolidated by a contract signed in early 1966 with Arthur Howes' company to co-found a music publishing company, and an independent contract signed with Philips by Alec Noel Productions. Old friend John Stewart had followed Scott to 'dear old Blighty', and they had many plans to work on.

The first act they were producing was rather close to home. "Now Gary is a funny character," Scott remarked. "He gets this thing going on stage and gets a lot of fan mail." But what he wanted right then was some musical recognition of his own, and the Stewart-Engel partnership was doing its best to ensure he found it.

"Scott let me do whatever I wanted in the studio, and would sit there and not say a word," Gary insisted. It may not have been the most proactive approach, but it seemed to bear fruit with 'You Don't Love Me' – an amazingly guitar-heavy cover of Tommy Raye's much-covered 1961 R&B hit,[24] which was issued by CBS but sounds like it belongs on the *Nuggets* anthology. Gary's beat-brat vocals rasp a John Stewart tune called 'Get It Right' on the flip, unremarkable apart from a brief saxophone break.

The A-side never garnered enough airplay to make it a hit, but in any case everyone's attention was now on the Walkers' next single release. 'The Sun Ain't Gonna Shine Anymore' was written by (New) Jersey boys Bob Crewe and Bob Gaudio, respectively the producer and backing vocalist of The Four Seasons.[25] When band leader Frankie Valli first heard the tune, he cornered it for his next solo release in early 1965. It stiffed – its generic "my baby left me"/"I can't go on" lyric was a little hackneyed by now – although Valli's vocal and the country-esque guitar opening were pleasant enough.

Valli always claimed he'd passed the 45 to John Maus to consider as a singles cover. John had no recollection of this, although he said all three brothers had heard the tune and were considering it. By the time it came to recording Ivor Raymonde's new arrangement, its full-on orchestration – including harpsichord and timpani – made it sound less like the mourning of just another teenage love affair than the apocalypse itself. Franz must have known they had something, as it's one of the few tracks he produced multiple takes for until the backing and vocals were exactly right.

("And I had such a big argument with the top people at Philips, who weren't gonna let us record the track again, man!" confirmed Scott. "And so I had to bite my knuckles.")

Scott and John switched places for the title-line chorus, the soprano sibling's tones perking up its merry melancholy. But the opening lines – "Loneliness is a cloak you wear / A deep shade of blue is always there" – were a baritone statement of identity, of sadness as a permanent state of mind that, for better or worse, became the public perception of Scott Walker.

This was an impression cemented by the now strangely dated promo video filmed in Stockholm, Sweden: intense but baby-faced Scott addresses the camera straight on, his expressionistic gesturing and pointing underlining every other phrase. A static John and Gary look ill at ease, as animated as the statues of angels and nymphs in the background. But nothing could detract from what would be regarded as the Walkers' signature tune.

Released on February 25, 1966, 'The Sun Ain't Gonna Shine Anymore' went straight to the top of the British singles chart and stayed there for four weeks. It was a remarkable achievement at a time when pop music was a vital expression of the culture. In the Top 10 when the record hit, pop-art was exploding from the guitar chords of The Kinks' 'Dedicated Follower Of Fashion', The Who's 'Substitute' and The Yardbirds' 'Shapes Of Things'; in the Top 30, male angst was expressed in more traditional form by C&W singer Eddy Arnold imploring 'Make The World Go Away (Take It Off Of My Shoulders)' and Gene Pitney (regarded as Scott's only rival in the pop-melancholia stakes) emoting about

'Backstage'; it was also a key time for young female vocalists, with Dusty's 'You Don't Have To Say You Love Me', Cilla Black singing the theme from *Alfie*, Cher's 'Bang Bang' and Nancy Sinatra sassing her way through Lee Hazelwood's 'These Boots Were Made For Walkin'.[26]

All of the above were trumped at the time by the Walkers' biggest hit, which even made a showing in the US *Billboard* Top 20. It was a track that very quickly entered the public consciousness.

(As if to underline this, it became an underworld legend that, on March 9, 1966, when prodigal East End villain George Cornell met his end in Whitechapel's Blind Beggar pub, the record was playing on the jukebox. Given the date this seems wholly feasible. What *does* seem like a self-mythologising embellishment is Ronnie Kray's claim that, when he fired a 9mm Mauser point blank through Cornell's brain, as the bullet exited his cranium the jukebox got stuck on the title line of the song.[27])

On the B-side, 'After The Lights Go Out' added something equally valuable (if less celebrated) to the Walker template. Opening to a murmuring bass and scraped percussion before going into a low-key Reg Guest arrangement, Scott as the song's narrator has his perception made painfully sharp by his lover's departure: "As the sun goes down my silent little room is growin' dim... / And the clock on the wall, I'd like to put its tickin' to an end."

It was as if he was afflicted by a bout of existential nausea. All the more remarkable, perhaps, that this was not one of Engel's earlier compositions but a lyric by John Stewart, the other half of the Alec Noel partnership.

In the wake of 'The Sun Ain't Gonna Shine Anymore', Scott himself would describe the appeal of the Walkers as one of "neurotic romanticism". While not yet recognised as the "neurotic boy outsider" that style commentator Peter York would later acclaim him as, there was little doubt that the lead vocalist of The Walker Brothers was by now pop music's neurotic romantic *par excellence*.

Notes

1   Note the music press tradition of replacing 'g's with apostrophes in Scott Walker interviews. It would continue for years – presumably as a means of communicating his smooth Midwestern/West Coast burr.

2   Powell would remain on the periphery of the Walkers' scene for some weeks, only returning home when it became clear that they were in fact taking London on their own terms.

3   Only at the end of the film is the mystery of what 'Rosebud' signifies in the life of newspaper tycoon Kane resolved. It's a humble snow sled but symbolises everything he's ever lost. Rumour had it that Rosebud was the pet name William Randolph Hearst (Kane's model and Welles' implacable foe) used for his mistress' vagina.

4   *The Virgin Spring*, with its story of rape, murder and revenge in the Dark Ages, is a painterly vision of the coming of Christianity to pagan Scandinavia. In the USA, its basic plot would be re-utilised for a couple of ultraviolent exploitation movies.

5   In the sixties, friction between Kinks songwriter/vocalist Ray Davies and lead guitarist brother Dave makes them seem now like more affable precursors to the Gallagher brothers in Oasis – though the elder Muswell hillbillies could erupt into violence, which got them temporarily barred from the US. On this occasion, however, the onstage row erupted between Dave Davies and drummer Mick Avory, who sliced the guitarist's head open with a cymbal.

6   In the summer of 1965, *Fab 208* would take the Walkers to Paris' Left Bank for a photoshoot. Scott agreed to it on the basis he could visit the Louvre.

7   Existentialism has been facilely written off as a late beat-era Left Bank fad, as if concerns with the nature of existence itself had a limited shelf life. Its concept of individual freedom was not some hippy-ish yearning to 'do your own thing', but a recognition that existence in a meaningless universe is only validated by personal commitment to a course of action. All else is 'bad faith'.

8   In 2004, Clayman, whose latter-day clients include former Walker rival Tom Jones, would be awarded the OBE by the Queen for services to the music industry; King would die in suspicious circumstances in the late seventies, an apparent suicide after leaving the entertainment industry.

9   If Ronnie and Reggie Kray were visitors to the Starlite Club in Stratford Place, London W1, it's more likely that King was paying them protection money. Some harassed nightclub owners would try to extract a cachet of danger from the fact that they were being bullied by the most parasitic of criminals.

10   *Radio Fun*, a British comic book in the tradition of *Comic Cuts*, featured a strip called 'The Adventures of Anne Shelton and Her Pianist Johnny Franz'.

11   The image of Scott Walker as a crooner of standards, sometimes paternally accompanied by Franz on the piano, would later be fulfilled by his 1969 TV series *Scott* and its corresponding album.

12   Recording artists at the time for 4AD – now Scott Walker's record label.

13 When interviewed in the mid-fifties, the young would-be star Scott Engel had complained that New York was "no place to shoot a gun" – many career criminals may have disagreed with him, but he was talking as an aspiring outdoorsman raised partly in Denver and partly in Texas.

14 The perennially photogenic Ms Dunford remains a model well into her sixties.

15 An exasperated Maurice King reputedly nicknamed Scott 'Scoot' on these occasions.

16 At the height of their teen-scream appeal in the mid-sixties, The Rolling Stones were known to play 'Three Blind Mice' beneath the cover of audience noise – instead of, say, '(I Can't Get No) Satisfaction'.

17 West was a contemporary of Ernest Hemingway, F. Scott Fitzgerald and Henry Miller – although the latter achieved recognition much later in life. As such, it's quite likely Scott is familiar with his work.

18 According to Scott, he and Ms Duncan wrote three songs in all ("They'll blow your mind!" he boasted at the time), but only 'You're All Around Me' saw official release as a B-side. It's likely the other two are among the uncredited tracks that appear alongside a handful of standards on the second half of disc three of *Everything Under The Sun*, the retrospective Walker Brothers box set. Lesley Duncan achieved greater recognition in the early seventies for her 'Love Song', covered by Elton John and numerous others. Having abandoned her career in the late seventies for family life, she died in March 2010 on the Isle of Mull.

19 R&B, as we've now learned to call it – a term which once suggested the guitar-based music of Muddy Waters or sixties beat groups – is often too beset by clichéd vocal histrionics to carry the emotional directness of the great soul singers.

20 Probably the closest thing the Walkers ever did to the sentimental 'Scotty Engel' recordings of the fifties, it reached its cheesy apotheosis when it became the theme tune to Mike Read's 'First Love' slot on his *Radio One Breakfast Show* in the eighties.

21 'Amphetamined alliteration' might have been more accurate, given Dylan's condition at the time. As with Lou Reed – who dismissed Dylan's lyrics as "marijuana throwaways" in his Velvet Underground years, but later opined that Dylan had never made an uninteresting album – Scott would moderate his opinion, although he clearly sees no reason for reverence.

22 In their joint autobiography John and Gary both insist that no such event occurred. The reasoning behind this is that nobody told them about it at the time.

23 Along the King's Road we have to assume the 'rocks' may have been bricks – or even stones.

24 The year after Gary recorded his version, Dawn Penn cut her classic rocksteady cover in Jamaica.

25 Crewe had written Four Seasons signature hits like 'Rag Doll' and 'Walk Like A Man'.

26 To all the above could be added Staff Sergeant Barry Sadler's 'Ballad Of The Green Berets', whose pro-US Army propaganda somehow crossed the Atlantic during the Vietnam War. Scott may or may not have appreciated the irony.

27   According to the 1992 Scott Walker biography *A Deep Shade Of Blue*, the Brothers had their own fleeting encounter with the Twins: though Scott was a Tony Bennett fan, he tired of 'villain' types continually playing 'I Left My Heart In San Francisco' in Maurice King's Starlite Club. When he ejected the record via a back button, he was supposedly threatened by a menacing guy in a suit who told him, "I don't think Ronnie would like that." The complainant was allegedly Reggie Kray.

Chapter 4

Portrait Of The Artists As Young Men

My own shadows surround me,
They won't go away.

Scott Engel and John Franz –
'A Young Man Cried' (1966)

The myth of the early Scott Walker as a kind of campy cabaret entertainer had its origin at the height of The Walker Brothers' success.

It was in March 1966 that their management booked them into the Tito Club in Stockton on Teesside, in England's Northwest. It was for a full week's residency and feelings were mixed. "Scott and I were upset by the idea of playing in cabaret," insisted Gary; "It was... a bad move for us as a group," seconded John.

It did at least make financial sense: the nightclub had a maximum capacity of 3,000; instead of tickets selling for a uniform price of under £1, as at the concert halls, the cheapest tickets at Tito's were selling for £10 – although this likely included a chicken-in-a-basket meal.

Scott, who admitted to being exceptionally nervous at the time, must have noted how the older audience were attentive to his performance, only cheering or whistling at the end of each song. Although supposedly reluctant to embrace the cabaret scene,[1] it would mark the first time that he moved away from the concert-hall circuit into the supper-club set.

Apart from the R&B/soul standards that the Walkers had kept in their set since the Sunset Strip days, Scott and John brought the house down with 'Summertime' – the George Gershwin song from his opera *Porgy And Bess*. Listen to the recorded version released later that year and you'll feel a dramatic tension in the sudden switching between lead singers; Engel and Maus are sweetly and evenly balanced at first, before a saxophone break by Barrie Martin of The Quotations momentarily takes off into free-blowing jazz. Little wonder that the Stockton crowd gave it a standing ovation.

Back 'home' in London, Scott had only the minimum of time to bitch about his social milieu to the pop press – "I spend most of my evenings down at Ronnie Scott's. You find a lot of pseudos and hippies there but not as many as the 'In' clubs" – before setting off on a 27-date tour.

In the tradition of sixties package tours, the Walkers were not the only big name at the top of the bill. More surprising was that the headliner was Roy Orbison, the USA's monolithic 'Big O' – a king of neurotic romanticism since before the Walkers had even played the Strip. Despite the brothers' current all-time-high popularity, it was the affable Texan Orbison who topped the bill.

Also on the line-up was 17-year-old Scots singing star Lulu (born Marie McDonald McLaughlin Lawrie), who recently had her first hit with a cover of The Isley Brothers' 'Shout'. "Not only was this 16 year old [*sic*] *mad* about him, but so was every 16 year old in the country," she much later acknowledged of Scott Walker.

In the pop weekly *Disc*, Scott and a chubby-faced young Lulu were photographed together as the readers' 'Mr and Miss Valentine'. In the actuality, his feelings for the much younger woman were more paternal. "I got to tour with them, with The Walker Brothers, so it was kind of a divine torturous experience," she laughs, "because he would kind of pat me on the head."

The opening night of the tour was March 25, 1966 at the Finsbury Park Astoria, later more famous as the Rainbow. Scott ensured that his mother and her sister were brought over to witness how far the trio had come in their single year across the ocean. Betty (or Mimi, as Scott was wont to call her) and Aunt Seal stayed at the Grosvenor House Hotel – where they were forced to eat supper in their hotel room, besieged as they were by Walker fans. Nothing in the juvenile career of Scotty Engel can have prepared Betty for the teen hysteria she witnessed.

'WALKER FAN MANIA!' ran one subsequent pop press headline.

"Last Saturday's Walker Brothers-Roy Orbison show at Hammersmith Odeon proved as eventful as any opening night!

"One girl fan got through the skylight during the second house[2] and [hung] suspended over the stage curtains, refusing to come down unless the Walkers spoke to her. Failing amplifiers and screaming girls added to the confusion."

The Hammersmith date saw Orbison's 30th birthday, with the Walkers and other artists on the bill attending a special midnight party in his honour at the Dolce Vita restaurant in Soho. Despite classic ballads like 'Only The Lonely', 'Running Scared' and 'Blue Bayou', which elevated heartbreak to a near-operatic level, only John had watched him reverentially from the side of the stage. Scott admired his work, but found his southern gentlemanly manners and his overall 'niceness' a little cloying. (He and Gary rather cruelly rechristened Orbison "the Big Slow".)

In any case, the Big O was quickly becoming a secondary feature on the bill. The kids were showing their impatience with this troubadour from the older generation, with one fan in Bradford later claiming they'd pelted him with sweets. Small wonder, perhaps, that when Maurice King asked him if the Walkers could close as the final act towards the end of the tour, he graciously conceded, "It's all the same to me" – just as he had to Brian Epstein three years earlier, when Beatlemania hit.

According to Gary, he and the physically sporty Scott had countered many nights of whisky drinking on tour by playing badminton – although John suffered a serious head injury that required hospitalisation, incurred while escaping a car surrounded by frantic fans ("the angry villagers", as Scott only semi-affectionately called them). The peak of the tour for Leeds was clearly the final night in Coventry: "Scott appeared on stage riding a bike, John was on piano and I did lead vocals.[3] It was probably one of our best shows."

In April, the month after the tour, it was a measure of the industry's current esteem for the Walkers that Maurice King played host at the *NME* poll winners' concert – with a performance by his 'boys', of course, who came third in Best Group (after The Beatles and Stones).

It was also the period that inspired a retrospective complaint from Scott, during his early solo days: "I was working like a badger. The other guys were just enjoying things. And it really made me angry that people weren't digging the music as much as the image."

The remark would draw offence from John, who by then had come to feel totally sidelined, and even the loyal Gary. But all the evidence suggests Maus and Leeds were more comfortable in the secondary role of celebrities – appearing at a motor-racing event at Brands Hatch, for example, knocking back champagne with the 'dolly birds'.

To Engel this kind of life was anathema. He didn't wear the obsession of the creative artist lightly – agonising over the choice of material and musicians, actively participating in song arrangements and production techniques, whether he'd be credited for it or not. To which can be added the neurosis of the novice songwriter – a status he had yet to transcend.

The almost ever-present sunglasses ("Everyone's on this daytime kick, it's awful") were no longer enough to provide him with a semblance of anonymity. "That's when he went into The Disguise

Period," said Gary Leeds. "One time he adopted the look of a building-site worker, complete with hard hat and long coat. But it was about 80 degrees that day, and everybody else was in shorts and T-shirts. Obviously, everyone was looking at him."

After the music press had inadvertently given away his latest change of address – to the McCartneyland of St John's Wood, NW8 – Scott was perturbed to hear Walker fans were scouring the streets for him. It prompted a further move back to west London. In the middle of the night, Gary and Maurice King helped him move under cover of darkness to a flat on the Fulham Road. His new peace of mind would not last long.

"Then sometime the next afternoon he rang up and yelled: 'They've found me! I can hear 'em screaming outside!'" confirmed Gary. What Scott himself had actually found, without realising it, was the Saturday afternoon home crowd for Chelsea FC at Stamford Bridge. Tens of thousands of men, mostly, screaming in unison – and not for The Walker Brothers.

In their spring 1966 tour of northern Europe, Scott would find some of the female attention more welcome. In late May/early June, the Walkers played two nights at the Carousel Club in Copenhagen, Denmark. It was here that a statuesque 19 year old came to their attention. "Both Scott and I noticed her," John acknowledged much later, "commenting to each other on how attractive she was, and we were all introduced to her. She may have been known to somebody connected to the show, because normally we didn't meet fans or audience."

Mette Teglbjaerg hailed from Lyngby, a northern suburb of Copenhagen. Pretty, leggy and curvaceous, in a way that women were still allowed to be even in the Twiggy era (without being labelled 'fat'), she impressed both singers. Scott was interested to hear that she was considering coming to London, to join her older sister. Their meeting at the Carousel may have clinched this.

In mid-July, the Walkers returned to the BBC's flagship chart show *Top Of The Pops* to mime to their new single, '(Baby) You

Don't Have To Tell Me'. Another troubled love song, it lacked the orchestrated angst of 'The Sun...' or 'Make It Easy...' – which was the appeal for Gary, who suggested covering the obscure US pop 45 by Bobby Coleman as a change of pace. (Its B-side was 'My Love Is Growing', a folk rock number co-written by John Stewart and sung by his best buddy.)

It also failed to repeat the success of the earlier epics (making it only as far as number 13 on the chart), but it was certainly more danceable. In fact, among the female *TOTP* audience gyrating along with Scott and John can be glimpsed a particularly animated brunette in outsize shades. Her sunglasses obscure part of her features, but in all other respects she resembles the few photos that survive of Mette in the mid-to-late sixties.

Whether or not it was her or just a pretty doppelganger, this marks a period when Irene Dunford seemed to gradually fade out and Ms Teglbjaerg took her place. "One thing that set her apart from most of the girls whom he met was that she didn't idolise him," John later reflected with obvious approval. "She wasn't starstruck but really cared for him. In fact, she took the mickey out of him when the occasion called for it. Also, she seemed emotionally stable, with a very even temperament, which benefited Scott..."

"... Femininity is a state of mind, not a mode of attire," Scott had insisted of his taste in women the previous year. "I don't expect her to come to see me every evening with her hair done. I like sensitive people, but most of all I like girls who try to understand or at least listen with some sympathy."

On the same day '(Baby) You Don't Have To Tell Me' was released, *Ready Steady Go!* devoted an entire edition to The Walker Brothers. Sadly, no videotapes of it exist – but Scott's downtempo version of The Beatles' 'We Can Work It Out' at least suggests an ambiguous attitude to the band he regarded both as overrated and as affecting balladeers.

As part of a glut of Walkers material in 1966, 'I Need You' was simultaneously released as the title track of an EP. An emotional ballad by Carole King and Gerry Goffin (contemporaries of 'Love Her' composers Mann and Weil at the Brill Building), it was a US hit for soul singer Chuck Jackson in 1964 and was given a serviceable treatment by Scott.

More worthy of note were 'Looking For Me' – principally for being the second Engel cover of a Randy Newman song, though its *West Side Story*-ish tale of trying to dodge your girlfriend's ex's buddies on the street is lively enough – and 'Young Man Cried'. The latter is a rare collaboration between Engel and producer Franz. An affecting piece of epic melancholia, even if its standard lyric ("You're gone again / and a young man cried today") is not quite the equal of its Cinemascope arrangement. This was the work of Reg Guest.

"Unlike Ivor Raymonde," said John, "who basically followed the arrangements of the original tracks and beefed them up a bit, Reg was far more imaginative, created tailored arrangements to enhance our recordings in every way possible, always taking what Scott and I did into consideration."

"My attitude to Scott was to let him be Scott and not interfere with his far-out ideas," acclaimed former session player Guest in return. "I let him be the way he was because as musical director I felt it was my duty to let him express himself."

"Johnny [Franz] was already starting to distract Scott away from The Walker Brothers with material and ideas intended to showcase his talent," John lamented later. But that particular train was already on the track, and at first it wouldn't be derailed.

The ongoing popularity of The Walkers had been underlined by their appearance on Lew Grade's popular variety show *Sunday Night At The London Palladium* the previous month. Their new EP was also picking up praise in the most unexpected quarters, as the following letter shows:

JONATHAN KING ENTERPRISES LTD
DIRECTORS:
Kenneth G. King   37 SOHO SQUARE
James E. King   LONDON W1
14th July, 1966
JK: CW
Miss Pat Jefferies
xxxxxxxxxxxxx
xxxxxxxxxxxxxxxx
London SW7.

Dear Pat,

Thank you very much for your letter. I am afraid that as a matter of principle I never ask Scott for his autograph for friends or anyone because he is busy signing autographs and doing business all day and likes to relax in the evenings. However, I suggest that you send it to Capable Management at 185 Bickenhall Mansions, London W1, and he will probably sign it personally as that is his manager's office.

I feel exactly the same as you do about their EP.

I will be finished at Cambridge at the end of next year and with a bit of luck will pass those exams too. Most of my vacation will be spent in plugging records I am afraid, which is another form of work, so your holiday will be more rewarding than mine.

Anyway, many thanks again for your letter. Sorry about the autograph, I am sure you understand and if you write to the above address you should get a result.

Yours,
Jonathan.

If the above reads as surprisingly thoughtful and courteous, it's because it originates from one of the more egocentric figures of the sixties British pop scene. Jonathan King had his first major hit under his own name (as opposed to the pseudonyms he later used) at 19 – his 1965 single 'Everyone's Gone To The Moon', a catchy, kitschy celebration of the space age.

Since then, he'd simultaneously pursued a pop career (as performer/composer/producer) and a journalistic sideline (for *Disc & Music Echo*) while taking an English literature degree at Trinity College, Cambridge. He and Scott had first met on a TV pop show, bonding over a shared recognition that they worked in one of the more ridiculous quarters of the entertainment industry – King with glee and Engel with a degree of enervation.

While the bearded, flamboyant King might venture forth in full period Cossack costume and Scott was mostly comfortable in the same old beat-up corduroy suit, they managed to find common ground.

"We were very similar in many ways," King later insisted. "We were exactly the same size and used to swap each other's clothes all the time.[4] We both, in a sense, had intellectual pretensions in that we didn't want to be just interested in pop culture... One of his fascinations was Jean Genet and it was through discussing the character of this rather bizarre man that we found we had a lot in common."

If Scott saw parallels with Genet, it was presumably because King was known to be gay in a society which still criminalised homosexuality.[5] King may have carried the cachet of a figure verging on social outsiderdom, as personified by Dirk Bogarde as the anguished barrister in the 1961 film *Victim*, with its glimpses of a gay underworld below the surface of inner London's streets.

But Jonathan King was actually an irreverent pop entrepreneur who later churned out harmless (if irritating) pieces of fluff like 'Johnny Reggae' by The Piglets; an inherent social conservative, he was perhaps the only former British pop star who'd record a loving tribute to Margaret Thatcher (she of the notorious Clause 28 – which banned 'promotion of homosexuality' by local councils) when she retired as Prime Minister.

Jean Genet, on the other hand, was a Parisian state-reared thief and male prostitute, christened 'Saint Genet' by an enthralled Sartre. In his memoir, *The Thief's Journal*, he wrote: "... Criminals are remote from you – as in love, they turn away and turn me away from the world and its laws. Theirs smells of sweat, sperm and blood... it was because the world contains these erotic conditions that I was bent on evil." Released from prison into the strangest kind of literary celebrity, in his plays Genet empathised with marginal figures often despised by the rest of the world: the Palestinians in *The Blacks*; two convicted murderesses in *The Maids*. Little wonder, perhaps, that English public schoolboy King should consider Genet 'bizarre'.

Scott, for his part, regarded Jonathan King as "the Cocteau of the pop business".[6] "He could never handle his own situations, but he could certainly handle mine," he'd later remark almost cryptically.

"I've never known anyone who hated stardom so much and from about the second day of knowing him, I was well aware that he was not going to keep putting up with it," King later observed of Engel. Just how accurate this was became apparent on August 15, 1966.

Immersed in recording the Walkers' second album, Scott did not respond to an early evening call from the band's driver, Bobby Hamilton. Alarmed, Hamilton kicked in the door and found an unconscious Engel in his flat's kitchen at Fulham. In a classic scenario, the oven door was open and the room smelled heavily of gas. Fighting to protect his own respiration, the record company minder dragged Scott out into the communal hallway and enlisted the neighbours' help in calling an ambulance.

On being revived, it seemed no long-term damage was done – although a croaky Scott was unable to sing for several days. On questioning as to whether he'd actually attempted suicide, a seemingly abashed Engel blamed "a lot of pressures and a personal problem. I think it all woke a lot of people up, includin' myself... But pressure wasn't the only reason. Nobody has the right reasons and I'm not tellin' anyone the right reasons."

The *Daily Mirror* had already fuelled speculation by reporting two weeks earlier that Scott's alleged marriage proposal to Irene Dunford had been turned down. ("I did not take him seriously because he was so unstable at the time," she'd later claim.) Due to Scott's disinclination to discuss his private life, the fact that the relationship with Ms Dunford was already superseded by his closeness to Mette Teglbjaerg was overlooked.

The response of the other Walkers was one of incredulity. To them, Scott's cryptic teasing spoke of an ulterior motive. "... Starting in 1966, a new and increasingly dramatic series of events associated with Scott began to 'feed' the press, so I've always wondered what came first," a cynical John later reflected. "If Maurice [King] did not know what was going on, then the whole event may have been a ploy on Scott's part to make the management treat him with a great deal more deference – as in 'Before we do anything else, we'd better check with Scott first.'"

"This so-called suicide attempt was, I think, just another publicity stunt to increase record sales," surmised the usually loyal Gary. "I was under the impression that Scott was too strong a person to do that kind of thing, or maybe I don't know him as well as I thought I did," he at least conceded.

"It was a very bad period," Scott later explained to *Disc & Music Echo*. "I thought everyone was trying to destroy my life. I had this idea that the press were people who misquoted me; fans were the ones who wouldn't stop ringing my phone, smashing my door and making me move flats... It was very immature of me. But to someone going through a paranoiac stage it all seemed to make sense."

For his part, Jonathan King had few doubts that Scott had intended to harm himself. ("I can't keep on having to dash to your bedside," he later claimed to have scolded him, "either commit suicide properly, in which case I'll never be pestered again, or you've got to stop.") Both men fuelled further speculation by taking a holiday together in Sitges, Spain, to help Engel convalesce.[7]

Sonny boy, such a sonny boy: Scotty Engel – heralded in 1951 (aged eight) by the *Denver Post* as the new Al Jolson.

Just like Eddie: young Scott Engel was a protégé of Eddie Fisher on his TV show – until Fisher took up with Liz Taylor and derailed his career. PRESS CLIPPING

'That wasn't anything serious,' said a mature Scott of his brief time as a child star. His fan club members might have disagreed in the late fifties. COURTESY ARNIE POTTS

THIS IS TO CERTIFY THAT

Elaine Igarashi

is a member in good standing
of the

**SCOTT ENGEL
FAN CLUB**

CHAPTER   PRESIDENT

The blonde face of pop heartbreak – an unlikely interpreter of the *chansonnier's* European angst? HARRY GOODWIN

When pop worlds collide: on the last sixties Walkers tour, their support acts diverge into the psychedelic blues of Hendrix and the sentimental crooning of Humperdinck. GAB ARCHIVE/REDFERNS

Portrait of the artists as three young men: Scott, John and Gary, The Walker Brothers, as photographed for their *Portrait* LP.
EZO HOFFMANN/REX FEATURES

On TV The Walkers presented the image of a band; in the studio their music was played by top sessions musicians, and onstage by tou[r] band The Quotations. KING COLLECTION /RETNA/PHOTOSHOT

Scott gets all Buddy Rich on Gary's skins; the former jobbing bassist was also a proficient multi-instrumentalist.
MICHAEL OCHS ARCHIVE/GETTY IMAGES

fans outside the June 1966 filming of *Sunday Night At The London Palladium*; the Walkers were a focus for hysteria, occasionally aying with personal injuries. ITV/REX FEATURES

Beat group or boy band? The line-up equates the Walkers with the sixties beat boom; the influence of Sinatra and Jack Jones took Scott somewhere different. CAMERAPRESS/E. TAYLOR

The blue-eyed boy of sixties pop and the backroom boffins who reinvented it: Scott with producer John Franz and arranger Peter Knight, at work on his solo output. DEZO HOFFMANN/REX FEATURES

'I really hear Sibelius here... I hear Delius.' Arranger Wally Stott's roll call of Scott's influences might also have included Bartok and the soundtracks of Jerry Goldsmith. DEZO HOFFMANN/REX FEATURES

Scott flanked by his friends Jackie Trent and Tony Hatch, composers of 'Joanna', on their 1968 TV special Mr & Mrs Music. Matt Monro completes the MOR line-up. ITV /REX FEATURES

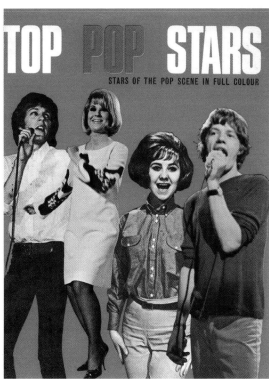

The inimitable Jacques Brel in 1961: Scott didn't try to imitate the Belgian's 'sweat and blood and anger', adapting it into the Anglophone pop of the late sixties.
LIPNITZKI/ROGER VIOLLET/GETTY IMAGES

1967's Top Pop Stars contrasts Scott with his contemporaries: nemesis Jagger, besotted Lulu and Dusty Springfield, whose repertoire sometimes mirrored his own. GAB ARCHIVE/REDFERNS

Scott clowns about in the Walkers days. His pierrot make-up pre-empts David Bowie's period in mime, and foreshadows the two artists' mutual influence on each other. BRUCE FLEMING/GETTY IMAGES

It's known that Scott got teetotal control freak King drunk on tequila in Spain, while he himself was loaded on the tranquillisers and sleeping pills doled out at the time by the medical profession. In terms of what we now think of as substance abuse, the performer was mostly not attracted by the voguish illicit drugs of the day – abandoning marijuana after a few sessions as it made his throat hurt.

Booze and downers were a different proposition, however, despite the fate that lay in store for stars from Judy Garland to Jimi Hendrix.[8] Scott would soon find that he could maintain his work rate on this chemical combination, as his tolerance to the pills increased. For all its dangers, the depressive twilight zone these stimulants created could also be a realm of creativity – at least for a while.

Back in the UK, the release that same month of 'Another Tear Falls' showed The Walker Brothers at their most lachrymose. The remake of a Bacharach and David song first crisply enunciated by refined Nat King Cole-alike Gene McDaniels (who augmented his performance in Brit movie *It's Trad, Dad!* with some serious cigarette smoking, in the days when such things were allowed), it was another classically atmospheric Guest arrangement of a standard lost-love lyric, this time introduced by sinister woodwind.

The B-side, 'Saddest Night In The World', did much the same thing only better. Beginning with a gently folky acoustic guitar, this further variation on the theme of the world being transformed by sadness when you lose your girl was bolstered by the backing vocals of its composer – one John Maus.

"Shop window girls smiled through the rain / And the wet, grey figure called me looks for a man he used to be." The former guitarist tapped into the essence of his vocal partner's romantic melancholy. John had written a perfect early Scott Walker lyric, even before the vocalist himself could pull off a similar feat.

Despite the quality of both sides of the 45, 'Another Tear Falls' didn't quite make it into the Top 10. It was a respectable showing, in the days when records really did sell in high quantities, but the maestros at Philips considered it a relative failure. Walker supporter

Keith Altham, at *NME*, suggested John Franz was cleaving too closely to a formula. Even Scott blamed himself for over-ornate orchestration, though it's hard to see what difference a more pared-down approach would have made. This was still one for aficionados of heartbreak.

"It gets kinda lonely, only there is no solution to the loneliness," Scott tried to describe his own state of mind in an interview the following year. "To stop being lonely you have to share your life and your mind with people, and I can't do that."

As imaginatively inspiring as a state of melancholy might be, it was obvious that Scott (whether in his daily life or in his role as a song's narrator) was not suffering the loneliness of the average poor sap who had no luck with women. His was the loneliness of the long-distance Walker – a much-adored pop singer who could virtually pluck girls from the trees, should he so desire. The distance he felt between himself and other people appears to have been a form of emotional alienation, an altogether profounder sense of being alone in a city of millions of people.

That autumn also saw the release of *Portrait*, the second Walkers album. Before they headed out on a promotional tour, a direct overture to manage the band was made by Brian Epstein, The Beatles' manager, which was turned down by Scott on the basis of a reluctance to be funded by "Beatle money". Despite the Walkers' (particularly Gary's) friendliness with the Fab Four, his ambiguous attitude toward the most popular band in the universe remained.

The album itself fulfilled much of the promise of the previous year – and of Reg Guest as an arranger, augmented by Scott himself. Despite this, the arrangement of the emotionally foreboding opener, 'In My Room', was based on the original English language version by Verdelle Smith (another black American singer with sharply crisp enunciation). While Guest was credited by many with the dread chords of Bach's 'Toccata In D Minor' running throughout the song, its tones of doom had already been present. Most stunning was how the Spanish love song 'El Amor', by Joaquin

Prieto, had been translated by Tin Pan Alley hacks Paul Vance and Lee Pockriss into a ballad of devastating despair. The abandoned (or possibly bereaved) narrator remains confined within his tiny apartment, going quietly insane awaiting the return of the wife he knows is gone forever: "Over there is the chair where I held her whenever she cried / Over there by the window the flowers she left – have all died."

It's a classic early Scott Walker performance, a Euro-ballad that combines its emotional sweep with a sense of domestic claustrophobia. (It's also a less sophisticated prelude to the time when Jacques Brel's lyrics would be translated into English.)

The first Engel original on the album, 'Saturday's Child', now seems uncharacteristically jaunty, with a bass riff apparently lifted from 'River Deep, Mountain High' (the latter recorded at the time Scott was hanging around the Spector studio). A lyrical blast at London's club and party set, it mirrors its time by making the object of its scorn a girl: "Saturday's child who used to say / That she could dance the world away... just hangs her head and cries today."

Scott's baritone takes precedence over John's lighter tones when they sing together, but there are still some great duets here: 'Hurting Each Other' is a cover of a 45 by Canadian band Guess Who, but more redolent of the sensitive Carpenters hit version that followed in 1972; Gershwin's 'Summertime' had become a high point of their current stage set, with an immaculate vocal arrangement by John; 'Living Above Your Head' is another uptempo cover, this time of the obscure Jay & The Americans, and once again it lets those flighty chicks have it: "Living above your head, girl / Something has got to go wrong"; Scott takes lead again on 'People Get Ready', the two big brothers' duet on The Impressions' gospel-inspired song of "a train a-comin'" – Engel may have been an existentialist, but he was also a social liberal whose emotions jibed with lyricist Curtis Mayfield's promise of divinely inspired social justice. (Gary later claimed they were among the few white performers Mayfield would license his songs to.)

85

John puts in a couple of sterling performances of his own on the Ray Charles ballad 'Just For A Thrill' and Leiber-Stoller's 'Take It Like A Man', previously recorded by Gene Pitney. Just as Maus reputedly chose 'In My Room' for Engel's angst-ridden soul, so Scott is said to have selected 'Take It Like A Man' for him, in which he comes over like a raspy, *laissez-faire* 'anti-Scott' ("Don't cry… she's gone!").

Scott's own rendition of the thirties jazz standard 'Old Folks', previously covered by many (including torch singer Mel Torme), was, according to John, "a song he'd always wanted to do". Sentimentally describing the twilight years of an old boy known colloquially as 'Old Folks', who spends his time fishing and wandering about town, it concludes, "Children's voices at play will be still for a day / the day they take the Old Folks away."

Those with hearts to touch will still be moved by it. But there were those who mocked how, in an age of purple hearts, LSD and guitar feedback, The Walker Brothers were retreating into mawkish show tunes. It may not have mattered to them that this was Scott's tribute to his father, still only in his mid-fifties, with whom he had recently been reconciled – or indeed that the tune may have signified Noel Sr.'s own recent parental loss. Over a year beforehand, when the Walkers were playing their first British concerts, the *Hamilton Daily News* had run the following notice:

SCOTT H. ENGEL
Obituary: May 29, 1965 Hamilton, Butler Co; Ohio… collapsed on 2nd & High Street and never recovered.

The obituary showed a fastidious-looking old geezer in rimless specs and bow tie. Grandpa Scott had been in his 85th year and remained active till the last.[9]

Less weepy but infinitely more moody, 'I Can See it Now' carries a typically muted sixties trumpet and handpicked strings. It's also the second of the few tracks to carry an Engel/Franz credit, celebrating romantic heartbreak rather than wallowing in it: "Maybe today a lonesome man / Is gonna find a dream again..." 'Where's The Girl?' is more effective still, with young Scott's voice reverberating in sombre regret: "The canary stopped singing the moment she walked out the door." Another Jerry Leiber and Mike Stoller ballad, this further remake from the Jerry Butler songbook carries a dated (and all the more poignant for that) stamp of a man left alone without his female half. ("You can tell that this apartment and I are in need of a woman's touch.")

The two singing brothers regroup their forces for the closing number, Tom Springfield's 'No Sad Songs For Me'. "[It] struck Scott and me as the most beautiful love song we'd ever heard," John later testified. "I sang lead on that, a departure from our usual format." It was also the first time that the Walker voices (in a duet this time) substituted the effortlessly dulcet tones of Dusty Springfield – who first sang the song as lead vocalist of her brother's folk group. "Pretty soon our love will be / Just a memory / It's all over" – sung as a melodic elegy, it's as if the closing track is marking the end of a life rather than just a love affair.

With a cover shot by society photographer Cecil Beaton which was replicated in a pull-out card, *Portrait* matched the Top 3 success of its predecessor. It was promoted by a 33-date tour, which Scott prepared for by having his formerly lustrous locks shorn short. The tour – a package supported by Dave Dee, Dozy, Beaky, Mick & Tich and The Troggs – was undertaken "out of greed" according to Engel, who already seemed to be tiring of the tour-record-tour routine. Not so, said the other brothers, with all of them being paid retainers of at least £40 per week. It was a good living wage, but all the same – they needed to record and tour in order to live.

As the dates wound towards their conclusion in late October/ early November, the schedules were derailed in a way that Engel can neither have wished for nor anticipated. On October 22, 1966, the Walkers were scheduled to appear as guests on BBC TV's *Billy Cotton Band Show* – a family variety show hosted by the jolly entertainer whose son (Bill Cotton Jr.) also happened to be the corporation's Head of Light Entertainment.

"Being on this show was a prestigious opportunity but, during rehearsals, Scott complained of having a bad headache," John later recalled. "We sent one of the television staff to get some tablets, specifying no aspirin, as Scott would have a terrible reaction to it… Within minutes of taking them he was having difficulty breathing and his face began to swell up. We had no choice but to leave, because obviously we would not be able to perform on the show."[10]

After his allergic reaction died down and his teen-dream features returned to normal proportions, the Walkers had to complete a further week of dates. Scott lasted out the schedule by retreating to his hotel room and marking out extracurricular creative plans. Among these were writing a screenplay for a "surrealistic pop film with a contemporary of Ingmar Bergman's". The filmmaker in question remains unidentified and it's perhaps a pity that we were never treated to The Walker Brothers' equivalent of The Beatles' *Magical Mystery Tour*, or The Monkees in *Head*.[11]

More practical and realistic were production plans for Alec Noel – the partnership with best friend John Stewart, by now a regular figure among the Walkers' camp in London. The single 'Light', by a Wolverhampton beat group called Finders Keepers, was produced after the tour for Fontana, Philips' pop offshoot label. Stewart-Engel laboured hard over the number (a mundane tune about "the light of my life", composed by Stewart) and the group were amazed at how a deep mix and chiming bells transformed it.

Production duties were also performed for Dutch band The Motions and a group with a female singer called Carol & The Memories, whose 'Tears On My Pillow' (c/w 'Crying My Eyes Out') was pitched somewhere between Spector and Merseybeat. None of these singles made for a hit, but Alec Noel at least remained a productive enterprise.

It wasn't to last, sadly.

While John Stewart was increasingly seen as 'the fourth Walker Brother' (to the extent that some people anticipated he might join the group), one absentminded motion put paid to it all. One day that November, he was crossing the road in Birmingham, part of Finders Keepers' Midlands stomping ground. Momentarily forgetful of how most traffic in Britain approaches a pedestrian from the right, he walked out in front of a car and was knocked down.

Scott rushed to his friend's hospital bedside, but injuries to his head and leg were substantial. Engel is said to have covered Stewart's private medical fees before flying him back to LA. He would never return to Britain.[12] Scott Engel was suddenly bereft of his closest friend, left ever more dependent for camaraderie on the maverick Jonathan King – himself something of an outsider.

The show had to go on. On November 29, 1966, the Walkers made their return headlining visit to the London Palladium for a Royal Gala performance in front of the Duke of Edinburgh. They acquitted themselves well with a medley of their greatest hits, lining up at the end of the show to exchange pleasant obsequies with Prince Philip and Princess Royal Margaret. The story got around that Scott had declined Margaret's invitation to party with them the next weekend.[13]

If something had to give in the tension between the nature of Scott Engel and what was expected of him by the entertainment industry, he pre-empted it himself the following month. "Reg Guest and I are hung up on the Gregorian chant," he'd told the *Melody Maker*. "It's one of the earliest forms of music and… when I play it softly it just takes me away from everything."

The fascination with ancient monastic chanting could later be heard in short vocal bursts on 'The Seventh Seal', from *Scott 4*. But for now, "just takes me away from everything" was as profound a need as terpsichorean study. Engel made an arrangement with the monks of Quarr Abbey on the Isle of Wight to spend some time on hiatus within their hallowed walls.

"The retreat has no religious significance. I am going simply to find time to think and to sort out my life," he explained at the time.

Studying early ecclesiastical music would be merely a part of this, but Gary Leeds later commented on how the atheistic Engel might have made a very good monk.

It was not to last long. The *Melody Maker* ran the following report in December 1966:

'FANS FORCE SCOTT TO QUIT MONASTERY'
Scott Walker has been forced to leave a monastery on the Isle of Wight – because of his fans.

Scott's plan to go to the monastery was exclusively revealed in the *MM* which did not disclose its whereabouts. Unfortunately, other newspapers did.

He had planned to stay for at least 10 days, primarily to study the Gregorian chants studied by the monks. But invading fans this week made it impossible.

On Monday, his publicist, Brian Sommerville, told the *MM*: "Scott has been asked to leave the monastery because so many kids invaded the place.

"He is bloody angry about it all. He seriously wanted to go there to rest and to learn about Gregorian chants.

"Now he has been asked to leave. Apparently the monks were spending all their time answering the telephone. Fans kept ringing up and others were trying to get into the place."

"[Scott] always enjoyed learning more about older Western music, and had a vast record library of classical and related recordings," John later confirmed. "He didn't discuss his trip there with me, but the whole thing turned into a ridiculous media-fest involving photographers and other press, who somehow got wind that he was there... [It] was a publicity dream, whether it was planned or not."[14]

Press treatment of the monastic sojourn only served to underline the image of 'Scott Walker – neurotic romantic outsider'. In one sense, his very reluctance to play the fame game was a gift to a publicist like Sommerville.

On the business front, at the height of the Walkers' success, Maurice King had formed his own music publishing company called Miracle Songs. The ultimate outcome was that any revenue from the Walkers' own compositions would be channelled via King and Capable Management – as their other earnings already were.

It was a classic fifties-style arrangement, hanging over into the decade that followed. That it was allowed to persist was largely due to the unworldliness of the group themselves.

"All the money that we earned went directly to our managers," John later admitted. "We never actually saw any of it, didn't think about it at the time... Scott and I had just come from Hollywood – otherwise known as 'rip-off city' – and were overly wary of scams, yet here we were, unquestioning. Later, sadly, we would find out that, like other artists in the sixties, we never saw all the money that we were due."

Scott was sanguine about the arrangement almost to the point of being boastful. "I don't even have a bank account," he said at the time.

Notes

1   Cabaret, in this milieu, tended to denote tuxedoed performers crooning as an accompaniment to diners eating meals. The term was redeemed over the ensuing decades by the Ebb and Kander musical (*Cabaret*) evoking the musical satire of Brecht and Weill during Germany's Weimar years, as well as by an eighties London cabaret scene which dared show its teeth on occasion. In fairness to the Walkers, they belonged to none of the above camps.

2   The evening, as opposed to matinee, performance, as some tour dates were doubles.

3   On other dates, Gary's 'lead vocals' amounted to a histrionic mime to Scott singing Sinatra's 'Strangers In The Night' offstage – then a current hit, which Engel considered way substandard to Ol' Blue Eyes' classic fifties Reprise albums.

4   Those familiar with the rotund latter-day King and the still slender Engel may find this extraordinary. In the mid-sixties, however, both were thin young men.

5   The 1967 Sexual Offences Act would selectively decriminalise many gay sex acts – though some have claimed that police persecution of homosexuals for 'indecency' continued unabated for years.

6   Jean Cocteau can also be said to have been a 'bizarre man', as well as an internationally revered artist. This post-romantic variously dabbled (almost always successfully) in poetry, drama and film. A homosexual contemporary of Genet, he supported the thief's release from a life sentence harshly imposed for a series

of petty crimes. How Cocteau compares with the man who made 'Una Paloma Blanca' a hit is not entirely clear.

7   "But I thought Scott Walker was gay?" is a cry that still goes up today, despite all evidence to the contrary. In the sixties, he may have amused himself by declining to confirm or deny such rumours, given the appealing outsider status of gay men. In turn, it served to fuel disinformation about 'The Walker Sisters' which reflected on John too.

8   When Hendrix's death is attributed to his drug use, it's often overlooked that the fatal combination was wine and prescription sleeping pills.

9   Engel Dry Cleaning ran for a long time from the same house in which Scott spent the first two years of his life. The local Hamilton paper carried its ad with an amateurish cartoon that showed an old fellow of similar vintage to Scott Sr. in moustache, tie, collar and hat: "MAN is the only living creature that can be skinned more than once," ran its oddly macabre slogan. It reads almost like a fragmentary line from a latter-day Scott Walker lyric.

10   The story that Cotton Jr. subsequently banned the Walkers from appearing on BBC TV, which supposedly stayed in place till their mid-seventies reformation and appearance on *The Vera Lynn Christmas Show*, appears to be a myth. Scott himself appeared as a solo artist on Cotton Sr.'s show one year after the event – singing the highly incongruous 'My Death'.

11   Given Scott's anti-psychedelic sensibility, perhaps any pop-movie opus would have ended up closer to Peter Watkins' sombre *Privilege*, with Manfred Mann's Paul Jones – which, as David Bowie has noted, is a sixties curio that grows better (and more prescient) with age.

12   Stewart had to undertake an extensive course of rehabilitation before becoming active again. When last heard of, he was working at Tower Records on Sunset Strip in the mid-seventies. His promising career in pop music was lost to him – contrary to a common misapprehension, he was not the folk-rock singer John Stewart who gifted 'Daydream Believer' to The Monkees.

13   John and Gary later denied that the invitation even occurred – though, given Margaret's party-girl antics with *Performance* actor/career criminal John Bindon and the scandalous allusions in recent film *The Bank Job*, it might have proved an eye-opener.

14   Relations remained cordial with the monks of Quarr Abbey. In the summer of 1967, Scott ran to the bedside of Father Altham Dean after he suffered a heart attack. "Supposedly he was given a key to the abbey, which he wore on his belt," acknowledged John. "… I asked him what it was for, and he said, 'To make people ask me what it's for.'" The key can be seen hanging from his belt on the cover of the deleted 1969 album *Scott: Scott Walker Sings Songs From His TV Series*.

Chapter 5

Alone/Solo/Seul

There are ships sailing to many ports, but not a single one goes where life
is not painful.

Fernando Pessoa (1888-1935) – *The Book Of Disquiet*

The music of Scott Walker is often described as 'cinematic', its
widescreen panorama having its origins back in The Walker
Brothers' days. But when he first composed for films, it wasn't quite
the art-house fare one would come to expect.

Betty Box was the producer of the Rank Organisation's 'Doctor'
films, starting with *Doctor In The House* – a lamely genteel early Britcom
series, at first starring Dirk Bogarde (before his characters became
synonymous with thin-lipped decadence and Nazism). By the time
the sixties were on the verge of swinging, domestic audiences were
grooving to something other than nice Dr Simon Sparrow.

"She was making a film called *Deadlier Than The Male*," explains
Gary Leeds, "one of the James Bond pastiches that were all the rage
at the time. Scott and John Franz put together a nice track that Betty
liked, then Scott and I went to see her. She lived just outside London
and her house looked like a stud farm, with stables and white fences."

It seems curious that Scott, who had reputedly turned down the chance to sing the John Barry-Leslie Bricusse theme to *You Only Live Twice* (assigned to Nancy Sinatra), should take up the cudgels for the first of an intended film series about Bulldog Drummond.[1] But the bait was the chance to co-write an original tune with Franz, suffused with the drama that the film (which Scott apparently walked out of at the premiere) mostly lacked: "She never cared / Beware, my brother, beware!"

He was also apparently miffed that Philips should treat it as the next official Walker Brothers release, in December 1966. But the really remarkable aspect is the B-side, which in many ways marked the gradual emergence of Engel as a solo artist.

'Archangel' carries an awe-inspiring gothic organ motif, which was played on the pipe organ at the Royal Albert Hall. Reflecting Scott's classical sensibilities, some compared it to a Bach fugue; others conjectured it may have been based on Dimitri Tiomkin's theme to 1964 sword-and-sandal epic *The Fall Of The Roman Empire* (there *is* a definite echo in the opening chords and the orchestral melody). But Reg Guest, who was best placed to know, recalled that Scott most likely requested of him, "I want it like Sibelius' Seventh Symphony."

The influence of Finnish composer Jean Sibelius – whose symphonies featured evolving themes that gradually find their way to the harmonic surface – would be increasingly notable in the young songwriter. But for now, 'Archangel' was a startling peek forward to a period (soon to follow) when rock musicians would be unafraid of displaying classical influences or, indeed, their own pretensions.

"Archangel ride in on the moon / Just to save me from this tomb": this grandiose statement of salvation makes a love song into a foreboding matter of life or death. Gary Leeds claimed it was "about a woman called Claire he had met at one of Maurice King's parties. She was the ex-wife of a peer, who later married an art dealer of some sort, a nice girl but totally mad. She used to hang out with Scott and had taken to bringing soft drugs to his flat. None of us used them, but Scott based this song on that."

Not a great love of Engel's but – for a briefly magical period – his muse. Leeds says that the Walkers were all annoyed that 'Archangel' was relegated to the single's flip side. Its innovative gothic pop was the first notable sole credit for its composer – who, according to busy conjecture in the pop press, may have been weighing up his options as to whether to leave the group.

'Hell of a Walker' was the heading for one interview with John, with the subhead 'Scott scares me'. With the piece ran a cartoon parody of the brothers, with Scott in a 'Jack Jones is Fab' T-shirt, reading Sartre's *Iron In The Soul*,[2] Gary in Harlequin ruffles and hat, and John with a surfboard.

In *Disc Weekly*, Rod Harrod had already asked, 'Well, *Should* Scott Go Solo?':

I put this question to the tall, good-looking Californian – undoubtedly the most popular member of the Walkers – at his St John's Wood flat last week. The effect was strange...

Immediate reaction was a staggering "Eh!" with a fast following "I don't know when I'll quit. Maybe tomorrow!"

He agreed that a number of people had suggested to him that he went solo and that if he WAS going to, now would be the best time.

"Maybe I'll have to go solo if the other two don't get back from their American holiday soon," he quipped.

"But seriously, I'd quit this business rather than go solo. Mentally I have a bit of trouble coping with the pop business as a member of a group. I'd NEVER be able to cope as a solo singer."

He seemed to be lunging into one of his frequent bits of self-analysis.

"I never was built for the pop business, I'm still not used to the life. All this image bit...

"If I had my time over again I definitely wouldn't become a pop singer. The emotional stuff really gets me down."

Scott did reveal that… there would be more splitting up on records in future.

"I believe John will do an EP on his own pretty soon. Then I'll do one shortly after," he explained.

"John likes to do the rhythm and blues type of thing. His knowledge of music isn't as vast as mine. I mean that in a nice way because rhythm and blues is the music he likes and has always sung.

"I like doing standards and the big romantic ballad type of stuff."

The two mooted solo EPs did actually emerge as one, immediately after 'Deadlier Than The Male'. *Solo John, Solo Scott* featured John pleasantly croaking through the much-covered 'Sunny' and Ray Charles' 'Come Rain Or Come Shine'. Scott did his by now standard "big romantic ballad" bit on another melodic (if inconsequential) film theme, this time to the 1966 romantic drama *The Gentle Rain*.

It was on the final track that the listener could hear another startling step forward. It was an Engel original, with the melody gradually emerging out of a Sibelian tumble of strings and brass: "Hello Mrs Murphy, that's a lovely dress you're wearing / Is it new?"

Scott's crooning of the banal chitchat that opens the song doesn't seem at all incongruous – he was merely locating the poetry within seedy British domestic concerns. For Mrs Johnson, their neighbour, is pregnant, but not by her husband. The gossiping neighbours whose words make up the lyric point the finger at the young man at flat number 22 – "less than half her age".

"Upstairs in 22 / The tall boy stretched just like a cat… Thinking of a dream he'd had." Scott's obvious sympathy for the young man evokes literary critic Cyril Connolly: "There is no more sombre enemy of good art than the pram in the hall." Engel, now more mature than the boy in number 22, had been almost universally desired by women in his young life; 'Mrs Murphy', in part, seems like a reflection on his own escape. And the brass-backed Reg Guest arrangement plays with all the forcefulness of the best film or TV soundtracks of the time.

"I'll tell you what it was like for me," the mature Engel explains to Stephen Kijak in *30 Century Man*. "I'd been watching Ealing comedies and I'd been watching people like old Margaret Rutherford, old Terry-Thomas and all these kinds of people. When we got here I thought, 'It's not going to be the same.' We arrived in winter and it was really bleak. And those kinds of people were running around, they were everywhere, so it was exactly like I'd seen in the movies. It was amazing, and it was really bleak and everything else. It was hardly swinging. It was only swinging in the scene, once you hooked into that."

Rather than crusty old eccentrics from an Ealing comedy, however, 'Mrs Murphy' is populated by everyday people facing domestic crises. It played far more like a tribute to the sixties kitchen-sink realism of Alan Sillitoe (*Saturday Night And Sunday Morning*, *The Loneliness Of The Long-Distance Runner*) or Shelagh Delaney (*A Taste Of Honey*), small-scale dramas that focused on the English working and lower-middle classes.[3] It was archive footage from this era that Kijak used to accompany the music of 'Archangel' in his Walker bio-doc.

"It's all over the song – the film is *The L-Shaped Room* with Leslie Caron," the filmmaker confirms. Ms Caron is seen walking slowly, resolutely down the kind of gone-to-seed inner London street that greeted Engel on his arrival.[4] "It's in the lyrics – 'Big Louise', 'Rosemary', these are kitchen-sink dramas; 'Mrs Murphy' – they're ripped right from those cinematic tropes, all a part of that culture."

Scott Engel, in his 24th year, was becoming a poetic observer of what, for him, had formerly been a foreign culture.

✶✶✶

In the early days of that weirdly pivotal year, 1967, The Walker Brothers were forced to suspend their British activities while the Home Office considered Capable Management's request for extension of their work visas. They had a new single released in early February – a cover of Lorraine Ellison's US soul hit 'Stay With Me Baby' – but were unable to appear live to promote it in the UK. It featured a creditably emotional Engel lead but somehow lacked the punch of the original. (Scott sings smoothly; Ms Ellison wails in despair.) Its chart showing reflected this, barely making the Top 30.

The B-side, 'Turn Out The Moon', is another Engel original, an upbeat heartbreak ballad ("Turn out the moon and the sun in the sky /… I'm through living a lie, without you"), but it doesn't approach the 'Archangel'/'Mrs Murphy' league.

Meanwhile, rather than have its boys languishing in some club somewhere, Capable put them on a tour of the Far East and Australasia, with Roy Orbison headlining once again. It didn't do much to calm Scott's growing fear of flying, which seemed to mirror his general nervous state of the time.

The Walkers had already endured numerous rough flights, which had Scott reaching increasingly for the whisky and sedatives. The only usually calm flyer was Gary, who held a pilot's licence himself and had a little cruel fun with his brothers' discomfort.

"Gary was quiet during just one flight, in 1967," John later remarked of the Australasian tour. "We were in New Zealand, travelling from Christchurch to Wellington, and an announcement was made that, due to severe wind and weather, the airport was closed to air traffic but we would be the last plane allowed in… The plane's descent to the runway was the scariest ride we'd ever had. It was tossed around like a little kite in a hurricane… Miraculously, we landed with the plane and everyone in it intact. Roy Orbison got out and kissed the ground[5]… As always, we headed for the nearest bar, Scott and I already being somewhat tranquillised – he with Valium, and I with Serenid – but nevertheless traumatised by the whole thing."

On the Far Eastern leg of the tour, Gary would later recollect, the Walkers first clapped eyes on lady boys in Singapore.[6] In Tokyo for a promotional visit, the culture was rather more traditional: "The geisha girls entertained us with old, traditional songs accompanied by Japanese instruments, and Scott asked to play the shamisen, a three-string, guitar-like instrument. To the surprise of all of us, he played all the music that the geisha had just performed.

"The next day, we were to do a prestigious TV show... Scott noticed a jacket hanging from a market rack; it was black with no collar, and buttoned up to the neck. He admired it, and was told that it was part of a Japanese school uniform, but bought it anyway." With 'In My Room' in the Japanese charts, Scott's adoring Eastern fans saw his adopting a school blazer as a compliment.

By the time they returned from their tour of the Pacific Rim, the Walkers' work permits had been extended and their third album, *Images*, was due for release in March – having been recorded only that previous December, at the time of the *Solo John, Solo Scott* release. It did little to ease simmering tensions within the group, but that's no reflection on it as a piece of classic vinyl.

Images opens, slightly incongruously, with the Walkers-do-a-girl-group, their cover of The Ronettes' 'Everything Under The Sun' (written, as was 'The Sun Ain't Gonna Shine Anymore', by Bob Crewe). After the pseudo-Spector (and alongside the odd lightweight track) comes the rarer treats: 'Once Upon A Summertime' is the English translation of French composer Michel Legrand's '*La valse des lilas*' ('the waltz of the lilacs'); its arrangement is romantically sublime, improving on the 1958 version by jazz singer Blossom Dearie (a friend of Scott's from the Ronnie Scott set – who'd write a song called 'Long Daddy Green' apparently inspired by him).

Opening side two, 'I Will Wait For You' continues this apparent tribute to Legrand. A further translation, this time of '*Je ne pourrais jamais vivre sans toi*' ('I will never be able to live without you') from the 1964 French hit movie *Les Parapluies De Cherbourg* (*The Umbrellas Of Cherbourg*), which introduced a young Catherine Deneuve to the world. This is one of the apexes of Scott Walker as an interpretive singer, and its cinematic romance is a million miles away from anything resembling a pop group. (Little wonder that John later complained of *Images*, "I didn't feel I was involved in it very much. I never knew what we were going to record until the day we went into the studio.")

'It Makes No Difference Now' is further testimony to the young Engel's Europhilia, a translation of an emotional ballad by Italian songwriter Iller Pattacini which, in its structure (though not its subject matter), is not dissimilar from 'My Way'. 'I Can't Let It Happen To You' is an original, written and sung by John Maus – his finest Walkers moment, with a hauntingly vulnerable lyric and achingly sparse organ and trumpet backing.[7] 'Just Say Goodbye' ends the album nicely, if conventionally, a cover of Petula Clark's collaboration with the professionally workmanlike Tony Hatch. Fading out on the title line, it leaves us with the classic 'lonesome Scott' image: "Just leave me on my own / To face the world alone."

And then there are the Engel originals: 'Experience' is a singular experience in itself. A Euro-cabaret number that sounds like a thigh-slapping bierkeller song, its wacky chorus aside ("Here's to memory, old age and every" – the latter word often mistaken for 'Emily'). Engel explained its lyric in an otherwise tongue-in-cheek *Disc* interview with Jonathan King: "It's my theory that the biggest problem in society today has to be with parents giving their children advice on things they know nothing about, as they've never experienced them themselves anywhere past their TV screens. This has a tendency to make their kids grow up to be as shallow individuals as they are, with a complete misconception of what's going on outside and around them." The existentialist of pop had spoken and most of us, it seems, had been found wanting.

'Genevieve' was, by his own account, John's favourite track on the album. It's classic early Scott Walker, just a whispered note away from taking its rightful place on his first solo album. Its delicate account of a transient lover leaving the young woman of the title drips with an atmosphere that's almost noir: "I guess I'll always be the same / A drifting man without a name / I once loved too – but that's all through." Its refrain begins "Genevieve, love hangs on a string"; the track itself floats on an undertow of strings, freezing the image of the young Engel as a gloomy romantic in time forever.

'Orpheus' is an altogether more joyous story of adultery than 'Mrs Murphy', touching on bawdiness, but no less cinematic. "I'll harpoon you like a whale / On a bent and rusty nail," the illicit lover promises, before the wave of ethereal strings takes the chorus into a more transcendent area: "I'll steal your dreams for my shiny gold chain / And you'll wake with your eyes full of rain."

It's not clear why Engel took the name from the Greek mythological archetype, the lyre player who travels to Hades to awaken his wife, Eurydice, from the dead.[8] When asked later if he was influenced by *Orphée,* Jean Cocteau's surreal 1950 film that updated the myth to include leather-clad motorcyclists, he replied, "Sure, that could have gone back to seeing the movie originally. Yet again, I really can't remember, because I was so out of it." For this was a time of booze, Valium and petty bickering with John. "But... cinema was a huge influence on those songs, in the broadest sense."

The song ends stridently on a marching note of callousness: "Remember me / See, I've already forgotten you!" It's more likely Scott was thinking of *Orpheus Descending* at the time, Tennessee Williams' play in which a snakeskin-jacketed wanderer named Val enters a town in the Southern states and causes chaos by having an affair with the wife of a dying man – or maybe *The Fugitive Kind*, the 1959 film adaptation with Marlon Brando which would re-enter his consciousness later in his career.

"I've got to say it just seemed like a very interesting parallel starting point," says Stephen Kijak as to why the sound and image of Orpheus open his Walker bio-doc. "When you line things up, 'Orpheus' obviously has very little to do with the myth of Orpheus – if you really listen to the lyric it's definitely about something quite different. Or is it, you know what I mean? The meaning just kind of swims around and it is a little ambiguous.

101

"It also kind of connects with the fact that we found a beautiful sculpture of Orpheus to start the film. Actually the sculpture is dedicated to Francis Scott Key [lawyer, poet and writer of 'The Star-Spangled Banner'] – the title of the sculpture is *American Orpheus*, it fits him as well. It's a real random dimension, it just seemed to make perfect sense when you lined the various versions of the myth up. It fits kind of perfectly into that. Of course, the song itself may be destroying or reinterpreting the myth – we kind of build him up in this grand mythological sense, then immediately subvert it by showing he's just a man sitting on a couch having a nap. You know what I mean? Never as specific as you might think, but more a playful collection of collisions and meanings that can work.

"The sixties stuff was mind-blowing," says Kijak of its cinematic imagery. "It was sweeping and epic. It creates a strange narrative world. The songs are just fantastic – like Jacques Brel, or when he's working with textures that sound like Morricone. He was obsessed with European cinema and all that was influencing him, bleeding into the sounds and the imagery."

Images was released with a Warhol-esque cover featuring the three brothers in duotone screenprints. It was of its time, but their time was very nearly up – save for one further extended period in which the years-old friendship of Engel and Maus would continue to splinter under the strain of more touring and heavy drinking.

The Walkers were booked to headline *Sunday Night At The London Palladium* for ATV once more. Swallowing producer Lew Grade's maxim ("Don't give 'em art! Give 'em what they want!") apparently whole, the Walkers appeared in a musical skit that featured them wearing straw boaters and carrying canes. The main number was a cringe-making take on 'My Kind Of Town' ("Our kind of town, London is!").

The obvious discomfort it caused Scott, who took the lead vocal, was mitigated slightly by him singing 'Lara's Theme' from *Doctor Zhivago*. But his reaction was both predictable and understandable.

"After seeing our last Palladium performance, I think I really got things into perspective and made up my mind to quit the group," he said soon after. "It's a nasty feeling watching a show like that. I was so embarrassed and full of shame for myself and the rest of the group. It was the last straw. I was disgusted. I want to be free."

The sense of bigger fish to fry was becoming tangible even to his bandmates. Engel was taking lessons in reading music from guitarist Tony Gilbert of backing band The Quotations, and was concentrating ever more intensely on his own compositions. With John Stewart departed, he kept up the independent production end himself – though the latest single he helmed, 'I Need To Be Needed' by Nicky James, was an unexceptional pop piece and sank without trace.

The next UK Walkers tour would, inevitably, be their last of the sixties. It began at the end of March.

"This is interesting," Walkers collector Arnie Potts points to one of his framed tour posters. "'The fabulous Walker Brothers onstage for one night only' at the Granada, I believe this was in Tooting, London. Now, the interesting thing is when the tour started the Walkers were the major act. However, because the tour ran for several months[9] this American chap came over, Jimi Hendrix, he was down the list when it started. By the time the tour was over, he wasn't officially the headlining act, but really he was. He was on the up there. Of course, by now we're coming to the end of their career, to be perfectly honest. They were on the downward slope at that moment."

Psychedelic blues and guitar histrionics were the future. Balladeering – no matter how innovative some of their new material – was starting to look like something from a different, older world. The final tour took in a bizarre range of styles and performers: Hendrix (who Gary took to immediately, describing him as "another one like Scott, just very, very shy"), new singer-songwriter Cat Stevens ("Are you getting the genius bit?" Scott joked to John, in a rare moment when they were talking) and cheesy pseudo-Vegas crooner[10] Engelbert Humperdinck.

103

Ultimately, fads and fashions were not the cause of the band's dissolution, but they could only serve to hasten it.

"Everyone kind of disintegrated in their different ways," Scott acknowledged years later. "You know, it probably started to happen after the second album, things started to get really 'difficult'."

By the time of the third album and its corresponding tour, John Maus described it as "kind of like a cold war... As the tour went on, everybody got really moody. Scott began constantly turning up late at the theatre, making Gary and me paranoid that he would finally just stop showing up at all."

One particular instance, when he turned up during the third number after tying one on at Tony Gilbert's baby's christening, broke down communications within the band. John, very far from being a teetotaller himself, was disgusted by Scott's *laissez-faire* attitude and stopped speaking to him.

The itinerary wore on until the final night, April 30, 1967, at the Tooting Granada. Philips recording star Shirley Bassey was there as a guest, but even she couldn't unfreeze the backstage atmosphere. Scott was observed hugging his own shoulders and clawing at his face, resembling some of his more melodramatic onstage gestures – or someone trying to reassure themselves during a panic attack. ("Thank God, it's over," someone claimed to overhear him mumbling to himself.)

Within three days it was announced that The Walker Brothers were to split. Their final single was released that month – 'Walking In The Rain', another inexplicable attempt to replicate The Ronettes, backed by 'Baby Make It The Last Time', an Engel co-composition that sounded oddly like it was one of their less distinctive pop covers. As with their previous single, it just about made the lower end of the Top 30.

Rumours abounded about the reason for the split, with one insisting that mainstream crooner Andy Williams was offering Scott a $2 million deal to take him back to the USA and make him the 'new Sinatra'.[11] "Scott turned it down. He didn't want that kind of stardom," Gary would later confirm.

"[John] Franz loved the purity of Scott's voice, as did we all," John Maus later acknowledged, "and he was moving towards creating a solo career for him, very much as he had done with Dusty Springfield when he took her out of The Springfields. I would have been the last one to stand in the way of Scott's career..."

In the immediate post-Walkers period, Scott was still the cover boy on the May 1967 issue of *Rave* – which namechecked Davy Jones of The Monkees and The Beatles without even mentioning him, so familiar was his face by now. "I guess I am scared," he admitted to *Rave* in a follow-up issue. "I wanna get the right message across right now, without fallin' into black or white, like Sinatra or pop. That is very important to me, to establish myself as myself."

In the run-up to the release of his first solo album, Engel gave an interview to Keith Altham of *NME*, rather stereotypically headed 'Scott Walker Hides Away in a Gloom-World'. "I'm one of those people who are just never happy about anything," he told Altham, further reinforcing the image. "I've got money for the band and all recordings are paid for by Phillips, but I didn't make a great deal of money and I can't eat at all the restaurants... Then there were bills for suits that got torn every night we played, hotel bills, big drink bills and entertainment bills. We came out with little money."

But when John Maus was working on his first (underrated and ill-fated) solo material, Scott Engel effectively disappeared. Still a fixture of northwest London, he was found unconscious in Regent's Park one night. Retrospective theories suggest he may have fallen over or blacked out under the influence of sleeping pills he was mixing with booze, which often failed to do their job but left him wandering nocturnally. (At the time there were more fanciful rumours about 'queer-bashers', as if the local Camden louts had taken to heart those stories about The Walker Sisters or Jonathan King.) "I never relax until I sleep," he admitted to the press. "I take lots of sleeping pills and drink a lot to relax and unwind."

He was also taking upward of a dozen vitamin pills a day by this time. His use of alcohol and pharmaceuticals may have veered toward excess, but this was still a young man with a pronounced sense of his own mortality.

✶✶✶

Scott Engel would return to the stage alone in August 1967, prompting the following telegraphed message from his mother:

TELEGRAM SENT PDS VIA WESTERN UNION – received
Middlesbrough 7 Aug 1967
SCOTT WALKER SIESTACLUB [*sic*] STOCKTON
SUCCESS LOVE YOU = MIMI +

His solo debut had actually taken place at the Fiesta Club the previous evening, Saturday 6th, where he once again used the northern cabaret circuit as a testing ground. He was backed by a tight band handpicked from the musicians who hung out at Ronnie Scott's. They opened with a cover version – 'Gonna Travel On' – which he would not commit to vinyl until a time when his solo career had taken a very different turn.

But for now he was very much the aloof professional performer. No autographs. No meet and greet the fans. Get the job done and get out.

As Engel explained to Altham, he'd been writing tracks for his debut album at Mette's flat in Copenhagen. "I'm writing my own odd, abstract stuff," he claimed in a statement that seems to have been made at least a decade too soon. "I don't want the Tom Jones scene.[12] I'll be skint if this LP doesn't work – but I won't switch to the old commercial scene."

For the most part, however, the first Engel solo album would still consist of cover versions. As to which songwriters would predominate among the new interpretations, he was only too happy to tell *Rave* that same month: "It was one of the happiest days of my life when a girlfriend gave me the first English translation I'd seen of [Jacques] Brel's lyrics."

Notes

1   Stiff upper-lipped son of Empire Drummond featured in a series of ripping post-World War One yarns by 'Sapper': "Detective, patriot, hero and gentleman" praised the blurb on one early novel, to which might be added "jingoist and racist" (he put the chinks and the darkies in their place, don'tcha know?). Ian Fleming claimed Bulldog as an influence on Bond, but the *Boy's Own*-style adventures were too fusty to combine sexiness and technology onscreen in the style of 007.

2   It's a witty cultural juxtaposition – all the more so for being true. ("I guess we're kinda sellin' Jack Jones through our hair," Scott had noted of the accomplished traditionalist.) For a contemporary version, imagine someone in a Michael Bublé T-shirt reading Michel Houellebecq's *Platform*. Even this doesn't quite hit it, as Bublé is basically a karaoke singer and the pessimistic Houellebecq is not honoured in France the way that the existentialists once were.

3   "It's so sixties as well," says long-time Walker person Marc Almond in *30 Century Man*, "that kind of kitchen-sink drama thing, that kind of black and white sixties film. If it was Britain it'd be a kitchen-sink drama, I think like a Ken Loach film, if it was America it'd be Tennessee Williams."

4   It's an aesthetic that also resonates with the sixties retro-iconography of The Smiths. The sound of Cicely Courtenidge singing 'Take Me Back To Dear Old Blighty', from *The L-Shaped Room*, can be heard at the opening of their album *The Queen Is Dead*.

5   The Big O, seen as a tragic figure (belying his good humour) in black clothes and shades, seemed to become the victim of a self-fulfilling prophecy: in 1966, after touring with the Walkers for the first time, his wife, Claudette, was killed in an accident when they were out on a motorbike; in 1968, the year after his last tour with the brothers, his two young sons would die in an appalling studio fire at his home in Texas.

6   No jokes about 'Big Rouise', please.

7   "I wasn't given adequate time to work with Reg Guest on the song," Maus later complained. It's disconcerting to think that the late John may never have recognised the true worth of what was, Scott's original material notwithstanding, one of the most beautiful Walkers recordings.

8   "Orpheus – a figure of myth, melancholy lover and transgressive musician. He is the only figure to have roamed the underworld and by the power and charm of his song returned again to the living," states the opening female narration of *30 Century Man*.

9   The tour ran for several months if the Far East and Australasian dates are included. Otherwise the UK dates ran from late March to late April.

10   Soon to be a genuine Vegas crooner, of course.

11   "To me, the greatest soul singer in the world is Frank Sinatra," Scott had praised him in the pre-'My Way' days. "I'd like to be able to put that styling into a song that Sinatra does in 'A Very Good Year'. That would mean a lot to me."

12 Mutual disrespect between Tom Jones and Scott Walker had been simmering for
    some time. Jones had claimed in the music press that all the Walkers' early hits
    sounded the same; Engel told Irene Dunford that Jones would lose his voice within
    five years if he didn't stop shouting his lyrics. "Every time I hear Tom Jones I want
    to jump out of a window," he'd complain to Altham. "I hear Tom Jones destroying
    a song and yet he and I are always being compared as singers." For his part, Jones
    was quoted in the press as saying a man ought to be willing to fight for his country
    – an apparent dig at Scott's Vietnam draft status by a man whose own country had
    abolished national military service.

Chapter 6

Dans La Rue De St Jacques

SS: *When you read the lyrics (contrasted with the way Scott Walker presents them: as if they're Las Vegas show tunes) they're really staggering. There's one called 'Next!' about a soldier in the French army who loses his virginity in a mobile whorehouse –*

BK: *With a gay lieutenant slapping his ass –*

SS: *– as if they were all fags. Every time he makes love he thinks of all the gonorrhoea that he's had.*

BK: *The original Jacques Brel song is French accordion fluff – if you heard it, you'd go, "Take this shit off!"*

Amok Books founders Stuart Swezey and Brian King, interviewed for *Incredibly Strange Music Volume I* (Re-Search #14, 1993)

After the Walkers first split, as the individual band members were casting round to make their next move, Gary Leeds was looking at forming his own band. Surprisingly, perhaps, he claims that Scott Engel, in one of his crises of confidence, asked if he could be the bass player.

"That was all he wanted to do," Gary would later say, "but the management and record company had other plans for him. I would talk to him on the phone now and then as we were both struggling and a little cash would have helped. We had trouble getting our money because the management controlled it."

Gary and Scott would still meet for drinks at night at the Playboy Club in Mayfair. Today it may seem like a cigar-smoking misogynist's playground, too 'naff' for politically correct sensibilities. Back then, when it was recently opened, it was the promise of a whole new world of hedonism (for those who could afford it) – Hefner's dream come to shabby little England.

"It's a strange story, but I'll tell it," Scott recounts to the Kijak documentary team. "We went to the opening evening of the London Playboy Club – why I don't know. I was there with Gary just drinking, we did a lot of drinking in those days. It opened on Park Lane and everyone was just invited. So we got involved with the girls, we took up with the bunnies. I met this German girl who was a Playboy bunny, and we went home, back to her place, and she was a really big drinker – I think it was Pernod, she was really into Pernod I seem to remember, and Jacques Brel.

"She translated him for me, a lot of things, that night. And I thought, 'This is fantastic!' It was a fantastic coincidence, about a week later I went up to see Andrew Oldham, I just used to go up to chat and drink Black Russians and things like that in the afternoons.[1] And I said, 'I heard this incredible guy the other night,' and he said, 'It's funny you should mention him, because I've got this demo by this man Eric Blau, and he's recorded this demo of translations of some of his songs.' And he played from it and it was an awful, crunchy old guy with a piano. I said, 'I'll have it!' I took it and ran with it. That changed me, changed everything for me."

Jacques Romain Brel was of an older generation (and indeed an older culture) to Scott Engel, born in Brussels on April 8, 1929. He was 11 years old when the Nazis took Belgium in May 1940. Sometimes latterly known as 'the French Sinatra' (wrong not only geographically but aesthetically), the Flemish French speaker is perhaps more accurately assessed as part of the 'can you name five famous Belgians?' game.[2]

The son of the owner of a cardboard manufacturing business, he rejected his bourgeois origins to follow his fortune in Paris as a *chansonnier*. At first his haunts were the low-rent hotels of Montmartre – the neighbourhood where Sartre and his lover Simone De Beauvoir held court.

The lyrics of Brel have an existential attitude toward much of life, as well as a Genet-like impulse not to flinch from all that's scabrous.[3] "I'm obsessed by those things that are ugly or sordid, that people don't want to talk about," he explained in his only English music press interview. "I like to take blows in the face too," he boasted in that Gallic style of treating metaphor as a reality.

Modern Liverpool quartet Dead Belgian – who play versions of Brel songs in a style pitched between raucous folk and barroom jazz[4] – have offered up their thoughts to this writer on Brel and his Anglo interpreters, particularly Engel.

"There was some guy who loaded stuff online," says band founder and percussionist Andy Delamere. "'Lightning something' was his user name. He wrote brilliant essays on it, so it was a great resource to see Brel perform. We've all done acting or written or performed stuff for theatre, so it was great. When you watch him it's all the spit, and then you listen to what he's actually singing, to the translation, and you're going, 'Fucking hell, you can actually sing that and get away with it?' 'Les bourgeois': 'The bourgeoisie are like pigs / The older they get the stupider they become' – the fact that he's obviously singing that to a bourgeois audience and he's got a suit and tie on. He was singing 'Les bourgeois' but he was as bourgeois as they come."

111

But Brel's songs are also imbued with a lyrical romanticism, an instinct to sniff out what makes life worth enduring (or even celebrating, at times). He shared a residency in Club Genevieve with French-Armenian Engel favourite Charles Aznavour, and strummed a guitar on his earliest hit, 1953's '*Quand on n'a que l'amour*' ('If We Only Have Love'). It could have been a more literate template for The Beatles' silly 'All You Need Is Love' – with love as a defence against humanity's own worst instincts ("Jerusalem will stand") rather than some lazy hippie slogan.

Brel's exclusively Francophone records (he never wrote or sang – or one assumes thought – in English) became known, perhaps ironically, to the English-speaking bourgeoisie via compilation releases such as *American Debut*. A demonstrative and dramatic vocalist, his performances were backed by orchestral arranger François Rauber and co-composer/pianist Gérard Jouannest, a member of the Communist Party who Brel jokingly called 'Nikita'.[5]

Brel's rare appearance at New York's Carnegie Hall in 1965 was witnessed by jobbing 20-something tunesmith Mort Shuman. As a former writing partner of the slightly older 'Doc' Pomus,[6] they'd created a roster of hits for a wide range of US artists – most notably Elvis, including 'Suspicion' and 'Viva Las Vegas'. Since splitting from the partnership, Shuman had washed up in London (where he'd written the odd chart hit like The Small Faces' 'Sha-La-La-Lee').

On his home visit to the US, however, he indulged a growing interest in the French *chansonnier* tradition by going to see Brel. "The only time I'd heard such virility in a voice was in black singers," praised Shuman. "I just had to find out what he was singing about. Then I had to translate it. Brel wrote about things that you don't normally hear people singing. He sang of things that you normally only found in philosophy or in novels."

Shuman's collaborator on the adaptations was playwright Eric Blau. But they hadn't quite got there first.

Brel's mockingly sardonic early sixties ballad 'Le moribond' has the dying man of the title asserting, "I want them to laugh and dance when they put me in that hole," and chiding the wife and friend he knows have been cuckolding him behind his back. In the hands of singing poet Rod McKuen, who first co-wrote songs sung by little Scotty Engel in the fifties, the black humour of the chorus was blanded out into "We had joy, we had fun / We had seasons in the sun."[7] This was for the 1964 US pop ballad version by The Kingston Trio, whose previous hit with traditional murder ballad 'Tom Dooley' made a sex killing seem like a bit of hi-jinks by a clean-cut young man.

'*Ne me quitte pas*' ('Don't Leave Me') was Brel's biggest hit of the sixties – an anguished (and allegedly autobiographical) plea for a lover not to turn away. The increasingly desperate deserted lover's promises include calling rain from the skies and raising dormant volcanoes.

In the hands of McKuen, this second early Brel translation became 'If You Go Away' – a more conventionally romantic but very affecting love song. Its myriad versions include those of Dusty Springfield, who sang verses both from McKuen and the French original, John Walker[8] and, in the wake of both, Scott Walker. (Scott's beautifully melancholic version appears on his third album, despite reputedly being recorded 18 months earlier with his first batch of Brel titles.) His version, as with most translations, commits the purist's sin of lamenting, "I'd have been the shadow of your shadow [rather than '*chien*' – dog] / If it might have kept me be your side." ("Only Frank Sinatra and I have ever sung that song right," McKuen later claimed of the translations.)

"Someone shouted out for 'If You Go Away' at a gig in Manchester – there's not a song called 'If You Go Away'," dismisses Dead Belgian's Andy Delamere. "'*Ne me quitte pas*' is a great tune. Sometimes I've talked about that just to say it's not a great love song – the character he's playing is just a stalker, pathetic, just the lowest, he'll do anything, it's desperate," he laughs. "But people don't get that. Brel's a literary figure, those words are incredible. I think everyone gets a little bit embarrassed about how emotional it is. I didn't want to make it precious, but I didn't want to make it camp – it *is* quite camp but there's that high emotion, the French aren't embarrassed by that."

"The literal translation really stands out," acclaims vocalist Fionnuala Dorrity, "and it's a very French way of saying and doing things. I think when it's switched around to make it suitable for an English audience, it does lose quite a lot actually. [Jazz singer] Barb Jungr did a new translation of '*Ne me quitte pas*' which is really, really close to the original, except she's obviously made it rhyme and scan. But the words are just as it's sung in the song. And it's amazing because it's not taking anything away."

Scott Engel was initially disappointed when Brel's only performance at the Royal Albert Hall clashed with the start of The Walker Brothers' Far East tour in December 1966. (Brel himself made his final live appearances before retiring from the stage in 1967 – just before Scott began to record his songs.) But it would be an adaptation by Shuman and Blau which opened *Scott*, his eponymous first solo album. "In a song, I now look for what I consider to be the truth," he earnestly explained at the time. "The people following me don't want sugar-coated rubbish." His route away from saccharine Tin Pan Alley would be via a diversion down the Rue de St Jacques.

'Mathilde' is a stampeding rush toward a poisoned boudoir. When performing to a backing track on *Dusty*, Ms Springfield's TV show, at the time of the LP's release, Scott's slender frame and spindly legs threw themselves into the jittery St Vitus Dance of Wally Stott's arrangement, before releasing his nervous tension at the end like a puppet with his strings cut.[9] "Mama, can you hear me yell? / Your baby boy's gone back to hell / Mathilde's come back to me!"

Engel would refer to the song's subject as "a sad old masochistic love affair", but in fact its bruises are more emotional. 'Mathilde' of the title is an all-devouring femme fatale; she's made our narrator miserable and still he can't wait for her return.

("There are some songs by Brel that I find really hard to do, like 'Mathilde'," says Fionnuala Dorrity. Given its sentiments from another age – "You want to beat her black and blue, but don't do it I beg of you" – it's perhaps unsurprising. "He couldn't act, he's a shit actor," Delamere disparages Scott's performance. "Watch him doing 'Mathilde' on the old footage." "He holds back quite a bit in the performance," notes Ms Dorrity of Engel's nervous tension. "It's just really camp," her bandmate concludes, "he's doing all these hand gestures.")

'La mort' is a sombre but tuneful existentialist statement by Brel, reflecting on how our finite mortality gives our lives meaning. "When you say to a Catholic that X or Y is no longer a Catholic," Brel himself said of his national faith, "they are always surprised. As far as they're concerned, only Sartre escaped the net." Despite his disparaging of religion, however, his translated lyric ('My Death') spoke of "whatever is behind the door" – the mystery of death that follows the uncertainties of life.

"Death waits for me in the lilacs that a gravedigger will toss over me to make the future," sings Brel; "My death waits among the falling leaves / in magician's mysterious sleeves" sings Engel in the Shuman/Blau translation. The Guest arrangement of Scott's version is heralded by ominous chords of doom from the medieval te deum 'Dies Irae',[10] which he may first have heard as a Gregorian chant, but both the original and the translation revolve around the draining sands of "the passing time".

"I realised all the phenomena of existence very young, and it was a hard thing for me," a middle-aged Engel would later recollect. 'My Death' is part of his coming to terms with that – with its skeletal orchestral arrangement and bass–guitar undertow, it's a romanticising of the fate that awaits us all. Almost incredibly, the artist would make his post-Walker Brothers return to *The Billy Cotton Band Show* to perform the song, coaxing the BBC variety audience's gaze down the poetic path to their own extinction.

"I just got into it via Scott Walker – *Scott Walker Sings Jacques Brel*,"[11] confirms Andy Delamere. "I bought it on tape and I got into all that. But I think I knew David Bowie's version of 'My Death',[12] which I loved. I just remember how dark it was and how rich."

As to their own visceral approach to the songs, including 'My Death': "We didn't want to be all precious, all kind of [whispering], 'This one is...' I didn't want it to be chin-stroking, but also I didn't want to camp it up. The way that Scott Walker sounds now, I find it a bit hard to stomach, and also Marc Almond — it's all kind of irony and we wanted to do it straight. Scott Walker's how I got into it. But I can't listen to it now, it's like listening to a big cream cake. It's camp."

"I love Scott Walker," clarifies Ms Dorrity, "I listen to him in The Walker Brothers and I listen to his solo stuff, but when I hear him doing Brel, and after listening to Brel's stuff... You can enjoy it for its theatricality, but whenever you start getting down to actual versions of Brel's work, you look at it and go, 'No, that's not really what he meant.'"

Scott climaxes with Brel's boozy, bawdy 'Amsterdam'. Matching the Belgian's quickening pace on his more manic *chansons* – which would be accompanied by huge hand gestures and the flashing of his buck teeth – Engel closes on the vignette of a drunken sailor who "drinks to the health of the whores of Amsterdam" and "pisses like I cry over an unfaithful love". It might not have played well at the London Palladium, but this was music as living, breathing, human drama.

After hearing *Scott*, Jacques Brel passed instructions to Mort Shuman to make all his translated material available to the young American. It began a series of semi-regular meetings in Hyde Park with Kenny Lynch, black London pop singer and Shuman's occasional co-writer, whereupon Lynch would pass Engel the latest Anglicised versions of Brel.

The intoxication with Brel would permeate Engel's first three solo albums – the plainly (yet perfectly) titled *Scott 1-3*, each containing three translations. In between the first two, the Engel team translated Brel's tragicomic, semiautobiographical '*Le chanson de Jacky*' into the thundering 'Jackie' – about a decadent figure who daydreams of being "a procurer of young girls", a saviour of mankind or returning to the innocence of childhood – but winds up "locked up inside some opium den / surrounded by my Chinamen". It made for the unlikeliest of single releases – at least as far as BBC radio was concerned.

"And if by chance I should become / A singer with a Spanish bum" began the Engel version, referring to the tight trousers of flamenco dancers, and it's this mild anal fixation that irritates Brel purists.

("When we did 'Jackie', we couldn't do 'cute-cute in a stupid-ass way', we couldn't stomach that," comments Dead Belgian's Delamere. "It's 'Beautiful, beautiful and an idiot simultaneously' – at the same time. Basically the words are just that. I love Scott Walker's version of 'Jackie' but it's like the music in *Thunderbirds*[13] – you can imagine the guys on Tracy Island putting it on in their 'pad', it's not 'dirty', it's not got any kind of dirt involved.")

The BBC presumably found 'Jackie' too 'dirty' for public consumption. It made it as far as number 22 in the charts in December 1967, with limited (night-time only) airplay. A bemused Engel found himself defending the lyric to sympathetic TV host Simon Dee on *Dee Time*, describing it as "beautiful" and Brel himself as "an art form" all of his own.

In early 1968, Shuman and Blau's dramatised revue *Jacques Brel Is Alive And Well And Living In Paris*[14] began a three-year run on Broadway. Shuman himself, a paunchy, moustachioed figure played one of the acting *chansonniers* – comical in 'Jacky', brooding in 'Amsterdam'.

("Brel's very funny," reflects Dead Belgian's Fionnuala, "they're clearly very funny songs. But I think Shuman's songs are a little bit saccharine, too sweet." "They're not European, are they?" says drummer Andy. "They're Americanised.")

But Scott Walker had got there first, recording four of the show's songs before they ever made the stage. His version of Brel's '*Au suivant*' ('Next') on 1968's *Scott 2* has been alternately criticised as both overly theatrical and not dramatic enough. In its time, however, it was as darkly Rabelaisian a performance as could be heard in the English language.

117

Set in a mobile army whorehouse, probably in the dying days of French Indochina,[15] it tells of a young man losing his virginity amid the stink "of corpses, of whisky and of mud". Given a dramatic build-up in its original French version,[16] its clinical line "I swear on the wet head of my first case of gonorrhoea" is a near-literal translation of the line referring to '*veroles*'.[17] In France, such scabrous imagery was tolerated as art; in England, it couldn't be played on the radio.

("He's not a great actor," demurs Delamere of Scott Walker's 'Next'. "Alex Harvey[18] acts – you get the meaning, you get the sense of it." "That's the difference," agrees Ms Dorrity. "Scott didn't put any aggression into it. He didn't put any of that same passion into it. He sang them very well but he sang them theatrically and he didn't put any real anger and hurt into it. I think what's missing from those is the performance – it's not the translation, it's not the orchestration or anything else to do with it, it's the sound of the man performing the song. He's quite cool with it, cool, theatrical and laid-back. Brel was fucking sweat and blood and anger!")

On the semi-classical *Scott 3*, in 1969, Brel would make his final appearance on a Scott Walker record with the final three tracks, ending with the languid 'If You Go Away'. Engel matches the Belgian's manic *accelerando* on 'Sons Of' ('*Fils de*'), a lullaby eulogy to lost childhood and children ("The same sweet smiles, the same sad tears / The cries at night, the nightmare fears"), opening on composer Jouannest's toy piano-like sound.

'Funeral Tango' is the black comic skit of a man watching the insincere mourners at his own funeral. Shuman played it for pathos in the show, but Engel has morbid fun with lines like, "Oh I can see me now / So cold and so alone / As the flowers slowly die / In my field of little bones."

"Did you ever have the desire to watch your own funeral?" he'd ask the audience of his 1969 TV show. "Listen to this."

("I think a lot of the translations are fine," concedes Delamere. "Some of them are a bit American. 'Funeral Tango' fits in fine, because we try to do all the death songs.")

"Brel was a reflection of the times I was going through," Scott explained in retrospect and in defiance of the purists, "all sorts of dark images, which I associated with Brel. His own interpretations of songs, in many ways, were very different from mine... My intention was to take the material and try and do something else with it."

By the end of the sixties, however, Scott Engel would move beyond and away from Brel. The last song he covered by the Belgian iconoclast was 'Alone' ('Seul'), a lyric about disintegrating relationships that, unusually for a translated work, seems to adopt a more universally philosophical perspective in its English version ("And we find we're alone"). But it was recorded only on (long since wiped) videotape for his 1969 TV series *Scott*, and never committed to vinyl.

"I heard through Brel's wife that he really liked the versions I'd done," said Engel. "I had a chance to meet him when I was in Paris one evening. He was doing [*Man Of*] *La Mancha*[19] – a show there. I was too nervous to meet him... I thought, 'I can't possibly... this is one of my big idols.' And I didn't do it."

Citing Brel's very basic melodies and comparing him to Bob Dylan,[20] Scott was distancing himself from the tradition in both folk and rock whereby the vocal was more a narrative performance than an organic component of a piece of music.

"It is grimy," says Matthew Wood of his own motley crew's contemporary approach to the music of Brel.

"And hopefully a little bit uncomfortable," seconds bandmate Delamere. "We did a gig on Matthew Street in Liverpool, there were 21 year olds and A-level students there. They were going: 'People don't know Jacques Brel – there should be a street like this,' because of Matthew Street and John Lennon.[21] I want to do things where you can hear the influence, like Leonard Cohen, or even The Divine Comedy," he strikes a percussionist's bell for emphasis. "Definitely Scott Walker, but it's just trying to choose which song. I love his songs that are influenced by Jacques Brel, better than his Brel versions. We could do 'The Girls From The

119

Streets', or 'Big Louise', 'Rosemary', I'd love to do 'Angels Of Ashes', it's a fantastic song, or 'Boy Child' – just for the flavour of it, I think it'd fit right in."

"We've been talking about doing stuff by other artists that have been clearly influenced by Jacques Brel," seconds Ms Dorrity. "I think he's been clearly influenced in terms of how he structures the songs, that orchestral feel to it."

"And also lyrically," confirms her bandmate. "'Such A Small Love' is a great song."

***

Scott, the first Engel solo album, debuted on September 16, 1967. It contained sleeve notes by original Walkers champion Keith Altham, which reflect both his enthusiasm and the earnestness of those times:

"This is the album which Scott called 'my obsession', and it is an LP for which you must open not only your ears but also your heart and your mind...

"If it were necessary to find any further proof that 'loneliness is not just a cloak he wears'[22] but a state of mind, it is here in his own compositions – 'Montague Terrace (In Blue)', 'Always Coming Back To You', and the cold ethereal beauty of 'Such A Small Love'.

"These three songs are almost an intrusion of privacy, and the points are barbed – but so superbly made that you must realise that like 'The bullfight' this is no idle 'sport' but a matter of life and death...[23]"

After several paragraphs of effusiveness, Altham continues:

"And while we applaud the result of this musical journey through Scott's mind we must not forget those sensitive arrangements by Wally Stott, Reg Guest and Peter Knight who have conjured 'musical spirits from the vastly deep' for these inspired orchestral settings.

"When Scott Engel (I use the surname because it is his real name and I know few more real people) sang with The Walker Brothers, he had a little-boy-lost image, but this album is a man's work, and the portent of greater things to come. Should some of the truth on this album offend, should the light be too bright for some, we might be permitted the device of using the words of another young man who wrote with the fire of burning youth:

"*'Beauty is truth, truth beauty – that is all.*
"*'That is all ye know on earth, and all ye need to know.'*
– John Keats."

Produced by John Franz and Peter Olliff, *Scott* made number three and remained on the album chart for more than four months. One of many positive reviews praised it as a melancholy "distillation of madness" – which seems a little strong now, given that the review goes on to observe how, "The songs sung by Scott are for the most part emotional ballads."

The track listing makes it essentially a covers album, every bit as much as those of The Walker Brothers. Cynthia Weil and Barry Mann's 'Angelica' is a sublime piece of romantic angst, outstripping even the intensity of Gene Pitney's version; "And then the cold winds came / And when I spoke her name… She couldn't hear me," the vocalist intones of the lover who may be absent or may be dead, to the insistent punctuation of Reg Guest's arrangement.

'The Lady Came From Baltimore' is a country-tinged ballad, anticipating the detour that Scott's career would later take. Telling the tale of a thief who "just came to steal her money, take her rings and run," but instead fell in love and "got away with none", it's a suitably downbeat romantic lyric by Tim Hardin – a tragic figure whose work Engel admired, "but not the man".[24]

'When Joanna Loved Me' is high-class schmaltz of the first order ("Every town was Paris… every month was May / but when Joanna left me / May became December"); it was also the first of many occasions that Scott would cover the repertoire of Tony Bennett, a romantic crooner second only to Sinatra himself.

'The Big Hurt' faithfully covers the beautifully brassy 1959 hit by Miss Toni Fisher, making high drama out of a simple break-up

("Now it begins, now that you've gone / Needles and pins, twilight till dawn").[25] André and Dory Previn's 'You're Gonna Hear From Me' is from the 1966 musical *Inside Daisy Clover* with Natalie Wood – a 'watch out, world, here I come!' number rather at odds with the album's intensity. 'Through A Long And Sleepless Night' is another soundtrack cover, from the 1949 movie *Come To The Stable*; more recently covered by Bobby Darin,[26] it benefited from a classically influenced arrangement by new man Peter Knight.

And then, of course, there are three Engel originals which, like the Brel songs in their own manner, are infused with an aesthetic truth.

"Everyone goes on about the Jacques Brel stuff," said Scott's eighties manager, Ed Bicknell, in the bio-doc, "but to me the most interesting thing on those Phillips records is Scott's own writing. Because he was kind of emerging as a songwriter and there were some *fantastic* songs."

"I'd heard of Scott and I'd heard of The Walker Brothers, but I'd never heard them," chimed in Angela Morley – the elderly lady formerly known as Wallace Stott.[27] "I had a call from a man saying he was Johnny Franz… and he said, 'Scott Walker is going to do some things on his own and I'd like you to come and work with him.' So I'd go into Johnny's office, I'd expected to see Johnny sitting at the piano and Scott holding his music. But no! I walked in to see this young man sitting on the floor with his arms out like that [extends arms], with a guitar and sheets of paper with words on all over the carpet, you know. And as he'd sing and strum his way all through these things, from time to time he would stop and he would say, 'I really hear Sibelius here,' you see, or, 'Here I hear Delius,' or, 'Here I hear…,' and all these classical composers that he was fond of, and somehow he just wanted that sound in the arrangements. We just thought that he was different, we didn't realise that he was… you know, a scout for like the avant-garde, what was to come."

The classic solo Engel track that first marked out his space in late sixties pop history, 'Montague Terrace (In Blue)' flows and weaves its way through a hypnotic string arrangement by Stott. When Scott later sang it on his TV show, he'd announce it as being about "two very dear friends of mine – a married couple who live in a small room about the size of a shoebox... who can still dream and this deals with their illusions of living in Montague Terrace."[28]

The focus of the lyric is less on the couple's dream home than the physical claustrophobia of their environment, described in biological metaphor: the man upstairs' "bloated, belching figure stomps / He may crash through the ceiling soon"; the girl across the hall's "thighs are full of tales to tell / Of all the nights she's known".

"The lyrics, the imagery was so strong and graphic," reflected Ms Morley (née Stott), "now and then I was a little shocked by it: 'Woo, is that allowed?', you know."

'Such A Small Love' is a funereal farewell to a friend, a close young male contemporary of the narrator. Gently mournful organ emerges from a quiet cacophony of strings: "Someone should have stopped the birds from singing today / Hammers from striking nails into clay." But there is as much wistful good humour here as there is melancholy. The dead man's girlfriend is present. "She is crying, but he knows that the girl cannot really have known his friend's worth over the years," described the songwriter at the time. She never shared their drunken "midnight mornings drenched in dago red".

'Always Coming Back To You', the final Engel original, is the most realistic of love songs, the universal tale of two lovers whose passion has passed but who keep returning to each other. "What was it like when we were young? / Sleeping in each other's arms, living in each other's dreams?" our narrator asks over a jangling harpsichord. But now he must search his lover's eyes, "just to see that they are dead" to him. It may sound bleak, but this is a love that most of us know; its repeated title line is an affirmation that love still exists beyond its early peaks.[29]

The weeks following the release of *Scott* saw its namesake playing cabaret dates and making his next recordings. In the sixties, the man who would come to be regarded as an irregularly productive recluse was possibly one of the hardest working artists in popular music.

Even a break spent in Moscow during the last week in September was for the purpose of studying the art of the Soviet Union. He was scheduled to meet Yevgeny Yevtushenko, the poet and 'people's artist' whose controversial poem 'Babi Yar' dared to speak of Soviet complicity in the massacre of Kiev's Jewish population during World War Two; Yevtushenko's contemporary Andrei Voznesensky was also due to attend, another feted poet in the Krushchev era who would have been crushed under the regime of Stalin, Krushchev's mentor.

Characteristically for the time, perhaps, the meeting never went ahead, with Engel crying off due to a crushing hangover. The writings of Yevtushenko,[30] however, would continue to influence the political thinking of the young American.

Back in London during the winter, Scott was found unconscious at home in Regent's Park the week before Christmas. It looked like it might be a rerun of the dramas of the Walkers era, before he was diagnosed with appendicitis at the London Clinic – and promptly discharged himself without being operated on. He was apparently well enough to perform the new single 'Jackie' on camp comedian Frankie Howerd's TV show, and to indulge in a peculiar skit based on the play *Cyrano De Bergerac*.

Engel would spend the festive season itself back in his girlfriend's home city of (wonderful, wonderful) Copenhagen. A photo of them taken at Heathrow shows Scott looking uncharacteristically relaxed in a blazer-style jacket and jeans, with the statuesque Mette, packed tight into a diamond-patterned dress, smiling at the photographer.

"There's a very childlike quality about this girl that changes my outlook and personality," he romantically appraised. What was unremarked upon was that the well brought up, middle-class girl had been persuaded by her man to return home to face a shoplifting charge. The press apparently knew but, with a sensitivity now lost in time, decided not to mention it.

Midwestern-born, cowpoke-statured Noel Scott Engel was going to spend time in his favourite city. He was truly becoming a European.

Notes

1   Andrew Loog Oldham, the acerbic motormouth manager behind The Rolling Stones in the early-to-mid-sixties, was then one of London's pop-cultural arbiters. In his memoir of the period, *Stoned*, he's very dismissive of Scott Engel, calling him "one sigh away from being a wanker". In *The Impossible Dream*, Anthony Reynolds' definitive history of The Walker Brothers as a band, his former Immediate Records partner, Tony Calder, contradicts him, claiming they were trying to sign the solo Scott: "I mean, what a fucking star, but I couldn't deal with him. Even Andrew couldn't cope with him. Scott Walker was the only artist Andrew shut up for."

2   Along with Hergé, Magritte, Georges Simenon and, of course...

3   Not that he shared Genet's sexual predilections. As his *'Au suivant'* ('Next') indicates, he found 'les fags' perverse.

4   "We work on a theatre ship," says band founder Andy Delamere. "I always wanted to do the songs, because we've got experience in theatre and just because of the drama in it. We did a cabaret night and there was a band doing a kind of *Jacques Brel Is Alive And Well And Living In Paris* – but really, *really* bad. Then it gestated for a while. I said I'd love to play with [lead vocalist] Nula [Dorrity], but she said, 'Let's not just play songs – let's *do* something. What do you wanna do?' I said, 'I'd love to do Jacques Brel songs,' and she'd never heard of Brel!" For a Brel novice, Ms Dorrity has learned to carry off the songs with a gutsy drama; most remarkably perhaps, for a non-French speaker, she combines the original Francophone lyrics with the English translations on 'Jacky', 'Amsterdam' and '*Au suivant'*. "To mix them up is really good, because otherwise we usually go into a bit more detail of what they're about," says Delamere. The Dead Belgian line-up is completed by accordion player Matthew Wood, who speaks French and makes his own translations of some of the lesser known songs like 'Jaures', about the murder of a French socialist politician. "We talked about doing 'Ces gens la' ['Those People There' – Brel's misanthropic portrait of a night-time crowd], but doing it as a translation with almost like prose over the top." "Matthew has tried to do a very, very specifically literal translation, he hasn't tried to rewrite or discard anything," acclaims singer Dorrity. Dead Belgian's 2012 album, *Love And Death: The Songs Of Jacques Brel*, is highly recommended.

5   As in Krushchev.

6   Lou Reed was a close friend of Pomus in his twilight years, commemorating his death from cancer in the *Magic And Loss* album.

7   When US pop singer Terry Jacks covered 'Seasons In The Sun' in the seventies, he removed all Brel's allusions to adultery from McKuen's final verse. The song still had a morbidly saccharine charm and became the biggest-selling Brel translation worldwide; Jacks followed with a similar emasculation of 'If You Go Away'.

8   It was the title track of John's sadly unsuccessful 1967 debut album.

9   In *30 Century Man*, Gavin Friday, Irish former vocalist of proto-goths The Virgin Prunes and latter-day Brel interpreter, expresses the following opinion: "A lot of people cite Brel as an influence – but really I think, subliminally, what they're really citing is Scott. You know, Brel was... Flemish, he sort of dribbled when he sang, he was sweaty; whereas Scott Walker took his songs and sang them like – a *Greek god.*" His ex-compatriate Fionnuala Dorrity is less complimentary of Friday's own performances: "I listened to two songs recently because he was doing Brel cover versions. One of them I just found very cheesy and not very passionate, not very fucking full of the vitriol and bitterness they should be."

10   'Day Of Wrath', as orchestrated by Berlioz.

11   A 1981 compilation of the Brel tracks from *Scott 1-3* – plus the odd addition of Engel/Semel's 'Little Things That Keep Us Together' (from *'Til The Band Comes In*). It sleeve replicated the classic cover of *Scott* – Engel with full head of hair bowed, swathed in shades and scarf – which was by then deleted.

12   Bowie, a long-term Walker fan, incorporated the Shuman version of 'My Death' into his 1973 farewell performances as glam-rock icon Ziggy Stardust. Strumming on an acoustic guitar, Bowie subverted the line, "My death waits like a swinging door / A patient girl who knows the score" to suit his voguish sexual ambiguity of the time: "My death waits like an old roué / Who knows that I will go his way." At the closing lines of the song, where Scott sings, "For in front of that door, there is you," Ziggy sang, "For in front of that door, there is..." "Me! Me! Me!" screamed dozens of little teenage voices at the Hammersmith Odeon. On the final track of *The Rise And Fall Of Ziggy Stardust And The Spiders From Mars*, 'Rock 'N' Roll Suicide', artistic thieving magpie Bowie takes elements of Brel's 'Les vieux' ('Old Folks' – Brel/Shuman: "The clock on the wall that waits for us all"/Bowie: "The clock waits so patiently on your song") and 'Jef', whose translated refrain is the same as that of Bowie: "You're not alone."

13   Indeed, the Stott arrangement has the brass-driven fury of the big TV themes of the time, particularly for ITC's shows. "That was *The Goon Show*, orchestra conducted by Wally Stott," the plummy-voiced announcer stated on BBC Home Service radio in the fifties; his days in broadcasting sometimes seemed to have run on into Scott Walker's records.

14   A parody of tabloid headlines such as 'Adolf Hitler Is Alive And Well And Living In Buenos Aires'.

15   As Scott was acutely aware, the withdrawal of the French during a communist insurgency had led the Americans to supplant them in the country now called Vietnam.

16   Driven along by a nerve-jangling xylophone – not an accordion, as suggested by Swezey and King in this chapter's epigram.

17   "Syphilis sores" in the more literal translation by Paul Buck for Marc Almond's 1990 album *Jacques*.

18 Alex Harvey (1935-1982), veteran Brit R&B singer and leader in the seventies of The Sensational Alex Harvey Band, put plenty of his native Glaswegian aggression into his 1973 cover of 'Next': "*Ah schwear on the wet head ae mah first case ae gonorrhoea!*" The title of the SAHB's 1974 album, *The Impossible Dream*, suggests he was probably as influenced by Scott Walker as he was by Brel.

19 Brel took the lead role in the French version of *Man Of La Mancha*, a musical adaptation of Cervantes' *Don Quixote*, from late 1968 to summer 1969.

20 Brel's 'J'Arrive' is a classic case in question: one of the more uptempo ballads in which he accepts and almost celebrates death, the refrain consists of the shouted title echoed by two loud notes.

21 Matthew Street is the site of the Cavern Club and of Liverpool City Council's statue of Lennon.

22 A slightly cringe-making allusion to 'The Sun Ain't Gonna Shine Anymore' – a song Engel would come to regard as a shroud rather than a cloak.

23 Scott Engel would spend a summer holiday in the late sixties in Spain to witness the bullfights, apparently enthralled by the Hemingwayesque spectacle of death in the afternoon. Jacques Brel's attitude to this cruel tradition can be heard in his song 'Les toros' ('The Bulls').

24 The Hardin songbook provided romantic tracks as disparate as The Four Tops' 'If I Were A Carpenter' and Emerson, Lake & Palmer's 'Hold On To A Dream'. Tim Hardin himself was a long-term heroin addict, who reputedly picked up the habit as a Special Forces 'adviser' in Vietnam; he died of an overdose at Christmas 1980, aged 39, over six years after cutting his last record.

25 Nick Cave would give the song a similar oomph as the theme to *Mojo*, the 1996 film set in fifties Soho, backed by the band Gallon Drunk.

26 According to original Walker Brothers drummer Al 'Tiny' Schneider, "He was quite affected when Bobby Darin came out... I think, secretly, that's what Scott really wanted to do. He wanted to be that type of cabaret entertainer." Seen from this distance, the brief Darin infatuation may have been the dying embers of teenage Scotty Engel's original ambition.

27 In the early seventies, Wally Stott decamped to Scandinavia to undergo a similar operation to Christine Jorgenson, who in the late fifties had been the first male-to-female sex change. Stott's operation briefly predated that of electronic composer Walter Carlos – who created the soundtrack for Stanley Kubrick's *A Clockwork Orange* in 1971, and before the end of that decade had become Wendy Carlos.

28 This particular west London terrace was apparently demolished in the seventies – although former *Record Collector* editor Mark Paytress signs off his highly informative sleeve notes to The Walker Brothers' *Everything Under The Sun* box set, "Montague Terrace Gardens, London".

29 Throughout the late eighties and early nineties, when Scott's Philips albums were not available, 'Always Coming Back To You' was preserved as a single B-side on

the basement jukebox of Bradley's Spanish Bar, in Fitzrovia's Hanway Street. This writer played it regularly.

30 A controversial figure both in the Soviet Union and the West; regarded as a force for openness and freedom by many, as an apologist for the communist regime by his detractors.

Chapter 7

An American Artist In Europe

I don't believe in heroism; I know it's easy and I've learnt it can be murderous. What interests me is living and dying for what one loves.

Albert Camus – *The Plague* (1947)

Flying towards me, wrapped in laughter / A woman's face, a terrible taste / Of the morning after kisses and goodbyes.

Scott Engel – 'The Plague' (1967)

S cott Engel arrived in Copenhagen as the Valium had still not quite worn off. He reputedly fell asleep in the arrivals lounge with a black Stetson pulled down over his eyes – a displaced cowboy in Europe.

While staying with Mette, her family and friends, he was privy to a police drugs raid on a Saturday night party they attended. Flying back and forth between Denmark and London to record, it would reputedly influence the lyric of 'Plastic Palace People', a song on his second album then in progress.

But before the prosaically titled *Scott 2* could see release, there was unfinished business to undertake. Prior to the break-up of The

Walker Brothers, Capable Management had arranged a Japanese tour for its disbanding artists. The obligation was dutifully undertaken by all three, and – just for a while – it was as if the band had never split. "There was no drama," confirmed John Maus. "We all did the 'hey, man' wave, and everything was back to normal, the way it had been in the days before things went wrong in the group."

The Walker Brothers and their entourage flew across Soviet airspace to reach the Far East. As they passed the terrain over the River Volga, Russian buff Scott is said to have gamely tried to converse with a group of women in their native tongue.

They toasted the New Year of 1968 while flying through the civilian air corridor of South Vietnam, while a Christmas truce was briefly in effect. When they finally touched at Osaka Airport, it was Walker mania all over again: 2,000 fans were in attendance, some with banners reading 'The Sun's Gonna Shine Once More!'[1] On the exit steps of the aircraft, the reluctant star held his arms aloft as if in victory.

"Japan was kinda scary because we could hear ourselves," Gary Leeds said, "but as soon as we stopped playing, there was this massive outbreak of screaming." Most remarkably, perhaps, on his return to the Land of the Rising Sun, 'Gallee Reeds' (as Scott would announce "the star of the show" onstage) was a fullblown pop star. All but forgotten by this time in the UK, the subsequent album release by his psychedelic pop band, Gary Walker & The Rain, would be in Japan only.

("I want to put over my own way of communicating aside from the psychedelic thing, because I don't believe those people convey real emotion," Scott had recently opined of the current trend in rock music. "Flower power, I believe, is a lie. It would be lovely if it were real, but the human race is so complex, it just could never happen.")

"We all did our solo bits on stage and, of course, Walker Brothers material," recollected John. "Gary performed his newest hit in Japan – 'Twinkie Lee' – and 'Dizzy Miss Lizzie', with Scott on drums and me playing my Telecaster."

The 10 shows in Osaka and Tokyo included a night at the prestigious 10,000-seater Budokan.[2] The Walkers' last Eastern stand saw them travelling at 200mph upon the famous bullet train, visiting Mount Fuji and historic Shinto temples. On their return to the UK, however, they would find that Barry Clayman (then in attendance on the tour) was leaving Capable Management and all three performers would be at the tender mercy of Maurice King.

Disc ran a report on the triumphant Nipponese tour which, nonetheless, emphasised the finality of the event: 'BROTHERS NO MORE' – Harry Cawtheray's account of the Walkers' Japanese tour':

A televised commercial for chocolate was fixed for the next day and the boys arrived at AOI recording studios where Scott Walker 'Perfectionist' immediately took charge of the sound session, working out harmonies on the piano, checking pronunciation of Japanese words, chalked out in huge letters on cue cards, balancing the sound and generally leaving a contingent of engineers, producers and ad-men wondering what was happening!

Lunch had been arranged at a noted Japanese restaurant where Scott, who had insisted on a huge electric fire being positioned within inches of him as he sat cross-legged on the floor, was attentively listening to an 'eating feasibility' report from Gary: "That's more seaweed. These are rubber bands. Here's a lump of glue."…

As the show ended, near riot broke out in the audience, fans clambering on stage, reaching out tearfully… Scott made his final 'thank you' speech – and all of us suddenly realised that this was not just the last night of the tour, it was almost certainly the last time The Walker Brothers will ever work together.

We travelled back to Tokyo still subdued, eating Engel's [25th] birthday cake. Immediately on arrival Scott and Gary rushed off to a recording studio, where Gary was to cut a single with one of Japan's beat groups, The Carnabeats, under Scott's direction.

"Look!" echoed Scott's amplified voice on the Look chocolate commercial. With chocolate bar in hand and mousy-ish hair looking distinctly darker,[3] he and John repeated the far from subliminal message – "Look chocolate!" – to the accompaniment of their own vaguely orientalised la-la-ing voices and a cartoon geisha girl. Crass commerciality was something to be avoided back in Britain, but in Japan, where the Walkers were demigods still, anything seemed to go.

As for Gary, he'd cover the recent Classics IV US hit 'Stormy' with The Carnabeats, produced by Scott – though he apparently only drummed on it, as the band's vocalist sang lead.

✱✱✱

Back in England, *Scott 2* saw light of day in April 1968. It opened with the Brel cover 'Jackie', which had suffered restricted sales due to lack of airplay – mainly due to the unflinching line "authentic queers and phoney virgins".

The single's remarkable B-side was not included, and would remain in obscurity for another two decades. 'The Plague' was inspired by Camus' novel of that title. While the great philosophical writer claimed his book was not some existentialist treatise but a story of humanity under stress, its depiction of a French-Algerian community trying to combat an outbreak of pestilence at times reads as an allegory about what people live and die for.

Engel's song adopted a more abstract conceit – the plague as a spiritual malaise rather than a medical epidemic. Opening with a tolling bell that sounds like it's straight out of Bergman, it's also far rockier than anything else with the name 'Scott Walker' on it at the time. The repetitive female 'la-la-la-la-la' backing accompanies an electric guitar with mild phasing, and an angst-ridden lyric – "How can I live an hour like this? / When anguish strikes me like a fist..." – and the almost defiant refrain, "I've got the plague."

The album was rather different. In the sleeve notes by Jonathan King,[4] the young pop entrepreneur quoted his friend approvingly:

"I'm afraid it's the work of a lazy, self indulgent man. Now the nonsense must stop, and the serious business must begin."

("I have no doubt that many years from now, over a space age dinner of vitamins," King also wrote, "he will say: 'Well, the last 50 years have been great fun, but now we really must get down to doing something worthwhile.'" It reads quite presciently from our current vantage point.)

Engel's 'laziness' only extends as far as the album following the template of *Scott*, three Brel songs and all. Otherwise, the elements that were present on his solo debut are developed further and the album exceeded its commercial success, reaching number one in the charts.

The MOR covers are still present, and exceptionally well handled: 'Best Of Both Worlds', the hit by his admirer Lulu, has Scott imploring his faithless lover, "Make your fickle mind up!" and giving the young Brit female ballad singers of the time a run for their money.[5] 'Black Sheep Boy' completes the minor infatuation with Tim Hardin's songs, its lyric about a drifter and transient lover sung in a similar rhythm and tempo to 'The Lady Came From Baltimore'. 'Wait Until Dark' is a love song co-written by Henry Mancini, the theme to the film of the same name (with Audrey Hepburn as a blind girl menaced by a criminal intruder – in the manner of theme songs back then, the lyric had nothing to do with the story). 'Windows Of The World' is a gentle antiwar ballad by Bacharach and David, previously recorded by their muse Dionne Warwick; lamenting how boys are often called to die for their country (without actually mentioning Vietnam), it makes an ineffective liberal plea: "The windows of the world are covered with rain / There must be something we can do." The album ends with 'Come Next Spring', a theme tune to a 1956 romantic drama with music by renowned film composer Max Steiner.

Despite the two film themes on the album, the most cinematic offerings were the four Engel originals. Arranged with extraordinary sensitivity by the Stott/Guest/Knight triumvirate, they create a vividly audiovisual world of their own (even if the visuals belong to the imagination of the listener). First is 'The Amorous Humphrey Plugg': the title character is oft described as a total fantasist, but the lyric seems to come from at least two perspectives. There's the tired wife looking after the kids, who tells him: "You've become a stranger / Every night with the boys"; there's Humphrey himself, who escapes from "Screaming kids on my knee / And the telly swallowing me" by imagining his implied adultery as something romantically grandiose: "Oh, to die of kisses, ecstasies and charms / Pavements of poets will write that I died in nine angels' arms"; and then the apparent third voice in the refrain – "... Stop a while behind our smile / In Channing Way" – may be the lover via whom Plugg[6] escapes his day-to-day, or possibly just the conciliatory wife again.

(As with many of the American expatriate's lyrics then, the setting seems indelibly British. But Channing Way is not listed among the London boroughs, applying instead to a neighbourhood in Berkeley, northern California.)

'The Girls From The Streets' has been frequently criticised for an overt Brel influence – but the differences are distinct too, and the song is a delight. The subject may be familiar, yet some of the verses – "His brandy brim voice whispers / Come with me I hold the key / The city's ours tonight" – have a self-conscious literary quality quite apart from the Belgian's bile and sweat. Its romanticisation of prostitutes[7] – "Cascading tears for every heartbeat / Tonight we'll sleep with the girls from the streets" – is, however, followed by a frantically speeded-up section that recalls the *accelerando* of Brel's 'Carousel' (whether in its original or Shuman version) and wouldn't seem out of place in a Euro-musical like *The Umbrellas Of Cherbourg*.

'Plastic Palace People' is a short audio movie in itself. Its shimmering string section follows Scott's gravity-defying voice as a boy floats above the rooftops, attached to a balloon: "Through cobbled stone streets a child races / And shouts 'Billy, come down from there.'" In its opening sense of wonderment it's like a children's fairy story. But the scenario also suggests Scott may have seen J. Lee Thompson's

1953 film *The Yellow Balloon*, in which a young boy sees his friend fall to his death, while chasing his balloon through bomb-pockmarked postwar London.

The childlike wonder of the balloon-themed verses is juxtaposed by the entirely different tempo of the chorus, about the Plastic Palace People themselves, who "sing silent songs" and "dream too long". Plastic Palace Alice, who "blows gaping holes to store her fears / Inside her lover's head", sounds likely to be a drug user – as, perhaps, are all the silent dreamers who seek to recapture the dreaminess of childhood via a kind of chemical regression.

It's the nearest that Scott Walker came to psychedelia (along with 'The Plague', perhaps), but this is psychological surrealism rather than any kind of trip – even the phased section of the vocal which says: "They rip your face with lies... like gods they bark replies," sounds more like an admonition than an enticement to blow one's mind. In the final fairy-tale verse Billy Balloon is burned, his underwear left hanging in the trees. The mingling of the two apparently unrelated narratives is hugely potent – the first instance, perhaps, of a *drift* of images which compound and intensify each other.

(At the time of the mid-seventies Walker Brothers reunion, Scott was a phone-in guest on London's Capital Radio. "Does it mean what I think it means?" asked one nervous lady caller of 'Plastic Palace People'. "Yes it does!" he answered instantly, without further elaboration. This might be construed as a blanket response to many later lyrics too.)

'The Bridge' is a piece of elegantly filmic melancholia, as the narrator watches from riverbanks for his missing Madelaine. There's a definite Brel influence again,[8] in the lyric that tells of how "Her sailors stained her cobblestones / With wine and piss and death desire." But there's no obvious literalness to Engel's words, no concrete conclusion to dispel the mystery of Madelaine.

As much as Engel was wont to disparage his own work for its "lack of continuity", *Scott 2* stood not simply as a great album but as a part of a powerfully evolving body of work. Philips (or more specifically John Franz) was prepared to give him his head at this time, and for that the albums which began with *Scott* (and would end with *'Til The Band Comes In*) stand alone in that period.

For all that, Scott Engel still seemed weary of the music industry – particularly of live performance – and fantasised in one interview about going to work in a Copenhagen beer factory. But he was still prepared to play the game when required of him.

John Maus later told how Scott recorded a romantic ballad and "was told it was going to be used as the theme in a movie with the same name, produced by Mike Sarne.[9] He didn't know it was going to be released as a single. 'Joanna' was not really in keeping with what he wanted to do musically – he just recorded the song for this project, but it was never used in the movie, so Scott was not very happy."

"I like to write one of these things occasionally," Scott defended the piece of straight sentimentalism. "Of course, this was done by [Jackie] Trent and [Tony] Hatch, but I adjusted the lyric."

Mainstream composer/producer Hatch has always backed Engel's assertion. "When my demo of the song was first sent to Scott, he suggested some subtle but perfect lyric changes." Indeed, he claimed composition of an entire verse about "the one they call Joanna", containing the lines, "You made the man a child again, so sweetly / He breathed your smile / Lived in your eyes completely." As he did for the reverberating closing line: "You may remember me and change your mind."

"Amazingly," confirmed Hatch, "he declined the offer and just said that he loved the song and was happy to leave us with the full songwriter shares." Jackie Trent and Tony Hatch may seem to inhabit an entirely different musical universe to Scott Walker: Hatch is remembered today as the theme tune composer for soap operas *Crossroads* and *Neighbours*, as well as for his panel role in seventies talent show *New Faces*.

But he and Engel were friendly acquaintances. Tony Hatch had been a regular at Philips' studios at Stanhope Place and watched the Engel-Franz partnership with interest, noting how the younger man's literacy and musicality jibed with the perfectionism of the

elder. Jackie and Tony would also be the support act at concerts by
Scott in Brighton. When they both hosted a TV special called *Mr &
Mrs Music*, Scott was one of their guests; when he was briefly granted
his own TV series he would return the favour.

So it's not entirely incongruous that Hatch and Trent's 'Joanna'
(with uncredited rewrites by Engel) should become the most popular
solo Scott Walker record of all time, reaching number seven in the
charts in April 1968, immediately after the release of *Scott 2*.

Manager Maurice King was thrilled, believing this to be the
calling card of his 'new Sinatra'. The artist would come to regard the
song as something of a bugbear in time. But within a year, it would
literally become his signature tune. When he appeared at the *NME*
Poll Winners Concert in May '68, after performing 'Amsterdam' he
stormed offstage when he realised the orchestra had no arrangement
prepared for 'Joanna'. Scott Walker now inhabited two different
musical universes simultaneously.

In his domestic life, Scott was sharing his St John's Wood flat with
Mette and a gigantic St Bernard named Rasmus, after her academic
father. The dog was apparently on record at the time as being the
largest example of his breed. (So difficult was it to contain him at
the flat that he'd have to be shipped off to Mette's father's farm in
Denmark.)

As John Maus, recently divorced and living with his second-
wife-to-be, was now back in London, Scott met with him more
frequently. With the friction of The Walker Brothers' disintegration
out of the way, they felt free to socialise and drink together.

"In the spring of 1968 Scott and I were each offered £100,000 to
do a show in South Africa before a segregated audience," John later
recalled, "but we both turned it down without a second thought.
We had previously agreed that we would never play under those
circumstances."

"Nobody will force me to perform in circumstances in conflict
with my own conscience," Scott confirmed at the time. It was at
least a decade and a half before the anti-Apartheid movement would

become a force in the music industry, but the ex-Walkers adhered to their consciences without any prompting or grandstanding.

Scott also nailed his political conscience to the mast when he came out in support of Democratic Sentator Robert Kennedy's bid to succeed President Lyndon B. Johnson to the White House. "I think Bobby Kennedy is the only man with the right ideas about peace and war," he told the music press, presumably hoping that, unlike LBJ, Kennedy was likely to limit American involvement in Vietnam.[10]

The performer had gone as far as placing an ad in *The Times* on April 3 – "Fellow Americans in London required to join campaign committee supporting Robert Kennedy election bid; 60,000 eligible votes in Britain are important and must be contacted" – giving a Covent Garden phone number.

Within two months, on June 5, 1968, Kennedy would share his brother's fate when shot dead during a presidential rally in LA.

"I just hate America," Scott told the pop press. "The assassination… just confirmed my opinions of the States, why I personally had to get out. I knew this could happen. There's so much inner tension in the people, such a fantastic pressure on society, loaded with demands that they can't give in to."[11]

One of the outcomes would be the election of Republican President Richard M. Nixon to the White House that following November, one of Engel's personal *bêtes noire*. But in the aftermath of the killing, Scott was already expressing the darkest pessimism: "All is lost anyway. We were doomed before we started."[12]

Back in the 'real world' of the entertainment industry, Maurice King did his best to distract his boy from unfolding world history and to get him treading the boards again. He booked him for four seaside gigs in June and July, two matinee and evening gigs each in Brighton and Blackpool. Scott would be accompanied by jazz saxophonist Ray Warleigh's band and supported by Jackie Trent and Tony Hatch in Brighton, for which the following typed agreement was made:

SCHEDULE

The Artiste agrees to appear at two performances at a salary of
£750.00.

one day(s) at The Dome Theatre, Brighton, Sussex, commencing
21st June, 1968...

SPECIAL CLAUSES

3. Performance times to be decided by the Management, but it
   is agreed that – Two spotf [*sic*] of 30 minutes each minimum...
6. All financial settlement to take place by £250.00 cheque
   to Capable Management fourteen days in advance and by
   balance by cheque within seven days.
7. Scott Walker to be accompanied by a band of at least twelve
   musicians.

£750 for two performances in one day was obviously not deemed
insulting then, as it would be now – although the insistence on at
least 12 backing musicians shows how far the money had to go. (In
fact Warleigh's band apparently consisted of no more than seven.)

Gary Leeds was also continuing to be productive – although that
hit record seemed as elusive as ever. Having cut a single with Japanese
band The Carnabeats after the Walkers' final Far Eastern tour (after
which he and Scott had returned to California to be with their
parents for a few weeks – one of the few times Engel has returned
to the US since the mid-sixties), Gary Walker & The Rain were
now gearing up for a full-scale tour of Japan. They would also have
a noted recording artist sharing the bill with them.

"From the money I will get on this tour, I could last a whole year
without makin' one concert appearance," Scott told *Disc & Music
Echo*. "I'm prepared to over-prostitute myself to get any money to
live on." The man in the baggy brown corduroy suit was hardly
living what the public would regard as a pop-star lifestyle anyway –
and he preferred it that way. Performing was a matter of expediency,
just enough to keep the wolves from the door and to allow him to
concentrate on composition and recording.

While Gary and his band flew to Tokyo, Scott deferred to his increasing fear of flying and took the Trans-Siberia Express. He set off equipped with a reel-to-reel tape recorder playing many of his favourite albums, and notebooks in which to plan his own next works. The rail journey would also offer him the luxury of a further transient visit to the Soviet Union. Except it didn't quite turn out like that.

"I got kicked out because I brought in tapes. Yes! I was spying!" he told the music press. "I had, uh, all these jazz tapes I'd made, and we entered the border in the middle of the night, and they got on the train like Nazis. They were doing the whole Nazi bit, and they took away my tapes and my tape recorder."

Scott's various vitamin tablets were also subject to a rigorous (if non-expert) examination, with a medical book consulted. "I love the Russian people, but the government... I'm worried about the Russian artist under this regime," he complained. As Scott was beginning to understand, the trouble with the dictatorship of the proletariat was that whoever was assertive enough to represent the proletariat would also, by definition, act as a dictator.

After having already spent 17 days on the train, Scott flew back to London directly from Moscow. Back home, he went into a state of nervous collapse. Gary and his band would have to tour Japan by themselves.

Scott recovered enough to record the first of two TV pilot shows for BBC1 at the Golders Green Hippodrome, two weeks later. It seemed like a natural follow-up to his appearance on *Dusty* the previous winter, when he and Ms Springfield had duetted on The Everly Brothers' 'Let It Be Me'. (By the time they reached, "Each time we meet, love / I find complete love," it had turned into a vocal clash of the titans.)

The first pilot set an eclectic tone, with Scott taking the stage to the tune of 'Joanna' and a selection of guests including his musical mentor:

"I'm very pleased to have the man who produces all my records at Philips, Johnny Franz, here with me tonight. John is very frustrated as he used to make a living playing the piano, but now he works as head of A&R, and of course I'm very lazy so I never work," Scott introduced Franz, with slight reticence, to mild titters at his self-deprecation. "We go over to his place some nights and take it out on his wife, and it goes something like this."

They performed 'I'll Be Around', a languid 1943 barroom ballad with Franz tinkling away behind Scott. This was followed by 'Genevieve', to effusive cheers from the younger female contingent in the audience at the mention of The Walker Brothers.

The show also set the format for a forthcoming TV series by featuring a guest performer: "It's been said many times before that my next guest has the potential to be the best female vocalist in Britain – Miss Kiki Dee!"[13] Ms Dee sang the Jimmy Webb bubblegum hit 'Up, Up And Away' before joining Scott on a duet of the emotional ballad 'Passing Strangers', previously a hit for jazz duo Billy Eckstine and Sarah Vaughan. (It would return to the charts in the wake of Scott's TV show.)

Scott finished the show with the classic 'If You Go Away', before signing off with a smooth piece of showbiz patter: "Thank you very much, you've been a wonderful audience. Now it's time for me to go away – good night." There were hysterical screams from female Walker fan members of the audience.

The first show aired in September (the second pilot followed in December, with a guest slot by Scott's Ronnie Scott's acquaintance Blossom Dearie), by which time Scott had been lined up for a further series of dates. ("I'm broke again and that's the only reason I'm doin' this tour.") There were certain stipulations set for these dates though, as pop journalist Bob Farmer reported of the opening night at the Finsbury Park Astoria:

'Scott tour – screamers keep quiet and LISTEN!'
    Full marks to the girls of Finsbury Park, London. They usually let Scott Walker sing uninterrupted at the opening of his concert tour last Friday before screaming their gratitude at the end of each song.

Compere Mike Quinn appealed for quiet before introducing the erratic American, but neither we nor he really supposed the audience would obey. Apart from the barest handful of ludicrous gigglers (whom Mr Walker would doubtless dearly have liked to punch on the nose) he got his hush.

And was it worth it? From the opening bars of 'Jackie' he gave a great performance...

As much as the three-week tour paid the bills, Scott had clearly outgrown package tours with ephemeral pop bands supporting him. For the rest of the year, he appeared only in London at a 'Save the Rave' charity gig at the London Palladium, sharing the bill with The Bonzo Dog Doo Dah Band,[14] and on a Christmas edition of Cilla Black's TV show.

He also found the time to produce old buddy John Maus, who had recently parted company with John Franz as a producer. To 'Woman', a tender but rough-edged John Walker ballad redolent of his great 'I Can't Let It Happen To You', Scott brought clarity and a subtle string arrangement reminiscent of some of his own quieter moments. It was released in November 1968, and Scott would also produce the follow-up, 'Yesterday's Sunshine', but, sadly, neither provided a hit for the increasingly underrated founder of The Walker Brothers. (According to John, Scott's ultimate ambition as a producer was to work with his teenage idol Elvis Presley, who had, Engel believed, the ultimate romantic balladeer's voice.)

He also took on a further handful of cabaret dates (which he described as "terrifying", due to the proximity of the audience) and went to Paris before Christmas to record the theme to *Cemetery Without Crosses*, French actor/director Robert Hossein's variation on the popular 'spaghetti Westerns' then being made in Almeria, Spain. The lyric was by Hollywood songwriter Hal Shaper, the music closer to Lee Hazlewood's *Trouble Is A Lonesome Town* album than the classic Ennio Morricone sound.[15] Shaper's jaunty ballad of revenge

142

and death is akin to 'Do Not Forsake Me Oh My Darlin' from *High Noon*: "But oh my darlin' if I should die / There's not a soul who will ever know that I loved you so was the reason why."

But the serious business of the season was to complete his next solo album, the eponymous *Scott 3*. By this stage, pop music hardly figured in his aesthetic. As Scott told *Disc & Music Echo*, his main influences were now, "Beethoven, because he was the greatest expert in his medium who ever lived, Shostakovich, because he was the last of the great symphonists and Brahms, because it is wonderfully intellectual music."

Scott 3 would be released almost a year after its predecessor, in March 1969. It would carry the following sleeve notes from the faithful Keith Altham, much celebrated for their endearing pretentiousness:

Narcissus in Metamorphis [*sic*][16]
Tearing at his well known image
Behind which he hides his unknown face
Grey rains and trains cascading crying strings
Tracing dribbling rivulets down beaded window panes
Yesterday that only those who live inside themselves know
Aged Renoir peers anxiously down upon an endless pink ribbon
Which fills the room with sounds of cellophane till Copenhagen is
In your ears and eyes and understanding mine today and yours
tomorrow...

You get the general drift. What's most interesting about Altham's piece is how the shape of the lines expands to a furthest point and then recedes back in again – almost like the blocks of text Engel would fashion for his more challenging pieces decades hence. The music journalist/PR man did also make the odd interesting observation about the songs' subject matter: "Colossal the requiem for Big Louise so sad his faded beauty huge loneliness"; "Awake Walt Disney and listen to the 30 Century Man the ice cream man cometh."[17]

Scott 3 almost matched the success of its predecessor, reaching number three on the chart. It's most remarkable in that it's almost an album of Engel originals – with the by now traditional Brel songs relegated to the last three tracks. The arrangements (uncredited this time) are all semi-classical in style, but range from soft-focus cinematic to the verge of atonality.

The opening 'It's Raining Today' is of the latter. The narrative that emerges from its cluster of stray chords is of fascination with a girl glimpsed from a train window. But Engel apparently wrote it as a memoir of his beat-era drifting across America. ("She smiles through the smoke from my cigarette," may be the non-smoker's means of coming over as Bohemian.) Essentially it's a romantic evocation of memory which most of us could relate to: "Those moments descend on my windowpane / I've hung around here too long."

'Copenhagen' is a beautifully sentimental celebration of what was now Scott's favourite city, at least in part because it was the home capital of Mette – whose smiling face features in the cameo brooch-shaped shots on the gatefold. But it was also the home of Hans Christian Andersen, whose fairy-tale world is evoked in the lyric: "Children aren't afraid to love / And laugh when life amuses them. / And our love is an antique song / For children's carousels."

'Rosemary' is a cinematic evocation of a spinster and her memory of short-lived lost love: "He smelled of miracles / With stained glass whispers / You loved his laughter / You tremble beneath him once again." Rosemary lives in a monochrome kitchen-sink world with her old mother and her elderly friends. She wants another shot at life but, like so many of us, placates herself by "watch[ing] the wind and seeing another dream blowing by". Scott claimed to base Rosemary on a friend of his, but one assumes he was too gentlemanly to use her real name. It's because of heart-rending personal snapshots like this (or 'Mrs Murphy', or 'Such A Small Love') that a Midwesterner briefly became the poet laureate of quietly desperate British city dwellers and suburbanites.

'Big Louise' is simply a historic moment. Its stately tempo is almost a still life, a respectful portrait of a transvestite prostitute who is never actually identified as such. We just know that, looking down from

144

her "fire escape in the sky", she's like the big-boned 'girl' seen in the gatefold: "She's a haunted house / And her windows are broken / And the sad young man's gone away." Just like some of the strangely proportioned, long-handed ladies that can still be seen living in Soho today. But Louise is as human as any of us. When Scott sings, "Didn't time sound sweet yesterday?", we know she's caught in the same whirling spiral of events and regrets that we are.

'We Came Through' is an ironic march of triumphalism at a *Champion The Wonder Horse* tempo.[18] It pokes fun at self-aggrandisers in a world of bloodshed and defeat – "And we're giants as we watch our kings and countries raise their shields / And Guevara dies encased in their ideals / And as Luther King's predictions fade from view... – to a closing cascade of gunfire that's '1812 Overture' meets the Alamo.

'Butterfly' is one of what Engel described as his haiku-like "miniatures": a 1.42 portrait of a girl racing across a beach during a rainstorm. "Like a butterfly lost in all this vast space. I tried to get close to Debussy or Delius. That fluttering feeling," he described.

'Two Ragged Soldiers' is another evocative short movie in itself, with Scott romanticising two Bowery bums (his inspiration, gleaned from *Time* magazine's photo journalism) as if they're the expectant down-at-heel heroes of Samuel Beckett's play *Waiting For Godot*: "One would speak of a lake where he used to go swimming / The other had no memories left for his mind." Engel spoke in the late sixties of how he was seen as a cynic with no sentimentalism in him (which seems extraordinary when listening to the records now); this track, like many others, belies such a shallow accusation. When he sings of how the 'two ragged soldiers' "laughed for a world filled with fantasy", he (along with us) shares their humanity.

'30 Century Man' is the now celebrated mock-celebration of the brave new world of immortality, where "you can freeze like a 30 century man". Stripped of the orchestration that permeates the DNA of the other tracks, Scott's pared-down voice, with just his six-string guitar, becomes rock 'n' roll surly. An opposite miniature, 'Winter Night', is a late autumnal lament to dying love with Brahmsian strings, a soundtrack to a weepy late fifties/early sixties film that exists only in the listener's imagination.

'Two Weeks Since You've Gone', the last Engel original, is like an extension of the previous track, the full-length confessional of a man who longs for his lover, rather than leaves her: "I could read all my sadness / In faces I knew... And if I walk these streets long enough / Will you happen to me again?"

And there, after the final flourishes of Walker sings Brel, ends a masterpiece. Scott would fret that 'the Establishment' (i.e. Philips Records) were sceptical of whether the general public could understand what he was relaying to them – but, for the time being, this was no impediment to his success.

Scott 3 would also find an unlikely promotional vehicle. In 1967, on the verge of his solo career, its creator had said, "I live the life of a recluse, not out of choice or any mistaken notion that I am creating an image or sympathy for myself, but because this is the way I am."

From March 4, 1969, this recluse could be seen over the space of six Tuesday nights in the UK's living rooms from 9.50-10.20pm. Expressing relief at having got through the pilot shows "without dying", *Scott* was a continuation of the format of the two TV specials shown the previous autumn. "This *is* Scott Walker," fanfared the BBC announcer to the tune of an orchestral arrangement of 'Joanna'.

"I think the BBC probably thought they were going to get a kind of Jack Jones sort of show," Ed Bicknell later remarked, "probably with [finger-clicking/drum brushes], that kind of thing, and there's Scott singing doomy ballads and refusing to do his hits."

"I suppose at the time Scott was considered to be a crooner," concurs Simon Raymonde, son of Walkers arranger Ivor, "but he wasn't like Jack Jones or Perry Como or Matt Monro, he wasn't Las Vegas, he was more, you know, Parisian or Left Bank."

Except it wasn't quite like that. For every 'It's Raining Today' (surprisingly showcased on the show) and Brel translation, there was Scott graciously introducing favourite Brit-jazz performers

146

like Blossom Dearie or The Dudley Moore Trio,[19] or his pop contemporaries like Gene Pitney or Trent and Hatch, or singing showbiz standards and Broadway show tunes with good old Johnny Franz at the piano.

For all the clashes with series producer Johnnie Stewart[20] (whose name used to run over the line drawing of a man sitting on a stool at the end of *Top Of The Pops* in the sixties), the tension seemed to create a musical balance that the audience enjoyed. (Viewing figures were said to outstrip *The Tom Jones Show*, on ITV.) There was no longer just one Scott Walker, but an innovative artist who shared corporeal space with a technically proficient crowd pleaser, and was at times rather at odds with him.

"I think he's developed his vocal prowess," assesses long-time admirer David Bowie. "He's just got the most amazing range and control. And he's been very clever, because he has the kind of voice that can topple over into Broadway: 'I see the sun in the sky!' And you get that kind of '*sky-yy!*' pronunciation. He never gets into that at all. It's a hard sell, that kind of voice in this day and age."

In the wake of both *Scott 3* and the TV series, Philips demanded another single from Scott – as they'd done when he followed the only slightly less innovative *Scott 2* with 'Joanna'. His agreement to record a song by British hitmaker Tony Macaulay[21] was apparently done under sufferance, not having the personal connection with Macaulay that he had with Hatch and Trent. The song, however, while pure MOR, was a little more interesting than 'Joanna'.

'The Lights Of Cincinnati' is a gently melodic paean to leaving the Midwest and your lover behind: "I remember still / I guess I always will / That winter's day I took the westbound plane..." Scott may have laughed on *Top Of The Pops* when he sang the line "I can see me there in that same old rocking chair," but behind the sentimental backing singers and harmonica accompaniment, there was at least a little personal history – Cincinnati was the neighbouring city to his birthplace of Hamilton, and Grandpa Scott had played the fiddle there long before his rocking chair days were through.

"If you listened to my single, you might get the impression that was the way I was going, but if you listen to my album you must see I'm not. Everything goes hand in hand in this business," reflected Scott of the now schizoid nature of his career. The record hit number 13 in the charts.

In June 1969, Philips issued *Scott: Scott Walker Sings Songs From His TV Series*, a selection of standards and covers rerecorded under the aegis of John Franz. There were no Engel originals and there was no Brel (not even the unrecorded 'Alone'), but there were some standout tracks: 'Who (Will Take My Place' is a translation of the Aznavour ballad 'Qui?', also covered in English by Dusty Springfield; oft dismissed as pure sentimentality, this reflection of an older lover on who will fill the space in his bed and his lover's heart if he dies is almost as moving in its way as the more brittle ruminations of Brel.

Scott jumps momentarily back into the Belgian's shoes in 'The Impossible Dream', at a time when Brel was still singing it in French ('La Queste') on the Paris stage; its famous lyric is a Broadway summation of the deluded knight Don Quixote's personal mission – "This is my quest, to follow that star / No matter how hopeless, no matter how far" – and Scott's vocal bravura makes it his own.

'The Look Of Love' is further Scott-Dusty crossover; he can't be expected to eclipse her version of the Bacharach-David tune, but his take is laid-back and lustrous; similarly, 'Country Girl' is a richly orchestrated ballad formerly a hit for Tony Bennett and Engel shows his affinity for that performer too, as he does with bossa noval legend Antonio Carlos Jobim's 'Someone To Light Up My Life'.

The album ends with 'Lost In The Stars', from the 1949 Kurt Weill-Maxwell Anderson musical set in the racially troubled South Africa; its imagery of God looking out over the country receives a moving treatment from the atheistic vocalist – who would reconfirm the potency of religious imagery on his next original work.

The cover actually contains one of the classic Scott Walker images: looking like a long drink of water all dressed in black, his hands-onhips pose reveals the key to Quarr Abbey hanging on a chain around his neck.

When he hit the seaside circuit in July, however, the dichotomy between the two sides of his career became obvious.

"I'm now going to sing a medley of my hits in the past year. I'm joining them together, because they are boring for me and this way they won't take long," he told a Blackpool audience of 'Joanna' and 'The Lights Of Cincinnati'. Still mixing scotch with nerve pills, he also treated them to two performances of 'Black Sheep Boy' without realising he'd done so. Some of the crowd reportedly asked for their money to be refunded.

While still living at his third-floor flat in St John's Wood, Engel was making regular trips back to Copenhagen with Mette and to an apartment they'd recently found in Amsterdam. His prolific workload was also completed by producing debut albums that summer for two of the jazz musicians who played behind him: *Ray Warleigh's First Album* by his alto sax player and *Fallout* by guitarist Terry Smith. Both were melodic without being radical, with riffs on popular songs (including one or two that had been sung by Scott), similar to how US jazz flautist Herbie Mann improvised on Sam & Dave's 'Hold On I'm Comin'' on his *Memphis Underground* that same year.

Back home in London, the two ex-brothers continued to associate. John Maus had moved back, living not far from where Engel resided. They would get together with Mette and John's second-wife-to-be (he was now divorced), with Mimi (Scott's mother Betty) coming over from LA to join them from time to time. It was around this time that Scott alerted his former partner to some underhand dealings by their shared management:

"Scott and I had always received our royalties every six months... now the cheques required both Scott's signature and mine. One day I received a call from Scott, who asked me if I knew that we had just received a royalty cheque at the office. I told him no. He disclosed to me that Maurice's plan was to deposit the cheque and split it with him, hoping I wouldn't find out... he was just beginning to realise that Maurice was not the best manager to be around."

By that late summer of 1969, the American Selective Service had also made it clear to Maurice King that Noel Scott Engel had to present himself to the draft induction board or else face extradition proceedings. King and Engel sailed via the *SS France* to New York, where Scott took the standard physical and psychological tests. He was deemed to be '4F' – after four and a half years of pursuing him, the draft board had decreed him psychologically unfit for service in Vietnam.[22]

Despite his manager's role in finally getting him exempted from mortal combat, Scott would abruptly leave Maurice King's management soon after. Already suspicious of his behaviour, Scott was confronted at the time by a New York lawyer demanding $10,000 he'd been promised by King for getting their case through the draft board. When Engel in turn demanded to know what was going on from his manager, the payment King had been trying to renege upon was eventually coughed up.

It fatally undermined any remaining trust between manager and client. At the end of the summer, Scott sent a solicitor's letter to Capable Management at Bickenhall Mansions, announcing that he was dispensing with King's services.

Maurice King was distraught. He'd lost his new Sinatra. Unlike his former partner, Barry Clayman, he drifted out of the music industry and tried his hand at other business. (He would die in June 1977, after several years of chronic alcoholism and barbiturate abuse. Suicide has been suggested but never confirmed.)

Scott Engel was now without management but was showing no signs of slowing down. Incredibly, he was about to release his third album of 1969 – the recording that many admirers consider his magnum opus.

"He absolutely became part of the culture," *30 Century Man* director Stephen Kijak told this writer of that late sixties period. "It's really amazing how deeply engrained that music and those songs were through all those decades – really part of the fabric of the British imagination in a lot of ways. If you're into the music of the sixties, he's there – he is always there, now in the most serious of ways. The thing is, I think England cherishes and nurtures its eccentrics a hell of a lot better than America, you know what I mean?"

That's certainly always said to be the case. In practice, however, the least conformist of performers and their audiences can sometimes alienate each other. In the late sixties, this suddenly appeared to be the case with Scott Walker.

'I Want To Get Out Of Pop' ran one headline in *Melody Maker*. *Disc* echoed the sentiment with the following:

> 'I Want To Be Alone Says SCOTT' talking to Mike Ledgerwood
>   Privacy is becoming a personal 'context' with Scott Walker. And he will go to inordinate lengths to ensure he gets it.
>   "I don't believe you belong to your public," he explained...
>
> Now, also, Scott hopes his face will be completely eclipsed from the scene. He wants to try and lose the original star 'image' built up so carefully with The Walker Brothers.

In the *MM*, during this most productive late sixties period, a disgruntled bunch, signing themselves '14 ex-Scott Walker fans, 28 Kent Street, Lower Broughton, Salford 7', composed a limerick-like poem that dripped with teenage vitriol:

> His claim to fame is somewhat hazy, / His attitude to life is lazy, / This pinnacle of mastered voice, / Conveys perfection with little choice, / His golden lights reflect / This glistening star so circumspect, / But all that glistens is not gold they say / And before his fame fades far away / One cold hard fact we wish to state: / They say that love's akin to hate. / He gives no thought for his fan's strife / As long as he can live his life. / He has no time to entertain / He's failed to show up once again. / Could the king have lost his crown? / Has this legend now lain down? / The lonely young long distance Walker, / The avid Brel and Sartre talker; / Don't underestimate our force / The end is nigh,

151

you're way off course. / Your reign is over – goodbye Scott. / Face it man – you've had your lot!

All of the above was in the period immediately predating the promised *Scott 4*, when Scott had cancelled a week's booking at the Golden Garter Theatre in Wythenshawe, Greater Manchester and announced that henceforth he was to be known under his birthname.

Even in the immediate aftermath of *Scott 3*'s release, and its commercial success, the chronically self-doubting Engel had fretted: "The melody lines were too long and people were puzzled... So *Scott 4* is gonna be much harder and tighter." When it arrived, even the sleeve notes this time were subject to a compact minimalism, consisting of a quote from Camus: "A man's work is nothing but this slow trek to rediscover through the detours of art, those two or three great or simple images in whose presence his heart first opened."

It served as a strong but simple statement of intent. The album cover showed an intensely gazing Scott – with head bowed slightly forward and the key chain around his neck – but credited the work to Noel Scott Engel. Again, it was a statement of belief in the work, though it would not be without its own ramifications.

The album came with a lyric sheet this time and a diverse selection of pictures: Scott at work in the Philips studio with Franz and Olliff; arrangers Stott, Knight and (new man) Keith Roberts conducting their musicians; Albert Camus, at some point between winning the Nobel Prize for Literature in 1957 and his death three years later; a soldier in Vietnam; Comrade Josef Stalin; Max Von Sydow as the Knight and his chess opponent, Death, in Bergman's *The Seventh Seal*.

"I was interested in film, European film, and I'd always been," confirmed Engel to Kijak regarding his long-time fascination with *The Seventh Seal*. "When I got here I found that everyone wanted to talk about American films, so I was the classic bore at the party. And even when I went to live in Scandinavia, I though well, everyone's going to be interested in talking about Bergman and Dreyer, and no one was interested, they all wanted to watch Woody Allen movies I think."

The opening track of the album, 'The Seventh Seal' is in effect a detailed synopsis of the film, set to a Spanish guitar and lonesome trumpet backing that evokes the spaghetti western soundtracks of Morricone. On that basis, it's like the theme song to some exploitation-movie style remake[23] – but it's also one of the most imaginatively and emotionally affecting pieces Engel ever recorded.

"Anybody hear of plague in this town? / The town I've left behind was burned to the ground / A young girl on a stake her face framed in flames cried, 'I'm not a witch.'" Bursts of Gregorian chant punctuate the existential horror, as if Engel and Franz had somehow managed to pre-invent the audio sampling process. The Knight's chess game with Master Death postpones his own end, but his quest to "feel God's heart in mine" seems doomed.

Scott 4, the most accessible of all the late sixties Philips albums, consists of Engel originals only. It also contains several tracks as remarkable in their own way as 'The Seventh Seal'. The classical influences are often present but sublimated, in comparison to the overtly string-driven *Scott 3*.

'Angels Of Ashes' is a hypnotic acoustic ballad, vaguely reminiscent of Leonard Cohen's 'Sisters Of Mercy' (which used convent imagery as a metaphor for prostitutes) but more literary than the Canadian singing poet. In his lyric, the singing existentialist[24] pursues images of supernatural redemption, rather than hookers in nuns' habits: "Let the great constellation of flickering ashes be heard / Let them burn with a fire, all it takes to confess is a word... You can say that he laughed, and he walked like St Francis, with love."

'Boy Child' is both breathtaking and all-enveloping, deservedly lending its name to a 1990 compilation of late sixties Engel originals. A work of wonderment, its string arrangement swells up to embrace the listener in a way that synthesizers or mellotrons (popular in the late sixties/early seventies) never could, as the plucked strings of a hammer dulcimer rise above it. Its lyrics are both simple and mysteriously opaque: "Echoes of laughter / Hide in the city's thighs... What can it cost to give a Boy Child back his sight?" The image of the Boy Child which "rides upon your back" is the early identity which follows us at all times, if we allow him/her to; tremulous, unsure, but always childlike in his or her curiosity.

In contrast, 'The Old Man's Back Again' is accessibility itself. An audacious, almost funky, bass-driven song, its subject matter is dictated by its subtitle ('Dedicated To The Neo-Stalinist Regime') and its historical period – mere months after the 'Prague Spring' political reforms of January-August 1968 had been crushed by invading Warsaw Pact troops, authorised by Leonid Brezhnev, Krushchev's successor as Communist Pary chairman.

Rather than a literal protest song, Engel imagines the military repression in metaphorical terms: "I seen a hand / I seen a vision / It was reaching through the clouds to risk a dream." He also sympathises with the Soviet soldier sent to suppress someone else's culture: "He'd like another name – the one he's got a curse these people cry. / Why can't they understand? / His mother called him Ivan, then she died."

"I don't like some of the things that are happenin' in Russia at the moment," Scott confirmed at the time. "It's neo-Stalinism... The Czechs, on the other hand, went about things the wrong way for a socialist state. What was done to them was cruel, but probably necessary in order to prevent the break-up of somethin' for which so many people have worked so hard and suffered so long."

He was sounding like Sartre, the epitome of the educated middle-class radical who argued with Camus that he could not condemn Soviet repression for fear of "disappointing the working classes". In his book *L'Homme Revolte* (*The Rebel*), the working-class intellectual Camus pointed out the absurdity of "slave camps under the flag of freedom, massacres justified by philanthropy".

Scott Engel would come round to Camus' point of view. But for now he just warned that "the old man's back again" – the 'old man' being the bear-like spectre of Uncle Joe Stalin – and, most audaciously perhaps, went out on a line of scat singing as if he'd just ended a political debate at Ronnie Scott's Jazz Club.

Scott 4 remains the most immediately affecting of the late sixties Philips period – and one which many people regard as his best, including Scott 4, the post-punk/country-rock band who saw fit to name themselves after the album. Part of the reason for this is the easy listening quality of the tracks between its standout masterpieces: the 'miniatures' 'On Your Own Again' and [Not] 'The World's Strongest Man' are pretty much defined by their titles. 'Hero Of The War' cocks a snook at the mother of an injured soldier whose husband formerly died in a war, but also (rather mercilessly, considering Scott's sympathy for the Russian soldier in the anti–Stalinist song) at the soldier himself: "It's so absurd feeling empty, / It's the emptiness of heroes like your son, / And what made him leave his mother for a gun?" Scott scats out at the end of this one too.

The final three tracks of the album show the direction that his songwriting might have headed in had this record been a commercial (rather than just artistic) success: 'Get Behind Me' is an only partially convincing attempt to rock out, missing the power of 'The Plague'; but 'Duchess' and 'Rhymes Of Goodbye' are beautifully crafted pieces of country rock, relying on Scott's understatedly powerful vocals and guitar accompaniment rather than any grandiose arrangements. "It's your bicycle bells and your Rembrandt swells... makes me feel like a thief when you're bleeding," he erotically praises the candle-lighting 'Duchess' of the former song. "The bells of our senses can cost us our pride / Can toll out the boundaries that level our lives... roaring through darkness the night children fly / I still hear them singing the rhymes of goodbye," runs the closing lyric, just a metaphor or two away from being an abstract.

The album was one of the greatest musical releases of the closing decade. And on its release, hardly anyone bought it. In fact it didn't even figure on the record charts.

"*Scott 4* tried to link lyrics by Sartre, Camus and Yevtushenko to Bartok modal lines, but nobody noticed," Scott would later wryly tell

Phil McNeill at the *NME*. "Those first three albums sold very well. When I made the fourth album I was livin' abroad [in Holland]… You gotta figure the state of mind I was in, in a foreign country, in total isolation."

It was a theory, at least. And everyone who ever heard the album seems to have a theory as to why it fared so badly.

"And so Scott was being pushed aside, I suppose, by the new wave of British rock bands that came along at the end of the sixties/early seventies," suggests Ed Bicknell, "because we then went into King Crimson, Emerson, Lake & Palmer, Yes – God, *Yes!*" He feigns vomiting.

"It got me, that's it!" says Richard Hawley of *Scott 4*. "What other artist, apart from really cheesy prog-rock, could get away with using a big fuck-off gong to start off with?" But if the term 'progressive rock' meant anything,[25] then surely *Scott 4* exemplified it? After all, Scott Engel had now embraced elements of rock music and was clearly starting to progress along more than one line.

"When everybody else was kind of like up their own arse with all that hippie crap – because love and peace is an ideal, it's not a fashion item, all that disappeared really, really quickly – everybody else was going to San Francisco, he was delving into the dark psyche of man."

But there again, Scott had started to delve into our darker corners ever since The Walker Brothers had split and had not suffered commercially for it. What happened with *Scott 4* was clearly something quite different.

"I have a theory about it, you can take it for what it's worth," says Engel himself, "but it was mostly written in 3/4 [time] and it just didn't lock onto anybody. And by the time the fourth album came around a lot of people thought, 'I'll pass on that.' When I do something like that, even when I'm doing stuff today, that's always in the back of my head, you know, people are not going to like it. And so I'm not disappointed – I'm more disappointed when I don't bring something off."

As a musician's explanation, it's as good as any. However, in Anthony Reynolds' book on The Walker Brothers he posits that both Scott and his fans, in the late sixties, had touched upon how 'killing' the Walker surname had caused confusion. This writer, being just about old enough to have first entered record shops in the early seventies, can vouch for that: this was before the computer age and all listings were printed; if the shop assistant (who wasn't always that switched onto music) hadn't heard of a record then you were told it didn't exist. If you asked for the new Scott Walker album when *Scott 4* came out, you'd either be given *Scott: Scott Walker Sings Songs From His TV Series* or you'd be told there wasn't one. If the store had alphabetical racks, if you looked under 'W' then you weren't going to find 'Noel Scott Engel' there.

All subsequent reissues of *Scott 4* would be credited to Scott Walker. But that was over two decades away. Within several months of its initial release, the album would slip into oblivion. A crucial recording career had been subverted by a name on a record.

✳✳✳

In the late summer/early autumn of 1969, Scott Walker's career spun on a coin. In Britain, his adopted culture, his commercial fall had been as abrupt as his rise. But he was a European now, and he wouldn't be going 'home'. Rather than climbing up the backroads into the Hollywood Hills, he'd temporarily live the life of a barfly, strolling along the streets of Amsterdam.

Besides, back in California at this time, American culture was continuing to spiral downwards into senseless violence. As Gary Leeds explains:

"Along with many other musicians and actors we used to have [our hair] cut by Jay Sebring, whose shop was in West Hollywood... None of us ever could have anticipated what would happen to Sebring in 1969. I remember Dennis Wilson of The Beach Boys telling me about a guy he met called Charles Manson. Dennis had picked up two girl hitchhikers who were part of what Manson called his 'family'... He was a writer and musician, and when Dennis heard some of his music he liked it. I believe he even recorded a couple of Manson's tunes with The Beach Boys. Later Manson met Terry Melcher, Doris Day's son, who was then staying at a house on Cielo Drive with Candice Bergen, his girlfriend. Manson wanted Terry, a record producer, to sign him up for a record deal, but Dennis and Terry eventually decided to have nothing more to do with Manson."

As much as Scott Engel was uncomfortable with the lifestyle of a star, to Charlie Manson it would become a matter of life and death. Layers of myth and mystique have been woven around the reasons why his LSD-addled 'family' did what they did, but the more prosaic explanation of rejection by the music industry still seems to hold true. As for Sebring, he'd apparently moved at this time from being a celebrity hairdresser to being a celebrity drug dealer, then hawking MDA, an early form of ecstasy.

"Sometime after Terry and Candice moved out of that house on Cielo Drive, Roman Polanski[26] leased it for himself with his wife, the [pregnant] actress Sharon Tate," continues Gary. "The house was the site of the brutal [August '69] murders of Sharon Tate and others, including Jay Sebring, who were slaughtered by members of Manson's 'family'... Scott and I couldn't believe that Sebring, our hairdresser and friend, had been killed. I guess we were quite lucky: we had once moved in that circle, and could easily have been in the wrong place at the wrong time."

"I couldn't stand the social climate of the States, we just didn't go together," Engel had said the year after arriving in England. "All the needless violence and killing... There's an enormous amount of brain deterioration going on in America and I hate seeing it, it got me down. I like some things about the States but I couldn't live there."

There would be no going home, even if he had to remain stateless.

Notes

1   This was the cover heading of issue four of *Scott Times*, a Xeroxed Japanese fanzine. Throughout the ups and down of Scott Engel's early solo career, a diminishing but hardcore cadre of Jap fans kept the faith.

2   Many of the concerts were recorded, but an album entitled *The Walker Brothers In Japan* would not be issued until 1987, on the sixties-retro Bam Caruso label.

3   His hair may have been dyed a darker shade in deference to his Japanese audience. But his former blondness seemed to be darkening with age, as can be seen in the front and back cover photos of *Scott 2*.

4   Scott Engel's friendship with Jonathan King – who once edited an issue of *Granta* literary magazine in late 1966, elicting a kind of post-beat Kerouac-style epilogue from his friend – remains back in the sixties. This seems less to do with King's subsequent infamy than Engel's need to stay locked in the present. In the seventies, when Scott became a covers artist and later moved on into a much more rarefied musical field, King was seducing young boys from the Walton Hop disco in leafy Surrey.

5   For further evidence, listen to Scott singing the Cilla Black hit 'A Fool Am I' on the previously unreleased Walker Brothers tracks of *Everything Under The Sun*.

6   Anthony Reynolds suggests the name comes from an obscure American children's fiction character.

7   The sensitive Engel, with his delicate taste in women, seems unlikely to have much experience of working girls.

8   Not least in the woman's name – though Brel's 'Madeleine' is a knockabout vaudevillian number about a girl who may or may not turn up on dates.

9   Former pop singer Sarne recorded the novelty record 'Come Outside' with Wendy Richard, later of *Are You Being Served?* and *EastEnders*, for producer Joe Meek. Sarne later became an actor and also produced several films – including the eponymous *Joanna*.

10   Recently declassified information suggests Bobby Kennedy played a major role in handling the Cuban missile crisis during his late brother John's presidency. His combination of playing hardball, realpolitik and diplomacy may even deserve the accolade 'the man who saved the world' – without his actions, it's unlikely Scott Walker would have made it to London. Or, indeed, that most readers of this book would have been born.

11   Sirhan Sirhan, convicted assassin of Bobby Kennedy, was actually a Palestinian migrant to the US. He allegedly confessed at the scene and blamed the Democrats' support of Israel for his crime. At trial he claimed no memory of the event. Doubts were raised as to how a shot fired into the back of Kennedy's head could have come from Sirhan in front of the podium, but he remains a prisoner into his dotage – the subject of theories about how pre-programming might create a 'Manchurian Candidate' killer prepared to take the rap.

12   This mildly controversial remark was given in interview to Nick Logan of the *NME*, later the paper's editor. It provoked enough of a response for Engel himself

to send an earnest missive to the paper the following week: "I may talk in riddles as I chase my thoughts like a madman, [but] I am no modern day Don Quixote, attempting to battle windmills... and I beg Mr Logan's forgiveness if I didn't make myself understood."

13 British soul singer Kiki Dee was chiefly known as a backing vocalist to Dusty at this point, although her early solo records received play on pirate radio. In the seventies she would find fame after signing to Elton John's Rocket Records and releasing a gorgeous version of the French ballad 'Amoureuse'. Much of her subsequent life has been linked to Elton, from duetting with him on number one hit 'Don't Go Breaking My Heart' to marrying his former guitarist, Davey Johnstone.

14 Vivian Stanshall of The Bonzos developed a similar cross-dependence on Valium and booze to Scott – a habit Engel would kick, though it stayed with Stanshall much longer. The downer habit is known to make holes in the memory: "Frank, it must be three years!" Viv later greeted old friend Frank Zappa. "It's been *13* years," Zappa admonished him.

15 Hazlewood himself may have influenced the spaghetti western sound – play his 1966 'Friday's Child' and the theme from that same year's *Django* back to back, then decide which is the chicken and which is the egg.

16 Altham is referencing the Italian surrealist painting *Narcissus In Metamorphosis* – principally because the myth of Narcissus gazing on his own reflection in a pool is reflexively evoked by the front cover shot of a pensive Scott reflected in a young woman's eye. The rest of the gatefold was a composite of images taken by photographer Chris Walter, loosely reflecting the song's subjects: "I remember we drove around London one Sunday morning in Scott's Mini, looking for gargoyles and tramps to photograph."

17 Disney had died in 1966 and famously arranged for his body to be cryogenically frozen, in the hope that the human race would one day overcome the affliction known as death. This is the subject of '30 Century Man' – although Scott references not Disney but Charles De Gaulle, who he seems to believe will survive immortally until the subject's resurrection. (General De Gaulle would actually die in the following year, 1970.)

18 An American b&w kids' TV programme popular in Britain at the time.

19 Other guests included Esther Ofarim, the Israeli singer of immensely irritating novelty hit 'Cinderella Rockafella'. Her presence on the show would, however, become significant.

20 "What about all the sick people in hospitals?" Stewart had asked when Scott wanted to perform Brel's 'Funeral Tango'. Indeed, Engel could have responded, what about the rest of us too? The mortality rate still stands at 100 percent and Brel was writing his songs for all of us.

21 Composer of 'Love Grows (Where My Rosemary Goes)' and myriad others. In the sixties Macaulay was something of a one-man hit factory. In the seventies, he was a good enough sport for his writer friend Dick Clement to spoof him in the film

of prison sitcom *Porridge*: "Tony Macaulay's on our team," boasts the manager of a 'celebrity' football squad, "have you heard of him?" "No!" spit back a prisoner and warder.

22 Rumours persisted that Scott evaded the draft by pretending to be homosexual – but there's no real evidence for this, even though many people used it as their get-out clause (including some rock stars).

23 It's arguable that US director Roger Corman had already remade *The Seventh Seal*, when he appropriated its plague imagery and came to England to make his version of Poe's *The Masque Of The Red Death* about 18 months before the Walkers arrived.

24 Existentialism is not necessarily synonymous with atheism – the former term was first applied to Danish philosophical writer Søren Kierkegaard, who made a commitment to Christianity in recognition of humankind's need for meaning in its existence.

25 The usual cultural connotations of 'prog-rock' are post-hippie noodling. But it was an umbrella term that covered a whole range of vices and virtues. Jazz-inflected experimentalists like King Crimson might have seen Scott as a fellow '21st century schizoid man'.

26 One of the greatest of the sixties wave of Euro-film directors, by then a migrant to Hollywood.

Chapter 8

Easy Come, Easy Go

"You're riding high in April / Shot down in May."

– Kelly Gordon/Dean Kay, *'That's Life',* as sung by Frank Sinatra

"The wheel is come full circle; I am here."

– William Shakespeare, *King Lear*

The man who now traversed the canals and bicycle paths of Amsterdam had reverted to being 'Scott Walker'. "Fuck it, I don't care, y'know?" he shrugged. "A name doesn't mean anything to me."

Maybe it didn't any more. For the time being though, his singing career still did. Even that was going through a kind of hiatus while he visited art galleries, walked his dog in the streets without fear of harassment, or downed bottles of Heineken with whisky chasers in local bars. "I had this thing once a year when I called everybody and said I'm quittin'," he told Chris Welch at the *Melody Maker* in March 1970. "The last time everybody said: 'We thought you already had.'"

When presented with a best male vocalist award (and a cup of hot sake) by perennially faithful Japanese magazine *Music Life* that same month, while in Tokyo to play a concert, he gave a (very approximately translated here[1]) appraisal of his immediate plans: "I will make *Scott 5*, but before I have to make one LP and also one single."

It's not exactly clear what he had in mind – but the mix of Engel originals and covers that would see release by the end of the year would be as close to *Scott 5* as he'd ever get.

"I [also] want to sing in other countries' languages, for example Hungarian, Russian and Japanese... and also of course French."

All these ambitions would fall by the wayside. But in the decades that followed, Scott Engel would become an artist who skirted around the edge of language – who found his own meaning in collages of sounds and words.

For now, however, when asked if he thought he had changed, he replied (in that quaintly translated English):

Now I don't think I'm going to fight things like before. Except pushing myself into things ... certainly like concerts, I'm quite fixed on that. At the last moment I retreated at the wall, I was scared of everything. It was always so. Before, sometimes, I lost my head.

Q. When are you happiest in your life?
I'm happiest when I think about the 'creativity of man' ... when a man creates something ... Of course I'm happy when I go see movies and I'm hearing music. Now I'm most pleased when I go see operas and movies."

Q. For you, what do fans mean?
First of all I dislike the word 'fan'. It's very disagreeable, the word should not be used, I think. Once I was one of The Walker Brothers, but now I think there are no hysterical fans. How do you feel if I call them 'the listeners of my records' or 'the audience of my concerts'? They can keep me alive or kill me ...

There then followed a series of questions and word associations that mainly relate to the end of the sixties, which subsequently ran in Engel fanzine *Scott Times*:

Q. What do you think about the activities for peace of John and Yoko?
S. It's only a devotion to egoism.

From the next word, please tell me the thing that you imagine:
1) God – Mankind
2) Death – Mankind
3) Love – Mankind
4) Woman – Out of Space
5) Human Being – Mankind
6) Man – Earth
7) Hippy – Hallucinations
8) Japan – I can't say it in one word
9) Religion – Fascinating
10) War – Fascinating
11) Scott Engel – Man
12) Sex – Exhilarating
13) Mother – Past
14) Father – Non-Existent
15) Politics – Good exercise
16) Fashion – Waste of time
17) America – Waste of time
18) Time – Waste
19) The Beatles – Overrated
20) Marriage – Necessary evil
21) Baby – Very necessary
22) Elvis Presley – Very necessary to my past
23) Bob Dylan – Beautiful[2]
24) Jean-Paul Sartre – Beautiful
25) Marijuana or Acid – Useful and distracting[3]

Asked if he'd had plans to appear in a film, he replied, "Yes, I was going to appear in a movie made in Czechoslovakia but I stopped it for one simple reason: I'm not interested in working as an actor at all." Instead, according to the translation, his ambition was to direct "movies of no form" (i.e. abstract films).

"I would love to direct," he confirmed in an English interview. "That's more of a reality now than ever before. I've seen some great continental movies recently, like [Visconti's] *The Damned*."[4]

Scott remained as disinterested as ever in contemporary American film trends: "I saw *Easy Rider*, but the only thing I liked about it was Phil Spector's appearance as the pusher at the beginning."

Film directing would remain an unfulfilled ambition, however. What *would* coalesce, in time, was a melding of musical narrative and abstract imagery.

✶✶✶

Back in London, for all that he now divided much of his time between Denmark and Holland, Scott was granted British citizenship in May 1970. His musical career may have been in stasis, but he had put down new roots.

As for his immediate musical plans, at first he was at a loss. He reverted to the 'plan B' he held in store for times when he was undergoing a crisis of confidence, offering his services as a bass player to bands. But Eric Clapton's new supergroup, Blind Faith, had already recruited their bassist, and neither Georgie Fame nor Alan Price returned his phone calls.

And so he began writing again. Observational songs, based on overheard snippets of conversation, or people he met in bars, or (most especially) the other figures who inhabited his block of flats in Holland. When stoked by his imagination and contained within an imagined environment, it began to gel into that quintessentially seventies artefact: a concept album.

In September Scott took a holiday in Greece, where he played on his acoustic guitar and developed character sketches of the disparate figures inhabiting his apartment block of the mind. On his record to Holland he called up Philips to tell the label he was ready to record again. He would be returning to London soon – with his new manager in tow.

Ady Semel was a sophisticated Israeli who dressed expensively, was well versed in classical music and reputedly spoke five languages. Engel had first met him when one of his charges, the exotic Esther Ofarim, had appeared on his BBC1 show 18 months previously.[5]

He also respected Semel enough to allow himself to be put back into live performance. After the fiasco the previous year, when he'd irritated his audience by reiterating 'Black Sheep Boy' (an incident he later blamed on painkillers for an injury sustained in a car accident), Scott happily took a cabaret residency at the Frontier Club in Batley, West Yorkshire.

(It later emerged that he'd been offered a lesser number of nights at the prestigious Royal Albert Hall at this time. As he admitted, "I never had the guts for the big concert stuff. I'd rather rationalise the frequency of my solo appearances to this one club every year for more money than some of the others combined.")

Descriptions of the gigs suggest he was professionalism itself. Perched atop a stool, he sang a smattering of early Walkers classics, his own most recent hit 45s, a touch of Brel and The Beatles' 'The Long And Winding Road' – a McCartney ballad he particularly admired, by a band he still considered grossly overrated.

Then it was back to Stanhope Place to record the new album in time for a Christmas release, most of which had been written in the space of two weeks. But this time Engel was working with a collaborator, as he explained – or at least a kind of lyrical editor.

"I came back from Greece with the tunes and most of the lyrics done and worked on them with my new manager," he told the *Sunday Mirror* in late November 1970. "He really stopped me going overboard on the songs which I have a tendency to do. He came up with some nice ideas, better ways of getting across my original idea… He acts as my censor, vetting all my lyrics and striking out the words likely to harm old ladies."

It was a big climbdown from his former refusal to compromise. But then Scott was likely to accept interference from the aesthetically attuned Semel in a way that he never would have done with the philistine Maurice King. As to how far Ady Semel actually participated in the lyric writing he was co-credited for, it's unlikely he went beyond toning down the most vivid imagery or language. (Others have suggested it was a purely financial arrangement the manager insisted on; more straightforward, perhaps, than how Colonel Tom Parker insisted on a co-writer's credit for Elvis on his earliest hits, while pocketing much of the royalties himself.)

Not that the album – intended as *Scott 5*, until changed (possibly at Philips' insistence) to *'Til The Band Comes In* – was a complete set of originals. Side one was a particularly vivid set of songs arranged by Wally Stott, while side two mostly consisted of five covers under the auspices of Peter Knight.

Semel, who by now was so omnipresent in his client's career that he actually sat in and made comment on press interviews, wrote sleeve notes which described the album as the combined narratives of "an old-age pensioner, a kept cowboy, a resigned girl lover, a telephone crank, a landlady's grasp of an unneighbourly stripper, an immigrant waiter". The unifying concept is the apartment block in which they all reside, though this cosmopolitan bunch are not only of different nationalities but sometimes seem to be inhabiting different countries.

The album opens with a short 'Prologue', which suggests Scott Engel's classical proclivities may be about to get full reign again. A cello quietly and mournfully scrapes in the style of Brahms while children's voices are heard, doors slam closed and a shouting adult voice is just about audible.

"I like film music," explained Scott, "I respect Jerry Goldsmith and I admire Alex North.[6] They belong to a bygone age, which was very rich and interesting." 'Prologue' segues into 'Little Things (That Keep Us Together)', which is cinematic music of a different kind, its insistently upbeat rhythm recalling the Pearl & Dean ad sections heard in British cinemas at the time. Its lyrics, though, are of the blackest pessimism: "It's on days like these / When your... brother falls from your hands / Jumbo jets can die / Killing 81 / Little things that help us get by" – our shared tabloid morbidity being the explanation of "Why the war's going on."[7]

The bleakness doesn't end there – although it's a more conventionally tuneful melancholy than on any of the *Scott* albums. "As old Joe sat a–dyin' / The baby down the hall was cryin' / "Someone had a party goin' on," runs the musicial obituary of 'Joe', one of the older tenants of the apartment block. The music is lounge piano crooning but, once again upbeat, with Scott taking his existentialism in his stride. (The line, "A postcard from Sun City was found laying by your side" was an obvious jibe at the promoter who tried to get him and John to play South Africa. It's unlikely that a lonely British pensioner, who lived on meals-on-wheels and had "no one left to call me Joe," would have contacts in what was then a playground of the rich and conscienceless.)

'Thanks For Chicago, Mr James' is simply stunning when heard today. Despite the fact that it was never issued as a single, its 'big pop' string arrangement and uplifting chorus (based around the title) can seduce you into believing you're listening to a big hit of the early seventies. Perhaps the reason for its neglect was that the grateful narrator of the song is a "kept cowboy" and the gay element is fairly overt: "Thanks... for all the shiny suits / And all the shiny names / The things a country boy can't grace / Without the look of shame." It was only half a decade before Glen Campbell would sing about a 'Rhinestone Cowboy', but Scott Walker was there first.

'Long About Now' is a beautiful oddity that seems to belong to *Scott 2* or *3* – except that it's sung from a female perspective by Esther Ofarim, as a dreamy precursor to the female vocalists who would later interpret the contemporary Scott. ("Long about now / He's... back from the rain / Burned to the ground / His ashes will rise black butterflies / Tapping at my window pane.")

The arrangements for the album are nowhere near as intricate as those which preceded it over the classic *1-4* – but there's a virtue to that, in that at times it's more accessibly poppy, and it's easy to imagine that Bowie may have given it at least one listen before recording his similarly eclectic *Hunky Dory* the next year.

'Time Operator' sets the tone of pastiche for the next two tracks. To a laid-back ersatz jazz backing, the narrator feeds chat-up lines to the recorded time announcer of the General Post Office's phone service. ("At the third stroke, the time will be..." It sounds almost archaic now, but it's as much of its time as downloadable apps would be today. It's also intrinsically British, whereas the apartment block seems to be a microcosm of the world.) Its seedily humorous tone – "And I wouldn't care if you're ugly / 'Cos with the lights out I couldn't see you," sings Scott, tongue-in-cheekly comparing himself to Paul Newman (as others had done) – leads into a track that's all-out burlesque.

'Jean The Machine' is simply good fun, its ragtime jazz parody already sounding familiar by the early seventies.[8] A Cold War-era comedy tune set to a striptease beat, it tells of a Hungarian 'exotic dancer' whose landlady believes she's a 'commie spy'. "Jean come back (we forgive you!)," runs the joyous ending, "Jean come back (Boy Scout's honour!) / Jean come back (Spiro Agnew!) / Jean come back (to the Bolshoi!)", and for a moment it's like Engel has joined The Bonzo Dog Doo-Dah Band.

'Cowbells Shakin'' is a leftover from Scott's miniatures. Running at under two minutes, its folk-country guitar covers the genuinely moving scenario of a former cowboy adrift without work: "And tell your fat momma the life we've been keepin' / Your head waiter brother won't give me a job / And I've walked these streets till I'm breakin'..." It abandoned the apartment block conceit (though, as stated, the building seems to be a universal microcosm), but it hinted of the highways and prairies where Engel's career would take a detour.

Side two eventually dispenses with the concept altogether, although not in the first two Engel/Semel originals. "Here on the outskirts of life / It's a world with voice of caretaker's wife," opens the title track, and its this loose concept that links the tracks. "The times we sat and sang of all the hidden things we knew / Did they ever come up true? / And it's the time to sing a song / Across the emptiness between us..." It's as if Engel is lamenting the death of his recent career, in vocal and musical arrangements that are less demanding of his listeners.

'The War Is Over (Epilogue)' is a concluding statement – though exactly what it's saying is characteristically not obvious. It's not a peace anthem per se, like the John & Yoko Christmas song of the following year: "Raise your blinds / The war is over / Let me get some sleep tonight." It sounds like a temporary respite in the drama of his characters' lives, a little relief before 'the war' begins all over again.

But the album still has time to run, and there are five cover versions which, if not entirely selected by John Franz or the Philips top brass, would at least be regarded by them as inoffensive enough for inclusion. "Cornball shlock," Scott would later dismiss them,[9] but their variable quality means that some are at least listenable. 'Stormy', a cover of Classics IV's 1968 US hit,[10] where Scott Walker pointlessly performs funk-lite. 'The Hills Of Yesterday' is much better, with lyrics by Paul Francis Webster and music by Mancini, taken from the Sean Connery-Richard Harris movie *The Molly Maguires*. Well sung and well orchestrated, it's to the standard of the lesser cover versions on the early *Scott* LPs. Then 'Reuben James' comes along and undermines the whole set-up – a lightweight hit for Kenny Rogers, it's country music for liberal folks, telling of a poor white boy saved by a black preacher. It also gives the impression that Scott Walker covering straight country was a bad idea (which was surely *not* the case).

Side two does at least end on two high points. 'What Are You Doing The Rest Of Your Life?' was co-written by Michel Legrand for the 1969 film *The Happy Ending*. Overtly sentimental, with flowery orchestration, it had already been covered by Jack Jones and Frank Sinatra – and here their young counterpart steps up to show himself, at the very least, their equal. 'It's Over' is a heartbreak ballad by folk-rocker Jimmie Rodgers that would become a hit for Elvis in 1973.

Anyone who feels a warm tingle at Presley's opening lines, "If time were not a moving thing / And I could make it stay," should hear Scott sing the song and take an even deeper emotional bath. But as to what relation it bore to what, overall, was a concept album, well...

Engel dutifully undertook a round of interviews and TV appearances for *'Til The Band Comes In*, one of his most tuneful and accessible solo albums. And it stiffed.

In a short space of time, the name 'Scott Walker' on a record had come to signify a living byword for lack of airplay and public indifference. A strange commercial void into which even some of the most compelling pop music could sink.

Engel himself was becoming fatalistically self-deprecating about it all. "Oh, here he goes again," he imagined a listener hearing the opening 'Prologue', "'Gloomy Sunday.'"

Scott and Mette left their apartment in Amsterdam, dividing their time now between Copenhagen (where she mostly resided) and London, where he had, perhaps ill-advisedly at the time, bought a large flat near Regent's Park: "I'd bought an apartment, which was giving me nightmares, a huge place I was wandering around in, like Xanadu."[11] Always fond of a drink and not averse to mixing it with sedatives, by his own account the early seventies became something of a blur for Scott Engel.

✴✴✴

On April 28, 1971 (her 61st birthday), Scott's mother, 'Mrs Betty', wrote a letter to her respectful correspondent Kazuie of the *Scott Times* fanzine. She advised her that Scott's fan club in London (which formerly had 16,000 members, more than that of the now-defunct Beatles) had closed down, but had been superseded by a new fan club in Manchester. She gave an interview around this time that Kazuie headed 'They keep In Touch with Telephone More than with Writing – "I wanna live with Mama"'. In touchingly pidgin English, the Anglo version of the interview ran as follows:

How does Scott write to you, often or not?
He writes to me once in a great while. But he phones me once in three weeks certainly.

When Scott phones you, what do you speak about?
We don't have such a serious talk. Scott won't tell me about his troubles or his works or the details of his works. I think he will think that I'll worry about him … But thinking about him who is troubled alone, I worry about him more. He usually phones me with such a simple reason that he would like to hear my voice suddenly …

I decided to ask if Mrs Betty would like to live with Scott in future. Mrs Betty considered for a while hearing my question but suddenly she told me like this certainly.
This spring when I enjoyed travel with Scott in England he said he wished I'd work with him forever. And I asked him if he was sad alone. He answered that this was sometimes so. Scott seemed that he wanted me to stay with him as he seemed to have had a lot of troubles. He would like me to be his comfortable place rather than his consultant. When I heard it from him I would like to stay with Scott going to England. But it was my momentary feeling. It is for himself that he goes the way alone that he would wish to go. If I'd lived with Scott in England, it would not be for Scott though my momentary wish would be satisfied … it would only trouble him. I cannot stand to trouble him. At first, if we did so, I would hurt him.

Now is it impossible for Scott to come back to America?
I cannot tell that. But I can tell to [be] American is not for him. Scott seems to have got accustomed to the life in England and likes such life.

The same fanzine dutifully reported their hero's professional activities later in the year, when he replaced a veteran of the late fifties/early sixties British pop scene onstage:

Adam Faith was due to appear but was taken ill and Scott took his place. This show was started on Sunday 29th August and closed on Saturday 4th Sept. It was said that Scott took the place of Adam Faith confidently. At the last night of the show, Scott wore black jacket with suede lining, black trousers, blue shirt and black shoes. He had a black belt but his key wasn't there. His songs that night were as followed: 'Amsterdam', 'The Long And Winding Road', 'Make It Easy', 'Stormy', 'Joanna', 'Cincinnati', 'Jackie', 'If You Go Away' and a curtain call, 'Lady Came From Baltimore'.

And then further into the autumn:

Scott appeared on BBCTV show *Top of the Pops*. This show was televised on 21st Oct … in order to introduce his new single 'I Still See You'. On 20th Oct Scott recorded 'I Still See You' with a navy blue anorak and moccasins, and he wore brown trousers, blue shirt (open-necked) and his key was around his neck on a chain.

'I Still See You' added lyrics by Hal Shaper to the theme music of *The Go-Between*, by Michel Legrand. Starring Julie Christie and Alan Bates, the 1971 film was an adaptation of L.P. Hartley's novel of illicit love and social duplicity in late Victorian England. It begins with the novel's most famous lines: "The past is a foreign country. They do things differently there."

When movie veteran Shaper (who had worked with Engel on 'The Rope And The Colt') offered the song to Philips, John Franz felt it would be a natural for his dejected charge. The job was accepted and Scott turned up with a young woman in tow (presumably Mette), bemoaning to Shaper how little time he was granted in the studio to perform his vocals. He was also in the process of getting soused, and kept pouring himself a drink from at least one vodka bottle he was carrying in a satchel.

Shaper was clearly perturbed. This was not the young professional with the get-the-job-done attitude he remembered from Paris in 1968. Scott, the frustrated songwriter, also insisted on making changes to the lyric: "The original line was: 'I see the fields / So green and fair / The silent ghosts / Are everywhere,' which fitted perfectly into the film, but Scott insisted on singing: 'I see the fields / In still green air / The silent ghosts / To dance their hair.'"

For all his indulgence, the voice is as warm and as resonant on the single as it is on any of his early seventies work, and as ever, it suits Legrand's fluid theme. The lyrical change, while partly nonsensical, is only really apparent if you're listening for it.

The B-side, 'My Way Home', is an Engel-Semel original. A superior song, it has been noted[12] that it bears a strong historical resemblance to the period described in 'It's Raining Today'. In fact, it's a more authentically 'on the road' lyric: "Watching greyhounds / Through the giant dawn ... Lost in a dream / Where windows open out on stars."

The rich arrangement might have fitted *Scott 2* or *3*. Nobody knew it at the time, but this was the last hurrah of the Scott Walker who had captivated listeners throughout the late sixties. Neither would there be another original Engel lyric recorded for six years.

Scott did his promotional duties on 'I Still See You', appearing on the 200th edition of ATV's *The Golden Shot*[13] as well as *Top Of The Pops*. All to no avail. The 45 mirrored the lack of success of all his recent recordings.

With his career apparently in stasis, Scott confined himself to the equally complicated business of living. Back in 1968, he'd told *Rave* magazine: "I want a woman to have my children, but without having to marry her ... I know how to handle children, how to educate them. They represent security to me. It's a kind of spiritual thing I believe in, to have something left of mine when I die. I could do more for children than the average person. I know how a child should be raised – in material security, free from pressures, completely relaxed with no mental hang-ups. These are all the things I wasn't!"

Scott and Mette's daughter Lee was born in Copenhagen on 30 August 1972. This writer has seen colour photostats taken from the Engel family album of the child's first Christmas:[14] baby Lee, on a sofa, looks in bemusement at the camera, already exhibiting her mother's Nordic features; Mimi (Betty) is there, looking admiringly up at her son (drink in his hand) as she clasps his arm, surrounded by seasonal decorations; in their very comfortable-looking apartment, Mette and Betty sit on the sofa, the younger woman holding her mother-in-law-to-be affectionately.

Scott's early aversion to marriage was overcome when he, Mette and Lee went to visit Betty at home early in the New Year of 1973. The wedding took place at a private ceremony in Las Vegas. ("In case I have to get a divorce, it'll be real easy," Scott joked to Gary Leeds.) There was no reception, but the happy couple flew back home to Copenhagen for a celebration with Mette's family.

There was now a dependent little mouth to feed. Art for art's sake would have to wait.

"The signals were out really that I had to try something different or else I'd have to go into this situation that eventually arrived, where I was making records for the company basically," Scott more recently told the Kijak documentary team. "To see out contracts, because they actually thought some of these records were going to do something. I didn't – no. At that time it started to bother me, not because of the success or failure or anything, but the fact that I wasn't going to be able to do any more albums like that. That was what really got to me, I wasn't going to be able to have all that at my disposal.

"After the fourth record, *'Til The Band Comes In* was kind of a signal of 'We're getting off you as a writer, we want you to do something else,' you know. That's when I started imbibing a little too much and things like that.

"John Franz, who was a dear friend of mine, came to me and said, 'Look, let them have a couple of albums they want, and down the line we'll sneak in another one.' It's that old thing and of course it never happened, you see. And so it got worse and worse, and I got worse and worse with the imbibing."

The first part of Franz's masterplan to save his protégé's career was *The Moviegoer* – an album of film theme songs recorded (once again, with some haste) at Stanhope Place soon after Scott's daughter was born. "I just sat back and copped money for whatever it was they wanted me to do," Scott said later in the seventies. "If they wanted me to do movie themes, man, I would pick the best movie themes that I thought were possible and I would do them."

In the event, *The Moviegoer* didn't so much demonstrate the range of Engel's cinematic and musical interests (which would have been truly interesting) as anthologise a load of songs from contemporary films of the late sixties/early seventies – although, as with 'I Still See You', some were lyrics that had never actually appeared in the films themselves. The cover showed Scott in cowboy's Stetson and rolled-up sleeves, with a 'rear stalls' ticket taken from the cinema. Combined with the seventies typography, it had a very budget-album effect.

Within a year, in fact, that's what it became, when it was reissued on the Contour Records label after no success with Philips. The sleeve notes read:

> His approach to these songs reflects the mood of each piece, varying from the powerful lyric to the pure story line. The orchestral backing never obtrudes, and allows the full scope of his tender voice and clear diction to take command and thrill you.
>
> With composers like Henry Mancini, Michel Legrand and John Barry, plus the talent of Scott Walker[,] you have a formidable middle of the road, easy-listening album.

The above is as fair a summation as any. The album was helmed by the Franz-Olliff team, with the substitution of Robert Cornford, founder of the London Sinfonia, for the arrangers on the classic *Scott* records. Despite the bargain-rack product that it ultimately became, some of the vocal performances couldn't help but give the album several high points.

'This Way Mary' added Don Black's romantic lyric to Barry's violin and cello requiem for the doomed *Mary, Queen Of Scots*. "This way Mary / Run, Mary / Our love was meant to be," seems particularly incongruous, given that "this way" is the direction that Mary, post-Reformation Catholic pretender to the throne, is taking to the executioner's block. Still, the sadness in Scott's voice gives the bland lyric its undertow of melancholy.

'Speak Softly Love', the English version of Nino Rota's love theme from *The Godfather* (as sung by Al Martino – who played Johnny Fontane in the film) is as sweetly handled as one would hope, with smooth vocals and Spanish guitar. Neil Diamond's 'Glory Road' is from *WUSA*, a now obscure (as with many of the pics represented here) but interesting picture with Paul Newman, adapted by Robert Stone from his politically liberal novel *A Hall Of Mirrors*. When Scott sings, "Hey friend, have you seen Glory Road?" and multitracks his voice, he briefly becomes a one-man Walker Brothers.

'That Night' is a well-orchestrated and sung (but not otherwise notable) theme from a film briefly controversial in its day – *The Fox*, from a D.H. Lawrence story about a clashing love triangle and lesbian affair. 'The Summer Knows' is a powerful performance with an arrangement briefly touching on discord, from a more anodyne film (wartime coming-of-age drama *Summer Of '42*).[15]

'The Ballad Of Sacco And Vanzetti' is another high point. Adapted from the Italian docudrama *Sacco E Vanzetti*, about the controversial conviction and execution for murder of two Italian anarchists in twenties Massachussetts,[16] Scott's low-murmured "Oh father, I am a prisoner," strips away the piety of original vocalist Joan Baez, the voice of earnest US liberalism, replacing it with spaghetti-western tension. (Understandably, since the music's composer was Morricone.)

'A Face In The Crowd' opens with traffic-noise discord that briefly suggests Edgard Varèse,[17] before going into the theme song from the Steve McQueen racing movie *Le Mans*. 'Joe Hill' isn't as bad as some suggest (it's certainly better than 'Reuben James'), but its cowboy-ballad encounter with the executed trade unionist of the title only just about puts over how Hill is mooted as a similar miscarriage of justice to Sacco and Vanzetti. Things *do* get really bad with 'All His Children', a Legrand-composed song from another liberal Paul Newman drama, *Never Give An Inch*. Black country singer Charley Pride may well have believed that we're all God's children, but Engel sounds unconvinced – to the point where it seems he's disguising his voice (or maybe he's just plain drunk).

Again, the final two covers are a couple of high points. 'Come Saturday Morning' is a refreshing 'let's hit the road' ballad, nominated for an Oscar, from Alan J. Pakula's otherwise inconsequential *Pookie* with Liza Minnelli.[18] 'Easy Come, Easy Go' is a genuine barroom ballad from *They Shoot Horses Don't They?*, Sydney Pollack's great adaptation of Horace McCoy's story of an exhausting Depression-era dance-athon. Scott carries it and closes the album beautifully, sounding like he's setting up the drinks – if he hasn't got one in his hand already.

As already intimated, the album did virtually nothing on its release. Scott headed back to cabaret at Fagin's Club in Manchester, in early 1973, to keep the coffers filled. With a family to support and a career that seemed to be slipping out of sight, he tried to remain philosophical. Indeed, he remained an existentialist: "I would rather have gone off totally and experimented with standards and had that experience than not," he later remarked. "It's just as important to exist as write… Existence is worth everything. So I wasn't dead, you know?"

Commercially, Philips may have found the latter remark debatable. But the label still hustled him back into the studio in early '73. The resulting album, *Any Day Now*, contained anodyne sleeve notes that referred to "this much misunderstood artiste" – misunderstood by whom, the 'artiste' may have asked? Philips Records?

Again, given the near-impossibility of the vocalist putting in a totally bad performance, there are inevitable high points. The Bacharach music of the title track plays like pretty cheesy loungecore today, but it's still as catchy as hell. (The song itself has a lyric by Bob Hilliard rather than Hal David, which calls his lover "my wild beautiful bird", and was previously a hit for Chuck Jackson, as well as covered by Elvis.)

'All My Love's Laughter' is the first time Engel covered a song by Jimmy Webb. It's regrettable it wasn't either of the Glen Campbell hits, 'Wichita Lineman' or 'By The Time I Get To Phoenix', love songs with an unusual evocation of time and distance. But this is one of Webb's own solo tunes with a modern country feel – "Don't lose your heart to that beautiful sinner / She walks without shining her light now" – and it contains some incredible pedal steel guitar playing for a song recorded in west London.

'Maria Bethania' is another standout track – though mostly for the wrong reasons. It's a tribute to a major singing artist in Brazil, in the classic bossa nova and samba styles (although her music has apparently taken on a slightly harder edge in recent years).

The song was written for her by her brother, Caetano Veloso, another famous musician in Brazil, who was exiled by the military government in the late sixties/early seventies, along with Gilberto Gil amongst others. (They spent most of their exile living in London.) Hence the chorus: "Maria Bethania, please send me a letter / I wish to know things are getting better." Which is very commendable and in tune with Scott's liberal conscience – apart from the odd cod-West Indian accent he adopts over the bossa nova beat, which kind of predicts Sting's mock-Jamaican tones in his early days. This is bookended by strange scat singing which seems to be based around the word '*dong*'. Quite how drunk one has to be to achieve all of this remains a matter of conjecture – but still, once heard never forgotten.[19]

At the other end of the scale, even a Scott Walker contractual obligation album has to contain one bone fide classic. Since his early championing of Randy Newman with The Walker Brothers, Scott had seen Newman turn from professional jobbing songwriter to solo artist in his own right. On *Any Day Now*, the Engel vocal does justice to (and partly transforms) the brief and mournful 'Cowboy', an out-of-time frontiersman's lament for the coming of urbanisation: "Cold grey buildings where hills should be / Steel and concrete closing in on me… Cowboy, cowboy… too late to fight now, too tired to try."

'When You Get Right Down To It' is pleasant but pointless, faithfully close to Ronnie Dyson's 1971 soul hit but too polite to add anything. The same goes for his version of David Gates'/Bread's 'If', which is too tastefully done to compete with Telly Savalas' gruff spoken-word hit version of 1975[20]. Ditto Bill Withers' 'Ain't No Sunshine' – nicely respectful to the original, but why bother? 'The Me I Never Knew' is an odd one – a cover of a Don Black/John Barry song from the 1972 British film of *Alice's Adventures In Wonderland*; the original did little justice to Lewis Carroll's wonderfully demented imagination and Scott's version is only a slight improvement. (It would be released as a single, but fell into the same void as all his recent records.)

As with the two previous albums, the final two cover versions almost justify Scott's gun-for-hire status of the time. 'If Ships Were Made To Sail' is the second track on the album by Jim Webb, almost making one wish for a similar long-term dalliance with the songs of Webb as with those of Brel or, to a lesser degree, Newman. Low-key and almost whispered to a simple piano backing, the listener can hear Engel's currently trapped status in Webb's dreams of ultimate escape: "I'd find a forest hill and clean fresh air / If I could go to Alpha Centauri / Then I would be a-living there."

'We Could Be Flying' is an altogether wackier dream of escape, and is notable only for that reason. Taken from a long-forgotten 1971 concept LP called *Wings* by French composer Michel Colombier, its lyrics were by Paul Williams: the diminutive US songwriter who, among other credits, contributed 'Fill Your Heart' to Bowie's *Hunky Dory* and (later) the lyrics to kiddie gangster musical *Bugsy Malone*.

Strangely, the track (which was presumably recorded a year earlier) was showcased in a London Weekend TV show called *2Gs & The*

Pop People in July 1972, which centred on a flared-trousered pop dancing troupe called The Second Generation.[21]

Scott walks godlike among them in a tightly tailored light brown suit: "A new kind of light surrounds us all / And if we could we'd all be flying / I've always felt that deep inside / We're trying, we're trying."

Accompanied by a post-psychedelic phased guitar freakout, people in multi-coloured trouser suits, Scott himself and hippie musicians are all superimposed very primitively, some arm in arm, onto cloud backdrops – including guest DJ/horror movie star Mike Raven in a Dracula cape.

At the end, Scott passes through the centre of the Second Generation dancers who gaze on him with adoration, before miming a Swingle Singers-type ba-ba-ba-ba backing. Scott may have ridiculed psychedelic drugs, but this is a very bad trip indeed – now available to watch online but recommended only for the strong in mind.

And then it was over.

Scott's contract at Philips was up for renewal, but the restrictions on him writing his own material had urged Ady Semel to seek a new deal elsewhere. He was getting no resistance from the top brass at Philips.

John Franz and Peter Olliff, who were still with Scott on *Any Day Now*, had collaborated with him since the mid-sixties on some of the most powerful popular music of the 20th century. But they, like him, knew the time had now passed.

Notes

1   Asked about his health, the apparent response was "I had a typhus long ago and I had a cracked physique recently" – presumably meaning a rib.

2   Scott's attitude toward Dylan by this point seemed to be that he was a skilled wordsmith but a harmonically limited musician.

3   The translator may well have meant "useless and distracting". While some have conjectured that Engel may have experimented with hallucinogens when writing some of the more surreal lyrics on *Scott 1-4*, he himself had nothing but scorn for the psychedelic generation.

4   The story of a decadent industrialist family under the Nazis, starring Dirk Bogarde.

5   The young woman was half of married duo Esther and Abi Ofarim, who had a number one hit with 'Cinderella Rockafeller' in 1968. According to Gary Leeds, Esther and Abi didn't regard themselves as "exclusively married"; Leeds was of the opinion that Scott and Esther had a fling before he got really serious with Mette – who he'd have known for almost three years by this point. But then Scott once opined that he didn't believe in permanent relationships as he didn't believe they really worked, viz that of his parents. By 1970, while still unwed, he'd come to regard marriage as a "necessary evil".

6   North was an orchestral composer for Hollywood, who worked for Stanley Kubrick on *Spartacus* but whose score for *2001: A Space Odyssey* was dropped; the original North score would later be recorded by Goldsmith, whose own music often entailed more avant-garde elements. A veteran of TV who created the scarily dissonant theme for the original *Planet Of The Apes*, much of Goldsmith's most noted work was still ahead of him when Scott Walker recorded *'Til The Band Comes In*.

7   Maybe Vietnam, which by then had dragged on half a decade with no end in sight – or perhaps, more universally, any war at any time.

8   It's not unlike 'The Ballad Of Bonnie And Clyde', a 1968 hit for Georgie Fame. It also echoes in later seventies music like the early 10cc (discovered by Jonathan King) and their own cinematic pastiches on albums like *How Dare You!*

9   "Like *The Planet Of The Apes* on TV / Like side two of *'Til The Band Comes In*," sing Pulp of pop-cultural disappointments on their 2001 piss-take of Band Aid/celebrity collaborations, 'Bad Cover Version'. The track was produced by Scott Walker and Peter Walsh, cementing Jarvis Cocker's group's status as an ironic Bonzo Dog Doo-Dah Band for the new millennium.

10   Their 'Spooky was formerly covered by Gary Walker.

11   Charles Foster Kane's palatial home in *Citizen Kane*.

12   By Reynolds in *The Impossible Dream*.

13   A particularly cheesy game show with comedian Bob Monkhouse.

14   I've no idea who gained access to the photos or how they took the copies, which are distinct if grainy – though it does illustrate the depth of obsession of some fans, even at this low point of Scott's career.

15   In his meandering though sometimes interesting book-length essay on Scott Walker, *Another Tear Falls*, poet Jeremy Reed makes the following point: "'The Summer Knows', and 'Come Saturday Morning', from *The Moviegoer*, are distinct inner readings of commendable material. The songs differed little in surface quality from the covers on his first solo album, numbers that included 'When Joanna Loved Me', 'Through A Long And Sleepless Night', and 'You're Gonna Hear From Me'."

16   Doubts about the fairness of Sacco and Vanzetti's trial remain a festering sore on the American liberal conscience. Shuman and Blau reference them in 'Marathon',

182

their rewrite of Brel's '*Les flamandes*' – though their scramble through world-historic events from the twenties to the post-war years has nothing to do with Brel's original lyric.

17 Anthony Reynolds also suggests George Gershwin's 'An American In Paris'.

18 Pakula went on to distinguish himself with paranoid thrillers like *Klute* and *The Parallax View* – and indeed *All The President's Men*, about the Watergate investigation.

19 It's widely believed the track 'Maria Bethania' is the reason Scott Engel has never allowed *Any Day Now* to be released to CD.

20 This may be just an idiosyncrasy of the author.

21 Presumably after The Young Generation – the premiere long-haired pop dancers on British variety TV.

Chapter 9

No Easy Way Down/No Regrets

"Country music is hypothesized to nurture a suicidal mood through its concerns with... marital discord, alcohol abuse, and alienation from work. The results of a multiple regression analysis of 49 metropolitan areas show that the greater the airtime devoted to country music, the greater the white suicide rate."

– Steven Stack and Jim Gundlach, 'The Effect Of Country Music On Suicide' (*Social Forces*, September 1992)

"The Walkers are dead and buried and better for it."

– Scott Engel, 1969

"Who should be standin' at the bar but John? We got rappin' for the first time in years, tossed a few ideas around and both went away interested in gettin' back together again."

– Scott Engel, 1975

The new deal Ady Semel struck for his charge was with the US corporation CBS – one of the giants of the music industry at that time.

184

"And the same thing happened at CBS," Scott recalls years later. "They gave me the impression that when I got over there I'd be able to write again, and of course that wasn't the case either, they wanted to stick me with a producer – very nice people, but yeah, you know. And so that ended that – I was just working off contracts."

Bruised by his wounded expectations, Engel came to realise his supposedly astute manager hadn't negotiated a clause in the contract to guarantee his input as a composer. He decided the best policy was to make the minimum two albums of covers he was obligated to deliver, and then leave.

But somewhere along the way, his commitment to his new material would ebb and flow. At the time at least, he didn't seem think of them as the "useless records" he'd later try to shrug off.

Probably chief among his reasons for making the best of it was his new producer, Del Newman. Of a younger generation than John Franz, Newman had previously worked as an arranger for many of the early seventies singer-songwriter generation – Paul Simon, Harry Nilsson, Cat Stevens, Elton John – and had also engineered for The Faces. Now he was making the move into production and would garner a reputation as an 'artiste's producer'.

As had already become apparent to Engel, the next album would be yet another collection of covers. For the most part, the musical direction had been mapped out too (though there would be exceptions) – country and western, taking its cue from the closing tracks of *Scott 4* and Jim Webb's 'All My Love's Laughter', on the final Philips album. "It's a return to my roots, because I was raised in Texas and I do know a lot about country music," said Scott at the time, rather glossing over his peripatetic childhood – though he'd later claim his new direction was imposed by the record company.

The latter Webb song had some haunting pedal steel guitar on it, but Europe's premier steel guitarist, B.J. Cole, remains unsure of whether he was responsible: "Not as far as I remember – but it could be. My memory is not complete in that sense, not for then," he tells this writer. But his ethereal twang would play an essential role on

Scott's first CBS album, *Stretch* – named after one of the longshanks singer's nicknames back in California.

"I discovered steel guitar through a record called 'Sleepwalk' by Santo & Johnny, which was a hit here in about 1963," says Cole, who hails not from below the Mason–Dixon Line but from the north London suburbs. "I just got passionate about the instrument. I wasn't really into country, but obviously, if I wanted to find more out about the pedal steel guitar I had to get into it because that's where all the good players were. It led me to work with a band called Cochise in 1969 and introduced me to a lot of well-known people, including Elton John. When he wanted a steel guitar on a record he asked me, and that really got me into the session scene, working with him on 'Tiny Dancer'.

"It was largely because I'd done sessions for Del Newman, the string arranger, that Del suggested I come in and do the session for Scott Walker on those two [country] albums. We did them at Nova Studios, I remember, near Marble Arch."

Engel was still known for putting a drop of the hard stuff away at the time, and anecdotes suggest a bottle of Old Grandad bourbon was a permanent accessory. But Cole has no recollection of boozy sessions.

"No, nothing like that – I wasn't aware of anything anyway. But you go in at 10 o'clock, come out at five and that's it. You engaged with the singer because he was there, doing vocals while you were playing. No chance to find out what was going on in the control room, for instance, because we were working head-down, reading the arrangements."

In any case, for all the vocalist's history of hard drinking, it was virtually unknown for him to become incapacitated while working. If, as Gary Leeds suggests, he was also maintaining his Valium habit up to this point, it may have been that a shot of bourbon and a tablet throughout the day were just enough to take the edge off his nerves.

"I remember that most of the musicians were playing together, it was not like an overdub situation, and he was delightful. I've never had a problem working with Scott, he's always been very friendly to me. At that point he was quite heavily into that [country] direction and into using the steel guitar and dobro quite extensively on those two records." B.J. Cole has the rare distinction of playing for Engel both during his gun-for-hire period of the seventies and on his highly idiosyncratic personal recordings of the present day.

Stretch contains some real heartbreakers. For a bourbon drinker, Scott, in his deepest, least melodramatic baritone, sounds at times like he's been authentically crying in his beer. The cover photo on *Stretch* shows him in blue denim waistcoat and shirtsleeves, wearing the tinted aviator shades that would become increasingly a part of his everyday apparel. He's stretching toward the ceiling and smiling, but much of the material in the grooves is far more downbeat.

Mickey Newbury's[1] mid-tempo 'Sunshine' is nicely steel-inflected by Cole, but its melancholia (the narrator asks to be left alone in the darkness) belies its title. Unlike the existential angst of the late sixties, however, this is the tangible sadness of the working man who finds life has slipped beyond his reach – the whole essence of much C&W music.

The other Newbury track on the album is downright despondent. 'Frisco Depot' is the downbeat narrative of a man too broke to travel away from the track where he watches the trains thunder by; too cold for comfort in winter and too parched in summer, in an unforgiving country that preaches Christianity but despises life's losers. Then there's his loneliness: "When you're alone, you ain't got much reason for livin'." Now all that life has to offer him is pain: "You find yourself searchin' your mind for the links to the chain."

'A Woman Left Lonely' is a cover of Janis Joplin's sad R&B ballad but, compared to the above, it's pure spiritual uplift with a touch of gospel choir to it. Scott also sings two tunes previously covered on Dusty Springfield's 1969 *Dusty In Memphis*, her amalgam of contemporary country and soul music: Randy Newman's 'Just One Smile' is a song of emotional salvation in Dusty's version; Scott's is more downbeat, his unfussy deep brown tones hitting Lee Marvin's level when he puts more emphasis on the fragile opening verse ("Can I cry a little bit?") than the redemptive chorus. Gerry Goffin and Carole King's 'No Easy Way Down' is a gospel-tinged song of sorrow to begin with; in Scott's hands, lines like "When each road you take / Is one more mistake / There's no one to break your fall" really are in the deepest shade of blue.

'Where Love Has Died' was formerly covered by 'outlaw' country singer Waylon Jennings early in his career, and is a truly sad lament for people stuck in loveless marriages with nowhere else to go: "Too many ghosts have walked the floors / Ghosts of a love that ain't no more... We keep living and never tried / In some old house where love has died." As with the other downbeat ballads, Scott's timbre here is devastatingly understated.

"Because I'd been playing in country bands in the sixties, I knew where it was coming from," says Cole of Scott's role as an interpreter of country heartbreak. "I didn't think it was unusual that somebody like that would be doing that sort of material. Him and Dusty were the best singers of their era. I didn't think he was out of context doing that. Scott is the best singer I've ever worked with – and continues to be so. He's just blessed with this unbelievable tone."

Engel sings Tom T. Hall's 'That's How I Got To Memphis' beautifully, the tale of a down-on-his-luck guy searching for his missing lover. But it's still strange to hear the man who so thoroughly rejected US culture singing interstate-traversing lyrics like, "I haven't eaten a bite / Or slept for three days and nights" so sincerely.

The purer country music aside, *Stretch* is a predictably mixed bag of covers: Bill Withers' 'Use Me' makes you wonder who thought it might be a good idea for Scott Walker to try white funk. 'Someone Who Cared' is a piano-based Del Newman original, and is really quite affecting: "Tomorrow came and you saved it for no-one / Yesterday's gone – you just threw it away... You may not know, but there was someone who cared / Not that you noticed, anyhow." Jim Webb's 'Where Does Brown Begin?' is a cringe-making effort by an otherwise great songwriter and a waste of the singer's interpretive talents: when race relations are reduced to similes about salt mixing with pepper, it seems like inspiration for the banalities of Stevie Wonder and Paul McCartney's later 'Ebony And Ivory'.

The album concludes on a low-key high point, with a second Randy Newman song, the last to be recorded by Scott Walker. 'I'll Be Home' is a simple statement of loyalty and intent, its basic title line ringing with unspoken hurt that the singer needs to heal. ("I think he's the closest style to what I write and he... has a wonderful feel for the human heart," Engel said of rough-edged sentimentalist Newman at the time.)

"I don't have any of my records at home because I find it difficult to listen to myself," Scott was quoted as saying on the CBS press release for the album. "But this is the first album where I can listen to most of it and say I really did my best on that." It's a startling statement – not necessarily because of the quality of the album, but because of all that had gone before.

"Well they were trying things out, it was a very new area for him, I think," rationalises B.J. Cole "He was dipping his toe in to find out if he could do it, as much as anything. Who's to say whether it worked or not? I don't think it worked commercially," he concedes. "Probably, if you asked him today, he wouldn't want much to do with it."

Stretch was released in November 1973 to the kind of indifference that, by now, Scott Engel was becoming used to.

In early 1974, he and Ady Semel began to agitate for the release of a second, more authentic selection of country songs. (Or at least 'authentic' in as much as they could be when recorded in London.) Del Newman had several of the tracks already in the can, but CBS was not keen. Sales of *Stretch* were slow to the point of being moribund. Scott complained in a *Melody Maker* interview that the label's A&R department had "rode shotgun on my ass", picking half of the tracks for *Stretch* themselves. This time he wanted to make a more autonomous selection.

After negotiations between Semel and label director Maurice Oberstein, CBS made the offer that Engel could complete the next album by writing some of the tracks himself. Perversely perhaps, it was no deal. Digging his heels in, Scott insisted the next album would either be entirely originals or else his own selection of covers. Relations with his new record company had come to an impasse quickly, only overcome by allowing Scott Walker to record a second country album. And this time, he intended to reflect what was going on in the genre at that very moment.

American roots music had become a big item with 'musos' in the early-mid seventies, the very antithesis of the glam rock that took hold of the charts. "There was The Flying Burrito Brothers, The Band and all those bands that really inspired me, like Little Feat – at that time they were what musicians were listening to," confirms Cole. "Scott was (probably with Del Newman) into that Texas contemporary country songwriter thing. He covered a lot of those early seventies outlaw country songwriters. It was sort of a very uncool thing to be doing at the time because it was quite new and nobody was really listening to that contemporary country stuff, until Willie Nelson made it credible."

What seems most remarkable today is that, of the 10 tracks on *We Had It All*, six of them had first appeared the previous year on Waylon Jennings' album *Honky Tonk Heroes* – including new songs by fellow outlaw country singer Billy Joe Shaver.[2] At this time in the UK, Jennings was a relatively obscure figure and Shaver a virtual unknown.

"It was the urban cowboy thing that made them more popular," confirms Cole of the later seventies period, "made people become more aware of that whole thing. It may not have been totally Scott's decision, but he was fascinated with the possibilities of it."

And so Scott Walker became, briefly, the most down-and-dirty outlaw singer south of the Edgware Road. His takes on the Jennings/Shaver material were variable but sometimes interesting, and occasionally powerful. On the latter's 'Low Down Freedom', he's a freewheelin' man who just has to leave his woman; 'Black

Rose', the tale of a sexual fling with the eponymous woman of the title, veers even further into clichéd territory, though it also contains the priceless lines, "Well, the Devil made me do it the first time / The second time I done it on my own."

Of the Shaver songs, it's the two downbeat ballads that, in Scott's performances, are predictably the most arresting. 'Ride Me Down Easy' is a hardbitten cowboy song about being "down to your last shuck with nothing to sell / And too far away from the train." Scott makes these kinds of sentiments universal via the rich brown timbre of his voice – though he's still a little smooth to pass for an ornery cowpoke. He tries a similar imposture on 'Old Five And Dimers Like Me', although, with the sense of his career being taken out of his hands, he could probably make the imaginative leap to sympathise with a line like, "Good luck and fast bucks are too far and too few between."

Of the non-Shaver tracks taken from the Jennings album, 'We Had It All' is a moving ballad of loss and regret: "Remember how I used to touch your hair / While reaching for the feeling that was always there." 'You're Young And You'll Forget' is a pleasant enough (though forgettable) cover of the Jerry Reed country-pop ballad. 'Whatever Happened To Saturday Night?' has the unusual distinction of making country-rock band The Eagles (then a fairly new proposition) sound more trad-country than they usually would. Closing track 'Delta Dawn' is an uptempo character sketch of a crazy 40-year-old lady whose "daddy still calls her 'baby'". Written by country songwriter Alex Harvey,[3] it'd recently been a hit for 13-year-old Tanya Tucker in the US and Helen Reddy in Australia – and is one of the unlikelier songs sung here by Scott Walker.

"I just think a lot of it works," opines B.J. Cole of this mixed bag, "I think it was valid. Maybe it could have been done better, more stripped down. It's of its era, it's of the early seventies. It's not a pure country record – but then it wouldn't be with Scott. It's not even country rock, it's almost like middle-of-the-road country in a way, [but] with contemporary songwriters, the outlaw country thing. But he wasn't singing it like an outlaw, as Waylon Jennings would have done for instance. There's a smooth style about it – he's a crooner. If he did that sort of material now he'd do it a different way, I'm sure."

That latter point rings with understatement. Still, there are two haunting standout tracks on *We Had It All*: 'The House Song' was originally recorded by sixties pop-folkies Peter, Paul & Mary (of 'Puff The Magic Dragon' fame). It's another tale of a couple passing over the line of separation or divorce, using the metaphor of an abandoned family home up for sale: "This room once rang with childish laughter / I come back to hear it now and again / I don't know why you're here or what you're after / But in this room, a part of you remains." Scott's version plays far more as a crying-in-your-beer country ballad than the original did.

The most powerful track by far is not really country at all, but a cover of a recent US hit by Canadian folk-rock singer Gordon Lightfoot. Best known for the haunting 'If You Could Read My Mind, Love', Lightfoot's 'Sundown' is a brooding song of sexual jealousy, of "a room where you do what you don't confess". Scott manages to improve on the original, multitracking his voice so that the refrain "Sundown, you better take care / If I find you've been creepin' round my back stairs," carries an almost menacing intensity.

We Had It All was released in August 1974. It did no better than its predecessor and CBS betrayed its feelings towards the album by using a more subdued cover shot of Scott left over from the *Stretch* photo sessions. The once superlative musical career of Scott Walker now seemed to be edging towards extinction.

★★★

While Scott was playing to an ever diminishing core audience, his former bandmates seemed to have fallen off the map of popular music.

In truth, John Maus had never really stopped performing, for all the discouragement his recording career had (mostly unfairly) received. When he'd had a surprise hit in Spain, he took off impromptu to the tavernas and restaurants of its rural regions, with a pickup group of female backing singers in tow. When that moment passed, he'd returned to Britain in late 1973 to tour the cabaret and seaside circuit with a band he called The New Walker Brothers – their vocalist was an urchin-like former *Opportunity Knocks*[4] winner named Jimmy Wilson who, despite being no more than about five foot two, reputedly did a serviceable impersonation of Scott.

Once again, it didn't last; the New Walkers fell apart in 1974, followed later by Wilson's death in a freak accident.

"During the summer of 1974, I was watching television, and on came the film *Deadlier Than The Male*," John later recalled, "the movie for which The Walker Brothers had sung the title song. As I heard it again, it struck me that we sounded really good, and I decided to call Scott... We had kept loosely in touch in the intervening years. I reached him at his home in Amsterdam,[5] and he too thought it was a good idea, so we planned to meet up in London within a few weeks. In the meantime, he said he would get in touch with Gary."

By the time the three former siblings regrouped in the summer of 1975, John, an enthusiastic drinker, rather endearingly claimed "the Bull & Bush was my base". By this stage, Ady Semel was also engaged in negotiations with CBS to get Scott out of what had proved an all-round disappointing arrangement. When Engel suggested Semel act as agent for a Walker Brothers reunion, there was no objection – but the fact that the Walkers were planning to reform remained a temporary secret, in case CBS should suddenly see them as a more valuable property than the solo artist.

Scott Engel, who'd previously refused to retrace his steps, was now prepared to go as far as returning to his sixties vocal coach, Freddie Winrose, to resume voice training. He'd also relocated semi-permanently to London, living in a hotel off the Edgware Road since running into domestic difficulties back in Copenhagen.

"Mette came from a wealthy family and was a strange girl," Gary later observed, "really possessive and jealous. She and Scott used to have terrible fights, and I'm sure that jealousy was a factor in their eventual break-up...

"He had been spending an increasing amount of time apart from Mette, in London, and she had been extremely envious of all the fan attention. When Scott did his shows, and she attended, she would accuse him of looking at different girls in the audience. He said to me, 'Of course I'm looking at different girls! That's my job, to entertain them.'"

It cut no ice. "Mette's jealousy would extend to girls in the street, leading to horrendous arguments. Eventually, Scott just couldn't carry on. The divorce was amicable and simple – I went with him to the Danish embassy, he just signed a few papers and, when we came out, Lulu happened to be driving by. She waved... After that, Scott never referred to the divorce, nor did he ever display any emotion. He continued to visit his daughter, Lee, regularly and ensured he played a major role in her upbringing."

With Scott released not only from his marriage but from his CBS contract, the new deal struck for the reformed Walkers by Semel was not, perhaps, the obvious one. Dick Leahy, a music publisher, had formerly made a success as A&R man of seventies Brit bubblegum label Bell Records – which had notable hits with Gary Glitter, David Cassidy and The Bay City Rollers.[6] As a young man, he'd cut his professional teeth at Philips, regarding The Walker Brothers both as his label's artists and, to a degree, as personal musical heroes.

Leahy was now starting his own label. GTO Records was initially launched with disco and soul acts like Billy Ocean, Gloria Gaynor and, later, Donna Summer, but he would also sign his old favourites the Walkers. The initial (potentially renewable) deal was for three albums. The immediate challenge, for a group with a lead vocalist whose songwriting abilities had long lain dormant, was to find the right material to record.

In the interim, GTO put the group on a retainer of £400 per month (a comfortable amount of money for the mid-seventies – particularly for John and Gary, the latter of whom had effectively left the music industry). They also moved them into a shared flat above Newton's bistro on 517 New King's Road, Fulham. Gary immediately reverted to his sixties level of wackiness by setting up a Bedouin-style tent in the centre of the living room. After all the bitterness of their final tour and ensuing dissolution, the three thirtysomethings seemed grateful to have each other's support again.

John, at least for a while, seemed to find the new domestic set-up amusing: "Scott still had his orange VW.[7] When he drove down the street, Gary would do his typical under-the-breath voice... saying, 'There goes Scott in the orange peel.'... the aerial got broken, so Scott stuck a coat hanger there... Scott did a lot of funny things without even realising it...

"One night Gary made a great roast and we told Scott that he had to clean up. We soaked the dishes, but the next morning they were still there. We got on at Scott to get started, but he said, 'I'm not going to put my hands into that dirty water.' He was helpless."

Dining regularly in the restaurant below, the Walkers made the acquaintance at this point of near neighbour Marc Bolan of T. Rex – the former chart-topping 'bopping elf' of the early seventies, now working his way back from a dip in his career via frequent TV appearances that would lead to his own *après*-school hours pop show, *Marc*.

"Hi, I'm Marc Bolan, the king of the boogie!" the five foot two glam-rock star introduced himself without compunction. Gary apparently tensed his muscles for Scott's reaction – but it was one of amusement. "The only person I ever knew Scott take an instant liking to was Marc Bolan," said Leeds with a touch of amazement. "Marc really made Scott laugh in a way that broke down all his barriers."[8]

When enticed round for a jam session at Bolan's boogie HQ, the T. Rex leader reputedly seemed taken aback at the musical chemistry that still existed between Scott and John as musicians and guitarists.

(How he regarded Gary's drumming abilities, which by this point had apparently all but vanished, was not noted.)

The ever-amiable Leeds was a regular visitor to the GTO offices; he'd later recall, "Billy Ocean… came running up and went right past me and went straight to Scott, and was all, 'Oh wow, you're the best singer in the world.'… Scott didn't know what to say."

Engel was notoriously harder to get to know. He and his label boss would occasionally play tennis, however, of which Scott remained a lifelong devotee. As a new divorcee, he also began a close friendship with Leahy's PA, young twentysomething brunette Denise Simpson. ("She was neurotic in a nice way," Leahy later reflected. "I can understand Scott and her getting on because I imagine they could look at the darker side of life together.") The relationship wasn't to last, but, according to Gary, "He then met a lady called Libby, who used to come to the flat in the King's Road. They were together for at least 10 years."[9]

The initial advance for the Walkers ran to £20,000 (in cash – presumably to circumvent somebody's problems with the taxman) and was to be split four ways: between Scott, John, Gary and Ady Semel.

The selection of material was a process of expensive trial and error. With few publishers or songwriters queuing up to help the Walkers relaunch a career that was now seen as of another era, Engel and Leeds would go on shopping expeditions to find suitable songs to record. "I guess we must have bought 3, 4, even 500 LPs," Scott later recounted. "And y'know what? I only wanted to keep about four out of the lot for my collection."

On an apparently regressive backtrack into the safety of a career he once knew, Engel also went to Philips' new studios to speak with old friend and mentor John Franz – who he wanted to record their new material. But Franz was tied down by corporate loyalty to Philips, as he was by the success of the label's current pet artistes, *Opportunity Knocks* winners Peters & Lee.[10] Scott would have to helm the production himself, assisted by engineer Geoff Calver.

When it came to recording, however, he was able to recruit session men like guitarist Alan Parker and drummer Barry Morgan who'd played on the original Walkers hits – replicating Franz's traditional mode of working by recording them all playing live together. When their single from the forthcoming album was eventually released, Scott and John would play live together in TV studios. For now, however, John's boozing seemed too out of control to allow him to be reliable in the studio.

"He'd start a thing and he'd come back in and he was like cock-eyed, man," Scott later intimated to the press. "So we'd have to keep cancellin' sessions. It happened again and again so finally I said: 'John, you're gonna have to kick it or that's it.'"

One of the first songs to be selected was US folk singer Tom Rush's break-up ballad 'No Regrets' – which, in a short time, would offer itself up as the title track of the forthcoming album.

"We listened to Tom Rush's version, which he sang solo with female backing singers, and really liked the idea of covering it," John later remarked. "It was a really good, creative time … even though we were still sometimes drinking more than we should."

In covering the song, Scott continued the understated style of his recent country LPs and restrained any hint of vibrato. His diction was clearer than Rush's on the original and he placed a more stated emphasis on the song's key lines: "I know you're leaving, it's too long overdue / For far too long I've had nothin' new to show to you," came the opener. It was like a calmly personal statement on the demise of his own marriage, with his calmness only mildly subverted by the sadness of the backing track.

Almost everyone who reads this book will know the refrain: "There's no regrets, no tears, goodbye. / I don't want you back. / We'd only cry again. / Say goodbye again." On the original album track, Scott's understatement is shadowed by an almost whispered backing from Suzanne Lynch of the vocal group Bones. At the insistence of Dick Leahy, who'd first presented them with the song, the single would carry a different mix which featured John as the backing vocalist.

"I can't remember the exact date we did it, but that was done at Air Studios in Oxford Circus," says B.J. Cole, who was once again called upon for pedal steel guitar duties. "I've only heard the Tom Rush original a few times. I mean, it's just a great song – I think Scott made it his own though. How can you think about anybody else's version when he's done it?"

Not a country ballad per se, it still opened to a melancholy sunset twang. "I only play at the beginning and at the end," said Cole. "I played all the way through when we did it – but they only used the bit at the front, at the first verse, and the outro bit – the bit that the DJs fade out as they're introducing the next song. Listening to the record, I probably had a free hand to play."

As to this writer's contention that Engel's understatement was the legacy of his country albums, B.J. demurs.

"I just think he got a bit older and had more control over his voice. Maturity does that – but he's a master. He applied himself to a song that's a little more introspective, and therefore he was a bit more intimate with it. I don't think that's anything other than a great artist going to what the song needed, really.

"When you're doing sessions like that, you don't necessarily follow the trajectory of the tracks that you've worked on. You don't tend to think in terms of whether it's going to be a success – I didn't know it was going to be a single at that time."

Neither did the Walkers themselves, before GTO earmarked it. The album *No Regrets* was released in October 1975. Rather than the typically moody shots of the sixties, the cover featured a laddish, all-grins group photo of John and Gary in denim and a bare-breasted, stick-thin Scott blocking his face with his hand and drinking from a can of Newcastle Brown Ale, the classic northern beer boy's drink. (Apparently all three were pretty drunk by the end of the session.)

The title track came out as a single in November. As it clocked in at just under six minutes, 'No Regrets' seemed to be outside the parameters of a radio playlist. But then, in December '75-January

'76, Queen's 'Bohemian Rhapsody' became a massive chart-topping hit – a track of similar length, though of a totally histrionic nature.

"Scott and Freddie Mercury are probably the two best pop singers ever," says Cole, drawing an analogy. "I'm talking generally, I'm not talking as though they're like one another – they're not. But if for instance I had to imagine two people going on to sing in a 'classical' context, to use the wrong word, in a way that would be respected by people of a higher artistic world, then they would be it."

But, as 'Bohemian Rhapsody' rose to the top of the charts and made pomp-rock history, 'No Regrets' had trouble even getting on the (then) all-important Radio 1 playlist. Only last-minute negotiations between Leahy and the station director allowed the British-produced version to supersede Tom Rush's dissimilar original, which had originally made the list.

With its elegantly understated string accompaniment and almost spoken baritone vocal (albeit with a typical seventies 'axe break'), 'No Regrets' gradually defied the gravity of its perceived limitations. It took three months to rise up the singles charts, but along the way it was helped by TV exposure including the venerable Dame Vera Lynn's Christmas show on BBC1.

"We performed 'No Regrets' and then 'Lover's Lullaby', which really seemed to captivate the live audience – you could have heard a pin drop," recalled John. "When we finished 'Lover's Lullaby', the audience leapt to their feet and gave us an enormous standing ovation... I later heard that, for some reason, the second song wasn't aired, which was a pity."

'Lover's Lullaby' is a lyric by seventies singer-songwriter Janis Ian, best known for her vulnerably sensitive 'At Seventeen'. "That song came closest to what we wanted to do," recalled Gary, "which was Schumann's 'Pretty Fly',[11] the children's lullaby from *Night Of The Hunter*, the film starring Robert Mitchum... They had clapped after 'No Regrets', but when we'd finished 'Lover's Lullaby' they just didn't stop applauding... Dame Vera said, 'Sounds like someone's been missing you. Welcome back.'"

Neither piece of footage now survives, both having been wiped. But there were numerous appearances on pop shows around Europe, including three on *Top Of The Pops*. Scott and John could be seen playing live and syncing up the words "Our friends have tried to turn my days to nights" and "We'd only cry again, say goodbye again" together. Outside of the studio, for a brief moment, The Walker Brothers were a band at last. Only John's drinking binges caused anxiety during the promotional itinerary – particularly when he went AWOL for three days in Edinburgh.

The single mix of 'No Regrets' reached its peak of number two in the charts in February 1976. The album fared less well, only reaching the apex of number 49. But *No Regrets* is a strangely atypical long player, even for a reformed sixties pop band. Despite the high points of the title track and the haunting 'Lover's Lullaby', it's essentially a seventies MOR record – with some of the slickly produced blandness that entails.

Scott gives a pleasant enough vocal performance on modern country singer Kris Kristofferson's 'I've Got To Have You' – but there's little that's soul-shaking here, not even to the extent of Engel's recent country covers. 'Everything That Touches You' (inevitably followed by 'touches me'), by Bowie/Pink Floyd musical arranger Michael Kamen, feigns big emotions but is by-the-numbers, as is a cover of a contemporary Dionne Warwick number, 'Burn Our Bridges'.

John provides another of the album's high points – Mickey Newbury's characteristically sad 'Lovers', about a couple who no longer even talk, let alone make love – and his cover of folk-rock singer Tracy Nelson's 'Hold An Old Friend's Hand' is nice enough. But otherwise, some of his vocal contributions (four as opposed to Scott's six) are on material that comes uncomfortably close to dross, particularly a rock-a-boogie take on one of Randy Newman's weaker tunes.

The album's one other peak is Scott's version of Emmylou Harris' classic 'Boulder To Birmingham', backed by unobtrusive but haunting steel guitar from B.J. Cole. A tribute to Ms Harris' late close friend and mentor Gram Parsons, the godfather of country-rock/former leader of The Flying Burrito Brothers and member of The Byrds, Engel's return to country is a resurgence of melancholic beauty: "I would walk all the way from Boulder to Birmingham / If I thought I could see, I could see your face," sing Emmylou/Scott in their different versions, as a tribute to the late, lamented Parsons, dead of an overdose at 26.

As Engel diplomatically conceded of the album during promo interviews, "There are a few nice things on it but I don't think anyone in the group is going around celebrating..."

(Inexplicably, some of Scott's best vocal performances on *No Regrets* were left off the album, not released until Walkers compilation CDs were issued many years later: 'I Never Dreamed You'd Leave In Summer' is as gorgeous as Scott Walker singing an early seventies Stevie Wonder ballad may be expected to be. Jim Webb's much-covered 'The Moon's A Harsh Mistress' has him intoning haunting love song metaphors: "The moon a phantom rose / Through the mountains and the pines / And then the darkness fell." It may have been the democratic six-parts-Scott-to-four-parts-John ratio that kept them off the original release – but then John's sweetly sentimental take on Randy Newman's 'Marie' was also excluded.)

It was the success of the title track as single that had concert promoters opening their chequebooks again. Scott was initially resistant to offers, but, as before, he was eventually enticed by band and management into lining up some cabaret dates. But first there was a follow-up album to record.

★★★

John Maus, who was by all accounts still drinking heavily during the recording of the second Walkers reformation album, described the initial song selection process of spring 1976:

"Dick Leahy came up with two more songs for us. The first was called 'Everything Must Change', and after we had made the backing tracks for that Scott started to put his vocal on the song. He did about four or five takes, then suddenly dropped everything, walked into the control room, and said he just couldn't sing the song because 'the lyrics are too inane' ... So that was the end of that song.

"Dick then presented us with the second song – 'To All The Girls I've Loved Before', which later became a massive hit for Willie Nelson and Julio Iglesias. But it was a case of *déjà vu* for Scott. We again made the backing track, he started singing, came back into the control and pointed to me, saying, 'John, get out there, you're singing this one.'... We played it for Dick, who was a little disappointed that it wasn't a joint effort, and we noted a little hostility from him from that point onwards."

The days of Scott Walker as a covers artist were starting to run down. But what might replace it at this stage was not at all clear. As for the songs that Engel did consider fit for his performance, Maus continued:

"Somebody had given us a song called 'Lines', written by Jerry Fuller, which really appealed to Scott, who thought it was one of the best songs he'd ever heard. Interestingly, the lyrics are clearly about cocaine addiction. We decided to name the album after the song..."

Scott, who'd previously disparaged hippie drugheads in the sixties, has subsequently come clean about his own experimentation with cocaine in the seventies. (John too said that, as far back as the sixties, he used to take a line of coke to wake him up before taking the stage, after one of the Walkers' heavy drinking sessions.)

In many ways cocaine is the classic drinker's drug: it doesn't alter the user's consciousness but (over-)animates him or her to the extent where he/she feels sober/clearheaded/omnipotent – until the inevitable comedown or the next line. All the negative effects – sleeplessness, palpitations, paranoia – are saved up for later. But when they hit (particularly if combined with an alcoholic hangover), they hit hardest; the longer the chemical deferment, the greater the long-term damage.

It seems curious that someone as highly strung as Scott Engel should be attracted to such a violent nerve stimulant[12] – but then, in the mid-nineties, he'd speak of "post-cocaine clarity", which was presumably the attraction for such a cerebral man.

There's no indication that Scott Engel was ever addicted to cocaine. In fact, as Gary Leeds says he'd maintained his Valium habit up to this point, it's more likely he'd have to resort to sedatives to deal with the side effects of the drug when he took it. But in any case, his choice of Fuller's song was no glorification.

"Oh Lord, I'm strung out / Soaking wet and hung out on the line," Scott sings of the narrator's addiction in as soulful a manner as a country singer might tell of being drunk and broke. The Engel/Calver production erupts in the chorus, pitched somewhere between gospel and the kind of atonality Scott would later experiment with: "And now I must stand free / But there's nobody here / But me to fill my bed." The addict knows he's got to break his habit, but he's already lost everyone who meant most to him.

'Lines' was, as Scott intimated to his bandmates, one of the most powerful tracks The Walker Brothers ever recorded. But the album it lent its name to was, like its predecessor, a mixed bag.

The title track was released as a single but, perhaps due to the subject matter, received little airplay and did nothing commercially. Of the other tracks sung by Scott, Tom Jans' 'Inside Of You' has come in for criticism for its literal depiction of the narrator entering his lover. But it's no leering proposition, rather a more melancholic ballad: "Prisoner of my past / Held by dreams that never last / I can only be myself / When I'm inside of you." It's the self-annihilation of sex, the *petit mort* that allows us to lose ourselves.

The second single of the album would be, many might assume, another hit for the Walkers – in fact, some people hearing it now seem to believe that it was. The familiar chorus of US MOR rocker

Boz Scaggs' 'We're All Alone' – "Close the window, calm the light / And it will be all right" – is delivered in smooth velvet tones by Scott. But it'd be pipped at the post by the US hit version by Rita Coolidge, Kristofferson's singing (and at the time romantic) partner. Never anything more than a good production of a mediocre song, it was kept from the UK airwaves. *Lines*, unlike *No Regrets*, would not find its own hit single.

Scott's other tracks are once again pleasant if hardly earth-shaking: the big production on reggae singer Jimmy Cliff's 'Many Rivers To Cross' leaves the song intact and soulful enough; its line about the striving man who is "Wandering... lost / As I travel along the white cliffs of Dover," may have had some resonance to a long-time voluntary exile in Britain. 'Brand New Tennessee Waltz' comes close to bluegrass with its country fiddle, but, with Jesse Winchester's lyric of "waltzing on air", is just a basic love song. As is the closing track, 'Dreaming As One' (first recorded by Woodstock veteran folk-rocker Richie Havens), where Scott and John resume their harmonious siblings double-act.

(Once again, a couple of outtakes from the album far outstrip its weaker numbers: ''Til I Gain Control Again' is a vulnerable country ballad first recorded by Emmylou Harris and, again, covered beautifully by Scott; John's self-composed 'The Ballad' is another aching number, which is much better than most of his rather weak offerings that did make the track listing.)

Scott was once more respectfully non-committal in his opinion of the album on the promo interviews: "The *Lines* album has about three dazzling tracks, but I think that the rest of the album doesn't come together right. We like 'Lines', 'Many Rivers To Cross', and [John's vocal] 'Taking It All In Your Stride'."

The album came in a tan line drawing of the three brothers' heads, based on a similar design used to promote a current movie: Jack Nicholson as a thief and Marlon Brando as a bounty hunter in Arthur Penn's 1976 Western, *The Missouri Breaks*. It ultimately made little difference to the album's commercial prospects, faring worse than its predecessor on its late summer '76 release.

Still under contract for a third album, Engel and Maus were called to a meeting with Dick Leahy. "He called us into his office one day for a meeting and strongly suggested that we try working with a co-producer, somebody he had in mind named 'Papa' Don Schroeder," John recalled. "Schroeder worked out of Nashville, Tennessee, and had produced several hits with a black duo, James and Bobby Purify, who had had a hit with 'I'm Your Puppet'. So off we went – Scott and I – to Nashville."

In the blizzard-bound southern winter of '76, the two Walkers met Schroeder with a view to refashioning one of their own classic covers of the sixties: Curtis Mayfield's Impressions song 'People Get Ready'.

"Scott and I had recorded the song in 1966 and were very familiar with it, so he went into the studio while I stayed in the control room. He did four or five takes until he got what he wanted, and when he took his headphones off I knew he was done... After we'd played it back a few times, Papa Don said, 'OK, now let's get out there and do it for real.' Scott shot me the 'I'm in total shock' look; as far as we were concerned, he had sung his ass off, so Papa Don's remark went down like a lead balloon."

Schroeder informed Engel that he always worked from the painstaking process of recording a song line by line and making a final assembly. It was no deal. The session was aborted; for the foremost of The Walker Brothers, the experience of being an interpretive singer had long since started to pall.

Back in England, all that was left was another round of cabaret to capitalise on the success of 'No Regrets'. For now, the Walkers were to be briefly represented by David Apps, the former agent for The Bay City Rollers.

Ady Semel, having long since tired of his client's lack of commercial success, had returned to his native Israel and has not been heard from since. (According to Gary Leeds, Semel received a message telling him his aged mother was critically ill. He took off and never returned.)

Apps booked the group for a cabaret tour of the Midlands and the North with a pickup band. The shows were to be tied to the success of 'No Regrets': no hits from the sixties; no solo material from any of the Walkers; just a smattering of tracks from the new albums and – intriguingly – a couple of covers from the repertoire of the newly famous Bruce Springsteen.[13]

Then the northern leg of the tour passed through Newcastle, before a week's residency at Fagin's in Manchester. The latter stint came to a half halfway through when John's drunkenness led Scott to the conclusion he could no longer rely on him. The Walker Brothers' reformation was falling apart; funds were running out and the advance on their third album wasn't due until early 1977.

Back in London, Scott Engel came under quiet pressure from Leahy to ditch the rest of the Walkers and get back to a solo career. His response seemed non-commital, but his neurotic anxiety was showing through: in a *Melody Maker* interview, he admitted that his own current favourite songwriters – the perennial Randy Newman and Joni Mitchell, whose *The Hissing Of Summer Lawns* was one of the albums of the mid-seventies – only made him feel daunted by their talent. It had been more than half a decade now since one of his own songs had been committed to vinyl.

"I'm slowly beginnin' to realise that that attitude is dumb," he admitted. "It's an inspiration to learn that Henry Miller didn't write *Tropic Of Cancer* until he was 33… I'm 33 and I'm ready.'"

But of course, the reason for the persisting influence of Miller as a novelist is that he was a true original. *Sui generis*.

Notes

1   The late Newbury was the songwriter who compiled three traditional US standards into 'American Trilogy', a signature tune for late-period Elvis.

2   The author is indebted to Lewis Williams' excellent 2006 Scott Walker discography, *The Rhymes Of Goodbye*, for this piece of musical detective work.

3   Not the Glaswegian who famously spat out 'Next', but a Tennessee songwriter who composed 'Reuben James' for Kenny Rogers – one of the lesser cover versions on *'Til The Band Comes In*.

4 The cheesiest British talent show of all time.

5 John seems to have confused Copenhagen with Amsterdam by this point.

6 Leahy would later consolidate his commercial acumen when he was instrumental in launching Wham!

7 The same Volkswagen he'd driven since the late sixties, after dispensing with his US Army jeep.

8 "I think Marc's girlfriend [singer] Gloria [Jones] had a twinkle in the eye for Scott, and I even suspected that Marc might have had an even brighter twinkle," reflected Gary. "Gloria would come on to Scott, who didn't fancy her but, being the perfect gentleman... did not respond." Bolan would die in a car crash with Gloria at the wheel, on Barnes Common in September 1977.

9 Scott Engel has long kept his private life (not unreasonably) private.

10 Lennie Peters, the male half of the MOR duo, had been blinded as a teenager. On their biggest hit, 'Welcome Home', he balanced this disability with the gruff tone-deafness of the working man's club singer.

11 The song sung by the little girl as she and her brother flee down the river in a canoe at night, watched by a croaking bullfrog: "There once was a pretty fly / She had some pretty children... but then the pretty fly / Flew away / Flew away." Film buff Scott Engel undoubtedly knew the haunting southern gothic fairy tale *The Night Of The Hunter*, the only film directed by actor Charles Laughton.

12 Gary Leeds tells of a strange incident with caffeine tablets when Scott was living in Amsterdam: "On one occasion he wanted to drive there from England because of his ever-worsening fear of flying, and asked me to go with him ... As we approached the border that separated Belgium from the Netherlands, Scott's orange VW Beetle seemed to be gaining speed rather than slowing down ... as we got ever closer to the border he was becoming itchier in the driver's seat, and he went straight through without stopping! ...

"I told Scott to pull over, and asked him what was the matter ... He told me he had taken some caffeine tablets to keep him awake on the long run. 'How many did you take?' I asked.

"'Three.' ... he had clearly drunk the equivalent of 200 cups of coffee. Of course, this was the last thing Scott wanted to hear.

"Matters were only made worse when Scott took three Valium to help himself calm down. He was like a dog when it gets really excited and shakes all over ... I had to take over the driving. Scott never took those caffeine tablets again, or even drank coffee." Given the user's natural nervous state, cocaine really didn't seem like a good idea.

13 Springsteen, then in his mid-twenties, had only released three albums by this point: *Greetings From Asbury Park, N.J.*, *The Wild, The Innocent & The E Street Shuffle*, and the recent *Born To Run*. But he'd been acclaimed as the latest 'new Dylan' – this time to a Spector-esque rather than folkie backing.

Chapter 10

The Cold Wave

"Listen to the cold wave roar from the seventies into the eighties."

—Vivien Goldman on post-punk music, *Sounds*, 1977

"Sometimes democracy must be bathed in blood."

– General Augusto Pinochet, Chilean President in the seventies

"Now somebody wants me to do a solo album of original material and I'm really strugglin' hard to complete it. It's a long haul back, man, to that dark and dark and dark… it really is… it's a real dark cavern."

– Scott Engel quoted in *New Musical Express*, January 1977

When the music press were conducting interviews with the reformed Walker Brothers, ostensibly to promote the *No Regrets* album, they'd found the courteous Scott willing to expound on most subjects – apart from the music.

Miles Davis, the trumpeter who for nearly decades had blown wild, free and then slipped back into a tight structure again; opening for rock acts and riffing on popular songs, the way 'Trane had with 'My Favourite Things'; more visible than ever but then suddenly dropping out of sight. (Davis' years of cocaine addiction might have had him sympathising with the poor schmuck yearning for salvation in 'Lines'.)

Henry Miller, the chronicler of modern man's psychosexual apexes, plexuses and nexuses; now mid-octogenarian and reaching a state of frailty, his devotee Engel sensing a coming loss. Then there was Alexander Solzhenitsyn, a latter-day literary interest: expelled from his native Soviet Union despite (or because of) having won the Nobel Prize for Literature; railing against the horror of *The Gulag Archipelago* in the trilogy to which the political prison camps lent their name; a soberly serious conservative, like his 19th-century antecedent Dostoyevsky,[1] his decrying of communism may have helped Scott Engel toward the Camus-like recognition that Marxism-Leninism promised the new Kingdom Come for which all were expected to suffer in its cause.

And The Walker Brothers' new music? Well, as we've seen, Scott was a little non-committal about that. The first album contained a few good tracks, but, y'know... The Walkers' next recording, he promised a little distractedly, would contain music that was much more "stark". But that statement made little sense after the *Lines* album – which, apart from the restrained hysteria of its title track, was mostly just more MOR.

He must have had something else in mind.

★★★

As the seventies began to move into their endgame, the doors that might have led back onto past glories were closing. On January 29, 1977, Johnny Franz suffered a sudden, massive heart attack that proved fatal. He was 54 years old. Scott's reaction was not recorded at the time, but he must have been despondent. Mentor, collaborator and friend, the Philips producer/A&R man was of a different era and had assisted the young Engel's search for the new by helping him reach into the past.

Nor did the current status quo sit all that steadily. Word had it that Dick Leahy might be selling GTO Records and returning to his interim career as a music publisher. The new beginnings for The Walker Brothers were starting to seem like a false dawn. Their current-day champion was getting out of the game and no one seemed interested in the renewal clause on their contract.

Three decades hence, filmmaker Stephen Kijak would ask Scott Engel about the sudden burst of creativity that was about to emerge seemingly from nowhere: "Were there songs you were holding onto, going, 'One day I'm going to get to write these,' or was it just the timing, something in the air?"

"It was something in the air," confirmed Engel, "but it really was a situation where I did say... the company's closing down, literally, the company's closed. So let's go for it, write anything you want. But then it all started coming back to me, you know, and I started thinking, 'I can write and do this again.'"

By this stage John and Gary had moved out of the flat on the New King's Road, leaving Scott to live – and now to compose – alone, in the flat above the noisy restaurant. All of them still shared a social life – or at least Scott and Gary would meet at Tramps nightclub, with no longer any fear of being accosted by fans or rivals.

For this was the late seventies. The Walkers were men of a bygone era, whose return to the music world now seemed like a flash in the pan. With their full heads of hair, John's medallion man-style jewellery and Scott's open-toed sandals, to the snotty kids in bondage strides who traversed the King's Road they were all 'hippies'. Out of fashion and out of time.

It may have suited Scott Engel that way. Better to be an anonymous relic of another era than perpetually sought out and pestered. His neuroses may have remained, but, as he grew older, they seemed less pronounced, bordering less on hysteria.

John and Gary had noticed his disgust at the dirty washing-up water while sharing the flat above the bistro, but Leeds was already well aware of his aversion to anything that might, in Scott's imagination, contain infectious microbes: "One of his biggest fears is of being disfigured or contracting some disease that would cause a slow death."

Engel would speak in later life of being painfully aware of "the phenomena of existence" – but coming to terms with it had been a seemingly long process (as it might be for any of us – with some people literally denying their mortality till the day they die). During the Fulham period, however, Gary Leeds had also noted an incident where Scott had behaved both humanely and with human resilience.

On hearing a screech of brakes outside their flat door, Scott had been the first one down the stairs. "A car had hit an old Indian gentleman and driven on without stopping," confirms Leeds. "The man was lying in the road with blood on his arm, and his eyes had a glazed look. Scott was holding the man's head, rubbing it and reassuring him that he was going to be all right... I called the ambulance and Scott wouldn't move until it came, kneeling there and talking all the time to the man and trying to help. I told Scott, 'That was a very impressive thing you did.' He said nothing."

He stayed silent but presumably fixed on the memory of his good friend John Stewart's accident a decade before. On the frailty of the human form. On the twisted shapes that existence can be bent into.

The recording sessions for the final GTO album took place over six weeks in the spring and summer of 1977, at Scorpio Sound in Euston. A new and relatively expensive 24-track studio, it came equipped with what was then (in those pre-digital days) state-of-the-art recording equipment. Technical staff recruited for the album included engineer Dennis Weinrich, who'd previously assisted producer Roy Thomas Baker in making Queen's obsessively multitracked 'Bohemian Rhapsody' a reality, and arranger Dave McRae. In the control room sat Engel himself, making esoteric conceptual requests of his staff that were sympathetically interpreted.

As with the previous two albums, inspiration was drawn from what the music scene had to offer at the time. In Scott's case, however, the focus was much narrower this time. He'd been writing in isolation (as had John, and even Gary, at his suggestion) and was taking inspiration from an artist to whom he himself had lent an influence.[2]

"I think it was a moment in music when there were new possibilities being explored," Kijak tells this writer. "If you look at what Bowie was doing, there was a parallel, I think they were kind of influencing each other in a way. Maybe Scott felt liberated by the possibility of what an artist like Bowie could do – the Berlin period was a real break with a certain part of his persona, and it was a real break with a way of songwriting. He explored something with a certain amount of freedom, and came up with something so fresh and new then. This didn't really jibe with what was going on in the mainstream of music, but who cares?"

From 1976-77, David Bowie had decamped from Los Angeles and left behind the correspondent cocaine addiction that was destroying him. His resulting 'Berlin albums', *Low* and *'Heroes'*, were heavily influenced by his collaborator Brian Eno – ex-Roxy Music member, electronic experimentalist and progenitor of the soundtracks for life he'd termed 'ambient music'. Both were inspired in turn by the German electronic scene that'd thrown up such innovators as Kraftwerk, Cluster and Neu.

In referring to the Berlin albums as 'electronic', however, we sell them short. What's most startling about them is how Bowie abandoned character-playing and narrative in his lyrics to offer introspective snapshots of his life that (on *Low* particularly) have a sharply impressionistic sketchiness. On the heavy tone poems that constitute the 'instrumental' sections on *Low*, the lyrics are hugely evocative but mostly phonetic, comprising apparently a foreign language that may not be real words at all.

"If it's direct – or if it was 'something in the air' – a lot of times these things are just happening," says Kijak of the Engel-Bowie connection. "There's not a really direct link: were they listening to *Low*? I don't know, maybe, maybe not. He never gives a specific

'We went in and planned this way' kind of thing. They're two artists who are obviously tuned into what the other is doing. I can't say for sure, but if you listen to the music, those albums, next to each other they're definitely kindred."

Side two of *Low* seems to share something in common with much of Engel's modern (i.e. post-seventies) music in how the conflicting tones and textures of the closing 'Subterraneans' make no concessions to the listener in terms of which element actually contains the melody.[3]

By his own account, it was *'Heroes'* that was often the point of reference for Scott and his technical collaborators in 1977. Newly released at the time of their sessions, it was a quick follow-up that was basically *Low Part Two* – in that it enhanced and expanded upon the approach of the first album. While the foreboding instrumental 'Sense Of Doubt' might have sat comfortably on side two of *Low*, the songs seemed more complete in that they took some kind of narrative and applied the cut-up technique[4] that Bowie had used on and off since his 1974 apocalyptic rock album *Diamond Dogs*. 'Sons Of The Silent Age', in particular, features a bleakly surrealistic lyric that cuts up various strands[5] in Bowie's Tommy Steele-style cockney before erupting into a joyously off-kilter rock 'n' roll chorus. It had no one specific meaning yet its collision of meanings and images seem to mean so much more than that.

But there was also, as Engel and Kijak agree, "something in the air". In the late seventies, the raw aggression of most punk rock would start to look very old fashioned in a very short space of time. The late music paper *Sounds* coined the term 'cold wave' to describe the stark, angular rhythms of early Siouxsie & The Banshees, but it might have been applied also to arty minimalists Wire or the US band Pere Ubu – who took their name from the proto-surrealist play *Ubu Roi*, and played an echoey version of 'What Shall We Do With The Drunken Sailor?' they called 'Caligari's Mirror'. 'Cold wave' might even have stretched to a band like Ultravox!,[6] who, while heavily influenced by Bowie, could come up with an allusively surreal and evocative piece of their own like 'Hiroshima Mon Amour'.[7]

"They weren't the only ones, you know," concurs Kijak of Bowie/Eno/Engel, "it was a really interesting time when new forms were being crafted and you started to feel that there were possibilities that hadn't been explored yet. Then look what happened in the new wave later. Scott was just on the cusp, but it was a shame that it was limited to those four songs. In many ways it just should have been a new Scott Walker album totally, but thank God we have those."

The resultant album, entitled *Nite Flights*, also included half a dozen songs of wildly varying quality (though of a vaguely sympathetic atmosphere to Scott's work) by Gary and John. Of Scott's seminal four originals, the title track would filter its way back into the consciousness of Bowie, the man who had arguably done so much to inspire Scott's half of the album in the first place – later covered for his 1993 album *Black Tie, White Noise*.[8]

The Walker Brothers, a revived ensemble of pop idols from the mid-sixties, might have seemed the least likely entity to be a part of some new musical vanguard – and in truth they were almost as far apart from the younger bands cited above as Scott would be from the ensuing decade's 'Sounds of the Sixties' revival tours with Dave Dee, Dozy, Beaky, Mick & Tich or Gerry & The Pacemakers. But on 'Nite Flights' both the rhythmic urgency and abstract anxiety of the era were encapsulated. John Maus' voice shadows Scott's so closely that it's like one coldly enunciating composite: "Be my love / We will be GODS on nite flights… Only one way to fall." Rather than some Bryan Ferry-ish sophisticate's love song, the wider lyric bespeaks a half-glimpsed nightmarishness that may be born from Engel's own fear of flying. But it's no voice from the black box – in his new mode of expression, abstract allusion and fleeting imagery are all there is. Flying is fear, but the song is not an aviator's nightmare as fear takes many forms: "The dark dug up by dogs / The stitches torn and broke / The raw meat fist you choke / Has hit the BLOODLITE."

The stitches torn and broke… the raw meat fist you choke. It's a visceral surrealism and it would replay and refine itself over the decades to come. For all that, the lyrics are no Bowie-esque cut-ups. From this point on, Engel would emphasise the pains he had to take to build, sculpt and hone his lyrics until a world of words is created that make little sense without their accompanying music but create their own hermetically sealed nightmare within it.

The four Engel tracks that begin the album start not with 'Nite Flights' but with the distorted guitar opening of 'Shutout'. Bending notes to the point of discord, pitched somewhere between heavy metal and psychedelic funk,[9] 'Shutout' is apocalyptic rock – in the sense of the original meaning of the term as a revelation of the unseen, rather than the end of the world. Scott's voice declaims ominously but without a trace of histrionics (or indeed vibrato): "Something attacked the earth last nite / With a kick that man habit-eye / Cut the sleep tight boys who dreamed and dreamed / Of a city like the sky." Its lyric has been described as science fiction – but if so, then it's the non-traditional SF marked out by William Burroughs and some of the 'new wave' authors who contributed to or followed from Harlan Ellison's seminal *Dangerous Visions* anthology in 1967, like Philip K. Dick. 'The earth' is not under attack in the manner of some Cold War-era sci-fi movie – it's reality and perception themselves that are under siege, our psyches vulnerable to the violence of language, the raw medium of communication which Burroughs once depicted as a mutant virus from outer space. (Note Engel's play on the junkie-talk phrase "kick that habit, man" – over the decades to come such wordplay would become both wittier and scarier.) "In the shutout," Engel finally implores, "how will we know the Great Doll?"

Indeed. Further proof that we're not in Kansas any more (nor in the wonderful land of Oz) follows with the flatulently parping sax that opens 'Fat Mama Kick'. Scott and John sing disconcertingly but not quite together, with the band sounding off-key but still tight. "Armed angels walk the city lights / Wait inside their master corpses / Peeled raw, betrayed," runs the surrealist SF lyric with the nightmare refrain: "DEAF-DUMB-BLIND, DEAF-DUMB-BLIND..." In an echo of Scott's earliest days of creativity with The Walker Brothers, the Royal Albert Hall's organ was hired for the day to augment the dark, mocking tones of 'Fat Mama Kick', much as it had previously taken a more prominent role in 'Archangel'.

There may be a more literal subtext to the track than its arrangement of grotesque imagery suggests. On early copies of the vinyl edition of *Nite Flights*, 'Fat Mama Kick' was dedicated to Bernard-Henri Levy,[10] who had recently published *La barbarie à visage humain* (*Barbarism With A Human Face*). The lines "The gods are gone / The air is thick / You cannot risk / The fat mama kick," may read as opaquely as the rest, but in their delivery they suggest the grotesque self-satisfaction of the police state, where the state is all and state-sanctioned barbarism rules.

The specific barbarism that Levy, then one of the bright young things of the '*Nouveaux Philosophie*',[11] refers to in his early book was that of the communist state. As an album track, the grotesque 'Fat Mama Kick' may mark the point at which Scott Engel lost all faith in the concept of state socialism as a potential salvation of humankind. There is an implicit recognition in all this that Sartre (as TV pundit Clive James would remark in the early eighties, on his late-night talk show) had somehow persuaded the European Left that torture under communism was less painful than under Nazism as it was in a good cause.

The fourth and last Engel track on *Nite Flights* depicts, in a much more literal sense, the other side of that same coin – where opposed ideologies meet at the taper end of their extremism, embracing the same barbaric methods. "I imagine these lovers in a conversation," said Scott of the narrative voice(s) in 'The Electrician', a track which was regarded at the time of its release, if it was regarded at all, as something of an oddity[12] and is now seen as a landmark. It can also be seen as a love song, as its composer suggests, but the love is one-sided and reflects the ecstasy of sadistic domination.

Sadistic *state-sanctioned* domination: "Baby it's slow," an ominous synth chord reverberates like the deepest, darkest bass. "When lights go low / There's no help, no." For our 'lovers', imagine at first Dirk

Bogarde and Charlotte Rampling in Liliana Cavani's exploitative but compelling *Night Porter*; he the former Nazi concentration camp guard, she his unwilling charge; locked forever in emotional and sexual power games.

"He's drilling through the spiritus sanctus tonight," sings Engel as the tempo lifts from static to staggering, undertowed by the echo of Maus' vocal accompaniment. The Latin phrase sounds like a designated part of the body subjected to unspeakable pain, but it's a human being's supposedly sanctified spirit. *If your body is mine to do with as I wish, then I shall fuck your soul,* the torturer seems to be telling his victim/unwilling lover.

"Through the dark hip falls screaming / Oh you mambos! / Kill me and kill me and kill me." Perspective switches from the torturer to the tortured. It's a dance of love and death – the wild Cuban gyrations of the mambo; the highly deadly African snake of the same name. The final ecstasy lies in surrender, in letting go of all resistance and all hope.

"If I jerk the handle / You'll die in your dreams / If I jerk the handle," in the torturer's orgasmic echo that last phrase seems to last forever, "You'll thrill me and thrill me and thrill me."

We might imagine De Sade with an electrical current box at his disposal. Or Harold Pinter's eighties play *One For The Road*, in which a military interrogator (named Nicholas) in a near-future fascistic Britain relishes lording it over the political dissident he's torturing, finally revealing that he's killed the helpless man's little son (his namesake Nicky).

And then, on the 'thrill me' line, 'The Electrician' becomes a thing of beauty. Spanish guitar and unsynthesized strings flower suddenly, orgasmically into bloom, describing the torturer's ecstasy as a collision between flamenco's romance and Mozart's spiritual affirmation.

It might be more apposite to think of torturer and tortured as the dinner party captive and his vengeful rape victim in Ariel Dorfman's more conventional piece of political theatre, *Death And The Maiden*.[13] For theirs is unfinished business left over from one of South America's numerous 'dirty wars' – precisely what Scott Engel had on his mind when he wrote 'The Electrician', one of his more literal latter-day pieces.

In preserving what was described as 'democracy' (or, rather, the dominance of the fledgling US multinationals) and labelling a perceived socialist threat as 'communism', the USA had been more than willing to provide 'advisers' during this period to annul Central and South America's dissident voices. It was an ideological world away from Stalinism but Engel saw that it depended upon the same Orwellian doublethink: 'freedom' as subjugation; 'due process' as pain; 'justice' as murder.

Through his horrified eye, the superpower games of his former homeland created an even greater cultural distance. His acknowledgement was not an innocently wounded protest song in the style of Joan Baez or the early Dylan, but an almost symphonic descent into the psychosexual that says: this is what humanity sometimes is; this is what it sometimes does.

He'd later compare his modern method of lyric writing, his assembly of sometimes opaque blocks of text, as akin to "a general assembling his troops on the battlefield", and perhaps the military analogy is most suited to 'The Electrician'.

Baby it's slow.
When lights go low.
There's no help.
No.

★★★

The rest of the tracks on *Nite Flights* can't hope to meet the power of 'The Electrician', or any of the other Engel songs.[14] But they're still worth hearing (at least once) because of their distance from The Walker Brothers of the sixties.

Surprisingly perhaps, it's Gary Leeds that comes off best in terms of anticipating what kind of album this was likely to be. (Scott kept his songs from his bandmates until they were ready to record.) "*Nite*

Flights is my favourite Walker Brothers album," he later enthused. "We got a new feel and sound that proved we could be quite original – so much so that when we presented it to the record company they didn't know how to categorise it."

Which in itself would prove the commercial kiss of death – but time has been kind to *Nite Flights*, and it stands up today as strongly as it ever did.

"We worked in three separate rooms, and no one knew what the others were doing," he attests, contesting Engel's own view of the work as a group album. "I wasn't as quick as Scott and John at writing songs, so I ended up with only two tracks. Originally the album was going to have the title of one of my tracks, 'Death Of Romance', which I still feel would have been highly appropriate because it marked a departure from romantic ballads." The title was prescient, though Gary's vocal was a little thin and reedy. Its sax motif again puts the listener in mind of Bowie, or perhaps the wheezing instrumental refrain of Gerry Rafferty's 'Baker Street' when it appeared that same year. "That song is based on experiences I had in Amsterdam, and the lyrics shook Scott to the ground: he absolutely loved it."

Engel made a personal contribution to all of the other Walkers' tracks: if he didn't supply backing vocals (his voice doesn't appear on any of John's tracks) then he was adding bass lines or keyboard embellishments. It was the rebirth of Scott Engel as composer/producer/multi-instrumentalist.

"'Den Haague' is about Monique Van Cleef," continues Gary, "a dominatrix who operated in the Dutch capital after being thrown out of America. I went to her chateau with a friend who was going to write a book about her. The song describes exactly what happened."

John Maus too saw the free hand on *Nite Flights* as a cue to explore the realm of sleaze – though his efforts were more fantasy-orientated. "For the first and only time in my writing career I wasn't writing songs about love," he later confirmed. "I wrote four songs for the album – 'Rhythms Of Vision', 'Disciples Of Death', 'Fury And The Fire' and 'Child Of Flames' – about bizarre science-fiction stuff.

Perhaps I was influenced by my choice of reading material at the time: Frank Herbert's *Dune*, Isaac Asimov novels and a lot of Dennis Wheatley's books."

In this sense, John's contributions are the most 'seventies' of all the tracks. Staying sober throughout composition and recording (though he'd later get back on the Scotch whisky – much to his relief, it seems), his disco-inflected soft rock sometimes strays into areas that, at best, recall the post-Roxy Music/Cockney Rebel 'art-rock' bands that predated punk.[15] "Just waiting to open / Her sacred stitch… You've lost to the bitch," he insistently but charmlessly sings at one point, briefly summoning the image of a decadent pop star in some late sixties or early seventies Brit horror movie.

Nite Flights would be released in a cover designed by Storm Thorgerson, the director of Hipgnosis[16], which was recognised in the mid-seventies for its eye-catching work for Pink Floyd and 10cc, among others. "We'd wanted something really unique and different for the album cover, and the company Hipgnosis, famous for its sleeve designs, suggested the idea of using an anamorphic lens to shoot close-ups of us, instead of the standard fish-eye format for which the lens was normally used," recalled John.

"We met up with [Thorgerson] to discuss ideas and told him what we thought would make a good cover," testified Gary, "but when Scott disagreed with some of the ideas that Storm put forward, Storm walked out. It was resolved only by Scott giving way, but he was definitely pleased with the finished cover, a gatefold that features fragmented black-and-white images of us that relate to the musical themes."

The metallic grey cover photos, shot through with silver lines, show the faces of each of the Walkers staring intently as if into the dystopian worlds of the album's lyrics. Each one of them is pulling on a cigarette – including lifelong non-smoker Scott, acceding to Thorgerson's request for effect.

Nite Flights, a classic album for all the variation between Engel's peaks and his pseudo-siblings' valiant efforts, saw release in July

1978 – which was also the point of its instantaneous commercial demise. Attempts to salvage 'The Electrician' as a single by reissuing it as part of an EP of all four Engel tracks (entitled *Shutout*) were similarly doomed. "*Nite Flights* was critically acclaimed, but didn't sell well," Gary concedes today, almost with pride. "At the time, it was our worst-selling album... it defied definition, and no one knew how to promote it... it was such a departure that it put all our fans in shock."

"I still consider *Nite Flights* to be sort of an unanswered musical question," echoed John. "I also think this album was the beginning of Scott's embarking on a whole new type of material for himself – not so much commercial, but more and more experimental. I liked the tracks he wrote for the album," he graciously conceded. "It was his first venture into avant-garde music,[17] and it signalled the direction in which he was going in the future."

"*Nite Flights* led Scott to his next page, the dark page as we call it," concurred Gary.

"The first time that he came back with a bang in my consciousness was *Nite Flights*," confirms David Bowie.

"It was the first four songs on *Nite Flights*," elaborates his seventies collaborator Brian Eno in Stephen Kijak's documentary film. "I remember taking those to Montreux, which is where I was working with David at the time[18] and saying, 'Christ, you've got to listen to these!' It was really going somewhere. We felt there was a kinship there, because there was a sort of marriage of sensibilities that came from outside pop music. They came from orchestral music or experimental music or electronic music, but marrying that with the idea of the pop song, although these were very, very, very spaced-out pop songs," he laughs.

"I have to say it's humiliating to hear this," he reflects onscreen, listening to the four Engel tracks again. "It is! I just think, 'Christ, we haven't got any further!' I just keep hearing all these bands that sound like Roxy Music and Talking Heads[19] – we haven't got any further than this! It's a disgrace, really."

"I assume that, of course, a lot of that enters the music of the times," Kijak opines to this writer both of the slowly filtering Engel influence and the edgy tensions of the late seventies, "it has to. And it is very much the beginning of a new chapter for him, and again I feel you can always sense the times in his music. It's not overtly political music, but even on *Tilt* and on *The Drift* he's reflecting on the state of the world and on human consciousness. He's very tapped into the feeling of the times, about the current malaise, if you will, or the pressing anxiety of a moment. I think he's always very much writing that."

But, despite its status as a profound artistic statement, *Nite Flights* still had to be promoted as a piece of record company product by GTO. In the run-up to the album's release, The Walker Brothers were to be put back into cabaret performances by David Apps, their manager of the time.

In his film, Kijak asks Engel about the absence of any *Nite Flights* material from the set lists.

"Well, nobody wanted to hear it!" comes Scott's almost amused reply. "That's the thing. If I recall, the tour was kind of a parting shot for everyone to make some money, I think, that's how far things had gone. So we knew that whatever public was there, nobody was going to want to hear *that*."

"Scott had been complaining to me, late at night, how John kept hounding him to go on tour," spoke Gary around the same time, "and he was adamant he couldn't take the chance because of John's drink problem. John, in turn, was constantly saying that Scott's nerves were shot and that he was afraid to go on stage. What Scott was really nervous about was John's inability to perform.

"There was some truth in what John said, and it may well be that it was at this time that Scott developed what has since been described as a 'total phobia' about live performances. He and I were now very dependent on Valium, taking the highest permitted dose. Everything was fine until that tablet started wearing off and then we became very, very edgy. This distorted our judgement, and Scott's built-in perfectionism made him near-obsessive. As in the sixties, he was terrified of the Valium wearing off on stage, and had panic attacks while performing... Scott was not the sociable type and liked keeping to himself, giving him more space to nurture his fears. My theory is that these factors put Scott off performing. The only way to resolve the problem was to take more Valium or give up playing live."

Over the ensuing years, Engel would apparently bring his reputed Valium dependency under control (as John would with his drinking – albeit much later). But his public performances would end with the tour. Gary Leeds recalls how John Maus would take more lead vocals than his fellow Walker on the summer '78 cabaret tour, and that Scott – still a vitamin-popping fitness fan, whatever his other weaknesses – mainly enjoyed forcing the backup band onto the tennis courts with him in the morning.

"Gary and I coerced him into doing some dates, which unfortunately backfired on us," John would later complain. "Scott didn't want to do The Walker Brothers' hits, of which we had to include at least a few, and refused to do any of his solo hits.[20]

"The cabaret dates turned out to be a disaster. Scott was obviously uninterested, on stage and off, which had a negative effect on the audience... Each night on stage I cursed myself for talking Scott into doing this. At least the band was good, thank God. I can't remember if David Apps was present or not but I wish he had ground the shows to a halt long before we were done. We really harmed our reputation by presenting ourselves the way we did: we looked unprofessional."

"The album hadn't sold, and things weren't looking good," Leeds recalls of the aftermath of the tour. "Scott didn't want to tour again after the last shows we had done. In the end, we just drifted apart. There would not be another reunion. There were a couple of times over the years when we got close to it, and needed to make some money, but it never happened."

"The album was a commercial failure," seconded John, "our royalties didn't compare to our successful albums, and GTO probably lost money on the venture. There was, however, a small, exclusive audience that really liked the material, particularly Scott's compositions... We didn't know at the time that GTO was being taken over by CBS, which wasn't good news for Scott, as not too long ago he'd gone to a lot of trouble to get out of a contract with them. We were still dependent financially on GTO, who paid for our flat, but we now needed to generate some other income... After several months went by, with no positive activity or plans for the future, I told Scott and Gary that I was going back to America... There was no discussion about breaking up the group, we just drifted apart."

★★★

In October 1978, another portal to the past closed. Jacques Brel, who'd been living in luxurious self-exile on a Polynesian island, had returned to Paris for treatment of the lung cancer from which he'd been suffering for several years. At 2.30am on October 9, the weakened man slipped into a terminal coma at the Franco-Muslim Hospital. All those poetic lyrics of human mortality were finally fulfilled. He would be shipped back to the South Pacific for burial, accompanied to the docks by a police motorcade.

Scott Engel would never sing another Brel lyric – though he was already in a very different place by this point. The novelistic approach of the deceased Belgian to his songs had been revolutionary in its time, but the twilight decades of the 20th century were demanding different modes of communication.

Several months later, on 17 March 1979, *Melody Maker* ran the following report:

David Bowie, in New York, finishing work on his next album, *Lodger*, with Tony Visconti, recently approached Scott Walker indirectly with a view to producing his next album.

Bowie was impressed by the European feeling of the last Walker Brothers' album which owed its critical acceptance to Scott's work. It is understood that while Walker appreciated

Bowie's interest, he turned down his help. He is working on his own solo album and is anxious to avoid contact with other musicians at the moment.

The MD of Virgin Records, Simon Draper, who had been alerted to the power of 'The Electrician' by Eno, had his curiosity piqued by the report. He would make overtures to Engel with a view to signing him to the label, and then...

And then, a period of silence ensued.

Notes

1 Scott Engel has long been an avid reader of Fyodor Dostoyevsky's novels and novellas. As with other devotees of 'the mad Russian', it's the psychological insight into the human condition and its intense contradictions that fascinate; few more profound arguments for atheism are found than in Dostoyevsky's works, where he also argues (Leonard Cohen-like) that we must not renounce God or all is lost.

2 Particularly in performing English translations of Brel.

3 Play 'Subterraneans', with its fragmentary guitar and bass chords, alongside the fractured guitar riff of Scott's later 'Jesse'. They're clearly not the same thing at all, yet their similar method drags the listener below the surface of the music.

4 First applied by William S. Burroughs to his own fiction, as adapted from the experimental techniques of his painter friend Brion Gysin.

5 Its line "[they] never die, they just go to sleep one day" is taken from Brel's '*Les vieux*' ('The Old Folks').

6 Note that exclamation mark. This was the early Ultravox! of John Foxx, not all-purpose eighties pop star Midge Ure – he of the pointlessly faithful cover of the Walkers' version of 'No Regrets'.

7 After the Alain Resnais art film that Scott Engel would surely be familiar with.

8 This full circle of the symbiotic Engel-Bowie influence came at a strange bookend of the former David Robert Haywood Stenton Jones' career. Having lost much credibility with former admirers via a bland mid-eighties adult-orientated rock period, Bowie tried to regain his former knack of combining disparate influences to startling effect. His version of 'Nite Flights', however, is so close to the original as to seem almost redundant – though it does play up the backing track to make it more rhythmically danceable.

9 Perhaps the early eighties incarnation of King Crimson with Adrian Belew (lead guitarist on Bowie's 1978 world tour) is the closest approximation of the guitar sound. All the more remarkable that Scott should coax it out of seasoned session men like Big Jim Sullivan and Les Davidson.

10 Or *Bertrand*-Henri Levy, due to a typographic error.

11 Levy, though loosely speaking of the French liberal left, was in the seventies a vocal opponent of the Marxism that held sway in French intellectualism since the De Gaulle era – an opposition which today he applies to fundamentalist Islam. As the son and heir of a multimillionaire industrialist, it's perhaps inevitable that he wouldn't keep faith with the dictatorship of the proletariat. Now in his early sixties, he plays the role of flaxen-haired 'celebrity philosopher' that only the French could produce (although sceptics have played up his celebrity while asking 'whither the philosophy?'). For all that, his humanitarianism seems beyond doubt and he was vocal in persuading the French government to intervene in Libya on the side of anti-Gadaffi rebels. In recent times, his recorded clash of worldviews with the pessimistic nihilist Houellebecq provides amusing reading in their literary dialogue *Public Enemies.*

12 'The Electrician' would be released as a single in August 1978 but would barely touch the lowest reaches of the chart.

13 Filmed in 1994 by Polanski.

14 There was also an instrumental Engel composition entitled 'Tokyo Rimshot', not released until the compilation Walkers CDs were issued in the new millennium. Based on melodic cocktail piano and synthesizer, it's like a jazzy precursor to The Yellow Magic Orchestra's 'Theme From Space Invaders'. It was reputedly also recorded in a vocal version that this writer has never heard.

15 The Doctors Of Madness are one such that come to mind – though both John's and Gary's songs occasionally resemble Richard O'Brien's camp but catchy numbers from his musical *The Rocky Horror Show.*

16 Hipgnosis employed the late Peter 'Sleazy' Christopherson at this time – a member of pioneering 'industrial collective' Throbbing Gristle, against whose harsh recordings The Walker Brothers would always sound (even on *Nite Flights*) like a reformed sixties pop group. As the decades wore on, however, and Scott Engel moved further into the field of regimented dissonance, there was not so great a separation between his work and that of Christopherson's later band, Coil.

17 Lovers of *Scott 3* or 'Boy Child' – or even certain brief moments on *Scott 1-2* – may beg to differ.

18 On Bowie's 1979 album *Lodger.*

19 His seminal role in early Roxy Music aside, Eno was also lauded for his production of Talking Heads' entire output and his own collaboration with band leader David Byrne.

20 At the final cabaret dates in Birmingham, a woman fan's calls for 'Joanna' were met by silent indifference from Scott.

Chapter 11

Season Of Ascetic

*"All through the wintertime he hid himself away... all through the
winter in his lonely clump of wheat."*

– Frank Loesser, 'The Ugly Duckling', as sung by Danny Kaye

Fisher: *"I'm going to see Europe again... for the first time in years.
But Europe is not the same. I have arrived at dusk. The trip has made
me restless. I cannot sleep. Water, water everywhere... and not a drop to
drink."*

Therapist: *"The story – what is the story?"*

– Lars Von Trier, *The Element Of Crime*, a screenplay produced
in 1984

The Scott Walker that began to slowly pique the interest of a cult
audience in the early eighties was a phantom presence.[1] At first
almost as inaudible as he was invisible, with all of his classic Philips LPs
long since deleted, his works had to be resurrected by an evangelist.

J.D. Beauvallet, founder and music editor of French magazine *Les
Inrockuptibles*, would later be instrumental in the revival of interest
in Walker's music that took place in the nineties. His own curiosity

was engaged a decade earlier: "I was too young to remember The Walker Brothers, I mean I know the songs, but I think like many people I discovered Scott through the punks – because the punk generation, through people like Julian Cope, people like Echo & The Bunnymen, they all really worshipped Scott Walker. So we thought, 'Why? Who is this guy? Why is he worshipped by our heroes, this old Californian guy, by our punk heroes?'"

In fact this was the slightly younger generation that immediately followed punk. Engel's personal Saint Paul was the latter-day Saint Julian of Tamworth. Julian Cope, lead singer and lyricist of psychedelic pop band The Teardrop Explodes, had been a part of the Merseyside scene which produced fellow post-punk bands Echo & The Bunnymen and Wah! Heat, whose vocalists, Ian McCulloch and Pete Wylie, had started off by rehearsing in a bedsit combo called The Big Three.

After Teardrop made hits of their first two catchy singles, 'Reward' and 'Treason', Cope displayed the amiable motormouth tendency of championing his favourite long-forgotten or neglected performers. His choices were often esoteric: one particularly engaging interview in *NME* (with Cope photographed in his 'jamas) ran like a playlist: from forgotten psychedelia to 'krautrock'[2] But it wasn't all wig-out music. Among his favourite solo vocalists were soul singer Don Covay and – in particular – Scott Walker, last heard of on a string of Walker Brothers cabaret dates after they delivered their audacious third reformation LP and promptly disappeared again.

Later in 1981, when the name 'Scott Walker' was becoming just a legendary rumour, with the artist unseen for years and the music seldom heard at all, Cope talked Teardrop's independent label, Zoo Records, into licensing a number of original Engel compositions from the unavailable classic Philips LPs.

Fire Escape In The Sky: The Godlike Genius Of Scott Walker featured the best dozen songs that Zoo could afford: 'Such A Small Love' / 'Big Louise' (after whose attic boudoir the album is named) / 'Little Things (That Keep Us Together)' / 'Plastic Palace People' / 'The Girls From The Streets' / 'It's Raining Today' / 'The Seventh Seal' /

'The Amorous Humphrey Plugg' / 'Angels Of Ashes' / 'Boy Child' / 'Montague Terrace (In Blue)' and 'Always Coming Back To You'.

It was as if a forgotten and almost forbidden part of pop music's golden sixties era had been preserved only in this one slightly shabby artefact. Betraying its small-label origins, the light grey cover featured only ornate typography (watching from a distance, Engel later admitted, "I guess I was embarrassed by [the subtitle]") and an empty space on the back where a picture might have been – reserved for a photograph that never showed in time for printing, it served to underline the sense of mystery and absence now surrounding the artist.

"I was sent Cope's compilation and I put it on and listened to this young guy singin'," Scott told the *NME* several years later, "thought, hey, that's not bad. But one play was enough." As his later output would demonstrate, he'd been set on a new path that began at the tail end of the seventies, with *Nite Flights*, and in any case, *Fire Escape In The Sky* would be deleted early after the struggling Zoo failed to pay royalties to Philips/Polygram.

When Stephen Kijak was making his bio-doc in the mid-noughties, he contacted Cope to talk about the subsequent Walker revival. The latter-day psychedelic druid gave no direct input but sent the following gracious email:

From: headheritage
Sent: Friday, December 10, 2004 7AM
Subject: scott walker film

Hey Stephen
Excellent to hear from you, and I'm very glad the film is going well.

My reason for releasing the FIRE ESCAPE IN THE SKY: THE GODLIKE GENIUS OF SCOTT WALKER compilation in 1981, was because I'd been buying up his LPs for between 80p and £1.20 all over Liverpool and Birmingham, and giving them to friends and/or anyone who would listen.

Furthermore, I really felt Scott had been utterly lost in terms of culture because of his willingness to include MOR slop right up until SCOTT 3.

All the subsequent compilations pushed his 'housewife' appeal and totally ignored the really great compositions.

However, by that time it was too late and my grey post-punk photograph-free design allowed people to enjoy Scott without feeling they were buying into some dodgy 60s MOR icon.

I really felt the job was done, and I'm very glad that Scott's career was reclaimed to such a great extent.

I am pleased that someone remembers that the FIRE ESCAPE IN THE SKY LP started the deluge.

Good luck,
JULIAN

Cope, who has led an intriguingly esoteric solo career post-Teardrop Explodes, including as an author of books on historical, occult or musical arcana, later described his lack of sympathy for the more recent music of Scott Walker.[3]

By the time of the next Walker album release, the *NME* tried to engineer a meeting between the two performers but Cope ultimately didn't go ahead with it. "His attitude was rather the same as mine when I had the chance to meet Brel in Paris," said Engel. "I just chickened out. He did for the same reason."

It seems to have had much to do with the wise option that says 'avoid meeting your idols'. Cope had already opined in an earlier article that he wouldn't want to meet another personal favourite, ex-Velvet Underground songwriter/vocalist/arranger John Cale, in case he got irritated by the Teardrop man's effusiveness and said, "Look, I'm *only* John Cale!" But in any case, the revival of interest in Scott Walker was about to slowly permeate pop culture now.

In 1982, camp electropop singer Marc Almond[4] of Soft Cell formed an occasional group called Marc & The Mambas to indulge his more esoteric musical interests; their debut double album *Untitled* features a faithful cover of 'Big Louise'. The bisexual Almond can't have been blind to Engel's obvious sympathy for the outsiders of gay culture; he would later make 'The Plague' a regular part of his solo act at a time when that phrase was often synonymous with AIDS. He'd also become a regular re-interpreter of Brel's songs – his more limited vocal range but pleasingly histrionic mode of performance making him a kind of gay alternative to late-sixties period Scott Walker.

"The thing that really got me into him was someone did me a cassette of his solo records, because his solo records weren't really available," says Sheffield-born post-punk vocalist Jarvis Cocker, who performed sporadically with his band Pulp in the eighties but would not see success till the nineties Britpop era. "This would be like the mid-eighties or something, and it happened that I had flu at the time, and I was in bed feeling sorry for myself. And it was very strange because, you know you get a bit feverish when you've got flu or something, and I thought, 'Maybe I've imagined that music? I can't believe that it really exists.'"[5]

Music to emulate the psychic immersion of fever dream would follow later in Engel's career. For now, a long tunnel had to be followed that would arrive back in the recording studio.

✶✶✶

In the early eighties, having signed a contract with Virgin Records, Scott would speak sanguinely in retrospect of his living conditions: "I was lucky to have so much time on my hands, time to read, to watch movies, to do things I like to do."

Viewed with the naked eye, however, his situation was rather more precarious. Having put some of his own money into the completion of *Nite Flights*, he received virtually no royalties from that album and ongoing funds from the first two GTO Walkers LPs (for which he wrote none of the songs) was minimal; his Philips LPs were all by now out of print, apart from the odd compilation which, as Julian

231

Cope points out, focused on his MOR output. In fact, diminishing funds prior to signing with Virgin had forced Engel to sell off his entire extensive collection of classical and jazz records.

And when he did sign in February 1980, demo tracks for the first Virgin album were not forthcoming – despite an advance of £20,000.[6]

The following year, Scott promised Virgin MD Simon Draper that recording would begin in the spring – when plants, flowers and other vegetation were in bloom and he would feel his creative energy replenished. Draper had no problem with that, but was perturbed at a subsequent meeting to be told, "They're shoutin' at me beneath my flat. Makin' noise and disturbin' me." Scott apparently blamed this psychological onslaught on Virgin.

Draper was momentarily struck by fear that his new signing was a paranoid schizophrenic, but on closer investigation the assertion made some sense. Engel's current flat was in a side road off High Street Kensington; in the office below was a counselling group for single mothers, philanthropically funded by Richard Branson. It was their noisier sessions which were disrupting the concentration needed to compose his new songs.

It was a tenuous, almost subterranean connection, but it was real. It was also a mode of thinking that would display itself more vividly on his later musical output.

By mid-1982, Virgin was becoming increasingly concerned at the lack of contact with Scott Engel. He had, however, become friendly with its PR Al Clark, who he'd meet in the tearoom of the Kensington Hilton to discuss their shared love of cinema, and A&R man Arnold Frolows (later renowned for Australian radio show *Ambience*), who was interested in modern jazz and became Scott's squash partner.

Engel's apparently leisurely lifestyle seemed at odds both with his contractual obligation and his financial state. Much of his advance from Virgin was already exhausted and he'd had to move from no less than three flats over the last three-year period after either defaulting on repayments or not meeting the rent.[7]

It was against this background that Clark tried to break the impasse by recommending that Scott solicit the help of Ed Bicknell as an intermediary.

"I had a friend at Virgin Records called Al Clark, who later went on to make *Priscilla, Queen Of The Desert*,"[8] confirms veteran rock industry manager Bicknell. "Al and I just used to talk music – this is in the early eighties. Somehow it emerged that we were both huge Scott Walker fans, and I'd been a fan of Scott not just from the Walker Brothers period but particularly the four albums he did for Philips, pretty much after he left the group. I just said I thought he was great and all the rest of it, and thought no more about it. About a year later, the phone went in my office and I happened to pick up. This voice came on and went [in mellifluous tones]: 'Hi, this is Scott Walker.' And I literally dropped the phone – it's one of only two occasions when somebody's called where I was really intimidated. Kind of picked myself up off the ground, picked the phone up and he was looking for management."

As an ardent music fan, Bicknell seemed far from precious in his regard for Scott Walker and The Walker Brothers: "It was great music to fuck to!" he insisted to the Kijak film crew. "It is – it's slow and it bumps along," he laughs, harking back to the uses he made of it in his university days. He was rather more daunted, however, by the prospect of meeting the man behind the orgasmic orchestral epics.

"There is a kind of received notion about him, his Garboesque leanings towards seclusion, the fact that he was always photographed wearing scarves and dark glasses and always seemed to avoid attention. And when he came in I was absolutely crapping myself! I was so nervous. I was kind of pacing up and down in the office, and he came in and we were kind of pacing up and down past each other. And I actually said to him, 'I've got all your records.' Which is the most obsequious and greasy thing you can say to an artist – but I literally had got all of his records.

"I must say we had some fantastically funny and interesting meetings. One of Scott's favourite places to meet was the old bar in the Kensington Hilton hotel, because it was completely dark. And we used to sit in a booth with the curtains closed, in total darkness. He'd be three feet from me and I couldn't see him."

The affably garrulous Bicknell soon realised the mechanics of the Virgin deal were not going to work out. "I managed Dire Straits, Mark Knopfler,[9] Bryan Ferry, Gerry Rafferty and The Blue Nile,"[10] he reels off a list of late seventies/early eighties names. "And Scott stands alone as being, as far as I can tell, completely unmotivated by money. I mean that not just in the musical sense but as a human being. I never ever got the impression that he would do anything for money."

Which, of course, had its implications for the Virgin contract. "It was one of the most disgraceful deals I've ever seen. I work in a business that exploits the talent and the consumer almost equally. This one was a 12-album deal,[11] and I calculated on the basis of Scott's work, what he could produce, he would probably be around 200 years old by the time he got to the 12th album."

Engel initially solicited Bicknell to get him work as a producer. When Virgin saw this as a delaying tactic, the manager went to work with Scott on a strategy of isolation which would allow him to produce material for the new album.

"The way I used to write albums back in the old days quite quickly, I believe now that I wrote my fourth album in about two months, maybe," Scott reflects. "That's very fast. I could be wrong there, but I seem to recall that. It wouldn't happen today.

"There's always urgency. It drives you really crazy, but you can't push it because if you do it doesn't work. It has to be exactly what it is and you've just got to sit around and do it. And years can go by and... nothing. It's different for everyone, maybe I'm just slow. But for me that's how it is. It's very difficult.

It was the arrival of a publisher's cheque which allowed him to replenish his diminishing resources and take off from London for a while. "And I remember he went to the New Forest, I think, and hired a cottage,"[12] says Bicknell, "and rang me up one day and basically said, 'I've got the songs – I'm ready.'"

After the eventual completion of the album, Engel would be interviewed by DJ Alan Bangs for British Forces Broadcasting Radio, who asked him of the six intervening years between it and *Nite Flights*, "Did you spend a lot of time during those six years actually on your own?"

"Uh yes, rather a lot of time," he answered pensively. "All the time, the six years, I was working towards what I call a silence, where it would come to me rather than me force it. It was very important that it flow to me, rather than me force it and so I was looking for the right atmosphere. And time and perception seemed to arrive at once. I've found that it's kind of a kaleidoscopic process, I don't know, I don't like to talk too much about the process because I don't really understand it. When it got to this album it got away from me, and I'm a little superstitious so I don't talk about this too much."

With a series of impressionistic lyrics now produced in total seclusion, all that remained was for them to be sonically sculpted into an album. It was to be a similarly painstaking process, though on a much accelerated scale. First he hired a hall in Islington to test that his maturing vocal cords could handle the word structures and tone poems he'd been composing. No longer *au fait* with developments in studio technology, Engel also required a new producer. The means of selection included listening to the production work of people currently active in the eighties.

Among these was a young engineer-turned-producer named Peter Walsh, who'd produced the classic early eighties political dance-pop of Heaven 17's *Penthouse & Pavement* album and turned former electro-rockers Simple Minds into a stadium act with their *New Gold Dream*. For all the extreme variability in this repertoire, Engel deemed Walsh's studio approach "more total" and a meeting was set.

"I met him in a hotel in Shepherds Bush," recalled Walsh. "'He'll be the guy with the baseball cap,' they said, sitting in this dimly lit restaurant, chewing a match. I was a little bit surprised by the amount of mystery that was there... I'd gone into the first recording without actually hearing any demos at that point, because there weren't any."

The album would be recorded at London's Town House, EMI and Sarm West Studios between October and December. It would cost Virgin several times what they'd already paid Engel for his advance. It would also, unfortunately, outstrip any profit they'd hoped to make on it.

"I realised that we weren't going to get a conventional record because there was no aspect of making it that was conventional," laughs Bicknell. Indeed, the studio sessions were dictated by an artistic agenda quite alien to most pop musicians.

"The guitarist on the session was heard to play the melody," confirms Walsh, "and Scott actually went crazy: 'Who's playing that melody? Stop the melody! I don't want to hear any melody – and nobody else is to hear any melody either.'"

"I even keep things from Pete till the end," Engel confirms of what is now a long-term working relationship with Walsh. "When you tell people, this banal thing starts to happen again. Somebody will pick up on a lyric and start joking about this, and suddenly the song is in another place. You know, it's not in the concentrated place it should be."

"So we actually recorded the whole album with the melody as a closely guarded secret," laughs Walsh of his 1984 Walker initiation. "As a producer, or co-producer if you like,[13] it's quite a big thing to be missing as you're working."

"It keeps everything a little more disjointed," confirms Engel, as if it were the most natural process in the world. "There's no chance of anyone 'swinging together' too much – which is not what I want, I'm not making groove records."

Scott was aware of improvisational sax player Evan Parker from his interest in the Euro-jazz scene. After being recruited to play on the songs 'Dealer' and 'Track Six' (many of the album's eight tracks would be ascribed numbers rather than titles – though some Engel-philes tend to refer to them by their opening lines), Parker admits, "I was a bit puzzled – why does he want me? Because I wasn't known to be a session player. I think the first thing he said is, 'This is not a funk session. I know your work. I'm thinking about clouds of saxophone, and I'm thinking about Ligeti[14] more than anything else.' So we drank some Chablis, I remember – a very good Chablis at room temperature, very interesting, maybe two bottles quite quickly. Meanwhile they're setting up the amp in the room that I'd played in, but the guitar player was in the control room. I'd never seen that done before."

The resulting album, *Climate Of Hunter*, is emblematic in its title of its creator's juxtaposition of words and possible meanings.[15] Engel acknowledged the influence of *Lieder* – the Teutonic melding of classical music and lyrics which composers such as Schubert or Mahler, whose mournful *Kindertotenlieder* ('Songs For The Death Of Children') is a classic of the genre. But no such overriding theme can be ascribed to *Climate Of Hunter* – an album that would perplex many.

From its opening sound of a cowbell shaking, the sharp clarity that Walsh brought to *Climate* made it a quintessential (if not overtly commercial) eighties album; years after the event, some of the elements (particularly the cleanly pounding sound of Peter Van Hooke's drums) seemed to date it to 1984. Played now it sounds contemporary again, as if the archivists of analogue music have rediscovered and reintegrated the sound of electronically polished eighties rock.

The cowbell opens 'Rawhide', an in-joke for a menacingly dramatic piece that has nothing to do with cowboy imagery (except as wordplay – raw hide = raw body): "This is how you disappear out between midnight," Scott sings with the unyielding clarity of his late Walker Brothers period, and there's a sense that he's singing not of his own elusive qualities but of an entire species. The organic construction of physical imagery on this album (later supplanted by images of movement or objectified tools on what followed over the next two decades) verges on the grotesque: "Foot, knee, shaggy belly, face, famous hind legs."

To quote Julian Cope's literary mentor, Colin Wilson: "It was... Robert Ardrey who first made the general public aware that one of the most basic impulses in all animals is the urge to establish an area that belongs to the family or the tribe, and from which all invaders are repelled." It was also anthropologist Ardrey, in his book *African Genesis*, who posited that the evolution from ape to Neanderthal to primitive human came as the result of our being aggressive, carnivorous killers. Something similar is going on here: "Cro-magnon herders will stand in the wind, / Sweeping tails shining, / And scaled to begin."

'Dealer', which follows, combines the coldly arpeggiated bursts of electric guitar that punctuate the album (courtesy of Phil Palmer) with Parker's drifting, nagging jazz textures. In his book *Another Tear Falls*, poet Jeremy Reed makes the obvious case for 'Dealer' as a drug-culture song – which seems only partway there, as the writer seems to accept.[16] Where he *does* seem to be correct is in its ephemeral/ ethereal use of drug-culture imagery: "Keeping ice junkies packed hard on a seam… Move a circuit on the white, / And he can't feel a thing," and the surreal picture of "hissing brains boiling up". William S. Burroughs, an on-off junkie throughout his life, appropriated the imagery of junk addiction, 'the sickness', as the perfect metaphor for our unnatural cravings and desires in our techno-consumer culture. These days we're all jacking up something, it seems; fortunately, for most people opiates are off the menu, but it's as difficult to dissuade a wage slave from working for the new iPad, say, as it was to wean them off their CD Walkman in the eighties.

As Engel said back in the day, this was "edge work", skating around the edge of meaning. But it now seems retrospectively attuned to a world where the word 'interface' was about to become a verb and where, in a decade, people would become literal addicts of the virtual reality of something called a 'worldwide web'. It's the cold, hard music of a still corporeal world where, as in 'cyberpunk' science fiction, technology and human flesh will have to learn to exist on equal terms.

But if there's an organic antithesis to all this, it's in the beautifully hypnotic closer to side one of the original vinyl album: "In the time of an exile / From the jails of another," sings Scott, his lightened baritone reaching skyward, almost towards soprano, as anyone with the necessary sensitivity discovers their nerves are tingling, "Where soundings are taken / Raw to his eyes."

The absence of a literal meaning or linear logic can't disguise the oneiric beauty of 'Sleepwalkers Woman'. Orchestrated by classically trained keyboard player Brian Gascoigne, this is Engel's *Lieder* – stretching back through a hypnotic lineage that passes through 'The Electrician', through 'Boy Child' and back into *Scott 3*. But as Engel said at the time, "now [i.e. in his forties] is the best age to sing at", before the inevitable decay of all things physical in his next decade. He never sang more powerfully than on 'Sleepwalkers Woman'[17] – pointedly without a possessive apostrophe, so that the woman who "will fold him away in his badly changed hand" may not be anyone who belongs to him – or anyone that exists outside of his dream.

"For the first time unwoken / I am returned" Engel intones several times over, sounding somehow exultant and elegiac at the same time. It's a mesmeric meditation on his own sense of alienation – a self-willed exile, as he acknowledges, from the time and place and culture that bore him. In Kijak's documentary, an extract from 'Sleepwalkers Woman' plays over shots of a lake that may or may not have been close to the cottage where he composed *Climate Of Hunter*; it's a haunting testament to how the human mind can seek solace in its own lonely detachment.[18]

The glacial nightmares continue, however, on side two of the (vinyl) album: "It's a starving reflection if he dies in the night," asserts 'Track Five', which opens to similar strange solitary sounds as the first side; "We chew up the blackness to some high sleep," announces the strange bio-oneiric imagery. "The ceilings are rising and falling / The ceilings are shining and slow / Peeling tongues from the ice hums," describes 'Track Six' which, apart from 'Track Three' (the token single), is the most urgent-sounding, guitar-driven piece on the album, augmented by Parker's sax squealings. 'Track Seven' (sometimes referred to as 'Stump Of A Drowner', its opening line) continues the bad dream but is the most shiny metallic eighties track of the lot, complete with what sounds like syn-drums.

On the final track, Scot Engel retreats into his past and into his own sense of isolation: "When I crossed the river, / With a heavy blanket roll," – it's strange to hear Mark Knopfler, Bicknell's boy, playing highly competent blues guitar here, a conventional British rock musician who adopts American affectations – "I took nobody with me, / Not a soul" – especially to a minimal lyric by Tennessee Williams, from his play *Orpheus Descending* – "I took a few provisions / Some for comfort, some for cold," – Engel asked a recording assistant to find the filmed version of the play where Brando kind of mumbles the song in tune, as he couldn't remember the title; in that pre-internet/ pre-DVD era it took several days of searching before a recording assistant found *The Fugitive Kind* – "But I took nobody with me / Not a soul." It offers the perfect lonely coda to so much that has been strangely impressionistic or obscure.

The cover photo of *Climate Of Hunter* finds Scott Walker apparently caught mid-gesture – extending a hand, looking expressively at the camera, youthfully middle-aged but still long-haired, without his trademark aviator shades to hide behind. On his promotional rounds for the album's release in March 1984,[19] however, he tended to retreat behind his shaded glasses again – or at least he did on *The Tube*, Channel 4's Newcastle-based eighties rock/pop show for Friday evenings. Interviewed not by hosts Jools Holland or Paula Yates but by pixie-ish Scot Muriel Gray (who went on to become a broadcasting media darling through much of the eighties), she was comically ill-informed and Engel's response is squirmy to watch.

After asking him lame questions about *Ready Steady Go!* and having once been a heartthrob, she nervously laughs about how "some of the tracks have got rather unusual names – because you've got 'Track Three', 'Track Five', 'Track Seven', 'Track Eight'. Why haven't you got names, Scott?"

"Yeah, well, I guess the old creativity kinda ran out," he genially shrugs. "I just thought they were finished as they were, and putting a title on them might have lopsided them or overloaded them. I don't know if this is original, somebody else might have done it."

"On the new album you're very much part of a band," she continues, "whereas in The Walker Brothers it was just three men singing [*sic*] and all this orchestration in the back. Are you happier doing this now? You don't ever get a yen to just get up and sing a song again on your own?"

"No, no, I'm not a get-up-and-sing-a-song singer," he laughs. "Pretty much a singer when the circumstances are totally right, especially now."

Going by his own itinerary, however, it seemed the moment had already passed. The excruciating banality of the interview was alleviated by the uncredited promo film for 'Track Three' – Scott Walker had entered the eighties video pop world.

"Delayed in the headlong / Resembled to breaking-point ..."

Scott's urgent vocals are echoed unseen by Billy Ocean,[20] the ex-GTO soul singer who praised the former Walker Brother as the best singer he'd ever heard. The video is noir-ish black and white, with Scott observing the action on a south London housing estate as he mimes to the song. A balding hawk-nosed actor leaves a car at night-time. Scott watches from the wall just around the corner – raising his face from his hands to mime urgently to the camera. He and the actor have both imprinted dark smudges on their foreheads – like some bloody mark of Cain.

"The blood of our split back without his prisoner / The distance rigged in his eyes..."

A still body seems to be lying under a sheet – cut to a wild-haired woman lying on a bed, staring toward the camera. The bald guy kicks over dusty ground which is like one big sandpit and drops to his knees to dig with his hands. He dips his face in darkish fluid which may be blood (the black and white photography obscures this). Another vehicle (apparently a Cortina – indicative of the video's budget) rounds the corner of the estate to find Scott singing alone and accompanying himself on bass in a very rock-video manner.

"From the host of late-comers a miracle enters the streets... He is shaking to wash the murder away..."

The driver of the other vehicle is a Michael Gambon lookalike with a tattooed hand, who drops two dice into the dust. The first man frantically digs for this obscure object of desire, before being pursued by the not-very-fast-moving Cortina through the post-industrial landscape as the short, frantic bursts of a guitar solo open up. The second man drops another obscure object into the dust – this time a piece of fruit (an apple?). The first man bites the dust just as the object does – and becomes the covered prone body we glimpsed shortly before.

It ends on the refrain, a wordplay subversion of a popular funeral hymn: "Rock of cast-offs, / Bury me, / Hide my soul, / And pray us free."

The video is very much a piece of low-budget eighties surrealist noir – its atmosphere has something in common with *The Element Of Crime*, the debut film by Danish director Lars Von Trier[21] and the first of his *Europa* trilogy. (As *The Element Of Crime* wasn't released till two months later, we have to assume it exerted no influence over the video's director – unless he saw it previewed at a film festival.) But the clipped, urgent tones of Scott's track might have made a novel stand-in for the usual Jan Hammer soundtrack on *Miami Vice*.

In a parallel eighties universe, *Climate Of Hunter* might have instituted a craze for surrealist noir (in both music and film) while 'Sleepwalkers Woman' would be praised for the sublime musical apex that it reached.

"I think there is a direct line," opines Stephen Kijak of the music's evolution, "especially if you follow it through to *Nite Flights* and *Climate*. In *Stretch* and *We Had It All*,[22] I've got to say I listen to those records more now because I just don't need all the other stuff so much. Now I've made the film it's like, 'Oh, I haven't really listened to this one so much.' Yeah, they're not his songs but some of them are fantastic. The voice is still there and clearly full of emotions –

either it's resolved or it's melancholy, because they weren't really happy years for him. But the actual creative work you can line up in the writing – from [*Scott*] *4*, *Nite Flights* and beyond. Obviously those intervening years altered him – you can't help but be changed by that stuff."

In the actuality, *Climate Of Hunter* gained an unenviably novel reputation as Virgin's worst seller of all time. Figures of 1,500 sales were mooted back in the eighties, but the sum total was closer to 10,000 copies internationally – still no world breaker. The record label was reputedly shocked by its failure to perform.

"You get unbelievable, or even believable people being picked up all the time who aren't selling records," complained a bruised Scott a few years later. "It's puzzled me. People expect a lot more sales out of me than are generated. So they're vastly disappointed. Whereas with other artists they'll eke it out."

Ed Bicknell tried to salvage the situation by suggesting a cover versions album of songs by contemporary writers[23] – like a step back into the final days of Philips or CBS. Predictably, Scott mulled over the idea but wasn't interested.

Once again – this is how you disappear. "I didn't immediately think next year we'll be doing the follow-up," reflected Pete Walsh. "I didn't expect to wait 10 years."

✴✴✴

It wasn't till 1986 that Bicknell again saw Scott, who'd been living in the west London suburb of Stamford Brook. When asked how he was occupying his time, he told his part-time manager he was painting.

"Oils or watercolours?"

"Oh no. Paintin' and decoratin'."

There may have been an element of leg pulling in this as, in the autumn of the following year, Scott Engel would begin a foundation course in fine arts as a mature student at the Byam Shaw School of Art in Archway, north London.[24]

In the meantime, however, as Engel had already been introduced to his admirer Brian Eno by Al Clark in 1981, Bicknell went all out to hook him up with Eno and his production partner Daniel Lanois – who had recently completed work on U2's *The Unforgettable Fire*, which would become one of the commercial blockbusters of the decade.

Sessions were set up with Scott and the producers at Roxy Music guitarist Phil Manzanera's studio in Chertsey, Surrey – and within two weeks they collapsed. At Engel's insistence, Bicknell had to put an injunction on EG Records, Eno's record label, to stop them issuing an album of the unused backing tracks Eno had prepared.

"I remember a quote when Scott turned down Bowie," says Stephen Kijak, "I think he self-deprecatingly said: 'I've ruined my career, I don't want to ruin his as well,' something to that effect – you know, ha ha. But I don't know – again, the unproduced albums, the aborted projects, they're not unique to him, these things happen *all the time*: they get together, they start to record, something isn't right, the collaboration isn't going to work, they move on, something else happens just down the road. And that I think was the case with Eno and Lanois – I can only imagine what it would have been like. I'm a huge fan of the work Lanois did with Emmylou Harris, *Wrecking Ball*, and they were coming after *The Unforgettable Fire*, so sonically it could have been a fantastic match, but it wasn't meant to be, sadly.

"He did find a fantastic partner in Pete Walsh, who's been at the helm ever since. Obviously Eno and Lanois are huge personalities in the studio and the thing is Scott himself, he doesn't get credit for producing a record but he knows his way around a studio. He's been involved in every aspect."

"We met and talked a little too quickly," said Engel himself a few years after. "I didn't like the studio anyway, it was way out of town, and, I don't know, it transpired that it became an irritation. [Eno] brought Daniel Lanois along and I just couldn't get along with that guy. It became too many cooks. I left very quickly before any major damage was inflicted. Except I got dropped from my record company deal."

The working relationship with Bicknell was also coming to an end – not out of any animosity, but simply because there was no work to collaborate on. "The thing about working with him was it was always interesting," reports Bicknell to Kijak. "It was never the standard way of doing anything. In the period I looked after him, I remember I made about £350 commission in five years – and I loaned him £500. At the end of it I had a net loss of £150 – and I'd do it again tomorrow, I'd do it like that.

"People say, 'Oh he should have done this!' Why should he? You know, if he's not driven toward that kind of [thing]... Scott Walker would be a complete non-fit with the way things are now. I mean, I think it would be tragic to see him trying to perform on the MTV Awards, between Dr Dre and Puff Diddly-Widdly."

In his small number of press interviews for *Climate Of Hunter* in '84, Scott had informed *NME* that he liked spending his time in pubs, watching people play darts. It became the latest urban myth about him: this was supposedly what the Invisible Man of modern music did all the time.

Before enrolling on his arts course, he could actually be glimpsed for the last time in public – or at least on the screen – for many years. Strapped for cash, he made the kind of bizarre commercial compromise that he would never apply to his music any more.

In cinemas during 1987, an ad for Britvic 55 (the sparkling version of the orange juice drink) played that featured a group of middle-aged hipsters from the swinging sixties strutting about in the fashions of their youth. It played to Dusty Springfield's 'I Only Want To Be With You', with Dusty herself (who that year had a hit with the Pet Shop Boys on 'What Have I Done To Deserve This?') as the driver of a sports car, giving the camera an embarrassed smile at the end; there was Sandie Shaw, last seen backed by three quarters of The Smiths on 'Hand In Glove', strutting about in kinky white boots; The Tremeloes fooling around a telephone box like a bunch of longhaired schoolboys; a figure credited as 'Man in Park' as Dusty drove past was a smiling Georgie Fame; and the 'Man in Café', looking apprehensively around him in shades, was Scott Walker. It was a strange epitaph to a brief eighties career.

Not that Scott didn't periodically try to become musically active; he had taken up again with his old friend John Maus. They were creating demos of John's latest songs with his current wife, Brandy, which later resulted in a single called 'Dark Angel', a clichéd rock ballad (with the odd eighties disco *boom! boom!* on the backing), issued on a small US label.

The demos he produced for John and Brandy were initially hawked to Geoff Travis, director of prominent independent/post-punk label Rough Trade, then home to the disbanding Smiths. Unsurprisingly, Travis wasn't interested in John's MOR rock – but signing Scott Walker was a different proposition. He wanted him for his smaller subsidiary, Blanco Y Negro, but this label had been bought out by Warner Brothers and the US corporate suits nixed the deal.

In the spring of the following year, Engel took one more tentative step toward getting back into music by signing with a new manager, entertainment lawyer Charles Negus-Fancey. The son of prolific low-budget British film director E.J. Fancey, Negus-Fancey had become increasingly involved in music via working for the Robert Stigwood Organisation, which was behind the hit film musicals *Tommy, Saturday Night Fever* and *Grease*. He was also, at the time he met Scott, the UK representative of Mort Shuman – the man who had popularised Jacques Brel in English.

Negus-Fancey would prove particularly patient over many years with his extraordinary charge. By the beginning of 1990, he was trying to resurrect the deal with Geoff Travis, this time with parent company Rough Trade, as brothers Jim and William Reid of The Jesus & Mary Chain (who cited The Walker Brothers' 'After The Lights Go Out' as one of their favourite tracks of all time) had expressed a wish to produce Scott Walker.

Again it came to nothing. Rough Trade's distributors were facing bankruptcy and the deal was blocked. "I have a totally different record I want to do now," Engel was quoted as saying around this time, "because I discovered all the new things I can use in the studio. But I have to wait. This is a waiting game."

No way back to the past. Pathway to the future blocked.

Notes

1   As we've seen, only one Noel Scott Engel seems to inhabit the world – but there are myriad permutations of Scott Walker.

2   The wave of post-psychedelic German bands like Can and Faust.

3   Cope described the ethos of latter-day Walker as "pale European intellectual" in his second volume of memoirs and denies interest in it. As an esotericist whose subjects embrace pagan prehistory and who is influenced by the occult writings of the polymathic Colin Wilson, he may share 'positive existentialist' Wilson's attitude to pessimistic existential playwright/author Samuel Beckett: Wilson reasonably states that humankind cannot live without hope and cites Beckett's hopelessness as near-criminal; Scott Engel, on the other hand, acknowledges Beckett as a major influence on his later work.

4   Peter Mark Almond coined himself 'Marc' after his idol Marc Bolan and had his first hit with a cover of Bolan's lover Gloria Jones' northern soul classic 'Tainted Love'.

5   Interviewed on *Later With Jools Holland* in the nineties, the archive pop clip selected for Cocker was Scott singing 'Mathilde' on Dusty Springfield's show.

6   Obviously a more considerable sum of money in the early eighties than it would be now – although its terms covered a staggering number of recordings.

7   It's unclear whether Scott had rented or bought these flats – although in the seventies he'd been a householder at a large flat near Regent's Park.

8   Clark produced the nineties comedy film.

9   Both as Dire Straits' frontman and as a solo artist.

10   The Blue Nile are an eighties-formed trio who play synth-pop on an epic scale. They have been periodically active throughout the ensuing decades.

11   Virgin claimed at the time it was for eight albums.

12   Engel's own recollection suggests a caretaker's cottage near Tunbridge Wells, Kent, in August and September of 1983.

13   Peter Walsh makes no bones about Scott Engel's own uncredited role as co-producer.

14   Gyorgy Ligeti – the Hungarian composer whose polyrhythmic 'Lux Aeterna' chorale was featured in the moon monolith scene of *2001: A Space Odyssey*, and which influenced 'The Bed' on Lou Reed's *Berlin* album.

15   Particularly in the lack of a definite article – it is *not* an allusion to *The Night Of The Hunter*.

16   Despite the old-fashioned tradition of middle-class arty types seeking to experience 'bohemia' by dabbling with heroin, it's hard to imagine Scott Engel ever giving himself over to such an all-consuming substance; nor is there any reason to doubt him when he says he's never touched it.

17   Despite the lack of commercial success experienced by *Climate Of Hunter*, post-punk/Gothic songstress Siouxsie included 'Sleepwalkers Woman' on her *My Top 12* for Radio One, soon after the album's release. She seemed taken aback by what she described as "such confident singing", completely *sui generis* in the world of modern popular music.

18   It may possibly be only this writer who can hear the brief melancholic passage of Danny Kaye's 'The Ugly Duckling', from the movie *Hans Christian Andersen*, in a section of 'Sleepwalkers Woman': "All through the wintertime he hid himself away / Ashamed to show his face, afraid of what others might say." But then the song's composer, Frank Loesser, was familiar with the *Lieder* form and Scott Engel's favourite city used to be Copenhagen.

19   This time around there would be no live shows to promote the album at all.

20   He had a big hit with 'When The Going Gets Tough' in the eighties.

21   A controversial figure who later headed Scandinavia's Dogme cinema movement.

22   Scott's country and western covers albums – see Chapter Nine.

23   The mooted figures included Mark Knopfler, Difford & Tilbrook of Squeeze, Joan Armatrading and Boy George. It sounds as if it might have been horribly inappropriate, had it come off.

24   Reputedly, none of the lecturers realised their student had been famous in a past life, until one pointed at a painting and said: "Scott Walker did that."

Chapter 12

Dislocation Is A Place

Sick of living/ unwilling to die
cut.
clean.
if red/
clean.
blood spurting
   dripping,
   spilling;
all over her new
   dress.

                    – opening section of a poem discovered etched into a
                          desk at the Riverside City College Library,
            San Francisco, March 1967, suspected of being
                        the work of the 'Zodiac Killer'

*"… For transports of the size with which Eichmann was concerned, he
had to work closely with officials of the German railways. Within the
ghettos set up by the Nazis in Eastern Europe, Jewish councils were
formed whose function was to supply the SS units with facts and figures.
They would be told how many people must report at such and such
a time and such and such a place for transportation to the liquidation*

249

> *centres. The Jewish elders were ordered to fill in countless forms in quintuplicate so that the machine could run with bureaucratic efficiency."*
>
> – G.S. Graber, *History Of The SS*

> *"I ain't no pussy / With the blues."*
>
> – Scott Engel, *'Man From Reno', 1992*

In the summer of 1990, the arcane Scott Walker of pop legend re-emerged from history. The vehicle was another compilation album in the vein of the previous decade's *Fire Escape In The Sky*. Entitled *Boy Child* – after his most ambitious early step towards the *Lieder* tradition, on 1969's *Scott 4* – it contained sleeve notes by the figure who'd taken on Julian Cope's mantle of the most vocal Engel-phile in modern pop culture.

"… Although on the one side he was the Jack Jones/Tony Bennett style crooner (both were firm favourites of Scott's) he broke away from that mould to record a series of solo albums that were both rich and dark with songs of death, desire, despair and isolation. His haunted disembodied voice was the supreme instrument for the interpretation of the 'lonely' song," waxed Marc Almond.

"The rumours – 'he's dead, he's mad, he's become a recluse, he's recording an instrumental album'… all add to the enigma of Scott Walker… Scott's recent recordings have been all too rare. He surfaced in recent years with the brilliantly disturbing *Climate Of Hunter*; sometimes it seems 'the sad young man has gone away,'[1] but just as Brel has been interpreted in many ways by different artists, so I hope will be Scott Walker."

Boy Child was as near as one could get to a definitive non-Brel anthology of the late sixties period, with a range of the strongest Engel originals from *Scott 1-4* and *'Til The Band Comes In*.

Almond, whose own drama-queen tones could rise from slightly warbling tenor to soprano-ish, also made reference to Engel's own "crooning deep tones and liquid vibrato". "Lazy journalists always used to say, 'He sounds Scott Walker-like,' about any singer that had a voice like a vibrato with a bit of reverb and a kind of a crooning quality. Because there is only one voice like that," he later elaborated in Stephen Kijak's film. Which was true enough, but had only really become a journalistic shtick over the past decade, since Cope's compilation had sold around 10,000 copies (in respectably quick time) and made the great absent baritone a yardstick for the select few who'd been exposed to it.

"I really know very little about him. I don't even know what he looks like," his elfin champion admitted in the mid-noughties. At the time of *Boy Child*, it was clear he was celebrating an almost mythological figure that he really didn't expect to return.

By then, of course, times had changed; Scott Engel was no longer the sad but androgynously handsome young man staring out of the girl's reflected eye on *Scott 3*, singing an accessible mini-oratorio about Big Louise. The decade of compromise that had followed had changed him, as we've already seen, into the most uncompromising of performers.

Crowd-pleasing was for the ephemeral. Scott Engel, though in seemingly good health and an admirable state of fitness, was approaching his 50th year, and he'd always felt mortality breathing down his neck. This was no time to be fooling around – or even to be recording music at all, if he couldn't draw the listener inward rather than having to step out to meet them halfway.

Further nostalgia was indulged when Fontana, Philips' resurrected pop label, released *No Regrets: The Best Of Scott Walker And The Walker Brothers* in 1992, which rose quickly to number four in the albums chart. Engel, in the interim, had been renewing contact with his old friends John Maus and Gary Leeds – though with no inclination for any further Walkers reunions, the latter now living in east London and working as a motorcycle courier – and taking a holiday in San Diego to visit his aging mother and Aunt Seal.

And still, at the pace which it takes small constellations to form, he was planning. And thinking. And, eventually, writing.

But to the music-listening public, the recent anthologies had made him a presence again, not just a rumour. This was compounded later in '92 when Fontana issued *Scott 1-4* on CD, followed soon after by *'Til The Band Comes In*.[2] He was no longer only a matter of legend – his music could be purchased again. There were articles about his past work (though never his 'lost years' as a covers artist) in the music press – and, predictably, pro- and anti-camps.

In the *Melody Maker*, Steve Sutherland struck a laddish tone, mocking everything Scott had done since The Walker Brothers and labelling him, with dull unimaginativeness, "daft as a brush". "Yes, there are people in the world who do not love Scott Walker," hit back Stuart Maconie in *NME*. "But what must their hearts be like? This is the voice... of mystery, suffering, heartbreak, nostalgia, yearning and joy."

It was also the voice of a romantic past; of a performer who, as far as his constituent parts went, no longer existed. But as far as the popular press were concerned, Scott Walker was a figure that existed in the past tense only – even if his corporeal body could be snapped moving along the street. When the *No Regrets* compilation hit the charts, Sunday tabloid *The People* carried a shot of a physically fit-looking middle-aged man in baseball cap, shades and padded windcheater, cycling along a leafy west London street in faded denim jeans and training shoes. To those who recalled him in his youth, this was clearly still Scott Engel. The paper even rather obtrusively set up a 'Walker Hotline' in case any readers knew his actual address. (Apparently none did.)

"I think he's got a way of disappearing," remarks *Les Inrockuptibles* editor J.D Beauvallet, whose magazine would soon mark the re-emergence of Scott Walker. "If he wants to be seen he's seen. I don't think he ever wants to be seen... People always said he had bought a fish and chips [shop] in London, people said he was an interior decorator." Or indeed that he was sitting in a pub watching people play darts.

Back at the time of his previous re-emergence, in 1984, Engel had insisted to *NME*: "I don't have the [old] records. People don't believe that, but I say you can come and listen to my apartment, like Gene Hackman."³

Now that the late sixties albums were common currency again, in the Kijak bio-doc a decade and a half hence he'd be asked if he could still hear the songs in his head that a younger generation of music lovers had cottoned on to, for example 'Montague Terrace' (In Blue)'.

"Someone will play it or you'll hear it on the radio and think back," he'd acknowledge. "But even these days, when people send me round digitally remastered versions of things they're reissuing for approval, which is very kind of them to do, I can't do it."

"We didn't grow up with The Walker Brothers' songs as a backdrop of the sixties," acknowledges Stephen Kijak of himself and his American peers, "they didn't become part of the seventies or eighties MOR radio. It's really not in the consciousness the way it is over there. It was more just through an underground hipster cult kind of awareness. In the nineties, when Fontana issued *Boy Child* and [reissued] *1-4*, they imported them to San Francisco. I was hanging out with musicians and it was kind of word of mouth. But once the new records were coming out, in the States they were issued on very cool record labels – Drag City put out *Tilt*, 4AD released *The Drift*, a very cool company, so you get that kind of generation. It was a very personal thing – you know, small groups of fans would pass copies around – a very cult awareness, always."

In London, in what may have seemed like an oddly retrograde step at the time, Charles Negus-Fancey had now negotiated his client a new recording deal with Fontana – the subsidiary of his original label from the sixties, now owned by Polygram. (In another echo of the past, the overall CEO was Maurice Oberstein – with whom Ady Semel had to negotiate to free Scott from his CBS contract.)

"Since the failure of your latest album, *Climate Of Hunter*, what have you been doing for 10 years?" asked Beauvallet in Scott's 1992 *Les Inrockuptibles* interview.

"*J'ai existé*," he answered – 'I have existed.'

Totally against all expectations, it was in France that the first stirrings of Scott Walker's new career were heard. *Toxic Affair* is a mildly diverting romantic drama with Isabelle Adjani as a wannabe writer who psychologically falls apart when her boyfriend leaves her; the film concerns how the self-absorbed young woman is forced to recognise how romance isn't everything, and to try to reconstitute herself.

Its soundtrack composer is Goran Bregovic, a Bosnian rock guitarist whose band and orchestral music would increasingly draw on the folk traditions of his homeland, as the former Yugoslavia splintered into a number of warring Balkan states.[4] The vocalist and lyricist he recruited to work with him on two songs for the film raised a few eyebrows.

'Man From Reno', a smoulderingly low-key song with a kind of slowed-down tango rhythm, became the first record by Scott Walker in eight years when it was released as a single. "Can't follow a man from Reno," warns Engel in his very controlled latter-day voice to a light female vocal backing, although his barroom pickup in the lyric is told she can follow a man from Zurich or Italy (or indeed Sarajevo). If the song is (only mildly) cryptic, that's intentional: the title is likely a reference to Johnny Cash's famous boast of murder in 'Folsom Prison Blues' ("I shot a man in Reno / Just to watch him die"). But it's one of the verses that really purrs with homicidal intention: "Zodiac killer / Needs that crack / He wants you back / He's waiting in the bars."

The 'Zodiac Killer' was an uncaught criminal in northern California responsible for the sadistic murders of at least six young people, often out on dates – and possibly for the deaths of many, many more according to his own cryptic letters. ("Like I have always said I am crack proof," he boasted in one of them.) *San Francisco Chronicle* cartoonist Robert Graysmith had become obsessed by the case during his time on the paper, writing a book called *Zodiac* which David Fincher would turn into a 2007 film about his obsession; the original book, published in the UK by the Mondo imprint in September 1992, was more concerned with how the Zodiac had made a psychotic art of cryptography – which seems to be the element that fascinated Scott.

'Indecent Sacrifice', on the B-side, is similarly languid and sinister: Took the model / And the murder weapon... Took the wallet / With the coral clitoris," it luridly intones before a Ferry-ish refrain of 'Give-in-up." If it played like soft rock, then its lyrics were much harder. "I ain't no pussy / With the blues" boasts the man who might be the Zodiac on 'Man From Reno', and it plays now like a portent of Scott Walker's career to come. Sensitive young romantics were about to become last century's thing.

Engel recorded his vocals at Matrix Studios in London, but Fontana would release the single in France only. Even so, it was the first hint of a career reactivated.

"Maybe at the time I just didn't feel like it was that major a step," concedes Kijak, who declined to cover 'Man From Reno' in his film. "Obviously it was at a time when he was moving toward *Tilt*. He was moving towards something in the lyrics – bits of it find their way onto *Tilt*, so he was certainly exploring something but he hadn't brought it to complete fruition yet, he was still finding his way through it."

It would be almost another three years before the second truly modern Scott Walker album was released.[5] But he was collecting concepts and ideas, some of them fragmentary or elliptical; trying different constructions of word patterns or juxtapositions of images.

As he'd tell *The Independent* on the eve of its release, evoking his early cinematic hero, "I've become the Orson Welles of the record industry. People want to take me to lunch, but nobody wants to finance the picture... In a sense I understand it. I keep hoping that when I make a record, I'll be asked to make another one. I keep hoping that if I can make a series of three records, then I can progress and do different things each time. But when I have to get it up once every 10 years... it's a tough way to work."

Engel would go on to describe his very unexceptional day-to-day life; for a supposed recluse, he could often be found (but not recognised) travelling on London Transport; he'd dedicated most of the last few years to his arts courses as a mature student[6] and, like most of us, to his personal relationships. "One very long-term," he told *The Times* of the woman Gary Leeds refers to as Libby. "Now I'm in another one. But I live alone and it's important that I do. I need my own space, as I think everybody does ultimately. It's the only way through a lot of this.

"It's been ducking and diving, always. But I've had a couple of good friends and I've borrowed money.[7] And whenever I'd get cheques in, I'd try to clear the debts. What I made from the sixties is enough for me to keep popping up every now and then."

"Scott was working on his album, *Tilt*, and we were in touch regularly," confirmed John Maus of this period. "He was trying to decide whether or not to go with the new digital technology or stick with analogue... In the end, he chose analogue because of the big sound he'd decided he wanted to achieve... He simply recorded everything – playing guitar and singing – on an old-fashioned cassette player and then worked things out with the arrangers, who would ultimately write everything out... Scott never disclosed the material he was preparing to record as a solo artist until he was in the studio, or with his arranger, so everything was kept under wraps until recording time."

★★★

Tilt, Scott Walker's millennial album, was released in May 1995. To try to circumnavigate the need for interviews, Fontana issued a promotional CD that featured Engel answering set questions:

Q1: Why has there been such a very long gap between the albums? How much of the delay was caused by musical reasons?
Yeah, this one's about 10 years I guess. Uh well, about two and a half years of musical reasons, because it takes me about that long to get the material together. Other than that, no. I just decided to stop for a while and concentrate on art, painting and drawing and things like that. What makes it harder is a lay-off like this, because you just have to reacquaint yourself with everything you do basically in that area, and then try to figure out a degree

and angle that you want to take, and that all goes with it. So you're hoping that it connects somewhere.

"I was an A&R man," explains David Bates, now director of DB Records, then at Fontana. "I think the first time I met Scott I wanted to sign him. I'd heard Scott was thinking of going back in the studio, and I thought it's worth having a meeting and finding out. And it was the most sober, sensible of all the meetings one could have. Scott was just saying, 'The only thing I won't do is sit in a demo studio churning out songs.' Oh, this is fantastic! And then The Pet Shop Boys had just had a hit with Dusty Springfield.[8] So I thought, I even have the language I can explain to my seniors of how this is going to make perfect sense. And the album that was in the offing, that happened about two or three years later, was *Tilt* – and I'm really glad," he laughs. "I would never have been able to explain that one away!"

Q2: In that 10 year gap, has the studio technology changed? Is it hard to make a new album under these circumstances?
Well it is and it isn't. Because first of all so much of this technology is transient. That shouldn't scare you too much, that doesn't bother me that much. So you can mix the old with the new fairly easily, and I catch on pretty quickly so that's not a big problem for me, and of course I work with people who are very *au fait* with that stuff, so what I don't know they know. I would try to get a band's performance as much as possible with most things, and now and then I'll layer something. But I try to get them all live because I'm looking for a depth of sound in the picture, rather than say something a synthesizer can give you which is rather a flat sound. So for this particular album I was looking for that. I only use a synthesizer when I'm absolutely pushed, and I have used it here and there, dotted it here and there. When we really can't find anything else and we've all conferred and we're all digging around for sounds, when we really can't find anything else then we'll resort to it. I don't have a closed mind to any of this, but when I say I didn't use synthesizers for

this, we're looking for a certain kind of sound and that wouldn't have been appropriate. So I'm not closing my mind to any of it.

Tilt was recorded at RAK Studios in London. Also present in the studio at the time were Engel-philes Radiohead, who were recording *The Bends*. Guitarist Jonny Greenwood was particularly impressed by Scott's backline: "It was the strangest collection of instruments lying around: 'How's he going to make a record with a timpani?'"

As Engel would tell *The Independent*, despite the long period of preparation he was still primed to make the actual recording within a maximum period of two months: "You're forced to limit the choices, to make radical decisions and take chances. That shows in a record. You can tell a lazy record."

As for the concept behind the title: "It's a good word, *Tilt*. It means so many things today. The way we might feel personally about ourselves and what we might do, radically. It covers a lot of area and that's what I'm looking for. It's like Picasso's universal face, y'know, you're always looking for one thing and then..."

Q3: After such a long lay-off, do you fear that your voice may have gone, or do you assume it's there when you call for it?
I hope it's gonna be there when I call for it, but because I wait so long before I've made a record, in this giant hiatus, I did spend about three months singing at home – which is something I don't normally do at all – and just warming it up and getting it. Because I know I'm gonna run into these highs here, and along the way I'd better get it to where I can do that. So I've just worked with it and brought it on gradually by myself there. So I just hoped I could get it when I got in the studio, because… I don't have the facility at home to hear it – there's nothing I have – I have one of these little Walkman tape recorders – that when I get in front of the mike it's going to come out sounding like something. And that's the most terrifying moment. When Pete Walsh says to me, "Well, it sounds fine, man," I know he wouldn't lie to me – so then it sounds fine and I feel better. In

the sixties, when I was doing records with The Walker Brothers, people were starting to say, "This guy can really sing," you know, so I thought I'd better go and learn something valid[9] ... I quite honestly try to unlearn anything like that; there are a lot of valuable things you can gain from that, breath control and things like that, but you have to unlearn a lot too...

"I had a phone call to say that the album's finished, and that I was expected at Metropolis [Studios in Chiswick] one late afternoon during the week," says David Bates. "As I walked through the door, Peter [Walsh] came down to welcome me and I wanted to ask how it was. But he said, 'Don't say anything! Scott is upstairs watching.' As I looked upstairs, from the top balcony looking down, he was obviously very nervous playing it back for the first time. A track came on – it was ['Farmer In The City'] at *full* blast. Wow! I had no idea what to make of the whole thing. I turned round and said, 'Is there any chance we can put it on the *small* speakers, a little quieter? I'm just finding it a little too much to take in.' So he agreed. And then Scott stopped it and said, 'Dave, I hope you don't mind, I'd like to listen to it on the big speakers again. Because when I make a record and I've finished, I don't really have any intention of listening to it again. So I'd just like to remember it this way if it's OK with you.'"

"I haven't heard *Tilt* since I made it," confirms Engel. "The moment I finish, I never listen to it again. Because look, I've written it over all those years, I've produced it, sung it, mixed it – I produced it with my friend Pete, of course. I never want to hear it again. It's a nightmare."

★★★

There is something of cinematic genius Stanley Kubrick in Scott's behaviour. In the all-consuming method of the process. In the end product being all-important but, ultimately, unsentimentalised. In the obsession that must ultimately (and perhaps mercifully) burn itself out.

259

Q4: Is Tilt *different from everything else you've done? Why is the album so gloomy?*

Well… I think it's just a carrying on from my past work. It's another departure in that way. I always think as well that there's a lot of dark humour in my records, because you have to have that attitude anyway to bring it off. If you approach it all with darkness then you won't bring the seriousness off – that's a strange thing to say but it's absolutely true. You have to have the balance of humour all the time and although it's not apparent, the undercurrent of that is apparent within it.

Q5: In this hi-tech society, music can go around the world much more easily … artists like Laurie Anderson use technology and multimedia to make their art.[10] *Will the people who like her, like* Tilt*?*

Uh, I think today it's more and more possible to have an audience for these kinds of records. They exist for all kinds of pockets of music we never had before, because there's so much more music. We are, as you say, living in a hi-tech information situation. These kinds of records will find their audience so I don't generally worry about that, I'm just trying to do the best job I can. Waiting for what comes to me and in that way using it. I heard a story recently – I can't remember the name of the major [label] but they signed a new band, and it's a story that's around and you hear it a lot. The guy from the major said: "Now remember, don't make it too commercial!" That's a great story, and it's more and more like I think it [is]. You gave Laurie Anderson, that's an excellent example – she has a market, there's no reason why I can't have a market, 'cos she doesn't all the time constantly keep a 4/4 going either. I just want to connect with as many people as I can with it, I know it's not easy but I'm always hoping.

Q6: How do you write? What kind of musicians do you need to help you play your music?

Well all I do is, when I'm composing the songs, I take a long time for the lyric. When I'm doing the melodies, I simply have a Telecaster at home and a little fibre-optic keyboard, it's not a synthesizer, it's just a piano. So I keep things simple and then, when I'm prepared, I get together with whoever I'm working with and notate it all, the topline. So generally speaking I have to use guys who can read. Now there are exceptions – musicians who are so wonderful in themselves like David Rhodes,[11] for instance, he doesn't read and he's kind of beyond music in a way. But if you have readers and they've got the topline and the general idea of the bars, we will fool around with it. So generally speaking it's an old-fashioned way of working. But that's the layout, they can actually see the layout, and the chords are there as well, because the chords for this album were very unusual and took a little more time in that many of the chords have no names – they were used especially in songs like 'The Cockfighter' and the song 'Bouncer [See Bouncer]'. So we don't know what the names of the chords are but you just grope around until you find the appropriate sounds for that. And that's why you have to pick players who are an extension of yourself – an extension somehow of your psychological sound – 'psychological' is kind of a bad word to use today, but, uh, the feeling of it, that extension. So for instance all of these players were very specifically chosen for that reason and they're wonderful players. What were we talking about? Oh yes, getting in and out of it – the reason why is because the lyric dictates everything on these tracks. The lyric will dictate everything to the end, even down to the cover of the record if you get the lyric right. So if the lyric dictates it, I'm in and out quickly on that one. So instead of just riffing and riffing, or making a track that goes on and on like that, I've reversed it and work the other way around.

The cover of *Tilt* is the first of his works not to feature Engel's face – although he (literally) showed his hand. Combined within David Scheinmann's photographic and image manipulation concept are bird's feathers and the eye of a stuffed bird of prey – an owl or hawklet. The effect is both mysterious and febrile.

Q7: You have said on a number of occasions that you don't like to talk about the lyrics. Why?

Well, I just think with anything like this that's very internal, it destroys the magic of it, if you like. Because I don't exactly know how these happened or what's going on there, and I'm a little superstitious about it. We're cheapening language that I waited a long time for, I waited a long time for those words. So they would be talking about something that we can't talk about, that really is unsayable. We're working around the edges with the words, and working with just the threads of language. So if we talk about it and try to lay it out, first of all it would be impossible almost, it would take us an interview or more for one song, to try and unlock it all. And second of all it's just something I don't care to do. I mean I can indicate things here and there for you perhaps. It's not autobiographical though, I don't think. My interest was [in] writing a song about Pasolini, 'Farmer In The City', who was murdered in a brutal way, but no one seems to know the bottom line on that, there are conflicting stories about it: where it was, was it a gang, was it a single person, what exactly happened, was it on this road, was it by a deserted football ground, what was it? So I'm quite a fan of his films, but the whole thing fascinated me as an internal exercise, I felt, "Well, I'll play around with this idea."

"Do i hear
   21
   21
   21 …"

Subtitled ('Remembering Pasolini'), 'Farmer In The City' opens on Scott's lilting voice as that of an auctioneer. Melancholic, almost abstract; floating aloft on waves of strings by the Sinfonia of London,

conducted by Brian Gascoigne.[12] The lyrics, as would be the case
from *Tilt* to the present day, are presented in a booklet as blocks
of symmetrically arranged words – almost as much the shapes and
symbols of a kind of concrete poetry as songs.

As Stephen Kijak suggests, they also contain a reference to Engel's
elliptical murder ballad 'Man From Reno':

"Can't go by
a man from
Rio
Can't go by
a man from
Ostia …"
(Lyrics of both songs also make a sinister reference to "brain
grass".)

As with most of the album, a metaphysical conceit accompanies
a central theme; the 'farmer in the city' (a man out of place who
"knew nothing of the horses / "Nothing of the thresher") is Pier
Paolo Pasolini, the Italian Marxist author and visionary neo-realist
filmmaker, who relocated from rural Italy to Rome in his young
adulthood. His vision extended from impoverished Roman streetlife
in *Accatone* to the grotesque allegories of *Porcile* (*Pigsty* – which
shares Brel's metaphor of the bourgeoisie as pigs but takes it to a
cannibalistic conclusion) and *Salo, or The 120 Days Of Sodom*, his
infamous final film which relocated De Sade's depraved imaginings
to Fascist Italy.

Pasolini was murdered in November 1975, soon after *Salo* was
completed, run over several times by his own car. As Engel suggests,
the crime was at first pinned on a rent boy (Pasolini was homosexual),
but then later attributed to right-wing thugs – and more recently
still, to a gang of extortionists. Images of his final night alive filter
in and out of 'Farmer In The City', including his young boyfriend
and cinematic muse Ninetto (not implicated in his death) and Ostia,

the scene of his demise. In this, the semi-operatic tone poems of *Tilt* become like aural art films in themselves.

"Fast forward to *Tilt* and it's cinematic in an entirely different way," concurs Kijak, "they are these weird imagined worlds. It's called abstract but I think it's entirely the opposite – it's concrete, specific. You can argue about the specific meaning, but the lyric and the sound is so powerful. If the old music is like classic European cinema then the new stuff has more of a David Lynch sensibility, something a little bit more nightmare-like, more dreamlike. To me it was epitomised by 'Farmer In The City' – there's something about his music that gives these very visual responses and they hit your subconscious zone where you're seeing things when you're listening to this music, you can't help it. Maybe that helps you try to figure it out, it works on a very cinematic level like that. It was great music for cinema."

The filmmaker's Lynch analogy may be particularly apposite. The all-American surrealist director has often opined that he doesn't wish to analyse his own work too much, in case his own particular magic is lost. *Tilt* may also bear comparison with Lynch's debut feature, *Eraserhead*, in that it creates an oppressive atmosphere which, on first viewing, some people find unbearable. On repeated viewings, the humour becomes more immediately apparent; as does the yin and yang of horror and occasional beauty.

"I feel he is somebody for whom this is a vocation and not a job, so I just think he would not be interested in putting out stuff that he hadn't really slaved over," Brian Eno laughs when giving his view of Engel's later work to Kijak for *30 Century Man*. "He very much believes in pain, I think! If it doesn't hurt then it wasn't worth releasing!

"For me lyrics, in most songs, are just a way of getting the voice to do something ... In Scott's songs that's not true at all, the lyrics just draw you further and further into the music. They're so rich and full of ambiguity that they actually withstand listening to again and again, like music does. They don't spell it out for you, so you haven't 'solved the problem' in the first two listens. That's why I say he's a poet – I'm sure people like Beckett thought about words in the same way. It's not to do with meaning, it's to do with making something happen ...

"He's also somebody who clearly has a vision of some kind. You know, you don't write these things as intellectual exercises, or to puzzle people or something like that. At the core of these things there's a picture of the world which is very, very dark and rich and confusing actually, there's a lot of doubt and undertones of anxiety in this world. Well it's not the normal topic of popular music, so it sort of eludes a big audience. But it is the normal topic of a lot of fine art actually, and fine writing if you like. But because it comes in a container, it's on a record, they don't spot it."

"What I really like about his songwriting is the way that he can paint a picture with what he says," says David Bowie, Eno's former collaborator – who has acclaimed *Tilt* as one of the greatest records he's ever heard. "I have *no idea* what he's singing about, I've no idea. I never bothered to find out and I'm not really interested, I'm quite happy to take the songs that he sings and make something of them myself. I read my own reasoning into the images and all that."

Q8: ... but the lyrics on Tilt *are really hard to understand.*
Well, let me just try another way around this. James Joyce[13] is a good example, he sort of changed the rules for all of us, I'm not doing anything that's more radical than that. Then you can go through lyrics today and I always give this example [laughs], Michael Stipe's of R.E.M. Nobody seems to give him much of a problem about his words – of course he doesn't write them down like I do. But I think I'm lucidity itself in comparison. So I don't understand what the problem is, because even if you listen to U2 or whoever it is, there's a puzzlement about all of the things that are going on now. And of course I've been going on for quite a long time, I know that, but I don't think I'm more of a problem than they are. As I said, the lyric led all of this. If it tells me to change the time or whatever, I will obey the lyric because that's where all of this stuff *came* from. So I'll be listening very

carefully to what that's saying to me. So if I feel the time should change, or if it's just a dropout or whatever, I'll do it.

"They're agony," Brian Gascoigne argues of the sessions for *Tilt* and, to a lesser degree, *Climate Of Hunter*. "He believes, and I take issue with him on this, that in order to convey very strong emotion in the music you have to be feeling it while you're making it. Well that couldn't be true, because otherwise the people who are playing Bruckner and Mahler every night would be basket cases by the time they're 30. And after three or four hours in the studio he is a basket case, because he lives the thing with such intensity of emotion. I always find writing the strings for Scott very irritating, because they're mostly holding one note for 16 bars. And yet he will make them go on and on and on, doing it again and again and again, until he gets the emotion. But in fact in the case of the string players, when he hears the difference it's irritation. I know one of them has described his session as like having your teeth drawn slowly, and he does put musicians through the wringer because he really wants that intensity."

Q9: Why are there so many percussion instruments and sounds on the album, in particular on a track like 'The Cockfighter'?
Well, the example of something like 'The Cockfighter', for instance: once again, the lyric made it appropriate to have this metallic sound, this sort of racket going on and there are several instances on the record where that happened. I thought it'd be interesting to use it too because you don't hear a lot of records with percussion. It's about an internal struggle, attack-and-defence struggle within one man. It starts with a nightmare, a man having a nightmare. And there are a lot of erotic images as well and banal sounds in the background. Finally, at the end of it, there's an idea that transpires – this is a time when everyone's talking about the Holocaust, I know I wrote this in '91 but it seems appropriate now.[14] And so again I wanted to talk about something that really can't be talked about, without a kneejerk reaction, without riffing 'dirty Nazi Germany' or something like

that. It's a very touchy subject, you have to approach it very carefully, it can go very wrong on you. So I came across this thought: I wanted to attack 'the ludicrous of the law', and I also wanted to play with time. So I picked two trials that were in the public consciousness in a big way at those times: one was this trial of Queen Caroline in 1820, the other is the Eichmann trial in our time. So by using questions from one trial and answers from another, I managed to suggest this without really talking about it, without anything really specific, to say, "This can't be talked about, this is unsayable – this is a way we can find through this." And then it comes through at the end of it, although they're both public things, because of using them this way they both turn into the private again. Into the internal where, uniquely, these things really start, this kind of horror starts. So that's what I was getting at.

'The Cockfighter' begins with sounds of murmuring and movement; the suggestion of physical noise in the room alongside you places it among the soundscapes heard on Radio 3's experimental music programme, *Mixing It* – for whom, naturally, *Tilt* was a major event.[15] The percussive attack, which comes suddenly out of nowhere, is when heard for the first time hard and fast and shocking.
"IT'S A BEAUTIFUL NIGHT
FROM HERE TO THOSE STARS," howls Scott, pushing his voice through the mix, and all traces of the old crooner are gone (for now at least). Physical and cosmological imagery collide with the cover imagery ("feathers on the side of my fingers") and the predicament of the two trial defendants – Duchess Caroline of Brunswick, who briefly became Queen Caroline on her adulterous husband George IV's accession to the throne in 1820, whose unhappy marriage was brought to an end by her husband's accusations of her own infidelities, despite her popularity with her subjects: "*Do you swear the breastbone was bare … Do you have any doubt that he slept in that bed*"[16] – and the epitome of the 'Banality Of Evil', as Hannah Arendt

subtitled her book [Adolf] *Eichmann In Jerusalem*, the Nazi bureaucrat who came to embody that tragicomic phrase 'Ve vere only obeying ze orders': "*I have a greenlight for fifty thousand … You were responsible for rolling stock … Do you know what happened to most of the children …*" The organ borrowed from London's Central Methodist Hall underpins the darkness.

"I would hesitate before saying there's a sadism that runs through the theme of the music," says David Bates, "because I don't think it is something quite as simple as that. But there do seem to be these abstract observations on people being put into positions of great discomfort." Perpetually including the composer himself, one could add.

Q10: The listener needs great concentration, just like the musicians did. In the end, is it all about lack of hope and despair?
It's hard work but there's a lot of people doing it, trying and keeping that memory there. Like I said, it has to be approached very carefully but it's no good getting kneejerky about this kind of thing, that's too simple and stupid. I knew that I'd have to have space for it, so that the words had the appropriate amount of space between them: "Spared … I've been spared …" So it took that amount of time to get to the centre section, which suddenly changes, it becomes like a sunny field, you know, woodwind, and then it goes back into what is really three instruments: electronic bass drum, and then there's the organ and guitar. And then we use some effects we took from the hurdy-gurdy. That's the one thing, there is always hope – but is a very hard course, all of this. When I look at some of these songs, it was daunting for me because singing is a terrifying thing to me anyway. When I think I'm going to have to cross these landscapes, it's a daunting proposition.

'Bouncer See Bouncer', with its truly obscure title, seems both a continuation of the previous narrative and the exemplar of the album's aural aesthetic:

"Spared
i've been
spared
all the nickling
all the dimeing"

It could be Engel's celebration of being spared the hustle and grind of everyday existence, of going back to being an artist. But it sure doesn't sound that way.[17] The "halo of locust" that the lyric refers to is heard buzzing malevolently around the opening and closing of the track; a single drum pounds monotonously in the background, like a downgraded version of the menace of eighties industrial music. Engel's never sounded sadder, not crooning but apparently on the verge of tears: "The sobbing that just might choke us ..." Then he intones, "I love this season without its cleft," and the London Sinfonia briefly takes flight – just as the string section did in the more literally sinister 'The Electrician'.

The album met with mixed reviews; some were left scratching their heads but it made the lower reaches of the album chart. "Majestic metal machine music," acclaimed *The Times*, evoking when Lou Reed briefly went way off the critical scale in 1976 with four sides of guitar feedback weighing in at 20 minutes one second each. What Engel was doing obviously wasn't as discordant as that.

Was it?

"What he's after is the boundary between chords and discords," Gascoigne explained after the event. "I mean anybody can play a chord or discord," he demonstrated by slamming his arm on the piano keyboard, "he will take a chord and hold it for 16 bars. It's halfway between a chord and a discord, I mean it contains four actual chords ... and when you fill in the only remaining note it's very different. So he's operating in the area where that makes a difference. The strategy is to get this great seesaw going back and forth, and the pivot for it is to get the musicians into the no man's land between melody and harmony conventionally and the squeaks and grunts of the avant-garde."

Q11: Singing as hard work! Surely not for Scott Walker?

Believe me, it is an effort. Not because it's a physical thing. I like to get the vocal down as quickly as possible – in my mind, when I go in to do the vocal I've only got one shot at it, that's the way I look at it. And that one shot across a landscape like 'The Cockfighter' or 'Bouncer' or whatever is a terrifying prospect to me, because I want to get everything, uh, 'there' as much as possible within this limited time. And I want to get even the terror of the voice on the record, so that is has an intensity. There are some tunes where some people are saying, "God, that's very high, you're singing very high," but again it's the lyric that drove that. If I'd have sung the centre section of 'The Cockfighter' it'd have been too bland, or there's are a couple of other instances there too in songs. If I take it to a certain height – where I'm not screaming, I don't want to scream because that's an overload of emotion – then I'm just about hopefully right. But of course there are parts of this album which are lower than this thing as well. So once again the lyric is dictating everything. If I know there's a certain timbre I'm not getting all the way through I will patch it, but very reluctantly. The idea though was that I try to get it as quickly as possible. So that is daunting for me. That's why when I come to the studio, you can ask my partner, Pete Walsh, the guy that I work with – I walk right into the studio, he has it set up so that I walk right up to the mike, he's got the tracks and I start. And that's it. I don't want to have cups of tea, I don't want to have polite conversation with anybody, I just want to do it. Or if I'm doing it live with the band I'll do it with that then! [clicks fingers] But I don't want any of that stuff going on. I want to catch this terrifying moment as much as possible; the impact of this feeling as much as possible. So that's just the way I work. I haven't always worked that way – in the old days sometimes we had to do four tunes in a session and I had to do it quickly, so I learn quickly anyway. But later on there was a mid–period where I didn't care much, so I floated vocals in mid-tune or whatever. But my last three records, that's the way I work.

"He hasn't gone classical and he hasn't gone jazz," opines David Bates. "It isn't really abstract, it's still songs and there's still a voice singing the songs, and there's still lyrics he writes out on the inner bag. It just doesn't make things clearer, it makes things a lot more confusing."

'Manhattan' being a case in question. It erupts into being with the church organ sound – "Here you / Are boy / Here you are," – being the earliest written track on the album.[18] In its switches of mood and suddenly shifting allusions, it might be seen as the template for *Tilt*, but of course, of the lyric's various international landmarks none are actually in New York City. Instead there's Bengal, Somalia, Burma, Kenya – all former seats of colonial empires. The track is subtitled '*Flerdele*', derived from *fleur de lys* – the French heraldic symbol with which, according to a 17th century code instituted by Louis XIV, slaves were branded on the shoulder.[19] One of the dramatically shifting verses combines nightmarish police state imagery with the negro spiritual 'Ezekiel In The Valley Of The Dry Bones':

"chief of police
a la collar –
bones connected ...
and hear the
word of the
lord ..."

'Face On Breast' is the strangest of beasts in this context – a pretty straight grunge-rock song with nicely distorted guitar, albeit still carrying the album's dark undertones. Opening to an image of a gliding swan, it incorporates erotically tantalising dialogue from Scott's favourite era of Hollywood, the forties: "Ya know how to whistle / Put ya lips together and blow."[20]

'Bolivia '95' is a rock song too, but multilayered and sinister. "Doctorie / Give me a C / For this babaloo," pleads the narrator, the latter being a paternal spirit in the voodoo-like Caribbean tradition of santeria. As for the 'C', well, we all know what Bolivia's national export is. The song is haunted by the necessity of impoverished communities growing botanical drugs for survival in the face of military intervention: "Save the crops / And the bodies / From illness / From pestilence / Hunger and war." (The plea for Doctorie to "opiate me" makes the lyric universal, not just pertaining to cocaine-producing Central America.) But Scott Walker doesn't do conventional protest songs; in fact he doesn't do conventional songs at all any more. The strangely eerie refrain, set to a menacingly low-key guitar riff in the style of Knopfler or Bregovic and a beaten snare, is "Lemon Bloody Cola"; it irritates the hell out of some but this writer finds it weirdly effective, suggesting a few things all at once: the Coke/cocaine euphemism; the symbol of US capitalism; even perhaps the emptiness of consumerism – as when the main character of George Orwell's *Coming Up For Air* samples a fish sausage: "It gave me the feeling that I'd bitten into the modern world and discovered what it was really made of ... Everything slick and streamlined, everything made out of something else."

'Patriot (a single)'[21] is almost a return to the orchestrated dramas of *Scott 1-4*. Citing January 19, 1991, it's another oblique sideways look at international carnage – in this case Operation Desert Storm, the first Gulf War (the title refers to the Patriot missile). Touching upon the sensitive croon of yesteryear, Engel poetically describes the chaos as "Cripple fingers / Hit the muezzin[22] yells." Then, in an extraordinary Brecht & Weillian section, the aural drama slows to a crawl as a piccolo whistles and Scott sings a kind of drunken Teutonic refrain:

"the
Luzerner
  Zeitung
  Never
sold out ..." – this being an apparent tribute to how the *New Lucerne Times* didn't follow the Western party line on the war.

'Tilt', the title track, might have been called 'Rawhide', if that title wasn't already used for the opener of *Climate Of Hunter*. It certainly plays like a parody of a fifties Western movie or TV show theme: "He was so strong / he was so bold / When they made him / they broke the mold." But Engel's anxious timbre, what's left unsaid and only alluded to bring the song into the uniform dark tenor of the album; the recurring phrase "they'll turn / the buffalo" seems to have some ominous meaning beyond its obvious prairie imagery.

In his reflections on his ex-partner's new music, John Maus said of *Tilt*, "There is no way to discredit what he does because there is nothing to compare it with." He made his own attempt, however, by comparing it with the *musique concrète* of Pierre Schaeffer; but whereas Schaeffer's mid-20th century experiments in sound adopted an everything-but-the-kitchen-sink approach which, if the kitchen sink was actually present in the room, might include the sound of its running tap water, the millennial Scott Walker was striving for a definite effect: "I want it to be like a heavy dose of flu."

It might not be the best selling point for a record album. But in terms of creating an aural environment that blocks out all else, its ambition (and its often startling effect) can't be denied.

Q12: Will you ever perform live in front of an audience again?
I think the real problem for me is having to do so much big singing in one go. See, I don't have a guitar player playing guitar solos forever, there's nowhere to take a rest, there's nowhere to hide. Once I start I'll be out there singing for a certain amount of time. A record like this, it probably would be possible to go in and do this in the Queen Elizabeth Hall with this nucleus band – even the big organ we've recorded live, we've sampled it so we could take it in there. My only concern would be people coming along for the wrong reasons. This would take about 45 minutes to perform – but if they were coming along expecting things from the past, and I

had to do that stuff as well, I don't think I'd want to do that. Because it's just too much singing, it's a different kind of thing. But there's a lot of my material from the past that might be interesting to check out again in another context, but very hard to bring off. But then these days it all gets harder because … you want more, so it all gets tougher. Uh … we all want a sort of fulfilment, which is always out there and it never stays, that's the problem. You get glimpses of it. You just want to try and capture it some way in art. So you're listening for [it], singing in neutrality and all kinds of things that come into that way. It's something we can't – once again what this album's about, it's an unsayable thing, we can't really talk about it. So it's a desire, and a longing.

Despite the *sui generis* nature of *Tilt*, Engel was still searching for those images to which he could open his heart, as described by the Camus quote on the cover of *Scott 4*.

And there was, in fact, one live performance delivered of material from the album. At the time of its release, he made one solitary appearance on *Jools Holland's Later*, singing the closing track. 'Rosary' is solo Scott, accompanying himself on electric guitar. As elliptical as anything that preceded it, it is also a song of desperate yearning, of emotional striving and frustrated desire. Some have made a drug song out of its imagery: "i'll string along … With all of the trembling vein / that you can bare," and its closing refrain of "And I gotta quit."

But that's an oversimplification.[23] 'Rosary' plays like anxiety raw and bare, in its purest form; the implied religious image of the Catholic faithful caressing their rosary beads for reassurance is obviously no accident. On *Later*, Scott's infamous stage fright translated into an intense performance: stroking nervously angular electric guitar chords somewhat redolent of Marc Ribot,[24] making the imploring non-verbal refrain, "oo whaoo whaoo whaoo."[25] It was also the last live performance of Scott Walker to date.

Midwestern-born; raised on the East and West Coasts – but a truly British icon. From the late sixties to the present day, Scott Walker is an integral part of Anglo pop culture. KING COLLECTION/RETNA UK

At a 1968 pop mag's St Valentine's Day awards, solo artist Scott poses with Lulu – the Scottish teeny pop singer who first met him on a Walkers tour. BALLARD/EXPRESS/GETTY IMAGES

With John Franz at the piano, the singer makes a full transition to MOR icon on his *Scott* TV series. Meanwhile, he was recording his most radical music thus far. CHRIS WALTER

Californian pop star reborn: Scott, all hair and teeth, during the July 1976 recording of the second Walkers reformation album. MICHAEL PUTLAND/GETTY IMAGES

The mid-seventies look personified: for Scott, John and Gary, the Walker Brothers reformation was a momentary way out of a number of personal cul-de-sacs. JORGEN ANGEL

The Walkers perform their last ever hit, 'No Regrets', on German TV. Success in the 1970s was short-lived, but the swansong *Nite Flights* LP pointed to the future. ELLEN POPPINGA - K & K/REDFERNS

Scott Walker in the eighties was little more than an urban myth – but he emerged in 1984 with *Climate Of Hunter*, an elliptical dispatch from an icy modern world. BRIAN RASIC/REX FEATURES

The last 'live performance': singing 'Rosary' on *Later With Jools Holland*, May 1997 – an angular song of metaphysical angst, with a refrain evoking *The Waste Land*. ANDRE CSILLAG/REX FEATURES

Promoting *Tilt* on Jools Holland's eclectic late-night music show: as Bowie remarked, the extraordinary impact of that album was in inverse proportion to its radio play. ANDRE CSILLAG/REX FEATURES

Scott with Jarvis Cocker in 2006, the antithesis of Walker-ish crooners – but then Walker was no longer a crooner himself, composing the psychic assault of *The Drift*. CAMERA PRESS

In lieu of a live Walker performance there was 2008's *Drifting & Tilting* at the Barbican: Dot Allison performs 'Buzzers', with its shadows of Balkan genocide. STUART MOSTYN/REDFERNS

Scott in the studio with Peter Walsh: friend, producer and principal collaborator since 1984. Their partnership most recently produced the comically infernal *Bish Bosch*. COURTESY IAIN AND JANE

Scott Walker the modern artist: an uncompromising performer possessed of a cosmological vision and a mordant sense of humour. CAMERA PRESS/PEROU

When *Tilt* was given a preview by selective invitation only at London's Royal College of Art, one of the attendees was Marc Almond.

"I hate *Tilt*, absolutely hate it!" he'd later report. "I went to a playing of it, a play-through of it, and I thought, 'Is this just me?' Everyone was sitting there silent and reverent and I just thought, 'This is terrible! This is absolutely awful!'" he laughs.

"For all these people who used to brag about being ambitious and being adventurous," retorted J.D Beauvallet in *30 Century Man*, "now there was a record for all the things they were standing for and all the things they were telling they were. It made people move fast, and now people who boasted of being avant-garde were old bag – or old hat," he corrects himself.[26]

"A number of people just walked away," Stephen Kijak recalls of *Tilt*'s tonal explorations of darkness. "Some people are just so attached and so invested in his melodic era that they just kind of want him to get back into it. And, of course, in a way, wouldn't it be great? But then again, I don't know. I'm quite fond of *Tilt*, so …

"And then when you listen to it up against *The Drift*, it becomes an even more melodic and pleasant record!" he laughs. "They age very well and they reveal themselves slowly. But it's fascinating when it's set in relief against the new work: what seemed impenetrable and abrasive is actually not at all, really. I turn to it now and yes, it's dark and foreboding. I like this kind of music – I love the sixties work, I love the current work. I guess it just depends on your musical tastes and what you're willing to take on. It's thrilling to me, even after having worked with him so intently for those years, I still turn to it and am thrilled by it and find new dimensions in it all the time. It's a very rewarding album."

✳✳✳

And then Scott Engel disappeared again.

The following years would not be breeding grounds for rumour or myth, as he could be occasionally detected in an outline or a whisper. In 1996, the ghost of his old crooner self could be heard on the soundtrack of *To Have And To Hold*, an Australian film about an obsessive love by writer/director John Hillcoat. The song was 'I Threw It All Away', a plaintive love song by Bob Dylan from his stripped-down country period album *Nashville Skyline*.

"Nick Cave[27] asked me to," Scott later told Kijak by way of explanation. "He said, 'Look, I want you to do two songs, one or the other' – one was 'My Way'," he smiles, "and the other was the Dylan song. I mean I'm not particularly a Dylan fan, but I was like, 'I'll take the Dylan song because I don't want to sing "My Way" *whatever*, man!' It was kind of the atmosphere he needed, because he needed a kind of drunken version of 'My Way' as well, which I could have done, you know."

These days, the old crooner version of Scott Walker was reserved for drunken movie soundtracks – although not for weddings, funerals or bar mitzvahs.

Notes

1   A quote from 'Big Louise'.
2   Inexplicably, the album that was effectively *Scott 5* would stay in print for only a brief amount of time before being deleted again.
3   The film buff is referring to *The Conversation*, Francis Ford Coppola's elliptically paranoid 1974 thriller about a surveillance expert who believes he's overheard a murder.
4   Bregovic is perhaps most familiar in the West for performing 'Ederlezi', the ethnic East European theme to Sacha Baron Cohen's 2006 comedy *Borat: Cultural Learnings Of America For Make Benefit Glorious Nation Of Kazakhstan* – which really doesn't do the eclecticism of his work justice.
5   Or the third if you count the first half of *Nite Flights*.
6   Unlike David Bowie's expressionistic portraits of Iggy Pop and Yukio Mishima in the seventies, none of Engel's works seem to have found their way into the public domain.
7   Presumably from Charles Negus-Fancey and his wife Cathy.
8   Actually in 1987, predating Fontana's signing of Scott by at least two and a half years.
9   Scott is referring to his lessons with vocal coach Freddie Winrose.

10   Performance artist Laurie Anderson had entered the world of popular music in 1982 with 'O Superman', a strangely compelling Top 10 hit mostly sung through a vocoder or spoken. Her subsequent works up to this point had combined electronics with installation art and a stage collaboration with cult author Robert Anton Wilson. Here she's obviously being used as a gauge by Fontana to indicate a market. Today she's also known as Mrs Lou Reed.

11   The guitarist on *Tilt*.

12   Previously the keyboardist and orchestrator of *Climate Of Hunter*.

13   It's arguable that the creative arc of Joyce as a writer follows a similar pattern to that of Engel: the conventional serious literature of *A Portrait Of The Artist As A Young Man* and *Dubliners*; the psychological prose and mythic archetypal lives of the characters in Ulysses; the stream of consciousness and wilful wordplay of *Finnegans Wake* – at its best echoed in the wordplay of Engel's own recent compositions; at its worst in the gibberish spoken by former US President George W. Bush.

14   The mid-nineties obviously saw the 50th anniversary of the end of World War II, as well as the establishment of a 'Holocaust Day' in various European countries.

15   Scott was also interviewed for the broadsheet press by one of *Mixing It*'s co-presenters, the late Robert Sandall; the programme has since relocated to Resonance FM under the title *Where's The Skill In That?*

16   This particular askew title is more likely derived from Rabelaisian wordplay on the adulterous element of the lyric than, say, any kind of reference to Charles Willeford's *roman noir* of the same title.

17   In *The Rhymes Of Goodbye*, Lewis Williams suggests the opening lines may be a continuation of the Holocaust strand of 'The Cockfighter'. *Skewed* may have been an appropriate (if less poetic) substitute title for *Tilt*.

18   In 1987 – as opposed to the bulk of the album being composed in 1991-2, and the closing track, 'Rosary', in '93.

19   Once again, the author salutes Lewis Williams for this piece of historical detective work.

20   Lauren Bacall to Humphrey Bogart in Howard Hawks' 1944 film of Hemingway's *To Have And Have Not*.

21   Of course it was never released as a single.

22   Islamic prayer caller.

23   As well as a potential libel.

24   Both in his own solo music and his work for Tom Waits.

25   It puts this writer in mind of T.S. Eliot's strange Thames river barge refrain – "Wallala leialala" – in *The Waste Land*, a poem that *Tilt*, in its clash of historical periods and imagery, and its underlying anxiety, has been compared to. (Strangely, the only popular music performer to have tackled *The Waste Land* seems to be Engel's contemporary P.J. Proby, in a splendidly Southern rendition recorded for Savoy Books; it was never issued, as it seems unlikely that Eliot's publishers, Faber & Faber, would grant permission.)

26   In fairness to Almond, he's never boasted of being 'avant-garde' – despite noise elements on the odd track like 'Your Love Is A Lesion' on The Mambas' *Torment & Toreros* LP. As a performer, he's more of a one-man archive of traditional pop music.

27   Nick Cave, one of the most literary – and still occasionally the most incendiary – of rock performers, had co-written and acted in his friend Hillcoat's harrowing 1988 prison drama, *Ghosts … Of The Civil Dead*; he'd also go on to write the original screenplay for *The Proposition* and the adaptation *Lawless* for the same filmmaker. Cave is known to be a big Walker Brothers fan.

Chapter 13

The Shock Of The New

"The subject of Elvis' twin can help us understand both the great power that Elvis had to connect with an audience as if he were reaching out to connect with his absent brother... Relatives and friends of Elvis in Tupelo have stated that Elvis felt guilty about the death of his twin brother, Jesse Garon."

–Vernon Chadwick, author *of In Search Of Elvis*, quoted in *Time* magazine

"The greatest work of art imaginable for the whole cosmos. Minds achieving something in an act that we couldn't even dream of in music, people rehearsing like mad for 10 years, preparing fanatically for a concert, and then dying... You have people who are that focused on a performance and then 5,000 people [sic] are dispatched to the afterlife, in a single moment."

– Karlheinz Stockhausen's response to the 9/11 attacks, as reported in the *Frankfurter Allgemeine Zeitung*

"Pasolini has made us feel even more trapped and helpless now than before, like the victims ... and like the masters, whose gaping internal emptiness has created this Dantesque/Sadean/fascist hell on earth.

Although it seems distant, it is spring 1945 and soon the 'four friends'
may end up as Mussolini did on April 28, 1945: shot, hung upside
down on a meat hook, and stoned by his own people."

– review of *Salo, or The 120 Days Of Sodom* by *Jim's Film Website*

In 1999, the ghost of the crooner incarnation of Scott Walker could be briefly detected in the ether.

Veteran movie lyricist Don Black had a track record in the James Bond series, including the theme songs to *Thunderball* and *Diamonds Are Forever* back in the Sean Connery era. Having previously written with revered soundtrack composer John Barry, he'd now taken up a similar collaborative position with David Arnold, who'd supplanted Barry in the Pierce Brosnan-era Bond films.

Their choice of vocalist for the end credits song to *The World Is Not Enough* may seem remarkable, in the light (or indeed in the dark shade) of *Tilt* – but Black had a tangential history of Scott covering his songs, harking back to the seventies.[1] The song, a regretful look back on lost love, was entitled 'Only Myself To Blame'; the famous Engel tones wafted in on a breeze of cocktail piano and muted trumpet, transporting the listener back to his classier cover versions of the late sixties/early seventies: "There is no greater fool in the fool's Hall of Fame, / And I've only myself… to blame."

The apparent intention was to a supplementary number to the main theme,[2] much as had been done with Louis Armstrong singing 'All The Time In The World' in *On Her Majesty's Secret Service*, the first 'official' non-Connery Bond film. It wasn't to be, however. The film's producer found the song, inspired by 007 falling in love with a villainess, too much of a 'downer' and the old Scott Walker stayed locked in his time zone, a figure from memory (although the track was included on the soundtrack album).

Less seemingly incongruous was Engel's collaboration with a French art filmmaker that same year. "It was a perfect match," insists J.D. Beauvallet of Engel working with Leos Carax. "It was almost

280

inevitable that he would fix on a complicity with Scott in the way that they're both complete mavericks in their own fields."

Carax, whose films are all basically love stories suffused with the intense stylisation of the French New Wave of the sixties, or the twenties/thirties style of German expressionist film, had long harboured an ambition to film *Moby Dick* author Herman Melville's novel of incestuous love, *Pierre, or The Ambiguities*. (*Pierre ou les ambiguïtés* in French – construct an anagram from the first letters and you get 'Pola'.) An obviously controversial novel in the 19th century,[3] in the 1999 film adaptation Carax would soften the provocation slightly (but only slightly) by featuring Guillaume Depardieu (late son of the celebrated Gérard) and Catherine Deneuve in starring roles as a wealthy mother and son. The incestuous element came with the male lead's fixation on the mysterious girl who steps out of nowhere and claims to be his long lost sister (Yekaterina Golubeva) – much of the film's controversy arose from how part of their sex scene together wasn't simulated, as Depardieu and Golubeva were a couple in real life. Even the film's chosen soundtrack composer was a singular artistic figure.

"I enjoyed doing the one I did for Leos Carax, but it was a nightmare," confirms Scott Engel. "He's as slow as I am so the process went on for years, and I kept having to meet him again and again. With me, you know, I can only do almost one thing at a time. So I was hung up for about four years just meeting Leos to do this soundtrack. I didn't mind 'cos I like him. How it came out in the end I have no idea."

It's extraordinary to think that film buff Engel hadn't seen *Pola X* by the time he was interviewed for *30 Century Man* (although he may well have done since). The film itself is an audacious mixture of styles, from the naturalism of the opening scenes to the infusions of *le fantastique* when Pierre follows his sister Isabel into a surreal Parisian underworld. Much of the soundtrack is surprisingly conventional orchestral music, arranged for the composer by Brian Gascoigne, which might have fitted into anything from old Hollywood films to

Hammer horror. It's in the use of sound effects that it bears greater relation to Scott Walker's most recent works: mostly (but not always) relevant to the film, it includes barking dogs, sirens, the World War II bombers which continued to haunt his recurring martial imagery, plus a sample from 'The Cockfighter' and even a brief apocalyptic rap sequence.

It marked the beginning of a series of projects which, compared to the previous decade, amounted to a kind of creative mania. In April 2000, the first spring of the new millennium, Teutonic cabaret chanteuse Ute Lemper's album *Punishing Kiss* saw release. It was a new collection that featured, aside from a song by her trademark composers Brecht and Weill, contributions by Nick Cave, early Walker devotee Neil Hannon (singing a duet with Ms Lemper, his band The Divine Comedy providing most of the backing), Elvis Costello, Philip Glass and Tom Waits. Two other original tracks were contributed by Scott Walker,[4] which he also produced.

"Those two songs I consider to be two of my best songs," he graciously concedes. "She was totally fearless, it was fantastic, showtime, take it on, it was great."

"I was a piece of clay and he basically moulded me into his musical vision," intones Ms Lemper like a latter-day Marlene Dietrich. "And it was sometimes frustrating, I had to scream it out when I thought this would be really nice to make this quiet. Or to make it quiet when I thought I need some emotion in this. I had to give in to a very abstract music style, what I'm not used to."

"The Russians are going," 'Scope J' announces twice in ghostly tones, Engel's lyrics inverting the Cold-War-era alarum, "Departing like merchants..." It might be a lament for a new world where capitalism has won and the former Soviet Union has dissolved into different levels of gangsterish oligarchy. But the geo-political images give way to a deeply personal mystery, encompassing the composer's poetically literal fascination with the physical.

"I don't really know what this is about," said Ute Lemper reading from her lyric sheets. "I don't really get it, but I like this: 'On the outside grows the first side of the inside grows the skin side / So the first side is the outside / The skin side is the inside / One side likes the skin side...'"

'Lullaby (By-By-By)' is just as lyrically clever, its images less diffuse: "Tonight my assistant will pass among you / His cap will be empty / The most intimate personal choices and requests central to your personal dignity will be sung." A kind of Brechtian perspective on the song's performance is combined with elements of show tunes and 'My Sweet Darling', a classical lullaby.

"In many ways it was the first glimpse of the new record," said David Sefton, executive producer of *Punishing Kiss*,[5] of Engel's contributions, "that was quite intriguing, falling as it did I guess almost exactly between the two albums. So it was interesting to see something that represented his output of the time. And now we know it was kind of a little glimpse into where he was headed."

But several years would pass before the release of the next Scott Walker album. Long before that, at the time of the Ute Lemper album's release, he'd underline his reintegration into the world of the performing arts by 'curating' one of London's more interesting annual events. Meltdown is an arts festival launched by Sefton in 1993, during his time at the South Bank's Royal Festival Hall. Recruiting high-profile figures from the music world, under their directorship each summer event combines contemporary music with a range of performing arts – theatre, cinema, dance, or whatever the proclivities of the curator – in an attempt to dissolve the barriers between high culture and popular culture.

Scott Walker's Meltdown Festival was about as catholic in its range as they come: from the mainstream Britpop of Blur, a temporary band put together by Jarvis Cocker of Pulp (who sang Scott's vintage 'miniature' 'On Your Own Again' and featured The Swingle Singers as guest artists) and the experimentally edged indie-rock of Radiohead to the hard-edged, politicised dance music of Asian Dub Foundation, former Fatima Mansons/Microdisney frontman Cathal Coughlan,[6] haunting Oregon singer-songwriter Elliott Smith, English nouveau-folk singer Tom McRae, Brit indie-rock band Clearlake, noise-rock band Clinic and Japanese 'retro-futurists' Cicala Mvta.

On the more rarefied musical front there was jazz-influenced modern classical composer Mark-Anthony Turnage, free jazz player/former Walker session man Evan Parker, free-form noise/jazz/noise/electronica player and Sonic Youth member Jim O'Rourke, minimalist guitarist/songwriter Bill Callahan (aka Smog), physically demonstrative Austrian noise-rock band Fuckhead, French Gregorian chant ensemble Organum and a cabaret performance by Hanna Schygulla, lead actress in Fassbinder films such as *The Bitter Tears Of Petra Von Kant*.

Wider cultural events included a French theatre production of Beckett's *Waiting For Godot*, Douglas Gordon's art-film tribute to Hitchcock's *Vertigo* (including James Conlon's performance of Bernard Herrmann's score) and dance performances by The Richard Alston Dance Company to an original score by Scott Walker (entitled 'Thimble Rigging' – later to be adapted as a track entitled 'Psoriatic') and all-woman troupe The Cholmondeleys (to a score by Orbital).

It was an extraordinary evening to be put together by an aging performer who'd only recently emerged from over a decade of reclusiveness. It also bought him closer to one of those who'd sung his praises in public – nerd-savant Jarvis Cocker.

"He was certainly an inspiration to me," confirms Cocker. "I don't think people should have idols – if you make someone an idol you take their humanity away, I think that's silly. You can admire people but they are just another human being... I had this thing where I loved pop music that I felt didn't really tell you the truth about the world, and maybe I was looking for truth in the wrong place but for whatever reason I wanted to find it there. So I'd been kind of stumbling around in the dark thinking this was probably worth pursuing. So when you come across somebody else who's done that very well, it's kind of an encouragement to you."

Cocker's long-time band, Pulp, had by now passed their peak in the Britpop era. For all that, he was still an engaging performer, as much comedic as musical, telling modern music-hall tales of working-class outsiders and lower middle-class misfits.[7]

"Because he's reclusive you just hear stupid bits of information, like I'd heard he only liked to sit in pubs and watch people play darts," says Cocker of the Engel of legend. "Which I thought was good, I thought that was quite interesting. Or that he'd enrolled on a painting course. You just hear these things that are in the order of urban myth or whatever. I really didn't know what to expect at all."

Out of a mutual respect for each other's dissimilar work, Jarvis Cocker found his enigmatic hero receptive to a suggestion he might produce the new Pulp album. "The record he did with us was called *We Love Life* – nobody bought it,"[8] laughs the spindly Britpop poet. "But I turned up at his manager's house[9] to meet him, he was sat there and he had a baseball cap on, I didn't expect that. The peak of the cap was pulled down here so I could only really see his mouth. And we started talking, I played him some bits of music and then I was encouraged, because as the conversation went on the brim kept kind of inching up, and maybe after 35 minutes we actually made eye contact. I came to see the hat as an indication of how comfortable he was feeling in a certain situation, 'cos when we got round to recording the record sometimes the cap would even come off. Then I knew things were going well."

Late fifties/early sixties-influenced singer-songwriter Richard Hawley was playing guitar for Pulp at the time. "He was really flexible and I liked working with him because he was quite direct as well," he reported of Engel. "I don't like people who go round the houses and bullshit.

"I remember when I first met him, he was kind of like this guy huddled at the desk with his baseball cap – 'Don't fuck with me.' I was thinking, 'Oh shit, man! He's gonna be a real hardball.' He wasn't, he was great... You just look in his eyes, man, and you know he's telling the truth...

"I don't think Scott really cares about the past, I think he's very much an artist who exists now, he's still relevant now. Obviously I like a lot of the old stuff but a lot of us are still picking up on what he did 10 years ago, he's way ahead of the game and he always was... I respect the fact that he's disciplined enough to know that there's no point in looking back – like Bob Dylan said,[10] 'Don't look back.'"

"When we worked with Scott producing it was different to how we'd done the previous records," concurs Jarvis. "He got us to all play together – which is what we were wanting to do – but he kind of gave us the confidence. Pulp were never a musicianly band and never ever will be, you know. And we kind of didn't believe that we were capable of all playing in the room at the same time... And then, for me personally, he was also very good in terms of my singing – as in my method before had just been to get as drunk as possible and then just sing it five times, and then the producer would piece it all together. But he encouraged me to not drink and try and get one performance, and maybe alter one or two lines... The contribution that I remember most clearly is there's a song on there called 'The Trees', and in the middle of it there's an instrumental passage. I said, 'I think in this bit it should have like the noise' – sometimes when you go out for a walk in the woods, the wind makes all the branches kind of sound together – 'It'd be nice to have the sound like that.' He said, 'Oh yeah.' So then he ended up in the studio with I think it was some drumsticks, the ones with like wires on the end, swishing them through the air as hard as he could with Pete Walsh trying to record it to get this sound – it sounds like very well disciplined trees, I must say, because it sounds like they're in time...

"One thing that I did pick up from when we were working with him, because he was already getting ideas ready for his next record and when nothing was happening he would go into the studio and play the piano and stuff. I kind of realised that maybe he's gone through doing stuff with melody and harmony, and it's like he would kind of find some weird chord on the piano. When you first heard it kind of sounded like a cat had landed on the piano – 'DER! DER!' or whatever. He would keep hammering away at it and I think... it's the kind of dissonance or interference between two notes that don't go together. In a way it's like a chorus or something, that's what he's into now. He's like still got the same passion about what he's doing, but whereas before maybe it was about harmony and stuff like that, now it's about disharmony. That's what he's got a genuine affection for."

It would be a total of 11 years between the release of *Tilt* and Scott Walker's next album – the same period of time as between the former and *Climate Of Hunter.* Apart from the performer's varied artistic activities, he would later explain that there was "a death in the family" during this period.[11] Most of the doors to his past were now closed.

In October 2003, Scott Engel was presented with a lifetime award by Q magazine for his contribution to music, presented by his latter-day friend and colleague, Jarvis Cocker.[12] Subsequent to this, with Polygram (parent company of Fontana) apparently disinterested in producing the follow-up album to *Tilt*, the Negus-Fancey Company negotiated a new contract with the 20-year-old English independent label 4AD Records.

It was a more simpatico relationship: 4AD had evolved from the left-field post-punk label formed by Beggars Banquet employee Ivo Watts-Russell at the very end of the seventies. Forever identified with the ethereal 'post-rock' of The Cocteau Twins and their spin-off This Mortal Coil, their early releases also spanned the cataclysmic swamp-rock of The Birthday Party (Nick Cave's band of Aussie renegades) and the glam-goth Bauhaus. As the eighties drew on, 4AD had specialised in US 'alternative' rock after picking up Pixies, and even had a big dance hit with 'Pump Up The Volume' by M/A/R/R/S.

By the time of the new millennium, adding the man who created the dark nouveau-classicism of *Tilt* to their roster would prove quite a feather in their cap.

★★★

In late 2004 to early 2005, Resonance FM broadcaster Henry Scott-Irvine was working at Metropolis Studios in Chiswick, west London. "I was working on a documentary titled *Punk Attitude* – it

287

was directed by Don Letts and I was an archive source and the co-producer. If you're talking to someone in America they get up eight hours later, which often meant I was there quite late at night on my own in an office. To describe Metropolis Studios: it's an old disused tramshed which I think was a power station at one point for the trams when they had them in London. So it's a big urban space with a lot of what I would call 'tanks', which were in fact recording studios, and in the middle of it all was a splendid first-floor balcony which was a meeting area with a bar, a restaurant and some tables for people to play pool and relax. One particular evening I came to a break, so I went to get a coffee. One of the studio engineers asked if I would like to join him and this other guy with a beard in playing pool. I told him I was dreadful at playing and I hoped they wouldn't take offence; he said that was absolutely fine and went off and played pool with this bearded guy. About an hour later he came in my office and said, 'You turned down the opportunity of playing pool with Scott Walker.'

"He was very bearded – about a centimetre in length and mostly brown, and his hair was a little bit longer than you'd normally expect. I did spot him wandering around after that late at night – he really looked like he could be one of the studio engineers. I believe he was there on and off over at least six months to maybe a year – I could spot him late at night when I was there many months later.

"I do remember seeing him at the bar, probably before I knew who he was. He wasn't a man you would see regularly hovering around to buy food or drink. That may be because we were both working where the studios were set up in total isolation, you really weren't aware of anyone else being around you in these small soundproof rooms with no windows. There was just one instance of him happening to be in the restaurant area or bar area at that very same moment, he was buying fruit juice when I was probably buying a large glass of wine. I think one of the engineers said he doesn't drink. It might just be because he was working – whereas some people like to drink non-stop when they work, I got the impression he didn't."

At the same time as the hirsute Engel was beginning work on his new album, documentary filmmaker Stephen Kijak was starting pre-production on his long-planned bio-doc, *30 Century Man*.[13] Kijak, who'd previously made *Never Met Picasso*, a gentle comedy with a gay sensibility, and *Cinemania*,[14] an affectionate study of New York film buffs, would later annotate the DVD release of his Walker film with the following words: "How does one make a film about a man described as an enigma, a recluse, a genius? A man who is still alive and spends more time out of the public eye than any working musician today."

Indeed, this writer asked, how did he?

"It was one of these things, almost like a 'be careful what you wish for' scenario. But I heard he was going to be making a new album – it was just the moment, I'd been thinking about him and his music for years, and knew I wanted to do something with it in some form – whether it was incorporating it into a narrative or something else. It just spoke to me in such a deep way, like it does to so many other people, and it's such cinematic music.

"But then, having started to do documentaries and hearing he was going to make a record – which is a once in a decade experience – it just seemed like a 'now or never' moment. And then you go through the process of trying to figure out access – I only wanted to do it if it was going to be official and sanctioned and with his participation. And then you virtually spend a year or so putting that together, but then when you realise the door has been opened and you're able to, that's when the fear starts. It's like, 'What have I done? Oh my God, I really have to do it to his level' – he sets a very high bar and as a filmmaker you wanna touch that bar. We'll never get to that kind of esoteric, beautiful, brilliant, enigmatic place that his music reaches, but it was on track. It was really one of these very personal labour of love-type documentaries that unfolded over the course of many years – probably six or so. I think I first reached out in 2001. We started filming initially, I believe, around late 2004. It must have been the early sessions for *The Drift*.

"I was doing a lot of work in Berlin, so I was able to travel to London and just meet his management. It was a very slow process of building a level of trust. They're just basic building blocks of doing a film like this – if you're doing it from the inside, if you really want to get involved, if you wanted him to be onside. It was [a case of] building a creative world that was in sympathy with the subject. There were collaborators that he'd worked with or he admired. I tried to use his aesthetic world to be a guide – Graham Wood, who did the animation[15] and worked on the music for the film, was an admirer of his. First of all we had to get Grant Gee involved – Grant actually filmed behind the scenes of Scott's Meltdown.[16] His management, Charles and Cathy, told us that Grant wanted to work with us. We tried to build it like it was all in the family – what's going to be the closest, what's going to feel the most personal? Even down to editorial decisions – it might seem a bit left-field, [as] it had its roots in art film."

Kijak remains the envy of aspiring Engel biographers in that he was granted the kind of access which mere writers never have been. The seeming completeness of his project, however, is occasionally the result of editorial sleight of hand, as even his subject conceded. "He's got so little material that I wonder what kind of movie he's gonna make," Scott pondered aloud to a German newspaper. "He never came to my home or was around my friends or anything like that."

Which may be a little unfair, as it's hard to imagine Scott Walker inviting anyone to film at his home. "We weren't being invasive and doing something that was going to tear down a wall," stresses Kijak, "because he has clearly built a very nice protective area between himself and the public eye. It's the way he wants it, but it was very much restricted to the respective music, specifically, and almost exclusively."

What *30 Century Man* does have is two days of concise interviews shot at the Negus-Fanceys' place, conducted by Kijak himself and by Meltdown founder David Sefton. These are fleshed out by interviews with Engel's admirers and, most effectively, by that documentary filmmaking staple, a generous use of archive footage – as well as

Wood's innovative graphics. There are certainly narrative gaps in the presentation of Scott's early life and his 'lost years'.[17] But what is most memorable about the film is its visualisation of the recording process of *The Drift*.

"At one point – ha!" Kijak recollects with a laugh at his own expense, "Charles and Cathy just kept saying, 'We'll let you know when there's something good for the camera.' I became very frustrated – 'Let us decide that, we're the filmmakers.' Everything's going to be good for the camera as far as I'm concerned. Of course they let us in that day and my God, it was an absolute bonanza!" he laughs

"We got the box, we got the beef – it was an incredible day to watch this process. So typical and so constructive – we saw all aspects, I felt, of this process. Observing these things being done was great stuff, and of course I would have liked to shoot more days, to really get into it. But in a way we got more than we could ever have used. It was great – and the two days we were in there were separated by about a year. At the time it felt like it just wasn't enough, but when you're actually working with it in the cut it truly is a really rich palette. The meat is such a legendary thing, isn't it? It's crazy – an extraordinary day."

As the recording process for *The Drift* got underway, Scott seems to have dispensed with the beard. Producer and long-time Engel friend Pete Walsh doesn't believe he donned it as a disguise. "He never stays in one place for too long," he tells this writer. "Different people have to have a reason to talk to him; he's always on the move, so he's never really in one place for too long," he laughs. "And you've seen him wearing the baseball cap, I think that's as far as the camouflage goes."

Walsh was centrally immersed in the recording process for *The Drift* detailed for Kijak's documentary. He confirms that, there among the aural representation of the human psyche's horrors, for a lot of the time they were having a bit of a laugh.

"Obviously some of the things that we get up to in the studios, trying to create new ways to record things, recording different sounds, lends itself to a fair bit of banter going with it," he genially reflects. "Some of the best results you get are when the musician or the performer is feeling relaxed and open to what the artist is trying to achieve. I feel it's not best achieved by making them frightened or pushing them too hard. There are some producers who think the opposite, I'm sure, whereby you only get to the real soul of it when you kind of crucify someone. There are people – it's quite widely known – who use those tactics. But not us."

Given the relentless psychic assault of *The Drift*, that might just have been a bridge too far. Its opener, 'Cossacks Are', however, plays like the very definition of accessibility compared to what is about to follow. Guitarist Hugh Burns' intricately repetitive riff is played backwards in a way which, in a more conventional song, might act as a bridge from the chorus back to the verse.

"A chilling
exploration
of erotic consumption."

A mass of critical plaudits relating to seemingly anything and everything are driven forward by drummer Ian Thomas' beat, again so repetitive that it sounds looped. If this was David Bowie singing you'd assume the lyric was a series of cut-ups. But the critical notices Engel croons almost operatically segue into something darker:

"With an arm
across the torso
face on
the nails...
'Medieval savagery
Calculated cruelty'
'It's hard to pick the worst moment.'

The invading image of "Cossacks... charging into fields of white roses" is leading us back into the field of conflict. The lyric itself may be obscure but, compared to what follows, the sound of it is easy listening.

As for *The Drift*'s lengthy recording itinerary and the gap suggested by Kijak, Walsh explains: "We usually take a long break before we do the orchestra – there's a lot of checking and talking and planning going on there. And it's a logistical nightmare trying to get it all set up, so there's usually a break there. I think there was possibly a break as well when Brian Gascoigne left the party[18] and Mark Warman joined, so we changed musical directors halfway through that album. So there might have been a little bit of a changeover period there. I don't remember disappearing off anywhere for any great length of time!"

The legendarily visceral percussion is revealed in *30 Century Man* when Scott carries a Tupperware box containing a side of beef into the studio. He tests the meat's acoustic qualities by jabbing several little right hooks into the animal flesh, which give off stark staccato smacks. The screen's subtitles read:

On the 28th of April 1945 Benito Mussolini was taken for execution by members of the committee of national liberation for Northern Italy. His mistress, Claretta Petacci, insisted on dying with him. They were shot, the bodies piled into a truck and taken to the Piazzele Loreto at Milan to be strung up by the heels side by side, their heads about six feet from the ground. They were mocked, vilified and riddled with bullets by the crowd that had gathered.

'Clar (Benito's Dream)' emerges from a swirling vortex of orchestrated sound which includes the flugelhorn, the Germanic signifier of death:

"Birds /
Birds /
This is not a cornhusk doll /
dipped in blood in the moonlight."

293

"It started when I was very young, maybe five or six, and my aunt took me to the cinema," explains Engel himself of the pathetic humanity glimpsed in the corpse of a fascist dictator. "Before the main feature started, in America they used to show newsreels in those days, there used to be some in the past, of World War Two and the aftermath. And then of course there were these two bodies hanging there, bloody things – it was quite shocking for me to see it, and I asked about it but nobody really wanted to explain it to me. It kept happening – every time I went to the cinema I'd see this shocking image and it stayed with me."

Newsreel footage shows *Il Duce* giving a strident speech applauded by fascists heavily packed into Rome's central square. It cuts to Benito and Clara lying wide-eyed and dead atop a jumble of fascist leaders' corpses – then to footage displaying the fickle loyalties of the crowd, with a similar-sized turnout gaping (with rather less enthusiasm) at the lifeless husks of the former leader and his lover hoisted up lampposts by their ankles. There were numerous shots taken of Mussolini and his mistress in death by the triumphalist partisans. The symmetrical topsy-turvy black-and-white photo shown in the film is almost a necromantic tribute. Others include a full-colour close-up of the corpses linked arm in arm, cardboard ID tags around their necks, like punctured gore balloons. This may have been briefly glimpsed by little Scotty Engel – albeit in monochrome on the movie screen.

> "The breasts are still heavy /
> The legs long and straight /
> The upper lip remains short /
> The teeth still too small."

Scott is seen tutoring percussionist Alasdair Malloy[19] on beating the meat: "You're gonna have to give it more like, 'Uh-UH! Uh-UH! Uh!-UH-UH!!!' Because if you wait too long between punches, you know what I mean? You can't do this too fast – it's got to be more varied and 'Uh-uh! Uh-uh! UH-UH! *E-uh! E-uh!*' Like that."

294

Malloy beats to a pugilistic rhythm that elicits a "Yeah, *yeah!*" from Scott.

"And then, I don't know," he elaborates on the childhood fixation on the murderous *Il Duce* and his lover, "more than a decade ago I read a biography and I thought, 'This is an incredible love story.' She was like someone today, like so many people today she was celebrity-obsessed, pictures all over her walls – especially of him, because he loved this sort of thing, meeting the press and doing these sorts of poses [he adopts a shoulders-back, breast puffed-out stance] and things. So in a sense she was a bit of an airhead, and of course in America at that time I remember my parents and people talking about Hitler and Mussolini – they thought they were sort of comic characters, the way they looked and everything, and he was essentially kind of a dangerous clown. But when they went to their deaths, she could have gotten away, he'd arranged for her to go. And she turned into this totally devoted different person, she went to her death with him and she could have gone. So in a sense it's a fascist love song, but it's strange, it's interesting."

To this writer, the meat-as-percussion is the aural realisation of the image in Orwell's novel *Nineteen Eighty-Four*, where O'Brien of the ruling Party says, "If you want a picture of the future, imagine a boot stamping on a human face – forever." Boot on face. Fist on flesh. Bullet on bone.

"I can only comment on the sonic side of it in this instance," says Walsh. "I can only say that he wanted it as real as possible. Short of actually having fisticuffs in the studio, it was the only other way we would get an honest representation of the sound. It was him being honest, it was him saying, 'I want it to sound exactly like somebody hitting a piece of flesh,' and that's what it was. Unfortunately, what you think is going to sound like a punch is not necessarily exactly what it is. Recording something like that, it doesn't give you a lot of depth, that sound, you just kind of get a slap."

Watch a boxing match. Grown men are throwing as much weight as they can behind their punches but you hear a very muffled sound in audio terms.

"I think it was the fact that we actually *did* it that sold the idea to him," says Walsh. "That's all to him, he's a very honest guy. To avoid using a pun, we wouldn't want to get too ham about it, getting some kind of puny *Batman* sound or something."[20]

"At the time, you didn't expect to see this doom and gloom-fest," says Stephen Kijak of filming the overwhelming audio-cinematic experience that is 'Clara'. "I've been in recording studios and in a way it's very much like production on a film – there's a camaraderie and you all pull together and try to achieve a goal. These guys love him and will do anything for him, and it's a great atmosphere. It's like a crazy, mad laboratory of sounds. Obviously we were only there for those couple of days and the album took a couple of years to put together, so I'm sure there were some very anxious moments and I'm sure the work wasn't always so easy. But it gets done, and the angst of those relationships, the experience, is a battle against time. I mean all of those outside-world pressures that are put on someone to achieve something in a short amount of time. We couldn't film the singing section but Grant Gee was able to photograph it, and again it was a very pressurised situation creatively – but physically the clock is ticking, these are expensive sessions, he wants very strange and abstract ideas out of these people, and it's finding a way to pull that out. But everyone pulls around him and they give it their all, the result is there, man, it's extraordinary stuff. I think it might be when he steps up to the mike and has to find something in himself to do these vocals, that's probably the darkest part of the process."

"No, no, we would kill ourselves, we would stop dead, if we were all in that mood all the time," asserts Engel in the film itself. "Of course there's humour laced through all the stuff. If it was all that kind of awful gothic stuff it would be terrible."

"But it's clear – these are supposedly abrasive, impenetrable, atonal records: bullshit!" insists Kijak. "There's like a melodic soul to 'Clara', there are just moments where out of the darkness fell this unbelievably aching melody. It's not at the top but it's still there in its DNA. And yeah, the journey, maybe it was tortuous and maybe it was necessary. But he's followed it through and it's fascinating. I feel like it's a very linear, very tight body of work, I don't think there's a split.[21] It's total evolution."

"You shouldn't take the songs too literally," says Engel. "Often I'll take a political idea, or an idea we all know, and that's a springboard to another place, to another sort of world, and that's the same in this case. So in the end it almost comes down to... a personal message of a self of some kind. I mean ultimately, your work is yourself. Everything in my world, because I have a very nightmarish imagination, I've had very bad dreams all my life... so everything in my world is *big*. It's way out of proportion."

In many ways, Scott Engel's viewpoint echoes that of pop-surrealist filmmaker David Lynch: grotesque images are a gateway to another world. Where they take the listener or viewer is largely subjective; what it all means is ultimately determined by the final element, the person who is taking it all in.

The tragically romantic phantasmagoria of 'Clara' is augmented by female voices near the beginning of the track, whispering about birds. At the end (of both the song and the film *30 Century Man*), Scott himself intones in natural clear speech.

"This morning in my room /
A little swallow was trapped /
It flew around, desperately /
Until it fell exhausted on my bed /
I picked it up so as not to frighten it /
I opened the window /
And I opened my hand."

No such escape for tragic, silly, loyal Clara.

The Drift, if it can be defined as a concept, is a never-ending process wherein seemingly disconnected entities and events collide and share the same existential space. The album's other key track is 'Jesse', whose key references are the 9/11[22] 2001 attacks on America (particularly the toppling of the World Trade Centre), Elvis Aaron

297

Presley and his stillborn twin, Jesse Garon.[23] A place was always set at the table for the absent Jesse and it's been suggested that Elvis regarded him as a presence his whole life.[24] In the song 'Jesse', which breaks the two-chord guitar intro to 'Jailhouse Rock' down to a recurring crawl throughout, he's our conduit to non-existence – a kind of Native American spirit guide whose non-presence we call upon from the wrecked image of the Twin Towers.

"I don't like out-and-out protest songs anyway," Engel says of the lateral imagery of 'Jesse'. "I mean there are a lot of albums that came out after 9/11, I don't like some guy strumming, preaching in my face. There's other ways to talk about these things – the same with the Mussolini thing, because fascism is in the air. It's worth people talking about it, but maybe if you give them something else to talk about they'll still be talking about it through a love song like that. But with 'Jesse' it's the same thing, you try to come from another place."

"Famine is a tall tower /
A building left in the night /
Jesse are you listening?"

The undercurrent of strings swells up in the refrain to a pitch both cinematic and menacing.

"So in 'Jesse' you have vertical and horizontal images – in the end you have the prairie and of course at the beginning you have the towers. But in the end it's a personal message of some kind from somewhere, it's an existential personal message."

"It casts its ruins in shadows …
Under Memphis moonlight …
In the dream /
I am crawling around on my hands and knees /
smoothing out the prairie."

"I was looking for an image for the Twin Towers, for a metaphor for that. Because of American hubris we build things sky-high, and it's full of muscle and whatever. Those two things had no reflective quality to me, spiritual reflective quality. Of course, Elvis' dead twin brother didn't either because he's not there – he couldn't see him, he spoke to him but there was no reflective quality. So that's how I came across that image and that's how I tried to tie those together. And of course in Memphis, once again, it's an ancient Egyptian city as well, so that all tied in."

"I think 'Jesse' has a very pictorial feel in the landscape that's there," says Pete Walsh. "I guess even more so for me because I kind of know what every sound does but I don't think I'm really able to go into it in that much detail, you know. If you do listen to that track in particular, everything's there for a reason. It's the same in all of Scott's music: no matter how mad or – well, not 'mad', I wouldn't say mad – how surprising it is, you can always justify something being there.

"It evolves – he's quite cautious about how much information he gives. Mainly because he doesn't want us to specifically go for a particular thing because of what it is. So he'll kind of be open about it and give the gist of it, but we don't set out to make it sound like that. I think the reason why Scott and I click so well is that I can interpret what he wants without him actually spelling it out to me. I think that's the secret of our collaboration really, I know the man so well and I can pretty much get into the area that he wants to get into internally."

In terms of visual imagery, Graham Wood's video for 'Jesse' features animated figures emerging as shapes from kaleidoscopic patterns that sometimes resemble a Rorschach test, including a baby or a foetus. All resemble how the mind strives to pick discernible figures out of the blur that comes with staring into darkness or the visions that form on eyelids closed against intensely bright sunlight.

'Jolson And Jones' depicts a hellishly surreal "grossness of spring". Its title and the antagonistically toned later verses were inspired by two performers linked with Engel's earlier life: Allan Jones, the movie musical star and singer, father of the crooner Jack Jones; Al Jolson, the much-loved singer of 'Sonny Boy', a song aggressively parodied in 'Jolson And Jones', and to whom little Scotty Engel was compared at the tender age of eight. In this strangest of lyrics, there's a refrain of "Curare!" – the naturally occurring poison which paralyses the respiratory system – and a nightmarish donkey ee-aw produced by Pete Walsh. "Donkey sounds was a major part of my life last year, trying to find the right mule," he laughs in *30 Century Man*.

Part of the cue for these strange colliding images can be found in this extract from *Unnatural: The Heretical Idea Of Making People* by Philip Ball:

> In 1814, an explorer named Charles Waterton brought back from an expedition to the Amazon samples of the deadly poison curare, which he proceeded to test on animals. A donkey was 'killed' by a dose and then wholly resuscitated... The implication is that 'death' may not be final and that surgical intervention can restore life.

(A hole was cut in the unfortunate animal's throat and bellows inserted to inflate her lungs – at which point she revived to see what was happening to her.)

Jolson and Jones, the latter approaching the end of his life, the former the end of his career, are stuck in a kind of seedy transmogrifying hell, "Where nice girls were turned into whores... Where deaf children were born." The narrator's footsteps are heard descending into "the paralysed street", before the unspecified aggression boils over into a clash between the two performers' best-known lyrics (Jolson's 'Sonny Boy' and Jones' 'Donkey Serenade') in the form of an attack on the mule, the dumb symbol of defiance against approaching death: "I'LL PUNCH A DONKEY IN THE STREETS OF GALWAY."

"Those [donkey] sounds took a long time to get," Walsh confirms to this writer. "That was an instance where I was not sure if I should be taking him literally or not. I had originally tried to use a saxophone to do it, and I think the donkey does relate to Allan Jones, there's something in there.[25] I think that was in a way a bit of his kind of tongue-in-cheek. I know the impression you get from it is this sort of nightmarish thing, but it's an example of how, when we were doing it, we didn't go through the nightmare at the same time."

The Galway line and the ee-aw seem to suggest so many things at once, including James Joyce.[26] "He's actually a real animal lover," Walsh says of Engel, suggesting the animal's suffering implies a particular kind of earthly hell; this writer thinks of the abused horse in the nightmare sequence of Dostoyevsky's *Crime And Punishment* and even Nietzsche's Turin horse, before whom the poet philosopher collapsed crying and put his arms around the suffering animal's neck before losing his mind completely.

'Cue' begins with the eerily exploratory trumpet Kijak uses to good effect in *30 Century Man*. It becomes considerably less comforting from there, contributing to *The Drift's* reputation as an album that actively elicits fear. At a deathly pace, Engel morbidly serenades us with images of biological infection in an impoverished Third World:

"Stars led to sky /
Lash led to eye /
Herpes to clit...
Through the dominant wards and nurseries
A flugelman moves."

A deathly quiet *a capella* section erupts suddenly into discordant strings. It's also the track that most overtly features those pounding, monolithic wooden boxes. As with the meat as percussion, "They were always there at the beginning," testifies Walsh of the original ideas. "Not right at the outset, but when we're trying to consider how to present an idea or record a particular sound we'll have discussions about how best to achieve it. The big box in fact was something that Scott remembered that we'd recorded on *Tilt*: 'You remember we were doing that thing, duh-duh-duh? Is it possible to recreate that?' I don't think we actually used it in the end. Sometimes he'll refer to stuff that was done in previous work and look at it and refresh it."

In *30 Century Man*, the building of the wooden sound box is shown at the Metropolis sessions in 2004. Pete Walsh is directing proceedings: "The image Scott has in his head is of this guy banging a huge glass on a bar counter, you know."

BANG! BANG! BANG!

"The thing with *The Drift* is that it doesn't really have any arrangements," acknowledges Scott. "There are some textures there, like in 'Cue'. It's big blocks of sound, the strings will be a big block of noise or they'll be noises. But there's no real arrangements, that's what I mean. I don't mean it's taking the fullness away, you use fullness when you need it. That's why for certain things you need an army of strings, because nothing less than that, it wouldn't give you that kind of effect."

On 'Hand Me Ups', the nightmare continues. It opens with a cacophony of percussion and features a particularly unharmonised male backing vocal. Among more obscure lyrics, it features an unnerving section about the uncertainties of raising children:

"What?
when you can't hear the bleating all night
Else he's strumming the springs of his cot
When?
what you can't hear is her tiny mouth squealing and shrieking with
laughter."
It ends, particularly strangely, on an image of crucifixion:
"I felt the nail driving into my foot while I felt the nail driving into my hand."

'Buzzers' is almost an acoustic ballad, but shot through with surreal horror. The origins of the horror are all too literal, however. As announced by a female newsreader on a radio broadcast, the Balkans are splintering into mutually antagonistic ethnic nation-states:

"'Milosevic couldn't care less if Bosnia was recognised,' a laughing Dr Karadzic later told a television interviewer. He said, 'Caligula proclaimed his horse a senator but the horse never took his seat.'"

302

Accompanied by gentle percussion, Scott gives a more brutally literal depiction of political torture than he did in 'The Electrician':

"Polish the fork and stick the fork in him

He's done boys."

'Psoriatic' is the track adapted from the Meltdown dance piece, 'Thimble Rigging'. It's accompanied by the sweeping grind of a cylindrical bin used for shucking peas and the almost traditional 'metal bashing' of industrial music,[27] in this case a hammer on a length of lead piping.

The images are many and bewilderingly various in 'Psoriatic': "a nimble rigger slyly rolls the pea," a conman suckering the saps who have to guess what thimble it's under; "Red is patchy / Snow's the silver" refers to the sores and flakes of the epidermic condition psoriasis itself; the post-World War One hit 'Ja Da' ("ja-da jing jing jing") is parodied in the manner of 'Sonny Boy' earlier; the line referring to an "anthrax jesus" (lower case) echoes the "vermin Holy Ghost" of 'Cue', evoking the controversial 1987 photo-portrait *Piss Christ* but updating it to reflect more recent anxieties.[28] All evokes all back and forth continually, creating circles of hell.

'The Escape' also begins like an acoustic ballad, but gives a sense of being stalked by a killer:

"The car

in front

follows

the long

way around ...

Prey moves

Predator moves."

The sudden uproarious refrain of "You and me against the world" is accompanied by rare synthesized effects. "I was trying to address secrecy, and deception and conspiracy theories," said Scott at the time, claiming not to be a believer but to be "interested in these

303

things out of curiosity". Slide guitar alludes to the *Merry Melodies/ Looney Tunes* theme of the classic Warner Brothers cartoons, but the macabre repetition of "What's up, doc?" at the end sounds like a predatory psychopath doing a particularly creepy Donald Duck impression.[29]

'A Lover Loves' is another coda to the album as per 'Rosary', accompanied by a two-note acoustic riff like a more minimalist early Johnny Cash. Despite its deceptive title, it offers no relief:

"Corneas misted (*psst psst psst psst*)
colour high
Motionless
(*psst psst psst psst*)
for seconds at a time."

The scenario is death and Engel seems to be reminding us that it's coming for every one of us – this being a man now in his early sixties who's lost both his elderly parents over the space of the last several years. The conspiratorial '*psst*' is to draw the listener in, but the implication is clear: there will be no getting away; we're not being let off the hook.

"This is
a waltz
for a
dodo,"

he tips the nod to an extinct species, also namechecking Disney's orphaned deer Bambi, Kaiser Wilhelm, the late German artist Joseph Beuys, communist revolutionary 'Red Rosa' Luxemburg and even the comic-strip character Tintin – all dead, even the latter who, like Jesse, never actually existed.

"Well it's very stark, and as I go on things get starker," Scott told interviewers Kijak and Sefton of the aesthetic of *The Drift*. "What Pete and I do is really keep refining that sound. We're pretty much set now in the noise that we've made of our own and people identify

[with]. Like Beckett did, we just keep honing things and honing things down, shaving down all the tracks and things like that. There's less personality as things have gone by, in the singing, so ultimately it's just a man singing now. There are no soul inflexions – not that there ever were many with me, but there's nothing like that. I just want to get to a man singing and when it has to have emotion, hopefully it's real emotion.

"Sometimes with a baritone voice it tranquillises people, it has that effect, people stop listening to what they're hearing. So if the voice is pitched as the lyric vertiginously, it's going to be very effective in place there. Anyone has to be very lucky to go through life singing, as opposed to other things, but it's a genuine terror that I'm not going to get it right. And I just want to do it once or twice if I can, and I just want to absolutely get it. I fail lots of times but at least I'm trying, you know...

"And of course we use baritone guitarists on here as well. So everything is very high end, very low end and voice right in the middle where it should be, you know. It stops people latching onto any kind of artifice, because there's a lot of it today, even in soul music and in so-called 'indie' stuff. You hear all these inflexions and it's cheesy. There used to be some great soul singers but now everything's clichéd. I don't want to have any clichés, so I'm trying to drain all of that away. So like I said, when you do really hit the emotional things, you can hear it on the records – it'll open out and you say, 'Oh yes, I caught that! Other times I didn't make it but that time...'

"So there's spaces in *Tilt*, but more spaces in this, for silence and language to emerge. And that's why the words are important, because you have to... feel the phenomenon of the words coming out of silence almost."

"I have to say I didn't sleep the night before the string sessions, not at all, and I doubt he did either," said Phil Sheppard, who conducted the orchestra on Scott Walker's most harrowing work thus far. "Some of the most high-octane, terrifying work I've ever done," he proclaimed.

"Because there's incredible pressure at the time of these sessions," explained 4AD CEO Chris Sharp. "You've got these people, it costs a fortune, you've got 36 people in there, you've got one day to get it all done."

It was the single days of string sessions at Air Studios that were imposing the pressure – but then the nature of the work itself was no picnic.

"You could see on the faces of the players that they were as uncertain about the project as I had been on the day I walked into the studio," explained new musical director Mark Warman with a smile. "When you tell them they've got to sound like World War Two bombers slowly approaching from 50 miles as a way of getting closer and closer, they understand that, by the time they're really close, they want to be playing those strings more violently than they've ever been asked to before."

In *30 Century Man*, Scott is seen conducting proceedings in the studio in a blue denim jacket and purple baseball cap.

"What I was struck by was that, for somebody who has a reputation for being incredibly deliberate and thinking long and hard about every creative move, how quick he was to react to how things were being played," said Sharp, "to suggest all kinds of ways of doing it, and knowing when not to, just to say go with it, this is fine. To watch that kind of instant ability to filter sound, to think, 'Is this what I want? Is it good enough? Yes, OK, go!' Or, if something wasn't right, to really just home in on what wasn't right."

"Because we strived so hard to get everything just right," confirms Engel, "it shouldn't be synthesized strings, it's got to be exactly what it is. And of course it would drive Hughie [Burns] crazy, he's one of the heroes of the record because he had to translate all of these chords, these horrendous things I'd written on the guitar, the baritone guitar which is without the normal tuning space. He'd have a nervous breakdown in one evening, I was trying to play this and I was like..." he laughs, contorting his hands.

***

In his foreword to the inner booklet for *The Drift*, Ian Penman, current *Wire*/former *NME*[30] journalist (who used to be regarded as something of a post-modernist himself) refers to Scott Walker as "the last modernist" – placing him on the literary level of Eliot's *The Waste Land* and Joyce's *Ulysses*, and on a musical par with Stravinsky's *The Rites Of Spring* – all innovative works, but of the post-World War One era.

"I don't think I'm a modernist, no," demurred Engel. "I know what he means – he's probably talking about 'bold gesture', and sometimes that's the case. I think that's what he means… I have a great admiration for the modernists, I love all that stuff, but it's simply not on now. From my personality, when I'm writing anyway, it's more like a Dostoyevsky or Knut Hamsun reaction, the Knut Hamsun of *Hunger*[31] probably. It's that more than anything else."

As to his own distinctive non-linear lyric writing, "I don't think of it as poetry because, generally speaking, poetry isn't written to be sung particularly. It can be a lot of things but this stuff always has to be written to be sung – which makes it extra difficult, because it's harder than poetry in a sense. And poetry is very difficult."

Asked by the Kijak team whether *Tilt* and *The Drift* can be considered experimental works, he demurred again.

"No, they shouldn't do… I'm experimenting at home, getting it all together and putting it all together, but not so much in the studio. No, it's very thought out in the playing. Anything can go wrong in the studio in the right way, so I allow for that to happen of course, I'm looking forward to that experience as well. But… there's not a lot of guys in black suits twiddling knobs, you know what I mean, and noodling around, we don't have time for that. So it's very disciplined and everyone has to be very clear."

"We all build on those things through our lives," opines Kijak of his subject's artistic influences, "obviously there was a certain kind of collection of influences in the sixties that direct the work. And as he continued on he brought other influences into play that reflect in the music. He's always absorbing and learning and taking things in – I know he loves the cinema of Bela Tarr;[32] if you want to make direct link between the harmonics and film maybe, it's all there. We were talking about Haneke when we were interviewing him, *Caché* (*Hidden*)[33] was a film that was in the cinemas. It's all part of a great lineage, the contemporary cinema and literature that he's absorbing now."

"Confusion still sounds dangerous… his most radical work yet," said *New York Magazine* of *The Drift* on its May 2006 release.

"He is a poet and a composer of the unconscious," acclaims Michael Warman, "and if one wants to look for logic in his work it would be more the logic of, in a sense, a dream-world. There is no one else doing what he's doing. I think the feeling that you get when you listen to Scott Walker's current work hasn't quite got a name yet. I'm very comfortable with that, I don't want to give it a name. It's a feeling."

"Recently I was in Paris doing some interviews," concurs Engel himself, "and the interviewers, at least three of them, said, 'They aren't songs any more – we don't know what they are, but they aren't songs.' And I said, 'I always think of them as songs.'

"They didn't, they just said, 'You're out there on your own now.' And I thought, 'Oh no, not again!'" he laughs

"It's like an intrepid explorer or something," explains Jarvis Cocker in his average-bloke-looks-askance-manner, "someone who goes to a part of the world no one's ever been to before. Now that part of the world might be very inhospitable and full of dangerous animals, or whatever. You wouldn't particularly want to live there yourself, but you've got to admire somebody who is prepared to take a path to there, and stick a flag down and say, 'This is where you can go.'"

"He really should be, as far as I'm concerned, recognised as not only one of our great composers but great poets as well," insists Brian Eno. "His lyrics are absolutely peerless to me, I think, and it's very surprising to me that he's still regarded as a slightly marginal figure. All right, he isn't very prolific, but the quality of the work he's done is so incredible."

In *30 Century Man*, Kijak asks his subject, "Do you think if *Scott 4* had been like a top-selling album you would have arrived at *Tilt* or *The Drift* today?"

"I'd have been sooner," Engel insists. "I would have been there a lot sooner. And that's the only thing, because I would have carried on instead of having nearly a 20-year hiatus. I must say, just to add to that, I don't blame anyone else for that. That's my bad faith and I've been paying for it ever since. I mean, for myself it is a serious issue with me, because... well, it's all down to me basically, all those wasted years. My dilemma now is to divert from this next record and go for a smaller form that I can do some touring with – or just let my imagination roll and forget about it, as I've always done. Or I'll know when I write the next record what it's going to be."

Speculation or rumours of a touring unit to take *The Drift* on the road circulated for a short while. But events would intervene.

"When I think of Scott Walker I think of the world of Eliot, or Beckett, or Joyce," acclaimed Michael Morris, co-director of the Artangel contemporary art project. "I also see connections with certain visual artists, say Francis Bacon:[34] interior landscapes, he deals in fragments, clues. In the hands of a lesser artist those influences would become pastiche, they would be on the surface. As it is, they're completely absorbed."

"We've heard rumblings from his instrumental work, which are for dance, which are no walk in the park," reflects Kijak on the likely nature of Engel's subsequent work. "Yeah, so who knows? But then there's that fantastic piece he did for *Plague Songs* – it was riveting. It was right after *The Drift* and it couldn't have been more different. 'Darkness' – the tambourine and the screaming choir, it was just *fantastic!* A completely different set of tools and it was great."

The Margate Exodus Day was an Artangel project, taking place on the Kent coast on September 30, 2006. As a representation in modern terms of the 10 biblical plagues, the event was accompanied by musical contributions later released on *Plague Songs*, a 4AD album. The other notable tracks included Brian Eno and Robert Wyatt's

'Flies', Laurie Anderson's 'Death Of Livestock' and The Tiger Lillies' harrowing 'Hail'. Scott Walker's contribution was the ninth plague, 'Darkness':

"Threadbare

little earth," he intones, and his selected choir scream his words back at him in the shrillest tones imaginable. It's like a call-and-response blues in a modern classical format, ending on the vocalist's deadpan line of "Get your coat."

The challenging dance soundtrack referred to by Kijak is *And Who Shall Go To The Ball? And What Shall Go To The Ball?* Performed by the London Sinfonietta with Walker collaborator Philip Sheppard on cello, it accompanied a London performance by the CandoCo Dance Company under choreographer Rafael Bonachela. In September 2007, Engel's 24-minute orchestral work (in collaboration with Mark Warman and Pete Walsh) was released as a limited edition CD. His liner notes reflect his continuing Baconian concern with the body:

> Apart from a slow movement given over to solitude, the music is full of edgy and staccato shapes or cuts, reflecting how we cut up the world around us as a consequence of the shape of our bodies. How much of a body does an intelligence need to be potentially socialised in an age of ever-developing AI?[35] This is but one of many questions that informed the approach to the project.

Reflecting his intended approach, the four-part soundtrack opens at first to scrapings and aural fragments that quickly die. It eventually progresses into an accelerando piece that evokes Polish composer Krzysztof Penderecki's groundbreaking 'Threnody To The Victims Of Hiroshima' – but eventually reaches a nerve-gratingly faster tempo.

The rest of the decade never did see that *Drift* touring band. Scott did give the odd mutually respectful nod to the modern indie-rock world: early twentysomething Alex Turner of The Arctic Monkeys formed a temporary band called The Last Shadow Puppets which owed much to 60s 'big pop' in general and late-sixties Scott Walker in particular; in a mutual interview with his friend Jarvis Cocker, he expressed a liking for the verbal and structural adeptness of Cocker's Northern compatriates the Monkeys ("You can hear they haven't stopped developing yet").

The indie world made its own tribute when, on November 13-15, 2008, various artists gave minimally theatrical performances of *Drifting And Tilting: The Songs Of Scott Walker* at London's Barbican. Damon Albarn of Blur sang 'Farmer In The City' in early Bowie-ish/Anthony Newley-ish style, answered "I'll give you 21!" by operatic baritone Owen Gilhooly; Cocker dramatically spoke/sang his way through 'Cossacks Are' while appearing to read the lines from a newspaper, making a good fist of "That's a nice suit / That's a swanky suit!"; as a pugilist pounded pig flesh, Gilhooly and Dot Allison divided 'Clara' up into Benito/Clara lines; Gavin Friday crooned his way through 'Jesse'.

And the composer? He was sitting anonymously behind the mixing desk with Pete Walsh.

"I think people are always asking him whether he's going to perform live, ever going to perform live again, and maybe that was one answer he gave," says Walsh. "Obviously everybody wanted him to get up onstage and sing a song. That was his way of kind of going out on the road and doing some," he laughs affectionately.

"It's probably why he doesn't want to perform these things," reflects Stephen Kijak. "They are not pop songs, these songs are such incredibly intense pieces. I don't even know if he recorded the vocals all in one take – I doubt it, I just don't think it'd be possible."

Notes

1   Scott had covered 'The Me I Never Knew', from *Alice's Adventures In Wonderland*, and 'This Way May', which applied Black's lyric to Barry's theme from *Mary, Queen Of Scots*.

2   By post-punk/Britpop band Garbage in this case – the soundtrack producers were at pains to sound contemporary.

3   Melville saw very little success in his lifetime, even with his religiously undertoned classic novel about the search for the white whale.

4   Only one, 'Scope J', is included on the Western release of the CD; the second track, 'Lullaby (By-By-By')', was reserved for the Japanese edition for some obscure reason.

5   The author is unsure of the role of an 'executive producer' on a record album as opposed to a feature film.

6   Whose 'Blues For Ceauşescu' shares the theme, if not the form, of the last track on Scott Walker's most recent release: 'The Day The Conductor Died'.

7   Cocker was once acclaimed as 'the new Morrissey'. Morrissey himself bristled at that, pointing out that Cocker can't sing – which is technically correct although, in the tradition of some of the best rock vocalists, he has a distinctive voice which tells a good tale. It also makes Cocker one of the odder figures to claim inspiration by the vocal virtuosity of Scott Walker.

8   In fact it spent three weeks in the Top 10 of the albums chart.

9   Charles Negus-Fancey's home/office in Holland Park – the site of most contemporary meetings, or rare interviews, with Scott Walker.

10   In 'Love Minus Zero (No Limits)', covered by The Walker Brothers.

11   In the early years of the new millennium, both Scott's mother, Betty (or Mimi, as he called her), and her ex-husband died in California; by the time of his demise, Noel Sr. had been a long-term resident of Bakersfield.

12   The only other recipients of this award were Phil Spector – who would subsequently be imprisoned for the shooting murder of actress Lana Clarkson – and Brian Eno: one shade of Scott Engel's past and one shade of a future that never was. In 2006, he would be presented with *Mojo* magazine's Icon Award for performers who "have enjoyed a spectacular career on a global scale".

13   Using the title of the minimalist *Scott 3* piece to emphasise, in Richard Hawley's words, just how "far ahead of the game" Scott Walker remained.

14   His next documentary film would be *Stones In Exile*, about the recording of The Rolling Stones' *Exile On Main Street*. As with *30 Century Man*, it would be shown in an edited form on BBC1's arts programme *Imagine*.

15   *30 Century Man* contains particularly evocative animated sequences for 'Boy Child', 'The Electrician' and 'Jesse'.

16   Gee was renowned by this point for his work on U2's Zoo TV tour and his documentary *Meeting People Is Easy*, on Radiohead. Working as director of photography on *30 Century Man*, he semi-simultaneously directed the equally recommended documentary *Joy Division*, in collaboration with punk/post-punk commentator Jon Savage.

17   This writer has sought to account for these periods in his own way. Without the subject's direct input, of course, one is arguably doomed to fail on these points but hopes to fail in a readable manner – or to "fail better", as Beckett would say.

18 Given Gascoigne's attitude to the *Tilt* sessions, he may have had enough of the 'agony' by now.

19 From Jarvis Cocker's Meltdown 2000 ensemble, A Touch Of Glass.

20 *Splat! Pow!*

21 From Scott Walker's early work.

22 September 11.

23 The hauntingly absent presence that was (or was not) Jesse was previously signified by the title of Nick Cave & The Bad Seeds' second album, *The Firstborn Is Dead*, and is at the core of its opening track, the distorted blues 'Tupelo': "In a shoebox buried with a ribbon of red."

24 In Alan Bleasdale's play *Are You Lonesome Tonight?*, about the final hours of Elvis' life, the tragic onetime king of rock 'n' roll wails that of the only two people who ever really loved him, one is dead (his mother, Gladys) and the other never lived (Jesse).

25 'Donkey Serenade'.

26 Joyce's beloved wife, Nora Barnacle, hailed from Galway, which served as the setting for his novella *The Dead*.

27 Viz the early eighties bands who placed the sounds of industry on a superior footing to rhythm and melody: Throbbing Gristle, Non, Einstürzende Neubaten, SPK, Test Department – even UK electro-pop combo Depeche Mode later incorporated metal bashing into their hit 'Master & Servant'.

28 Immediately post-9/11, the cattle disease anthrax seemed to become an apocalyptic weapon of jihadist terrorists – though the supposed instances of 'anthrax powder' sent through the post turned out to be hoaxes.

29 A Disney character of course, not Warners'.

30 In the days when it was the most credible of the 'inkies', not the glossy magazine it is now.

31 Both Dostoyevsky and the (later) Norwegian Hamsun remain 'modern' novelists in terms of describing their characters' inner psychology – but have little in common with the experiments in form of the modernist writers. Hamsun will also probably be forever associated – as will the great French novelist Céline, a doctor who was courageous enough to treat Jewish patients during the Vichy era – with his eccentrically sympathetic attitude towards Nazism in his dotage.

32 The Hungarian Tarr's initially social realist style became gradually more meditative, based around seemingly interminable long shots. He has announced his desire to retire from the cinema and says his last film will be 2011's *The Turin Horse* – fixating on the fate of the family of the cab driver who Nietzsche witnessed mercilessly whipping a horse before his mental collapse. Tarr says its theme is "the heaviness of human existence" – which might be applied to much of his later work.

33 Michael Haneke is the French director of such psychologically disturbing works as *Funny Games* (filmed in both French and American versions) and *The Piano Teacher*. *Hidden*, to give his 2006 film its English title, is a dark thriller in which some major aspects remain ambiguous or unexplained. The shared existence of

313

Parisian intellectuals Georges and Anne (the archetypal names Haneke always gives to his bourgeois couples) starts to unravel when a posted videotape shows them their home life is under surveillance; the manipulated events culminate in the disappearance of their young son and revelation of a guilty secret from Georges' own youth.

34 The distorted flesh aesthetic of Bacon as a painter often appears almost fetishistic in his works; the positioning of the body in Scott Walker's modern lyrics is more of an existential question, of the space in the world that an individual body is allowed to occupy or is forced into.

35 Artificial intelligence.

Chapter 14

Exizstenchooliszt

"All I want to do is sit on my arse and fart and think of Dante."

– Samuel Beckett

"The first lady's words when it became clear their fate was sealed were less dignified: 'Go back up your mother's cunt!' The bloody end of the Ceaușescus, riddled with bullets, is immortalised in easily accessible news footage. It would be celebrated by those they had persecuted and mourned by those to whom the communist era had granted an affordable standard of living."

– Gavin Baddeley and Paul Woods, *Vlad The Impaler: Son Of The Devil, Hero Of The People*

"If you're not being non-annoyingly pessimistic in this beautiful world of ours, you are definitely not in full possession of the facts."

– Scott Engel, shortly prior to the release of *Bish Bosch*

In the early spring of 2009, the old crooner wafted in again on the ethereal breeze.

Bat For Lashes, an apparently heavily Siouxsie/Kate Bush-influenced group that was effectively young English songstress

315

Natasha Khan and attendant musicians, issued their *Two Suns* album, its songs centring on a failed love affair and astrology.

The melodramatic final track, 'The Big Sleep', features a piano tone redolent of silent movie accompaniments and borrows its title from Raymond Chandler's hardboiled/romantic metaphor for death. "How can this be the last show?" pleads Ms Khan. "How can it be?" a dramatic male accompaniment echoes her.

She apparently never met Scott Walker, now the elder statesman of 'alternative' music. The mere fact that he agreed to provide his duet vocal via an MP3 file demonstrates how approachable he is by younger musicians he considers worthy of his time – even those one might not connect with his later, most uncompromising period. According to Ms Khan, he sent her a follow-up email, joking, "I hear that your album went in at number five in the UK. Such huge congratulations. I must be losing my edge."

He was about to demonstrate otherwise, however.

"If one is going purely by the output of albums and comparing it to when we're working together then the picture is not completely true," insists long-time friend and co-producer Peter Walsh, "because we have done projects between recording his solo projects, you know. There was the set of Barbican concerts called *Drifting And Tilting* in between the two albums, and I think even during the album we did a project, the *Duet For One Voice* at the Royal Opera House. So there is quite a continuous working relationship there, but it doesn't encompass solely the albums."

Cocteau's play *Le bel indifferent* was originally written as a single-handed piece for his friend Edith Piaf, which she performed shortly before the Wehrmacht took Paris in the spring of 1940.[1] In the hands of choreographer Aletta Collins, it was refashioned as part of a Cocteau double bill (with *La voix humaine*) so that the 'indifferent beauty' is the woman in a dysfunctional relationship, her cheated-upon lover's entreaties falling upon silence.

"I must admit to not really being an admirer of Cocteau,"[2] said Scott Engel. "I am, however, an admirer of Aletta Collins and her work. So when Aletta asked me to collaborate with the intention of deconstructing the original script for dance, I was grateful for the challenge to help take what is essentially, in my humble opinion, an antiquated piece of misogyny (in this case, woman as willing victim) and try to turn it on its head and use its traces to create something new."

The soundtrack music was a synthesis of many of the modern classical composers that have influenced Scott Walker in his recent work: there are traces of Varèse, Schoenberg, Ligeti and Penderecki. For all that, particularly given the eerie trumpet tones, this is most recognisably the composer of 'Cue' on *The Drift*.

As producer Walsh says, the work on a new album was already underway by the point of the play's run in June 2011. In fact the writing process had begun in 2009 – but the by now characteristically bleak (if also absurdly humorous) work would be interrupted by some genuinely depressing news. On May 7, 2011, John Maus had died of liver cancer at the Californian home he shared with his wife, Cynthia, and their four children.

For all the artistic differences between them and the rivalry in the latter days of the Walkers' sixties stardom, the two had remained lifelong friends. "[John is] very high up in some kind of trucking company," Scott had told *The Times* several years earlier. "He has an enormous home; he's doing very well. He's doing much, much better financially than I am, I guarantee you."

"I know Scott perhaps as well as anyone and he is a recluse," Maus had said of his former musical partner, "but he is not weird in any way. He is a very private person and wants to stay that way. I think he is a lot more together than most people who are very public showbiz personalities."[3]

For all John's later success in the workaday world, he'd never truly left music behind; having trained as a sound engineer, he'd built a recording studio in his home and recorded his last album of love songs in 2007. In that same year and in 2009, he'd returned to the UK to join old acquaintance Dave Dee on the Solid Silver 60s Show.

And now the original Walker Brother had gone. There truly were no doors left open to the past.

***

When the new album was eventually announced by 4AD in late September 2012, Engel would ponder aloud, "I was thinking about making the title refer to a mythological, all-encompassing, giant woman artist." Unlike certain other radical sound sculptors,[4] Scott Engel's socio-political instincts seemed to remain instinctively progressive.

But it was not to be. For the metaphorical wordplay and metaphysical conceit that would carry his new work, he chose a phrase that the politically sensitive might even accuse of misogyny, should they be so inclined. As ever, things would be neither so simple nor so obvious.

Bish (n. sl.), bitch
Bosch, Hieronymous (c.1450-1516), Dutch painter
Bish Bosh (sl.), job done, sorted

Bish Bosch, as a title, showed how much of the late-period cockney vernacular Engel had soaked up in his adopted city. It also confirmed what might have been gleaned from his last three[5] albums: that the Engel worldview was reaching a hybrid peak of the grotesque and (to lighten things up in the darkest way possible) the comically absurd.

"Bosch apparently could not invent enough hideous monstrosities, his sense of reality was quite literally haunted by visions and distortions which defied any law of nature," said art critic David Larkin of the man christened Jeroen Anthoiszoon van Aken, in his 1973 anthology *Fantastic Art*.

Anthropomorphised molluscs and scary birds in uniform; sawn-off mutant overseers consisting only of a head and limbs; the skewered unrepentant and women impaled through their anuses, as Christ and his sycophant apostles look on piously from the cloud above in *The*

Last Judgement; the souls of the damned filing around giant eggshells and transmogrified human heads in *The Garden Of Delights*, as one lost soul tries to resist the sexual overtures of a pig in a nun's habit.

So, the devotional paintings of a late medieval believer in Heaven and Hell[6] and the skewed satire of late-period Scott Walker occupy the same territory?

Nah. Probably not.

But what Engel, now approaching his 70th birthday, shares with the visionary of damnation is the ability to telescope the entire jolly cesspool of existence. To make disparate historical entities and different eras collide with each other in a manner that might startle the absurdist playwright Pirandello, or possibly elicit a sly wink of recognition from Samuel Beckett over the top of his pint of Guinness.

Musically, Scott is aided and abetted by his usual accomplices in this slapstick atrocity of an album: Burns on guitars, Thomas on drums and Malloy[7] on percussion, augmented by fellow survivors of *The Drift*, James Stevenson[8] on baritone guitar and John Giblin on bass – with the addition of Guy Barker on trumpet, and B.J. Cole, from the seventies C&W period, on pedal steel guitar for one track. Musical director Mark Warman plays keyboards as well as conducting the orchestra.

"If I use the big orchestra I'm using it for noises or textures, or big pillars of sound, rather than arrangements," confirms Engel and it's no understatement. This one plays its way right out of music, into surrealism and the queasiest of black belly laughs.

"The recording process is not quite as intense as maybe the music indicates sometimes," confirms Pete Walsh. "I think both of us feel that you only get good results when you're not under stress, so there would be a certain relaxed repartee going on, certainly in the control room and in the way we directed the sessions for the musicians in the studio.

"But there are times when organising the personnel is difficult; he likes to work with a musical director, Mark Warman on the last two albums, and particular musicians. I think if you imagine trying to get all these people in the studio, and me, all together for a period of time, it actually takes time to organise it.

"Because he has a lot of it in his head he's cautious that it doesn't become disjointed, because otherwise he might lose the flow, do you know what I mean? And when you've got titles that are over 10 minutes long – in 'Zercon''s case over 20 – you need to keep a handle on where you are in the arrangement. You can't be dealing with recording the first five minutes one week and the last five minutes four weeks later. In that way he likes to be disciplined, get things done on the creative side. But there is now also [the fact that] the music business has redefined itself, budgets are not the same, so we actually can't afford to stay too long in an expensive situation. So he likes to plan it, cover all angles and then go in and do it."

In his accompanying notes on the release, Rob Young, editor of *The Wire*, observes that, "Scott insists none of his work is in any way autobiographical." It's a 180-degree turnaround on his attitude at the time of *The Drift*, whereby he noted that what an artist carried around in his head was a good part of the sum total of his existence.

"He's interested in art and history," confirms Walsh, "and he's probably prowling through the art galleries and making his own judgments. I think it's one thing to actually carry those things around in your head, it's another to be able to express them in a way that other people can identify with or get some kind of gratification from."

The same must hold true of *Bish Bosch* – the only sense that it's not autobiographical is that Scott Engel hasn't literally had his entrails strewn incontinently around for us to pick through and examine. But otherwise, what's going on here represents an amusingly jaundiced worldview as personal to him as that of the much-mooted Beckett and his hopeless antiheroes, stranded in dustbins in *Endgame* or lying alone in the dark in *Krapp's Last Tape*, knowing that nothing can be done; given the blackness of the humour and the vividness of the imagery, this writer refuses to believe Engel isn't equally familiar with Louis-Ferdinand Céline's exaggeratedly funny misanthropy in *Death On The Instalment Plan* and *Journey To The End of The Night*, or Alfred Jarry's grotesque, green shit-spraying monarch in his play *Ubu Roi*.

The album contains the title scrawled minimally in white on a blackboard. It opens with 'See You Don't Bump His Head', the type of advice liberally offered while holding a vulnerable small baby (and try not to smear his brains all over the wall too). The sequenced drumming goes at more beats per minute than the most deranged vintage acid house. But this is no smiley dance music – the only acid going on around here is vitriol.

"Scott would definitely not want to be seen as competing against anyone," Pete Walsh contradicts the author's perception that the opening may take its cue from the electro-dance or industrial music of the eighties and nineties. "Very much in that respect, I think he's a leader in that kind of music and other people are possibly following him. But, however, he does have his eye on the current scene: what's hip and what's good and what he likes. So he definitely doesn't turn a blind eye to those other influences that you mentioned."

"While plucking feathers
from a swan song,"

croons Scott and that croon is turning awful nasty. The elder statesman will not be going gently into that good night. The refrain recurs continually, skating the sacred and the profane:

"a mythic instance
of erotic impulse"

and

"shit might pretzel
Christ's intestines."

It's no adolescent black metal sentiment but a similar mockery of the solace of religion to those once given by Joyce and Beckett.

"...On the snow
'Rummy' flaunts
his unmanly
dribble,"

mocks Engel of Pentagon armchair warrior Donald Rumsfeld and the lyric sheet tells us this is "Montgomery Clift's missing line that was cut from the scene in *From Here To Eternity*, where he's cautioning soldiers who are placing the dead Maggio (Frank Sinatra) in the truck." (Rummy's not fit to pick up a real soldier's corpse.)

'Corps De Blah' is a tour de force of surreal pastiche and vulgarity. Engel sings lyrics that are at once specific and at the same time seemingly disconnected from each other line by line – physically literal but almost solipsistic until bursts of meaning break through. Or break wind.

From the start,

"Hence
            went
and cracked
an atom age
old egg
beneath my nose,"

the lyric reeks of a certain rancid flatulence.

"I'm wading through
blue, vacant veins
of Sterzing,"

is more suggestive of age and moral, as well as physical, corruption. .

"Sterzing, the Tyrolean village mentioned in 'Corps De Blah', was notorious as a bolthole for Nazi war criminals in the aftermath of the Second World War," read the album's notes. "At the same time, Scott takes a delight in crude humour, and the album is awash with insults and sardonic putdowns, slapstick, body parts and bad smells," notes Young.

By the time we get to

"Ah, my old
Scabby Sachem,
a sphincter's tooting our tune . . .
"We'd slosh, we'd slide,
We'd cling
round a Kellogg's floor,"[9]

we can likely add Rabelais' *Gargantua*, in its glorious vulgarity, to the endless Engel library. The percussion at this juncture is pretty lively, if no breath of fresh air.

"The farts on 'Corps De Blah' are kind of an honest, if not comical, allusion to the lyric," describes Walsh. "I guess in a way you could think of it as a shock factor, but Scott is quite literal and does want to be at times very literal with the lyric. I guess there was no other way of putting a sound on there that suggested that, so we just went for the real thing, you know."

Or a very convincing series of sound effects, one assumes. Much of the track gives a disturbing evocation of physical rottenness, backed by electronics, bursts of metalesque guitar and Alasdair Malloy using a chisel as percussion. Scott gives an almost light operatic performance on 'Corps De Blah' and it's akin to a very delicate glazing on a cake made of shit – not that it's any indication of the track's quality; we're just moving way out of some listeners' comfort zones.

'Phrasing' is one of the most concise and effective tracks on *Bish Bosch*, equal to similar moments on *Tilt* and *The Drift*.

"Pain is not alone.
P-a-i-n is n-o-t alone,"

sings Engel in a beautifully phrased mutant lament. There's more grotesque physical imagery

("There's a protein song
howling through the meat.")

and one thinks of Engel's interview comment in recent years about the pure existence of animals, although he doesn't share the sentimentality or piety of vegetarians. Images of the Klan sending roses from the south and

"Did ya spot
the die-cut
crosses?
Did ya?"

are bookended by a rhythmic percussion section with exotica sound effects (tropical birdcall?) that sounds like a pastiche of Booker T. & The MGs' 'Soul Limbo' – collapsing the history of popular music in upon itself to create something altogether more darkly unique.

Pete Walsh doesn't hear it.

"Scott will very rarely mention other artists in the studio as a reference, you know," he protests. "I have worked with other artists in the past who can't describe a sound in any other way to you, they have to say 'that sound in blah-blah-blah'. Scott very rarely uses references, if he's actually got it in his head I wouldn't really know about it – we don't consciously go out to recreate anything we've heard. There might be references to effects and reverb – usually when Scott uses a reference it's because he doesn't want to sound like somebody else."

OK, put that one down to the writer having listened to too much different music over too many years. One thing we perhaps agree on is the sardonic, almost nihilistic spirit of the closing sentiment:

"Here's to a lousy life."

Cheers. You can almost see Beckett raising his glass to the rest of us.

What follows is the most audacious piece thus far – perhaps in Scott Walker's career. Even by Engel's current standards, it's both esoteric and obscure enough to warrant a lengthy explanation by its composer in the album notes; its combination of top-heavy elements really shouldn't work – in fact it nearly topples over.

And it's a veritable masterpiece. The author puts it to the producer that the opening of 'SDSS 1416+13B (Zercon, a Flagpole sitter)' is outright funny – almost as if the composer is enjoying pre-empting an attack on his own work:

> "*Silence*
>
> What's the matter,
> didn't you get enough attention at home?
>
> > *Silence*
>
> If shit were music,
> you'd be a brass band.
>
> > *Silence*
>
> Know what?
> You should get an agent,
> why sit in the dark
> handling yourself?"

"It is at times tongue-in-cheek, you know," acknowledges Walsh, "and it is in a way a reflection of his character, he is quite intense and dark but there is that other side to him that enjoys humour and comedy and that comes out sometimes in the music as well. If you're looking for it. In the intro there is a kind of underlying side to it, there's a particular scene going on there that's in his head. On face value it's maybe humorous, but deeper down there's other sides to it. I think he sees it that any performer could be heckled in that way."

As Scott Engel says of the recording process for the hellishly clear *Bish Bosch*: "What we did was record the drums, bass, percussion, strings and vocal in digital and analogue simultaneously. Because we knew there were a lot of silences in it, especially in something like 'Zercon'... So in those spots we just cut off the analogue, and where we had the silences we just used the digital. And then we turned on the analogue again when everyone was playing together. Everything was recorded that way, so it's about 80 percent analogue."

"I think the analogue side of it is that we both feel it's giving us a more realistic and truer reproduction of what we're trying to put across," concurs Walsh. "I think that sometimes in the digital domain things come back a little bit too sharp, a little bit too clear, and in a lot of areas that doesn't actually help to stay in that grainy, if you like, black-and-white world if everything's too clear. So he's very fond of the analogue, but we did use a combination on this album, whereby I think the only thing people find a bit difficult to accept now on the analogue is the actual hiss, the tape hiss, the noise. Where there would be very quiet moments on the album we'd try to make the analogue work; where it wasn't as quiet as we could make it, that's where the digital came in very useful. When we needed it we would use digital to enhance the experience. So when you've got all those really quiet textures going on, quite delicate, the last thing you want added to that is a load of tape hiss, do you know what I mean?

"On previous albums, what I've had to do, because they've all been totally analogue, is produce the high frequencies if it's not there, but in this case we actually have a full bandwidth for using both analogue and digital."

There's rather more to this sprawling 20-minute track than bilious humour – as witnessed in the liner notes:

In the spring of 449, the historian Priscus writes of being part of a group of high-level envoys who'd been dispatched from Rome on a goodwill mission to the court of Attila the Hun. He reports back of attending a banquet where the main entertainment of the evening was a stuttering, lisping, Moorish dwarf jester called Zercon who the Huns found to be hilarious. He had two holes where a nose should be, and hobbled around on deformed feet. He had had the sense to turn these deficiencies into assets and became a living legend.

"To play fugues
on Jove's
Spam castanets.
V IX IX
I VI IX I
Cattle are slaughtered,

Entrails examined,
spread out across the moon."

Amidst the superstition of examining animals' entrails to divine the future, Scott uses Roman numerals as a refrain instead of any kind of conventional chorus: "Vee, Eye-Ex, Eye-Ex!"

Attila derives from Atta – Father in both Turkish and Gothic – plus a diminutive – ila; it means 'Little Father'.

For Romans and Barbarians alike, storks were portentous creatures.

"No more
dragging this wormy anus
round on shag piles from
Persia to Thrace.
I've severed
my reeking gonads,
fed them to your
shrunken face...
For a Roman who's proof
that Greeks fucked bears."

In the fortress town of Aquileia a temple had been built to 'Venus The Bald' to honour its women who donated their hair to make ropes for the town's machinery in the fight against the rebel Maximin.

The word Barbarian derives from the incomprehensible bar-bar-bar noises made by outsiders in lieu of language – an expression of snobbery and elitism.

"Heard this one?
This'll kill ya,
about the ropes of hair
care of
Venus the Bald
tugging Mercs across the plain . . .

Syrinx screaming
all around,
BAR! BAR! BAR!"

Flagpole-sitting was a fad in the early 20th century.

The fad was begun by a former sailor, Alvin 'Shipwreck' Kelly, who sat on a flagpole either to dare a friend, or as a publicity stunt. His sit lasted 13 hours and 13 minutes. It soon became a fad with other contestants setting records of 12, 17 and 21 days.

"DID YOU EVER THROW..." to... "HIS OWN MOTHER?!" quote attributed to Louis B. Mayer.[10]

"The one
about the saint
stranded high
upon his pillar.
Thirty summers,
Thirty winters,
his constant visitor,
his mother.
But he'd stare into the distance,
ignored her calls from down
below ...
'DID YOU EVER THROW YOUR OWN
MOTHER'S FOOD BACK AT HER?!'
'DID YOU EVER TELL HER,
TAKE THIS JUNK AWAY?!'
'WHAT KIND OF UNNATURAL SON
WOULD DO THAT TO HIS OWN
MOTHER?!'"

Star-struck astronomers from the University of Hertfordshire have discovered what is possibly the coolest sub-stellar body ever found outside the solar system. The discovery, a so called 'brown dwarf' known as SDSS1416+13B, has an estimated temperature of 500 Kelvin, or 227 degrees Celsius.

"I was interested in this thing about someone trying to escape his situation," Engel clarifies his cosmologically berserk vision, "in this case Attila's wooden palace, which he regards as an immense toilet – and achieve a kind of spiritual sovereignty, and a height beyond calculation. As the song moves forward he imagines himself at different stages of height: he imagines first that he escapes and finds himself surrounded by eagles; then there's the mention of St Simon on his pillar; then he jumps to thirties America where it's become a flagpole-sitter ... 'Flagpole-sitting' – trying to spend several days alone on a platform at the top of a pole – achieved a brief craze status in the thirties.

"At the end of the song he eventually becomes a brown dwarf, known as SDSS1416. As with the majority of my songs, it ends in failure. Like a brown dwarf, he freezes to death."

Among the song's sinister and comical quiet phases – where silence is used as an instrument – and the blown rams horns of Roman times that augment the electronics, the voice of a performer often regarded as a crooner goes into a splenetic rant in the middle section.

"If you listen to the middle of 'Zercon'," says Pete Walsh, "where the voice is all distorted, where it's kind of screaming into the mike, I could understand if people said that's a kind of metal sound like Rage Against The Machine or something, yelling into the mike."

Maybe. For this writer's money, I'll go with the description Mark Paytress is groping towards in his early review: "In its more gruelling moments, [it] evokes a condemned man singing a half-remembered Van Der Graaf Generator epic as he is led, bound and bleeding..." – and this is a *good* thing. Van Der Graaf, with their mercurial leader Peter Hammill, came the closest to fulfilling the promise of that hoary old term 'progressive rock'; they were one of the few rock bands to convincingly assimilate both jazz and classical elements, and Hammill wasn't afraid to take on philosophy or science in his lyrics sometimes.

'Zercon: A Flagpole Sitter' goes beyond all this. In its musical universality, it holds a chaotic lyrical scope only limited by the mind's free association of words and ideas – as with the original twenties Surrealists, or the more creatively minded schizophrenia sufferers.

In this kind of inner landscape, 'Epizootics!' is relatively more accessible (and, like 'Zercon', wildly enjoyable). With its cartoon images of epidemics (an 'epizootic' being a spiked peak within the outbreak) in the Americas and down on the street corner, if we go by Gary Leeds' testimony about his fear of disease then this sounds like Engel facing his worst nightmares and having a lot of fun with it.

"Scratch and Jesus,on the corner,
pushing each other around.
Shoving like sluggers.
Touching like muggers.
Pushing each other around ...
Knock me.
Boot me,
down in the land of darkness."

The brassy three-note sequence is film-noir cinematic, like Elmer Bernstein by way of Barry Adamson or John Zorn. It also opens to twanging pedal steel guitar that marks the return of B.J. Cole to the Walker fold after more than 35 years,[11] brought into a radically different way of working.

"The new track was taken apart and done in detail intricately," confirms Cole. "He wanted a certain effect, of a sliding Hawaiian-style part, but he did it a note at a time rather than a chord – he would take it apart and play one note at one interval, and then one note at the next interval in the same session. He wanted to create a feeling, an impression of a Hawaiian guitar but without it being Hawaiian.

"He wants the sound but he doesn't want the implications. But I'm used to that because a lot of people that I work for are intrigued by the possibilities of the steel guitar, its sliding ability, but they don't want it to sound country – certainly David Sylvian didn't want it to sound country on *Gone To Earth*.[12]

"I played Scott a track from my [recent] solo album[13] and he appreciated it. I'm in a similar position in a way in playing the pedal steel, because I'm working on a lot of experimental stuff as well. I'm pushing against the assumptions and stereotypes that people have of pedal steel guitar being country or being American, and I'm trying to do Debussy and Satie on it. He's pushing against people's assumptions and stereotypes about what he's done before and his early music that was so successful."

The track also features a rare instrument called a tubax. As Engel explains: "It's a combination of a tuba and a saxophone, and there's only two in the country. It's a monster thing, you actually have to sit on the floor, it's enormous. But it means you can get below the bass, very very deep."

In the sessions, Cole was unaware of the cartoonishly nightmarish context in which his steel guitar would find itself:

"Maman Neigho was frightened by Hawaiians,
When all the veins ran out.
When too much bone structure went missing . . .
Adipocere in a zoot..."[14]

As Young's liner notes acknowledge, "There's plenty of rough and tumble and visceral argy-bargy, too," and it underlines how many years the artist has now lived in not-so-merry England:

"Oops, pardon the elbow
Let's just shift you over here.
Sorry,
I'm so clumsy.
Take that accident'ly in the bollocks for a start."

The bloke who wrote this ain't no pussy with the blues. But in the spirit of such perversity, 'Dimple' belies its innocuous-sounding title:

"November in July.
Eyes glistening
in darkness,
like freshly
crushed flies,"

he croons, about as overtly gothic as the modern Scott Walker gets.

"Fourteen bones
held together
by avian phlegm,"

continues the imagery of bodily decay.

"I read somewhere no matter how much your face descends with age," says the composer, "the dimple remains in the same place. In this case I'm using it as a metaphor for a constant presence, and building a kind of mythological face throughout the first part of the song."

He's also combining it with the (by now) anticipated incongruous elements: timpani percussion meshed with dropping steel ball bearings into a glass tray; the odd word of Danish;[15] even quotes from the thirties Jimmy Durante song 'Inka Dinka Doo', echoed menacingly on a backing vocal.

On 'Tar', the cryptic title headlines a pedantic argument over details in The Bible. The nerve-scratching horror FX make it about as laid-back and swinging as death metal, the sound oscillation complemented by vigorously scraped machetes (with curved edges like scimitar swords) used as percussion.

"The women came
to the tomb
at dawn.
Booty chatter!
The women came
when the sun
had risen,"

argues Engel with himself, augmenting his ill-tempered theology lesson with horrific images of a 'Colombian necktie' (cut throat).

"There
but for
the grace
of god
goes
God,"

endeth the sermon, cribbed from the secular context of post-war British politics.[16]

"On that particularly, there were logistical problems," Pete Walsh confirms of 'Tar'. "It was around the time of the riots in London when we were recording all that, it was a bit of a hot kind of subject. But I think the swords are accepted – they're also used in gardening as well," he laughs. "They could have been used for cutting down pampas. [But] I don't really think anybody wanted to be seen walking around with them on the streets of London at that time."

In August 2011, the streets of many London boroughs were going up in flames, supposedly as the result of the shooting of a drug dealer by police in Tottenham – though the protest apparently manifested in massed looting from Foot Locker. Just down the road to Chiswick's Metropolis Studios, there was civil unrest in Acton – and, bizarrely, an elderly man was punched to death in leafy, middle-class Ealing for trying to put out a fire in a dustbin.

Bish Bosch was made in the right place at the right time.

'Pilgrim' is almost one of Engel's old 'miniatures', with its single theme of describing childish cruelty to small creatures as a parallel to scientific vivisection:

"Heya, heya, heya, heya...
Room full of mice...
Blowing up bullfrogs

333

with a straw.
Staring
into their eyes
just before they..."

"I'm not particularly fascinated by brutality," insists Scott Engel. "I mean, at times I'll use it on a comic level, or it'll be angry, but I'm never striving for it – it just happens. I don't know why – that's for an analyst!"

That may be debatable in terms of the album's closing track – but even here, the brutal end to a brutal political reign is described in oblique terms.

'The Day The Conducator Died' is ironically subtitled 'An Xmas Song' – for that's when Nicolae Ceauşescu,[17] Romania's communist dictator from 1967, 89, was summarily executed along with his wife Elena.

"I am nurturant, compassionate,
caring.
O Not so much.
O Very much,"

Engel subverts his natural croon once again, lending a mock-profundity to magazine 'personality test' questionnaires. Against these banalities are set a haunting (and unexplained, except in the album's accompanying notes) refrain:

"Nobody
waited for
fire."

The song ends macabrely on Christmas bells playing 'Jingle Bells' – commemorating the death by firing squad of Ceauşescu and his wife on Christmas Day 1989.

"I think that lyric on the last song is just fantastic," says Pete Walsh. "'Nobody waited for fire,' you know. You don't immediately know what he's talking about; you think, 'Fire, burning, what?' and then you realise what it's about, you think, 'Fucking hell!' I thought it was brilliant how he managed to get that in there: the fact that they just couldn't wait to kill him was a sign of what a monster he was."

Indeed. If you were a political dissident at the tender mercy of Ceaușescu's secret police, or an HIV-infected child in one of Romania's state orphanages, it'd be difficult to feel otherwise. In *realpolitik* terms, it was also a sign of how Ceaușescu's former political aides couldn't wait to get rid of him so as to form a new government.

"But that's what all great lyricists are about: it's a way of suggesting his ideas without being too specific. I think he's just interested in history, you know," says his producer of Engel's admission to being fascinated by dictators and their deeds.[18] I guess he's probably interested in what drives these people; he's always searching for answers. Obviously I remembered the allusions there from the album before, but it's not something about which I'd say, 'Oh yeah, he's fascinated by this!' or, 'He's obsessed by it!' I think it's just something he's interested in, the thing that's driving these people – there is a story to tell and to talk about."

As for the overall musical nightmare that is *Bish Bosch*, its clash of musical styles and myriad cultural or biographical allusions, the artist still known as Scott Walker insists: "There is always meaning for me there; I don't write haphazardly. I'm pretty sure everything is right and balanced, as far as I can get it. I won't throw anything in that shouldn't be there."

"He's an enigma, is Scott," opines B.J. Cole, the only musician to have played on Engel's recent works and during his seventies 'lost years'. He's always pushing to go somewhere new all the time. Whether it's better than what he was doing before, I'm not sure," he laughs.

"He's sticking to his guns until his audience comes to *him*. The last three albums or so have been that, haven't they? They start out being unlistenable – until you get it, and the idea is they won't buy the first two but [on] the third one, hopefully this one, the audience and his

335

fans will get it and they'll go, 'Ooh! Now I understand number one and two, since *Tilt*.' That seems to be the way it is, as I see it."

"I think on this album, in particular, [his lyricism is] stunning," says Walsh. "I think possibly the subject matter is a bit closer and a bit easier to grasp on this album. I think I remember on the other albums I would hear the words and try to create my own vision of what it was all about. He doesn't divulge too much even to me about the content and where it's all come from. Obviously if there's something I really need to understand he'll tell me. But I find that the lyrics on this album are a lot more easy to formulate an idea about. In a way, even though there are no choruses there's a sort of repetition in many songs. They're more structured and I think maybe a bit more sexual at times. He's always full of surprises!" laughs Engel's producer.

"The thing that always amazes is how somebody who is actually very personable and very outgoing when you're one-to-one with him is capable of being so dark, and he's got such a 'sunny voice'. He'll probably hate me for saying that!" laughs Cole.

"I wish he was able to get out and perform it live. That's always been his problem, hasn't it? Because then people would get it quicker and would be able to get to the bottom of it better, by hearing him put on a production which would probably be a mixed-media artistic experience with theatre and dance and things like that. When you're coming out with records once in a blue moon and people have to get it on the basis of these shard-like, impressionistic things that he puts on record, it's very hard for them to understand where it's coming from."

Walsh, who accompanied Engel on his last live appearance,[19] only agrees up to a point: "I think everybody would have hoped this time round – once again, 'Rosary' lent itself to a live performance, you know, and I think he did it really well. I was actually there and I did the sound for it. Just the two of us turned up to do it and there was no big kind of entourage or whatever. I don't think there are any songs on this new album that would be so easy for him to actually go out and do."

336

"Whatever he does, he's a crooner," insists B. J. Cole in his final assessment, "he can't escape it really. Unfortunately, he's one of the best ever in history. Therefore he has that much more to undo."

"I think on face a lot of people don't get it," accedes Pete Walsh, "but when people get it they really are fully immersed in it and can't get enough of it because it is so timeless."

And the man behind the work?

At the time of the release of *The Drift*, in 2006, aged 63, he was asked by BBC2's *The Culture Show* if he expected to be delivering an album in another 10 years' time. "I probably won't be alive then," he answered almost diffidently, displaying the famous sense of his own mortality.

In 2012, on the release of *Bish Bosch*, his mood had lightened – albeit only slightly.

"I'm a pessimist, in that I know it's not going to end well," he tells Rob Young. "But most of my songs are spiritual at the core. I try not to be too cynical about things, because it's too difficult otherwise. You have to be able to work your way through it – you have to be able to see what's there, and deal with it."

As long as existence continues to torment his imagination, it seems the works will always follow.

As long as existence continues.

Notes

1   The closeness of the gay artist and the morphine-addicted 'Little Sparrow' was such that Cocteau's death, in 1963, is frequently attributed to his choking upon hearing of the demise of Piaf.

2   He is nonetheless familiar with his film *Orphée*, as we have seen.

3   As *The Times* had said of Engel, it's "very strange... that you should be thought of as reclusive just because you don't want to be a celebrity."

4   And certainly unlike the early 20th-century modernists he's previously been compared to.

5   Or three-and-a-half, if you include The Walker Brothers' swansong.

6   Bosch occupied the rank of 'Sworn Brother' in the Brotherhood of Our Lady.

7   Now there's a figure out of Beckett for you – at least if you changed the 'a' to an 'o'.

8   Stevenson is a veteran of the seventies punk rock scene, having played in Chelsea, one of the first wave of punk bands.

9   Dr John Harvey Kellogg was a famous enema enthusiast and reputedly developed his cornflakes for our biological spring cleaning.

10   Head of production at Metro-Goldwyn Mayer (MGM).

11   He played on Scott's two country albums and The Walker Brothers' *No Regrets* in the mid-seventies.

12   At the time B.J. Cole played on Sylvian's semi-ambient 1986 album, the ex-Japan vocalist was a friendly acquaintance of the similarly reticent Scott Walker. As B.J. says, the influence of Walker can be heard in Sylvian's music – though his warbling early vocal style always sounded rather more like Bryan Ferry.

13   The album is *Transparent Music 2*, recorded with keyboard player Guy Jackson; the track is a languidly multi-textured piece called 'Monolith', featuring trumpeter Arve Henriksen. One suspects that Cole would like Scott Walker to contribute a vocal to his works – he should go ahead and ask; after all, if Bat For Lashes can do it...

14   I.e. 'grave wax' (the putrid slimy substance as the skin starts to rot) in a baggy forties jazzman's suit.

15   Remember that Copenhagen used to be Scott's favourite city.

16   Churchill on Labour minister Sir Stafford Cripps.

17   Ceauşescu styled himself as 'the Conducator', a Romanian equivalent to 'Leader' or 'Fuhrer' since the reign of King Carol II.

18   For which also see 'Clara', 'The Cockfighter' and 'The Old Man's Back Again'.

19   Performing 'Rosary' on *Jools Holland's Later*, May 1995.

Selective Discography

SCOTTY ENGEL

Single
When Is A Boy A Man? (Parker/Greiner/Scheck)/ Steady As A Rock
(Lee/Elli)
RKO Unique 386 (1957 – US)

SCOTT ENGEL

Singles
The Livin' End (Mancini/McKuen)/Good For Nothin' (Sparks)
Orbit 506 (1958 – US)/Picture sleeve. Vogue Pop 45/78rpm –V9145
(1959 – UK)

Charley Bop (Franklin/Loring)/All I Do Is Dream Of You (Freed/
Brown)
Orbit 511 (1958 – US)/Picture sleeve. Vogue Pop 45/78rpm –V9150
(1959 – UK)

Bluebell (Livingstone/Webster)/Paper Doll (Black)
Orbit 512 (1958 – US)/Picture sleeve
Vogue Pop 45/78rpm – V9125 (1959 – UK)

*Kathalene/The Livin' End
Polydor DP-1552 – recorded 1958/released 1967 – Japan.
Single release credited to Scott Walker.

The Golden Rule Of Love (Kohen)/Sunday (Rodgers/Hammerstein)
Orbit 537 (1959 – US)/Picture sleeve

Comin' Home (Burnette)/I Don't Want To Know (Burnette)
Orbit 545 (1959 – US)/Picture sleeve.

Take This Love (Engel)/Till You Return (Engel)
Hi-Fi 586 (1959 – US)

Anything Will Do (Arno/Day/Hart)/Mr Jones (Loudermilk)
Liberty 55312 (1961 – US)

Anything Will Do/Forevermore (King)
Liberty 55428 (1962 – US)

Devil Surfer (Taylor)/Your Guess
Martay 2004 (June 1963 – US)/Challenge 9206 (October 1963 – US).

EP
I Broke My Own Heart (McFarland/Stewart)/What Do You Say?
(Devorzon/Ferguson)/Are These Really Mine? (Skylar/Saxon/
Cook)/ Crazy In Love With You (Benton/Otis)
Liberty 2261 recorded 1962/released 1966 – UK.

Album*
LOOKING BACK WITH SCOTT WALKER: Too Young (Dee/
Lippman)/I Don't Want To Know/Comin' Home/Bluebell/Paper

Doll/Sunday/When I Kiss You Goodnight (Cooper)/Sing Boy Sing
(McKuen/Sands)/Too Young To Know/Take This Love/Till You
Return/When You See Her/All I Do Is Dream Of You/Everybody
But Me (Burnette)
Ember 3393 – recorded 1958/59 – released 1967
★*Credited to Scott Walker.*

SANDY NELSON (with Scott Engel on bass)

Single
Let There Be Drums (Nelson)/Quite A Beat (Nelson)
Imperial 5775 (1962 – US)

THE MOONGOONERS (John Stewart and Scott Engel)

Singles
Moongoon Stomp (Young)/The Long Trip (Stewart/Engel)
Candix 335 (1962 – US)

Willie And The Hand Jive (Otis)/Moongoon Twist (Stewart/Engel)
Essar 1007/Donna 1373 (1962 – US)

THE CHOSEN FEW (featuring John Stewart and Scott Engel)

Single
Wish You Were Here (Stewart/Engle – *sic*)/Jump Down (Stewart/
Engle)
Marsh 201 (1962 – US)

THE ROUTERS (with Scott Engel on bass)

Single
Let's Go (Pony) (L. & R. Duncan)/Mashy (Gordon/Saraceno)
Warner Bros 5283 (1962 – US)

THE NEWPORTERS (John Stewart and Scott Engel)

Single
Adventures In Paradise (Newman)/Loose Board (Stewart/Engel)
Scotchdown 500 (1963 – US)

THE DALTON BROTHERS (John Stewart and Scott Engel)

Single
I Only Came To Dance With You (Smith)/Without Your Love
(Engel/Stewart)
Martay MT2001 (1963 – US)

I Only Came To Dance With You/Greens (Taylor)
Tower 2181 (1966 US)/Capitol 15440 (1966 UK)

Album
I ONLY CAME TO DANCE WITH YOU:★ I Only Came To Dance
With You/Chick's Choice/Ham Hocks/Swingin' At The Batcave/
Wallflower/Without Your Love/Diskoteque/Greens/Lottin' Dottin'
Da Da/Nashville
Tower 5026 – recorded 1963/released US 1966
★*Doubt has been cast on whether any of the tracks (mainly instrumentals)
not already released as single A-sides or B-sides actually feature Engel and
Stewart. Certainly the sleeve note's claim that John Stewart was "an original
member of The Walker Brothers" was way off the mark.*

THE WALKER BROTHERS
(*UK releases unless otherwise specified*)

Singles
Pretty Girls Everywhere (Church/Williams)/Doin' The Jerk (Engel)
Philips BF1401 1964

Love Her (Mann/Weil)/The Seventh Dawn (Ortolani/Webster)
Philips BFR1409 1965

Make It Easy On Yourself (Bacharach/David)/But I Do (Guidry/
Gayten)
Philips BF1454 1965

My Ship Is Coming In (Brooks)/You're All Around Me (Engel/
Duncan)
Philips BF1454 1965

The Sun Ain't Gonna Shine Anymore (Crewe/Gaudio)/After The
Lights Go Out (Stewart) Philips BF 1473 1966

(Baby) You Don't Have To Tell Me (Antell)/My Love Is Growing
(Stewart/Van Leeuwen) Philips BF1514 1966

Another Tear Falls(Bacharach/David)/Saddest Night In The World
(Maus)
Philips BF1514 1966

Deadlier Than The Male (Engel/Franz)/Archangel (Engel)
Philips BF1537 1966

Stay With Me Baby (Ragovoy/Weiss)/Turn Out The Moon (Engel)
Philips BF1548 1967

Walking In The Rain (Mann/Spector/Weil)/Baby Make It The Last
Time (Engel/Duncan/Nicholls)
Philips BF1576 1967

No Regrets [single version] (Rush)/Remember Me (Dayam)
GTO GT42 1975

Lines (Fuller)/First Day (Dayam)
GTO GT67 1976

We're All Alone (Scaggs)/Have You Seen My Baby? (Newman)
GTO GT78 1976

The Electrician (Engel)/Den Haague (Leeds)
GTO GT230 1978/Picture sleeve

EPs
I NEED YOU: Looking For Me (Newman)/Young Man Cried
(Franz/Engel)/Everything's Gonna Be Alright (Mitchell)/I Need
You (Goffin/King)
Philips BE12596 1966

SOLO JOHN, SOLO SCOTT: Sunny (Hebb)/Come Rain Or
Come Shine (Mercer/Arlen)/The Gentle Rain (Dubey/Bonfa)/Mrs
Murphy (Engel)
Philips BE12597 1966

SHUTOUT: Shutout (Engel)/The Electrician/Nite Flights (Engel)/
Fat Mama Kick (Engel) – GTO GT295 1978

Albums
TAKE IT EASY WITH THE WALKER BROTHERS: Make
It Easy On Yourself/There Goes My Baby (Nelson/Patterson/
Treadwell)/First Love Never Dies (Morris/Seals)/Dancing In The
Street (Stevenson/Gaye)/Lonely Winds (Pomus/Shuman)/The Girl
I Lost In The Rain (Gates)/Land Of 1,000 Dances (Kenner)/You're
All Around Me/Love Minus Zero (Dylan)/I Don't Want To Hear It
Anymore (Newman)/Here Comes The Night (Pomus/Shuman)/
Tell The Truth (Pauling)
Philips BL7691 1965

PORTRAIT: In My Room (Prieto/Pockriss/Vance)/Saturday's
Child (Engel)/Just For A Thrill (Armstrong/Raye/Williams)/Hurting
Each Other (Udell/Geld)/Old Folks (Robison/Hill)/Summertime
(Gershwin)/People Get Ready (Mayfield)/I Can See It Now (Engel/

Franz)/Where's The Girl? (Leiber/Stoller)/Living Above Your Head (Sanders/BlackVance)/Take It Like A Man (Leiber/Stoller)/No Sad Songs For Me (Springfield)
Philips BL7732 1966

IMAGES: Everything Under The Sun (Crewe/Knight)/Once Upon A Summertime (Legrand/Marney/Mercer)/Experience (Engel)/ Blueberry Hill (Lewis/Stock Rose)/Orpheus (Engel)/Stand By Me (King/Leiber/Stoller)/I Wanna Know (Maus)/I Will Wait For You (Gimbel/Legrand)/It Makes No Difference Now (Pattacini/ Newell)/I Can't Let It Happen To You (Maus)/Genevieve (Engel)/ Just Say Goodbye (Clark/Hatch/Delanoe)
Philips BL7770 1967

THE WALKER BROTHERS IN JAPAN: Land Of 1,000 Dances/I Need You/Everything Under The Sun/Tell Me How Do You Feel? (Mayfield/Charles)/Watch Your Step (Parker)/Uptight (Wonder/ Moy/Cosby)/In My Room/The Lady Came From Baltimore (Hardin)/Living Above Your Head/Dizzy Miss Lizzie (Williams)/ Twinkie Lee (Bright)/Hold On I'm Coming (Hayes/Porter)/ Annabella (Maus/Nash)/Yesterday (Lennon/McCartney)/Reach Out I'll Be There (Holland/Dozier/Holland)/Make It Easy On Yourself/Saturday's Child/Walking In The Rain/The Sun Ain't Gonna Shine Anymore/Turn On Your Lovelight (Scott/Malone)/ Ooh Poo Pah Doo (Hill)
Bam Caruso double album AIDA 076 – recorded 1968/released 1987

NO REGRETS: No Regrets [album version] (Rush)/Hold An Old Friend's Hand (Weiss)/Boulder To Birmingham (Harris/Danoff)/ Walkin' In The Sun (Barry)/Lover's Lullaby (Ian)/I've Got To Have You (Kristofferson)/He'll Break Your Heart (Mayfield/Butler)/ Everything That Touches You (Kamen)/Lovers (Newbury)/Burn Our Bridges (Ragovoy/Laurie)
GTO GTLP 007 1975

LINES: Lines (Fuller)/Taking It All In Stride (Snow)/Inside Of You (Jans)/Have You Seen My Baby? (Newman)/We're All Alone (Scaggs)/Many Rivers To Cross (Cliff)/First Day (Dayam)/Brand New Tennessee Waltz (Winchester)/Hard To Be Friends (Murray) / Dreaming As One (Palmer/Smith)
GTO GTLP 014 1976

NITE FLIGHTS: Shutout/Fat Mama Kick/Nite Flights/The Electrician/Death Of Romance (Leeds)/Den Haague (Leeds)/Rhythms Of Vision (Maus)/Disciples Of Death (Maus)/Fury And The Fire (Maus)/Child Of Flames (Maus)
GTO GTLP 033 1978.

Five CD Box Set Compilation
EVERYTHING UNDER THE SUN: Pretty Girls Everywhere/Doin' The Jerk/Love Her/The Seventh Dawn/Make It Easy On Yourself/There Goes My Baby/First Love Never Dies/Dancing In The Street/Lonely Winds/The Girl I Lost In The Rain/Land Of 1,000 Dances/You're All Around Me/Love Minus Zero/I Don't Want To Hear It Anymore/Here Comes The Night/Tell The Truth/But I Do/My Ship Is Coming In/The Sun Ain't Gonna Shine Anymore/After The Lights Go Out/(Baby) You Don't Have To Tell Me/ My Love Is Growing/Looking For Me/Young Man Cried/Everything's Gonna Be All Right/I Need You/The Sun Ain't Gonna Shine Anymore [alternate version]/Another Tear Falls/Saddest Night In The World/In My Room/Saturday's Child/Just For A Thrill/Hurting Each Other/ Old Folks/Summertime/People Get Ready/I Can See It Now/Where's The Girl?/Living Above Your Head/Take It Like A Man/No Sad Songs For Me/Deadlier Than The Male/Archangel/Sunny/Come Rain Or Come Shine/The Gentle Rain/Mrs Murphy/Stay With Me Baby/Turn Out The Moon/Walking In The Rain/Baby Make It The Last Time/Me About You (Gordon/Bonner)/Everything Under The Sun/Once Upon A Summertime/Experience/Blueberry Hill/Orpheus/Stand By Me/I Wanna Know/I Will Wait For You/It

Makes No Difference Now/I Can't Let It Happen To You/Genevieve/
Just Say Goodbye/Looking For Me [alternate version]/The Sun Ain't
Gonna Shine Anymore [alternate version]/Lazy Afternoon (Moross/
La Touche)/In The Midnight Hour (Cropper/Pickett)/A Song For
Young Love (B. & D. Post)/Let The Music Play (Bacharach/David)/
The Shadow Of Your Smile(Mandel/Webster)/Hang On For Me*/I
Got You (I Feel Good) (Brown)/I Got Lost For A While*/A Fool Am
I (Testa/Carraresi/Callendar)/Wipe Away My Tears*/Lost One*/
No Regrets/Hold An Old Friend's Hand/Boulder To Birmingham/
Walkin' In The Sun/Lover's Lullaby/I've Got To Have You/He'll
Break Your Heart/Everything That Touches You/Lovers/Burn Our
Bridges/Remember Me/Loving Arms (Jans)/I Never Dreamed You'd
Leave In Summer (Wonder)/The Moon's A Harsh Mistress (Webb)/
Marie (Newman)/Lines/Taking It All In Stride/Inside Of You/Have
You Seen My Baby?/We're All Alone/Many Rivers To Cross/First
Day/Brand New Tennesse Waltz/Hard To Be Friends/Dreaming
As One/'Til I Gain Control Again (Crowell) /The Ballad (Maus)/
Shutout/Fat Mama Kick/Nite Flights/The Electrician/Death Of
Romance/Den Haague/Rhythms Of Vision/Disciples Of Death/
Fury And The Fire/Child Of Flames/Tokyo Rimshot (Engel)
Universal 00268 2006
*No composer credit given. John Maus conjectured that these were probably
unreleased solo tracks by Scott.*

SCOTT WALKER

Singles
Jackie (Brel/Jouannest/Shuman)/The Plague (Engel)
Philips 1628 1967

Joanna (Hatch/Trent)/Always Coming Back To You (Engel)
Philips 1662 1968

The Rope And The Colt (Hossein/Shaper) /Concert Pour Guitare*
Philips B.370780.F – France 1968

★Both A and B-side from the soundtrack of the film Cemetery Without Crosses *– the latter is not a Scott Walker recording.*

The Lights Of Cincinnati (Macaulay/Stephens)/Two Weeks Since You've Gone (Engel)
Philips 1793 1969

I Still See You (Shaper/Legrand)/My Way Home (Engel/Semel)
Philips 6006-168 1971

The Me I Never Knew (Black/Barry)/This Way Mary (Barry/Black)
Philips 6006-311 1973

A Woman Left Lonely (Oldham/Penn)/Where Love Has Died (Owen)
CBS 1795 1973

Delta Dawn (Harvey)/We Had It All (Fritts/Seals)
CBS 2521 1974

Track Three (Engel)/Blanket Roll Blues (Williams/Hopkins)
Virgin VS 666 1984/Picture sleeve

Man From Reno (Engel/Bregovic)/Indecent Sacrifice (Engel/Bregovic)
Fontana CD 682382-2 – France 1993

EPs
GREAT SCOTT: Jackie/When Joanna Love Me (Wells/Segal)/The Plague/Mathilde (Brel/Jouannest/Shuman)
Philips cassette MCP-1006 1967

AND WHO SHALL GO TO THE BALL? AND WHAT SHALL GO TO THE BALL?: Instrumental music written by Scott Walker for the dance piece performed by CandoCo Dance Company. Choreography by Rafael Bonachela.
4AD limited edition 2007

Albums

SCOTT: Mathilde (Brel, Jouannest, Shuman)/Montague Terrace (In Blue) (Engel)/Angelica (Weil/Mann)/The Lady Came From Baltimore/When Joanna Loved Me (Wells, Segal)/My Death (Brel/Shuman)/The Big Hurt (Shanklin)/Such A Small Love (Engel)/You're Gonna Hear From Me (A. & D. Previn)/Through A Long And Sleepless Night (Gordon/Newman)/Always Coming Back To You (Engel)/Amsterdam (Brel/Shuman)
Philips 7816 1967. Reissued on Fontana CD 510 879-2 1992

SCOTT 2: Jackie (Brel, Jouannest, Shuman)/Best Of Both Worlds (London/Black)/ Black Sheep Boy (Hardin)/The Amorous Humphrey Plugg (Engel)/Next (Brel/Shuman)/The Girls From The Streets (Engel)/Plastic Palace People (Engel)/Wait Until Dark (Mancini/Livingston/Evans)/The Girls And The Dogs (Brel/Shuman/Jouannest)/Windows Of The World (David/Bacharach)/The Bridge (Engel)/Come Next Spring (Adelson/Steiner)
Philips 7840 1968. Reissued on Fontana CD 510 880-2 1992

SCOTT 3: It's Raining Today (Engel)/Copenhagen (Engel)/Rosemary (Engel)/Big Louise (Engel)/We Came Through (Engel)/Butterfly (Engel) /Two Ragged Soldiers (Engel)/30 Century Man (Engel)/Winter Night (Engel)/Two Weeks Since You've Gone (Engel)/Sons Of (Jouannest/Brel/Shuman)/Funeral Tango (Jouannest/Brel/Shuman)/If You Go Away (Brel/McKuen)
Philips 7882 1969. Reissued on Fontana CD 510 881-2 1992

SCOTT: SCOTT WALKER SINGS SONGS FROM HIS TV SERIES: Will You Still Be Mine? (Dennis/Adair)/I Have Dreamed (Rodgers/Hammerstein)/When The World Was Young (Gérard/Vanier/Mercer)/Who (Will Take My Place?) (Aznavour/Kretzmer)/If She Walked Into My Life (Herman)/The Impossible Dream (Leigh/Darion)/The Song Is You (Kern/Hammerstein)/The Look Of Love

(Bacharach/David)/Country Girl (Farnon)/Someone To Light Up
My Life (de Moraes/Jobim/Lees)/Only The Young (Ahlert/Fisher)/
Lost In The Stars (Anderson/Weill)
Philips 7900 1969.

SCOTT 4: The Seventh Seal (Engel)/On Your Own Again (Engel)/
The World's Strongest Man (Engel)/Angels Of Ashes (Engel)/Boy
Child (Engel)/The Old Man's Back Again (Engel)/Hero Of The
War (Engel)/Duchess (Engel)/Get Behind Me (Engel)/Rhymes Of
Goodbye (Engel)
Philips 7913 1969 – credited to Noel Scott Engel.
Reissued as a remastered Fontana CD 510 882-2 2000 – credited to
Scott Walker.

'TIL THE BAND COMES IN: Prologue (Engel/Semel)/Little
Things (That Keep Us Together) (Engel/Semel)/Joe (Engel/Semel)/
Thanks For Chicago Mr James (Engel/Semel)/Long About Now★
(Engel/Semel)/Time Operator (Engel/Semel)/Jean The Machine
(Engel/Semel)/Cowbells Shakin' (Engel/Semel)/'Til The Band
Comes In (Engel/Semel)/The War Is Over (Engel/Semel)/Stormy
(Buie/Cobb)/The Hills Of Yesterday (Webster/Mancini)/Reuben
James (Etris/Harvey)/What Are You Doing The Rest Of Your Life?
(A. & M. Bergman/Legrand)/It's Over (Rodgers)
Philips 6308 035 1970.
Reissued as Water Music CD 226 2008. ★Sung by Esther Ofarim.

THE MOVIEGOER: This Way Mary (Barry/Black)/Speak Softly Love
(Rota/Kusik)/Glory Road (Diamond)/That Night (Schifrin/Gimbel)/
The Summer Knows (Legrand/A. & M. Bergman)/The Ballad Of
Sacco & Vanzetti (Baez/Morricone)/A Face In The Crowd (Bergman/
Legrand)/Joe Hill (Grossman)/Loss Of Love (Mancini/Merrill)/All
His Children (Mancini/A. & M. Bergman)/Come Saturday Morning
(Karlin/Previn)/Easy Come Easy Go (Green/Heyman) – Philips 6308
120 1972. Reissued Contour Records 6870 633 1973.

ANY DAY NOW: Any Day Now (Hilliard/Bacharach)/All My Love's Laughter (Webb)/Do I Love You? (Pelay/le Govic/Dessca/Piolot/Anka)/Maria Bethania (Veloso)/Cowboy (Newman)/When You Get Right Down To It (Mann)/If (Gates)/Ain't No Sunshine (Withers)/The Me I Never Knew (Black/Barry)/If Ships Were Made To Sail (Webb)/We Could Be Flying (Colombier/Williams)
Philips 6308 148 1973

STRETCH: Sunshine (Newbury)/Just One Smile (R. Newman)/A Woman Left Lonely (Oldham, Penn)/No Easy Way Down (Goffin/King)/That's How I Got To Memphis (Hall)/Use Me (Withers)/Frisco Depot (Newbury)/Someone Who Cared (D. Newman)/Where Does Brown Begin? (Webb)/Where Love Has Died (Owen)/I'll Be Home (R. Newman)
CBS 65725 1973
Reissued as a double album with *We Had It All* on BGO CD 358 1997

WE HAD IT ALL: Low Down Freedom (Shaver)/We Had It All (Fritts, Seals)/Black Rose (Shaver)/Ride Me Down Easy (Shaver)/You're Young And You'll Forget (Reed)/The House Song (Bannard, Stockey)/Whatever Happened To Saturday Night? (Meisner, Henley, Frey, Leadon)/Sundown (Lightfoot)/Old Five And Dimers Like Me (Shaver)/Delta Dawn (Harvey)
CBS 80254 1974
Reissued as a double album with *Stretch* on BGO CD 358 1997

CLIMATE OF HUNTER: Rawhide (Engel)/Dealer (Engel)/Track Three (Engel)/Sleepwalkers Woman (Engel)/Track Five (Engel)/Track Six (Engel)/Track Seven (Engel)/Blanket Roll Blues – Virgin V2303 1984. Reissued on Virgin CDV 2303 2006.

TILT: Farmer In The City (Engel)/The Cockfighter (Engel)/Bouncer See Bouncer (Engel)/Manhattan (Engel)/Face On Breast

(Engel)/Bolivia '95 (Engel)/Patriot (A Single) (Engel)/Tilt (Engel)/
Rosary (Engel)
Fontana vinyl 526 859-1/Fontana CD 526 859-2 1995

THE DRIFT: Cossacks Are (Engel)/Clara (Engel)/Jesse (Engel)/
Jolson & Jones (Engel)/Cue (Engel)/Hand Me Ups (Engel)/Buzzers
(Engel)/Psoriatic (Engel)/The Escape (Engel)/A Lover Loves (Engel)
4AD double album CAD 2603/4AD CD CAD 2603 2006

BISH BOSCH: See You Don't Bump His Head (Engel)/Corps De
Blah (Engel)/Phrasing (Engel)/SDSS14 16+ 13B (Zercon, A Flagpole
Sitter) (Engel)/Epizootics! (Engel)/Dimple (Engel)/Tar (Engel)/
Pilgrim (Engel)/The Day The 'Conducator' Died (An Xmas Song)
(Engel) – 4AD CAD 3220CD 2012

Selected Compilations
FIRE ESCAPE IN THE SKY: THE GODLIKE GENIUS OF
SCOTT WALKER: Such A Small Love/Big Louise/Little Things
(That Keep Us Together)/Plastic Palace People/The Girls From
The Streets/It's Raining Today/The Seventh Seal/The Amorous
Humphrey Plugg/Angels Of Ashes/Boy Child/Montague Terrace
(In Blue)/Always Coming Back To You
Zoo 2 1981

SCOTT WALKER SINGS JACQUES BREL: Jackie/Next/The
Girls And The Dogs/If You Go Away/Funeral Tango/Mathilde/
Amsterdam/Sons Of/My Death/Little Things (That Keep Us
Together) – Phonogram 6359 090 1981. Reissued on Fontana CD
838 212-2 1990.

BOY CHILD – THE BEST OF 1967-70: The Plague/Montague
Terrace (In Blue)/Such A Small Love/The Amorous Humphrey
Plugg/Plastic Palace People/The Bridge/Big Louise/We Came

Through/The Seventh Seal/Boy Child/The Old Man's Back Again/
Prologue/Little Things (That Keep Us Together)/Time Operator
Fontana 8428323-1 1990
Reissued on Fontana HDCD 2000

NO REGRETS: THE BEST OF SCOTT WALKER AND THE
WALKER BROTHERS 1965-1976: No Regrets/Make It Easy On
Yourself/The Sun Ain't Gonna Shine Anymore/My Ship Is Coming
In/Joanna/The Lights Of Cincinnati/Another Tear Falls/Boy Child/
Montague Terrace (In Blue)/Jackie/Stay With Me Baby/If You Go
Away/First Love Never Dies/Love Her/Walking In The Rain/
(Baby) You Don't Have To Tell Me/Deadlier Than The Male/We're
All Alone
Fontana 510 831-1 1992

CD Box Set
SCOTT WALKER IN 5 EASY PIECES: A THEMED 5-CD
ANTHOLOGY:
CD1: IN MY ROOM: Prologue/Little Things (That Keep Us
Together)/I Don't Want To Hear It Anymore/In My Room/After
The Lights Go Out/Archangel/Orpheus/Mrs Murphy/Montague
Terrace (In Blue)/Such A Small Love/The Amorous Humphrey
Plugg/It's Raining Today/Rosemary/Big Louise/Angels Of Ashes/
Hero Of The War/Time Operator/Joe/The War Is Over
CD2: WHERE'S THE GIRL?: Where's The Girl?/You're All Around
Me/Just Say Goodbye/Hurting Each Other/Genevieve/Once Upon
A Summertime/When Joanna Loved Me/Joanna/Angelica/Always
Coming Back To You/The Bridge/Best Of Both Worlds/Two Weeks
Since You've Gone/On Your Own Again/Someone Who Cared/
Long About Now/Scope J★ (Engel)/Lullaby (By-By-By)★ (Engel)/
★Sung by Ute Lemper.
CD3: AN AMERICAN IN EUROPE: Jackie/Mathilde/The Girls
And The Dogs/Amsterdam/Next/The Girls From The Streets/
My Death/Sons Of/If You Go Away/Copenhagen/We Came

Through/30 Century Man/Rhymes Of Goodbye/Thanks For Chicago Mr James/Cowbells Shakin'/My Way Home/Lines/Rawhide/Blanket Roll Blues/Tilt/Patriot (A Single)
CD4: THIS IS HOW YOU DISAPPEAR: The Plague/Plastic Palace People/Boy Child/Shutout/Fat Mama Kick/Nite Flights/The Electrician/Dealer/Track Three (Delayed)/Sleepwalkers Woman/Track Five (It's A Starving)/Farmer In The City/The Cockfighter/Bouncer See Bouncer/Face On Breast
CD5 SCOTT ON SCREEN: Light★ (Engel)/Deadlier Than The Male/The Rope And The Colt/Meadow★ (Engel)/The Seventh Seal/The Darkest Forest★ (Engel)/The Ballad Of Sacco & Vanzetti/The Summer Knows/Glory Road/Isabel★ (Engel)/Man From Reno/The Church Of The Apostles★ (Engel)/Indecent Sacrifice/Bombupper★ (Engel)/I Threw It All Away★★ (Dylan)/River Of Blood★ (Engel)/Only Myself To Blame★★★ (Black/Arnold)/Running★ (Engel)/The Time Is Out Of Joint★ (Engel)/Never Again★ (Engel)/Closing★ (Engel)
★From the soundtrack of *Pola X*. ★★ From the soundtrack of *To Have And To Hold*. ★★★From the soundtrack of *The World Is Not Enough*.
Universal box set 2003

As A Contributor
PLAGUE SONGS – one track: Darkness (Engel) – Artangel/4AD CAD 2616CD 2006.
Bat For Lashes: Two Suns – backing vocals on one track: 'The Big Sleep' (Khan)
Echo CD 2009

Acknowledgements

The author wishes to thank the following for their invaluable contributions to this book:

Peter Walsh, for describing the methods of his long-time working relationship with Scott Walker as co-producer; Rich Walker at 4AD, for arranging preview access to *Bish Bosch* and the Pete Walsh interview; Stephen Kijak, for an interview on how Scott Walker became the subject of his film *30 Century Man*, a film referenced extensively at several points in this book and which remains essential viewing; Arnie Potts, for access to his extraordinary Scott Walker/Walker Brothers collector's archive, including the rare *Scott Times* fanzines; Marlene Carmack at Butler County Historical Society, for tracing the Engel family history via Ohio state archives and providing newspaper articles from Scott Engel's early life; B.J. Cole, for his uniquely contrasting account of working with Scott Walker during the seventies and, far more recently, on *Bish Bosch*; Fionnuala Dorrity/Andy Delamere/Matthew Wood of Dead Belgian, for their entertaining views on Jacques Brel and his Anglophone interpreters; and Henry Scott-Irvine, for his anecdote about Metropolis Studios at the start of the *Drift* era.

Thanks are also due to Lewis Williams, for encouragement; Charles Negus-Fancey, for courteously explaining his client's benign non-participation; Tony Hatch, for confirmation of anecdotes relating to 'Joanna' and working with Scott Engel in the late sixties; Alistair Plumb, for his explanation of the song 'Maria Bethania' in relation to Brazilian music; and last but very far from least, thank you to Baz and Chris at Omnibus for your encouragement and forbearance.

Select Bibliography

The author found the following titles invaluable in researching his subject:

Clayson, Alan: *Jacques Brel: La Vie Bohème* (Chrome Dreams, 2010).

Paytress, Mark: booklet notes for *Everything Under The Sun* by The Walker Brothers (Universal, 2006)

Reed, Jeremy: *Scott Walker: Another Tear Falls* (Creation Books, 1998).

Reynolds, Anthony: *The Impossible Dream: The Story Of Scott Walker & The Walker Brothers* (Jawbone, 2009).

Walker, John & Gary: *The Walker Brothers: No Regrets* (John Blake Publishing, 2009).

Watkinson, Mike & Anderson, Pete: *Scott Walker: A Deep Shade Of Blue* (Virgin, 1994).

Williams, Lewis: *Scott Walker: The Rhymes Of Goodbye* (Plexus, 2006).

Young, Rob: album notes for *Bish Bosch* (4AD, 2012).

Articles from the following magazines and periodicals were also particularly useful: *Music Life* (Japan), *Scott Times* (fanzine), *Melody Maker, New Musical Express, The Wire, Q, Mojo, The Independent, The Times*

FILMOGRAPHY

30 Century Man (directed by Stephen Kijak, 2006)

Index

359

Orbit Records 10, 12–13
'Orpheus' 101

'Paper Doll' 12–13
Parker, Alan 197
Parker, Evan 236–7
Pasolini, Pier Paolo xiii, 262–4
'*Patriot (a single)*' 272
Pattacini, Iller 100
Paytress, Mark 329
Penman, Ian 307
'People Get Ready' 85
Petacci, Clara 293–4, 295
Philips Records 44–5, 47, 147, 148, 175–6,
    178, 181
'Phrasing' 323–4
'Pilgrim' 333–4
Pitney, Gene 67–8, 147
'The Plague' 132, 231
Plague Songs 309
'Plastic Palace People' 130, 134–5, 228
Polanski, Roman 158, 161n
Pomus, 'Doc' 112, 125n
Portrait ix, 84–7
Potts, Arnie 11, 103
Powell, Claude 42, 69n
Presley, Elvis Aaron 2, 11, 112, 142, 167,
    170–1, 297–8, 313n
'Pretty Fly' 199, 207n
'Pretty Girls Everywhere' 31, 44
Prieto, Joaquin 84–5
Proby, P.J. 26, 27–8, 34–5, 39n, 277n
'Prologue' 167
'Psoriatic' 303
Pulp 182n, 231, 284–6

The Quotations 55, 58, 73

Radcliffe, Jimmy 61
'Rawhide' 237–8
Raymonde, Ivor 54, 67
Raymonde, Simon 54, 146
Ready Steady Go! 46, 77
Reed, Jeremy 182n, 238
Reed, John 25
'Reuben James' 170
Reynolds, Anthony 157
Rhodes, David 261
'Rhymes Of Goodbye' 155
'Ride Me Down Easy' 191

The Righteous Brothers 24, 31, 36, 44
The Rocking Horse Winner (film) 5
The Rolling Stones 33, 36, 56–7, 70n
'Rosary' 274, 336, 338n
'Rosemary' 144
Routers, The 24

'Saddest Night In The World' 83
Sands, Tommy 13
Sarne, Mike 136, 159n
Sartre, Jean-Paul 49, 154, 216
'Saturday's Child' 57, 85
Schneider, Al 'Tiny' 28, 30, 38n, 128n
Schroeder, 'Papa' Don 205
'Scope J' 282–3, 312n
Scott x, 114–15, 116, 120–3
Scott 2 117–18, 132–6
Scott 3 118, 143–6
Scott 4 xi, xii, 152–7
Scott Times fanzine (extracts) 159n, 164,
    171–3
Scott Walker: 30 Century Man 13, 58–9, 60,
    97, 101–2, 107n, 126n, 222, 239, 289–
    91, 293–4, 301–2, 306, 309, 312n
Scott Walker Sings Jacques Brel 115
Scott Walker Sings Songs From His TV Series
    148
Scott-Irvine, Henry 287–8
'SDSS 1416+13B (Zercon, a Flagpole
    Sitter) xiii, 324–30
Sebring, Jay 38, 157, 158
'See You Don't Bump His Head' 321–2
Sefton, David 283, 290
Semel, Ady 166, 181, 189–90, 193, 205
'The Seventh Dawn' 35, 37
'The Seventh Seal' 89, 153, 228
The Seventh Seal (film) 43–4, 151
Shaper, Hal 142–3, 173–4
Sharp, Chris 306
Shaver, Billy Joe 190–1
Sheppard, Phil 305, 310
Shindig (TV) 32, 35
Shrimpton, Chrissie 57
Shuman, Mort 112, 114, 115, 116, 117,
    118, 182–3n, 246
'Shutout' 215
Sinatra, Frank 6, 10, 13, 21n, 36, 41, 50, 57,
    91n, 104, 105, 107n, 111, 113, 2121,
    137, 150, 170, 332
Sinatra, Nancy 68, 94